Praise for *The Crown in Crisis*

"Excellent, well written, deeply researched . . . a dynamic revisionist history . . . that is both heartbreaking and glamorous, scholarly and very entertaining."   —Simon Sebag Montefiore

"Alexander Larman's well-researched and well-written *The Crown in Crisis* is both scholarly and highly readable. He has mastered the sources superbly, and his analysis of the extraordinary story is full of thought-provoking insights."   —Andrew Roberts

"A compulsively readable and comprehensive account. Anyone who wants to deepen their understanding of one of the key events of the twentieth century, whose reverberations are still with us today, must read this engagingly fun and detailed book."   —Anne Sebba

"A gripping day-by-day account . . . compelling."
                                        —Ysenda Maxtone Graham

"Larman's retelling zips along, infusing a well-known narrative with impressive suspense. An enduringly relevant chapter of British history, brought to life with panache."   —*The Observer* (UK)

"Larman is an amiable and talented young writer . . . rendered with brio and dispatch . . . always interesting."
                            —David Aaronovitch, *The Times* "Book of the Week"

"A fresh look at a time of catastrophe for the royals, with new ideas about a plot to assassinate Edward VIII . . . Larman shows a delicate touch too in not banging home the obvious contemporary resonances. Instead he lets us find our own fun."   —*The Guardian* (UK)

"Forensically researched . . . Larman has done a fine job of explaining the religious, social, and political issues involved."
                                        —*Business Post* (Ireland)

"A gripping new book on the abdication crisis reveals how the ambitious former champagne salesman wooed Wallis to ingratiate himself with King Edward VIII." —*Daily Express* (UK)

"In this absorbing new book, Alexander Larman takes us through the whole, tangled story with great clarity."
—*Reader's Digest* "Recommended Read"

"Alexander Larman brings together unpublished archive material and witness testimonies to reveal exactly what went on at the palace almost a century before 'Megxit.'" —*The Daily Telegraph* (UK)

"An engaging, detailed, and suspenseful read; one that is equal parts empathetic and entertaining. You will be gripped."
—*The Independent* (UK)

"Alexander Larman has done a thoroughly researched job in retelling this oft-told tale and has made some fresh discoveries that shed new light on the affair." —Nigel Jones, *BBC History Magazine*

"Many of the central characters so vividly brought to life in Alexander Larman's *The Crown in Crisis* appear as if drawn from a period matinee at the Aldwych. . . . Both judiciously weighed and ceaselessly entertaining." —*The Critic* (UK)

"A suspense thriller about the abdication, complete with end-of-chapter cliff-hangers that leave you on the edge of your chaise longue . . . a thrilling, eloquent and witty tale." —*The Chap* (UK)

"An entertaining, multilayered study of the abdication crisis of 1936 . . . Larman captures the era's delicious wit, spite, and malice."
—*Kirkus Reviews*

Also by Alexander Larman

The Crown in Crisis: Countdown to the Abdication
Byron's Women
Restoration
Blazing Star

THE WINDSORS
AT WAR

The King, His Brother, and a Family Divided

ALEXANDER LARMAN

ST. MARTIN'S PRESS
NEW YORK

First published in the United States by St. Martin's Press, an imprint of
St. Martin's Publishing Group

THE WINDSORS AT WAR. Copyright © 2023 by Alexander Larman.
All rights reserved. Printed in the United States of America. For information,
address St. Martin's Publishing Group, 120 Broadway,
New York, NY 10271.

www.stmartins.com

Library of Congress Cataloging-in-Publication Data

Names: Larman, Alexander, 1981- author.
Title: The Windsors at war : the King, his brother, and a family divided / Alexander
  Larman.
Other titles: King, his brother, and a family divided
Description: First U.S. edition. | New York : St. Martin's Press, 2023. |
  Includes bibliographical references and index.
Identifiers: LCCN 2022052677 | ISBN 9781250284587 (hardcover) |
  ISBN 9781250284594 (ebook)
Subjects: LCSH: Windsor, House of. | George VI, King of Great Britain, 1895-1952 . |
  Windsor, Edward, Duke of, 1894-1972. | Great Britain—Kings and rulers—
  History—20th century. | World War, 1939-1945—Great Britain. | Great Britain—
  Politics and government—20th century. | Windsor, Edward, Duke of, 1894-1972—
  Family. | George VI, King of Great Britain, 1895-1952—Family.
Classification: LCC DA28.35.W54 L37 2023 | DDC 940.53/42—dc23/eng/20221101
LC record available at https://lccn.loc.gov/2022052677

Our books may be purchased in bulk for promotional, educational, or
business use. Please contact your local bookseller or the Macmillan Corporate
and Premium Sales Department at 1-800-221-7945, extension 5442, or by email
at MacmillanSpecialMarkets@macmillan.com.

Originally published in Great Britain by Weidenfeld & Nicolson, an imprint of
The Orion Publishing Group Ltd

First U.S. Edition: 2023

10 9 8 7 6 5 4 3 2 1

For Alan Samson.
'A god from afar looks graciously upon a gentle master.'

'Oh, brothers! I don't care for brothers. My elder brother won't die, and my younger brothers seem never to do anything else.'

Oscar Wilde, *The Picture of Dorian Gray*

And Cain talked with Abel his brother: and it came to pass, when they were in the field, that Cain rose up against Abel his brother, and slew him. And the Lord said unto Cain, Where is Abel thy brother? And he said, I know not: Am I my brother's keeper?

Genesis 4:8-9

Contents

Dramatis Personae

Royalty and their circle

George VI, King of the United Kingdom, the Dominions of the
  Commonwealth, and Emperor of India
Queen Elizabeth, his wife
Princesses Elizabeth and Margaret, their children
Edward, Duke of Windsor, former king and continued irritant
Wallis Windsor, his wife
Queen Mary, the royal mother
Prince Henry, Duke of Gloucester, her third son
Prince George, Duke of Kent, her youngest son
Princess Marina, Duchess of Kent, his wife
Mary, Princess Royal, Countess of Harewood, Queen Mary's
  daughter
Charles Edward, Duke of Saxe-Coburg, Edward's cousin
Lord Mountbatten, Edward's cousin
Bessie Merryman, Wallis's aunt
May Elphinstone, Queen Elizabeth's sister
Sir Alec Hardinge, private secretary to George VI 1937-43
Lady Helen Hardinge, his wife
Viscountess Milner, her mother
Sir Alan 'Tommy' Lascelles, assistant private secretary to George
  VI 1937-43; private secretary 1943-52
Eric Miéville, assistant private secretary to George VI 1936-45
Walter Montagu Douglas Scott, Duke of Buccleuch, Lord Steward
  1937-40

Douglas Douglas-Hamilton, 14th Duke of Hamilton, Lord Steward
    1940–1964

Edward 'Fruity' Metcalfe, confidant to the Duke of Windsor

Alexandra 'Baba' Metcalfe, his wife

Albert 'AG' Allen, solicitor to the Duke of Windsor

Sir Walter Monckton, lawyer and Director General of Propaganda
    and Information Services

David Storrier, bodyguard to the Duke and Duchess of Windsor

Betty Lawson-Johnston, friend to the Duchess of Windsor and
    the Duke of Kent

Jack Lowther, the Duke of Kent's private secretary

Military

Dwight D. Eisenhower, Supreme Commander of the Allied
    Expeditionary Force

Lord Portal, Chief of the Air Staff 1940–46

Major General Sir Richard 'the Wombat' Howard-Vyse, head of
    British Military Mission to French High Command 1939–40

Field Marshal Edmund Ironside, Chief of the Imperial General
    Staff 1939–40

Lord Gort, Commander-in-Chief of the British Expeditionary
    Force in France 1939–40

Lieutenant-General Henry Pownall, his chief of staff

Field Marshal Alan Brooke, the prime minister's military adviser
    and Chief of the Imperial General Staff 1941–5

General Hastings Ismay, the prime minister's military assistant

Field Marshal Bernard 'Monty' Montgomery, senior army officer

Sergeant Andrew Jack, sole survivor of the flight that killed the
    Duke of Kent

Infante 'Baby Bee' Alfonso, Duke of Galliera, Spanish prince and
    aviator

Walter Schellenberg, SS Brigadeführer and Nazi spymaster

Politicians

Neville Chamberlain, Prime Minister of Great Britain 1937-40

Winston Churchill, First Lord of the Admiralty 1939-40; prime minister 1940-45

Clement Attlee, leader of the Labour Party 1937-45; deputy prime minister 1942-45; prime minister 1945-51

Lord Halifax, Foreign Secretary 1938-40; British ambassador to the United States 1940-46

Anthony Eden, Foreign Secretary 1937-38, 1940-45

Sir John Simon, Chancellor of the Exchequer 1937-40; Lord High Chancellor 1940-45

Duff Cooper, First Lord of the Admiralty 1937-38; Chancellor of the Duchy of Lancaster 1941-43; British ambassador to France 1944-48

Lord Beaverbrook, newspaper magnate and variously Minister of Aircraft Production, Minister of Supply, Minister of War Production and Lord Keeper of the Privy Seal

Leslie Hore-Belisha, Secretary of State for War 1937-40

Henry Margesson, Secretary of State for War 1940-42

Sir Archibald Sinclair, Secretary of State for Air 1940-45

David Lloyd-George, former prime minister

Ramsay MacDonald, former prime minister

Oliver Stanley, politician, President of the Board of Trade 1937-40; Secretary of State for the Colonies 1942-5

Sir Alexander Cadogan, Permanent Under-Secretary for Foreign Affairs 1938-46

David Lindsay, Earl of Crawford, former Conservative chief whip

Sir Samuel Hoare, Home Secretary 1937-39; British ambassador to Spain 1940-44

Philip Kerr, Marquess of Lothian, British ambassador to the United States 1939-40

Sir Horace Wilson, senior civil servant, head of the civil service 1939-42

George Lloyd, 1st Baron Lloyd, Secretary of State for the Colonies 1940–41

Ernest Bevin, Labour politician, Foreign Secretary 1945–51

Robert 'Bob' Boothby, Conservative politician

Henry 'Chips' Channon, Conservative politician and diarist

Harold Nicolson, Conservative politician and diarist

Leo Amery, Conservative politician

Charles Dundas, Governor of the Bahamas 1932–40

Roundell Palmer, Minister for Economic Warfare 1942–45

Alexander 'Sanny' Sloan, Labour politician

Sir John Wardlaw-Milne, Conservative politician

Sir Eric Phipps, British ambassador to France 1937–39

Sir Ronald Campbell, British ambassador to France 1939–40

Sir Nevile Henderson, British ambassador to Germany 1937–39

Sir Walford Selby, British ambassador to Portugal 1937–40

Franklin D. Roosevelt, President of the United States 1933–45

Eleanor Roosevelt, his wife

Harry S. Truman, American president 1945–53

Joseph Kennedy, American ambassador to Britain 1938–40

J. Edgar Hoover, director of the FBI, 1924–72

Harry Hopkins, Roosevelt's foreign policy adviser

John G. Winant, American ambassador to Britain 1941–46

Wendell Wilkie, presidential envoy and Republican presidential candidate

Adolf Hitler, Führer of Germany 1933–45

Rudolf Hess, deputy Führer 1933–41

Hermann Göring, Reichstag president 1932–45

Joachim von Ribbentrop, German ambassador to Britain 1936–38; Reichsminister of Foreign Affairs 1938–45

Reinhard Heydrich, 'the man with the iron heart'

Konstantin von Neurath, German foreign minister 1932–38; Reich Protector of Czechoslovakia 1939–43

Julius 'Zech' von Zech-Burkersroda, German ambassador to The Hague 1928–40

Fritz Hesse, press attaché to the German embassy

Eberhard von Stohrer, German diplomat
Erich Pheiffer, German intelligence officer
Joseph Stalin, General Secretary of the Soviet Union, 1922-52
Benito Mussolini, Italian dictator, 1943-45
Édouard Daladier, French prime minister 1938-40
Philippe Pétain, chief of staff of Vichy France 1940-44
Ramón Serrano Suñer, Spanish Minister of the Interior
António de Oliveira Salazar, Portuguese prime minister
René Massigli, French ambassador to the United Kingdom
    1944-55

Society - high

Clementine Churchill, wife to Winston
Randolph Churchill, her son
Lady Maud 'Emerald' Cunard, society hostess and German
    sympathiser
Lady Diana Cooper, wife to Duff
Cecil Beaton, society photographer and diarist
Sir John Reith, director general of the BBC 1927-38
Sir Frederick Ogilvie, director general of the BBC 1938-1942
Fred Bate, head of the European section of NBC
Thomas Argyll 'Tar' Robertson, head of 'XX' committee of MI5
Herman and Katherine Rogers, friends of Wallis
Sir Osbert Sitwell, writer and wit
Noël Coward, playwright and actor
Sibyl Colefax, socialite
Cosmo Lang, 1st Baron Lang, Archbishop of Canterbury
John Dauglish, Bishop of Nassau
Charles Bedaux, industrialist and Nazi sympathiser
Fern Lombard, his wife
Ricardo de Espiritu Santa e Silva, aka Ricardo Espírito Santo,
    Portuguese banker, friend to the Duke and Duchess of
    Windsor
Miguel Primo de Rivera, Spanish aristocrat and playboy

Sir Harry Oakes, Anglo-American millionaire gold-mine owner
and murder victim

Axel Wenner-Gren, Swedish entrepreneur

Marguerite Wenner-Gren, his wife

Lady Jane Williams Taylor, Bahamas 'distinguished social leader'

Prince Paul of Yugoslavia, disgraced Yugoslavian prince

Albrecht Haushofer, German playboy in London

Karl Haushofer, German academic and fascist guru

Count Alfred de Marigny, French-Mauritian playboy, Bahamas
resident and suspected murderer

Colonel R. A. Erskine-Lindop, Bahamas police commissioner

Society - low

George McMahon, would-be royal assassin

May McMahon, his wife

The Reverend Robert Jardine, 'the Fighting Parson' and 'the
Duke's Vicar'

Margaret Harris, Sergeant Andrew Jack's niece

Etienne Dupuch, editor and publisher of Bahamas newspaper *The
Tribute*

Captain W. E. Melchen, chief of Miami Homicide Bureau

Captain James Barker, his assistant

William H. Harman, Pennsylvania engineer; unimpressed by the
Duke and Duchess of Windsor

Introduction

A couple of years ago, I was having a haircut. The barber - a literary man - was pleased to hear that I was working on a book about the royal family in World War II, but he had a particular interest in one issue.

'Was the Duke of Windsor really a Nazi?'

I was unable to respond pithily; when someone is cutting your hair, you are more than usually vulnerable to something going awry if your response is an unexpected one. But the answer is neither an unequivocal 'yes' or a dismissive 'no'; rather something more ambiguous. When I was writing my previous book, *The Crown in Crisis*, the discussion of Edward VIII's political sympathies took up a substantial proportion of the narrative. If he was not at least a Nazi sympathiser, then it was deeply unfortunate that he willingly spent quite so much time in their company.

But the tale of his abdication and its build-up ended in December 1936, with Edward no longer monarch and exiled to Europe, travelling away in the night. During my research, I kept seeing glimpses of fascinating documents in archives that promised to elucidate his inclinations but also hinted at far greater discoveries to come. I have never written a sequel before, but when I concluded *The Crown in Crisis*, I knew that the story I had been telling was not - could not be - finished. The question that reader after reader has asked me is 'What happened after Edward and Wallis left Britain?' Here, they have their answer.

The question of the duke's Nazi loyalties and associations can now be answered in satisfying and conclusive detail, thanks to new information that has come to light over the previous decade. And

I cannot say that I have warmed to him during my research. I have been accused of harshness towards Edward, whom I described in *The Crown in Crisis* as 'a wretched, quixotic ruler, an obsessed and demanding lover and, bar the odd instance of compassion and decency, a selfish and thoughtless man'. My only regret is that I have been too generous towards him. If there is a public figure of comparable standing who displayed the lack of self-awareness, non-existent consideration for others and disdain for any reasonable standard of behaviour as the Duke of Windsor, their name should live in infamy.

But the duke's failings are only one aspect of *The Windsors at War*. If *The Crown in Crisis* was a book about the moral, social and political weight of kingship, this is ultimately a story about a squabbling and dysfunctional family being tested to the limits under unimaginable pressure. The fascinating psychodrama of the uneasy relationship between King George VI and the Duke of Windsor – the man who struggled to be king and the man who had given it all up for a woman – featured only tangentially in the earlier book. Now, thanks to access to rare and never-before-published letters, diaries and memoranda, I can tell its story with the candour and detail it deserves.

Inevitably, this period encompasses far more than sibling rivalries. The Second World War has been written about by countless historians before, and the central narrative can seem almost overfamiliar. Yet the role of the royal family in the conflict, both public and private, is curiously under-reported. As I delved into it, I was astonished at the new and never-before-published information that I discovered, from the candid letters of the king's private secretary, Alec Hardinge, to revelatory information about the Nazi sympathies of some of the most intimate members of the royal circle. I feel privileged to be able to bring this explosive material into the public eye for the first time.

This is a story on the broadest of canvases, spanning nearly a decade and featuring a cast of characters who represent everything from duplicitous chicanery to clear-sighted, even heroic principle.

It has been a pleasure to meet many of them for the first time, and to reunite with old friends from *The Crown in Crisis*. The great lawyer Walter Monckton returns, still trying to do his best for the increasingly ungrateful duke, and I was delighted that Diana Cooper and Chips Channon are able to offer their (invariably waspish) observations on proceedings once again. And for the conspiracy-minded, there is a reappearance by Edward VIII's would-be assassin, George McMahon, still professing his undying loyalty to a man he tried to shoot.

The Windsors at War is a book made up of many interwoven narratives. It is an account of treachery, and of cynicism. It is a tale of decent people doing thoughtless and inconsiderate, even dangerous things when faced with an intolerable amount of pressure, and of their getting it wrong as often as they succeeded. I have attempted to strip away the flummery and protocol of the royal family and examine them afresh, as flawed, often capricious human beings, whose internal struggles could seem petty and self-indulgent at a time of national crisis.

But it is also a story of heroism and honour, of principles maintained against near-impossible odds. It demonstrates how the king, Queen Elizabeth and those loyal and stoic figures around them – even the underappreciated Hardinge, whom I hope I have rehabilitated here – were faced with the dual difficulties of having to act as symbolic figureheads for a nation while confronting personal and familial challenges that would test even the most robust of individuals. I have tried to show, paraphrasing W. H. Auden, how private faces in public places are more appealing than the reverse. I hope that I have been as sympathetic and balanced a chronicler as possible – even to the Duke of Windsor.

We remain fascinated by royalty. The international outpouring of grief that was sparked by the news of Elizabeth II's death on 8 September 2022, at the age of ninety-six, was a genuine expression of communal mourning, rather than performative attention-seeking. Would that the Queen's quiet, unostentatious dedication to duty that she offered her country for seven decades had been adopted by the rest of her family. Instead, their actions have excited comment and discussion all over the world, not always of a favourable kind. From the Duke of York's legal travails to the continuing exploits of the Duke and Duchess of Sussex, the monarchy has been dogged by scandal and embarrassment in a fashion that has been unanticipated for decades.

But as I write this in the year that saw both the grand success of the Platinum Jubilee and the reaction to the Queen's death, it is possible to balance often prurient interest in the antics of the renegade members of 'the Firm' with a recognition that the monarchy, at its best, is an ever-fixèd mark in both British society and in history. The Queen herself appears in this book, along with many of her family, and I remain grateful for her gracious permission to include extensive quotations from documents in the Royal Archives (as with *The Crown in Crisis*).

All the same, *The Windsors at War* is an independent minded and fresh examination of the time, not an exercise in public relations. Britain now has a new King, and one who has a phenomenal precedent to live up to. I hope that if he has the opportunity to read this book, he would view it as a fair account of an extraordinary period in which good overcame evil after one hell of a tussle.

Albeit one that came within an ace of being fatal for his family.

Prologue

'We All Wondered Why We Weren't Dead'

13 September 1940

It took courage to fly as low and as fast down the Mall as the German pilot did, dodging the clouds as he sped, but his task that Friday morning was a daring one: the destruction of Buckingham Palace. It was an executive decision that had been made by Reichsmarschall Hermann Göring the previous week, as he took control of the bombing of London.

Should the airman succeed, ideally killing the king and queen at the same time, it would be both a propaganda and a military triumph for Hitler. The risks were great, but so was the prize. The bomber readied the 55kg cylindrical explosive bombs, known as SC50s, and hoped that they would blow the building to pieces.

The approach only took a matter of a few seconds, but it was all the pilot needed. He drew his Heinkel He 111 as close as he dared to Buckingham Palace, unmolested by anti-aircraft guns, and let his cargo fall onto the target. Then, his mission accomplished, he flew away, hoping that he had managed to achieve what so many of his fellow aeronauts had only dreamt of doing.

King George VI, or 'Bertie' to his familiars, and Queen Elizabeth were no longer strangers to the prospect of death rained down from the air. Like their subjects, they had been horrified by the Blitz, which had begun the previous week, on Saturday 7 September. It had turned towns and cities into gap-toothed shadows of what they had been only hours before. In London alone, over 300 people were killed in a single night, with 1,337 badly injured and countless more wounded or rendered homeless.

The devastation could barely be measured in human or financial cost. Yet it was only the overture to what would become a twenty-three-day, fifty-seven-night attack on Britain, orchestrated by the Nazis with the intention of reducing an entire country to fear, from the lowliest of beggars to the highest in the land. Nobody would – could – be spared.

On Monday 9 September, the first intruder arrived at Buckingham Palace, in the form of a bomb that fell into the garden courtyard. It landed only a few feet away from the king's study, which was located on the floor above. He gazed at the interloper with fear, but it did not detonate, so he continued to work at his papers as if nothing untoward had happened.

He soon discovered what could have occurred. The next night, the bomb finally exploded. The ferocity of the upward blast blew out the windows above and turned the garden, once a source of royal pride and solace, into a mess of rubble and earth. Precious stained-glass windows were destroyed. Even the swimming pool was laid to waste. Only the wire netting that defaced the windows of the palace prevented further damage to the family's private quarters.

Courtiers and politicians urged the king and queen to be cautious, even if it verged on the cowardly. Flee London, they said, for the safety of Windsor, or head further away still. It would be too great a loss to the country if anything happened to either of you.* Their words were listened to, and then disregarded. As the queen remarked to the politician and diarist Harold Nicolson, 'I should die if I had to leave.'[1]

Yet underneath the bravado was confusion and doubt. Security at the palace was all but non-existent, and the advent of the Blitz

---

* It was also suggested that the princesses should be evacuated, but the queen responded peremptorily, 'The children could not go without me, and I could not possibly leave the King.'

had left the usual elements of protocol and ceremony in chaos. Decisions had to be made in seconds, rather than over the course of days. There was no chain of command to debate the wisdom of the royal actions. The king and queen agreed upon a compromise. They would go to Windsor for a couple of days with fourteen-year-old Princess Elizabeth and ten-year-old Princess Margaret while the worst of the debris was cleared up, and then return on Friday to London, ready to resume their responsibilities and duties, while their children remained behind in Windsor. That would satisfy everyone.

It nearly proved the greatest mistake they ever made.

When the royal pair returned to London on the morning of 13 September, an air raid was in progress. The weather was poor, a mixture of cloud and rain, and they hoped it would impede visibility for any attack. As they entered the palace at quarter to eleven, they did not head for their usual rooms towards its front, as the windows had been smashed by the bomb a few days before. Instead, they made for a smaller sitting room in the inner part of the building, overlooking a quadrangle.

The king's private secretary, Sir Alec Hardinge, notified them that there was a 'red' warning in operation, meaning that an attack was believed imminent, and entreated them to head down to the air raid shelter. The king, still less cautious about the prospect of attack than those around him, insisted that they gather a few possessions before they went, and the queen joined him in his sitting room.

As they prepared to leave, the king was troubled by an eyelash getting stuck in his eye. He asked for the queen's assistance in removing it, just as Hardinge, papers in hand, entered the sitting room to chivvy his superiors down to safety. Before they could leave, however, they heard the whirring sound that signified the arrival of the Heinkel bomber.

All anyone could think to say in the circumstances was 'Ah, a German',[2] before the trio heard two noises. First was the sound of the plane preparing to unload its cargo, followed by the scream of the SC50s as they tore down into the palace quadrangle. As two of the bombs exploded, shattering stone, masonry and glass in their wake, they sent up what the queen called 'a great column of smoke and earth'[3] into the air. It was clear that this was no near miss, but a direct hit on an iconic symbol of London and of Britain. Göring's plan had succeeded.

Its consequences would have segued from symbolic to devastating if the king and queen had been killed, but luckily they were unharmed. As they backed away from the windows, aware that glass might fly into the room and cut them to pieces, they realised that they had been spared purely by chance. As the prime minister, Winston Churchill, later wrote of the attack, 'had the windows been closed instead of open, the whole of the glass would have splintered into the faces of the King and Queen, causing terrible injuries'.[4]

The royal pair and Hardinge rushed into the corridor. They lingered there with two pages, taking care to be as far away from the windows as they could. The king and queen remained calm, through either fortitude or shock. There was a crisis, but it could be overcome. As they walked down to the shelter, they saw the extent of the devastation: two enormous craters had appeared in the courtyard, and one of the bombs had destroyed a fire hydrant, meaning that flames and water were laying waste to all around them.

They held their nerve. The only sign of the fear that both felt was that the queen's knees trembled, even as she enquired about the welfare of the housemaids and other staff. ('I <u>was</u> so pleased with the behaviour of our servants . . . they were really magnificent,'[5] she wrote to Queen Mary.) Six bombs had landed in total: two in the quadrangle, two in the forecourt, one in the chapel and one in the garden. They could have killed dozens of people.

Whatever fortune had spared their lives had been extended to the other inhabitants of the palace that morning, most of whom were unharmed, save three men who cried out for bandages. It transpired that they were workmen who had been attempting to repair some of the damage to the chapel that had been caused earlier in the week. A bomb had exploded directly above them, but they had been shielded from the worst of the impact by being underground, although one worker, Alfred Davies, subsequently died of his injuries. He was the sole casualty of the most successful direct bombing raid the Germans ever made on Buckingham Palace.

Immediately afterwards, the king and queen set out by car to the East End of London to assess the carnage there. They were both affected by the 'ghastly' damage they saw, with hundreds of their subjects either dead or trapped beneath ruins, and countless people bombed out of their homes. The queen wrote to Queen Mary, 'I really felt as if I was walking in a dead city ... it does affect me seeing this terrible and senseless destruction - I think that really I mind it more than being bombed myself.' Even as she praised the people she encountered for being 'marvellous' and 'full of fight', she was struck by the realisation that 'One could not imagine that life could become so terrible.' She vowed, 'We must win in the end.'[6]

As they returned home, compassion and pity were joined by pragmatism. Hardinge knew the importance of regaining the initiative, certain that Hitler would rejoice at his propaganda triumph. He wrote to his mother-in-law, Viscountess Milner, making light of what had happened as far as he could. 'What days we live in! We have had lots of bombs in this place, but only three people were slightly wounded. I felt quite shaken up one day - when three bombs dropped in the quadrangle 30 yards from me.'[7] And he persuaded the queen to put out a statement to the press that demonstrated the spirit of no-nonsense courage that the behaviour of the royal couple was to epitomise throughout the war, accompanied by carefully stage-managed photographs of the two of them looking stoic amidst the rubble of the palace. Her statement said simply, 'I'm glad we've been bombed. It makes me feel I can look the East End in the face.'[8]

When word spread, it had the desired effect amongst their

subjects, who felt that they stood in solidarity with their rulers. One woman said that 'If they hurt the King or Queen or the Princesses, we'd be so mad we'd blast every German out of existence.'[9] The politician and diarist Henry 'Chips' Channon, no admirer of the couple, wrote that 'the bombs on Buckingham Palace have made the King and Queen more popular . . . everyone realises that they do their duty in difficult circumstances'.*[10] Louis Mountbatten, who would himself meet his end four decades later at the hands of a similar atrocity, remarked that had the Germans known the 'depth of feeling' their actions would lead to, they should have been advised 'to keep the assassins off'.[11] But it was also a symbol of the potency of the Nazi regime that an attack like this could be planned, executed and come within an inch of succeeding. As Churchill said, 'This shows the Germans mean business.'[12]

Despite relief at the king and queen's survival, there was no time for celebration. Underneath his facade of stoicism, George VI knew how close they had come to death. He wrote in his diary that day that 'We all wondered why we weren't dead', and called it 'a ghastly experience, & I don't want it to be repeated', observing that 'it certainly teaches one to "take cover" on all future occasions, but one must be careful not to become dugout minded'.[13] Yet although he slept well and hoped for no traumatic after-effects,[†] he later noted that 'I quite disliked sitting in my room on a Monday or Tuesday. I found myself unable to read, always in a hurry, & glancing out of the window.'[14] As he expressed his hopes that the tours that he and the queen made offered a mixture of inspiration and solace, he wrote glumly that 'nobody is immune'.[15]

Once fear and adrenaline had been replaced by anger, the king

---

* Typically, Channon also referred to the king as 'the dullest, most boring but well-meaning little man on earth', although he called the queen 'glamorous, unspoilt and gracious'.

† He wrote in his diary the following day that when he heard the noise of a bombing practice he instinctively ducked; 'yesterday's experience was still too clear in my mind to avoid doing so'.

demanded to know how exactly a German bomber had managed
to make a direct hit on the palace, especially in the day's cloudy
conditions. He had been a pilot himself before he was sovereign –
the first member of the royal family to qualify – and knew that such
a targeted attack could not have taken place by chance. It required
both skill and inside information, which led him to the conclusion
that whoever had planned the assault had been assisted by a traitor
who wished for the deaths of the royal family and all those around
them.

His first thought was that a distant relative with Nazi sympathies
could somehow be involved. He knew that his German cousin
Charles Edward, Duke of Saxe-Coburg, was a Nazi, but the so-
called 'traitor peer' had been *persona non grata* with the royal family
for decades. In July 1917, George V had even altered the family
name from the House of Saxe-Coburg and Gotha to the House of
Windsor, both as a patriotic gesture and to remove any taint of pro-
German sentiment. It seemed unlikely that Charles Edward would
have suddenly decided to mastermind such an attack.

The king's suspicions then turned to his Spanish relation
Infante Alfonso, Duke of Galliera, a distinguished aviator who had
commanded Franco's aerial forces in the Spanish Civil War and
had the aviation experience necessary to train pilots to accomplish
a mission of that nature. Although there was no clear link between Alfonso and the Germans, or any reason for him to aid the
attack, the king terminated his lease of a grace-and-favour house
in Chiswick, the King's Cottage, which was instead given to the
Archbishop of Canterbury, Cosmo Lang, for his retirement. It was
a petty gesture, but it was at least a nod towards retaliation.

Yet the king feared that his true nemesis was someone altogether closer to home, albeit in exile and isolation in Europe,
having left England nearly four years before. He was someone
who knew Buckingham Palace – he had even, albeit briefly, been
resident within it himself – and his Nazi sympathies were a dangerous facet of his character. The king had heard the rumours that
this man, frustrated with the life of a playboy, wished to return to

his country by whatever means he could. Nor did he ignore MI5 reports that suggested that, should Hitler succeed in conquering Britain, he was prepared to offer this figure his heart's desire in exchange for 'assistance'.

The man whom the king feared had betrayed him, directly or otherwise, was his brother: 'David' to his friends and family, but known to the rest of the world as the former Edward VIII, now Duke of Windsor. Relations between the two had been increasingly difficult since Edward had abdicated the throne on 11 December 1936, and had now resulted in estrangement. Yet it seemed unthinkable that his own sibling - a man who had once ruled Britain - could even contemplate such an action.

The king made no mention, to his wife or anyone else, of his suspicions. He did not need to. As the war, for so long becalmed, lurched into its next stage, the battle lines were now drawn. Country against country, nation against nation. That it should also pit brother against brother seemed inevitable.

Chapter One

'The Other One'

For a man with no interest in religion, the Duke of Windsor's public and private lives were inextricably bound up with the actions of clergymen. Walter Blunt, Bishop of Bradford, preached a sermon on 1 December 1936 that led to the media's policy of silence on Edward's love affair with Wallis Simpson being abandoned,* and the presence of the vicar Robert Anderson Jardine at his wedding to Wallis ensured that the event attracted even greater attention than it would otherwise have done. Had Jardine been less eager to thrust himself into the spotlight, the wedding would have been a quiet civil ceremony, and many of the difficulties of subsequent years might have been avoided. But action follows inclination, and so the Fighting Parson - who acquired his nickname through his time as an army padre in World War I - found himself out of his depth.

In his memoir, *At Long Last*, which was never published in Britain due to fears of libel, Jardine recounted the moment when he decided to support the Duke and Duchess of Windsor, and thereby make himself notorious. The vicar of a working-class parish in Darlington in the north of England, he was in his late fifties in 1936. He admired the former Edward VIII and said of his relationship with Wallis that 'many felt and saw that this constant companionship brought the King supreme happiness and that it might be a case of true love'.[1]

---

* For further details, see *The Crown in Crisis*, Chapter Nine.

While Jardine's daily business in 'the Athens of the north', as he termed Darlington, kept him remote from the discussions of Edward's conduct during the abdication – 'I was trying to mind my own business and leave that of the King alone . . . to my mind, this discussion of another man's affairs was repugnant'[2] – he was aware that to his parishioners, 'Edward was and always had been their friend and idol'.[3] He was himself sympathetic to 'the Little Gentleman', as he called him, and considered it a shame that the now Duke of Windsor was forced to endure 'a long and lonely wait' at the Schloss Enzesfeld, a castle near Vienna, as Wallis's decree nisi had yet to become legal. Any reunion between the two of them would have jeopardised the legality of the divorce. If that had happened, the abdication would have been pointless.

Jardine enjoyed the reports of the coronation of George VI on 12 May 1937 ('one of England's greatest traditions of ceremony, grandeur and pomp'), but he was more interested in the predicament of the previous king. He was informed by his superior, the Bishop of Durham, that no ceremony for Edward and Wallis could be sanctioned in his or any other diocese, on the direct instructions of the Archbishop of Canterbury. It was therefore announced in the press by Edward and Wallis's friend and official spokesman Herman Rogers that 'there will be no religious ceremony when the Duke of Windsor and Mrs Wallis Warfield are married at Monts . . . Mr Rogers said he could give no reason *why* there would be no religious ceremony.'

Jardine professed himself 'so upset and angry . . . that I lost all interest in my breakfast'.[4] Retiring to his old army tent in the garden, he prayed for guidance, which duly arrived. He decided that it was his duty to write to Rogers and offer his services officiating at the wedding, consequences be damned. As he remarked to his wife, '[I am] only an unknown vicar of a working class parish [who offers] to perform a ceremony which should be held in a Cathedral and presided over by dignitaries of the church', but the Fighting Parson remained a pugilist. He vowed that 'with God's help, I am fighting for the happiness of my one-time earthly King'.[5]

Although he mistakenly believed that 'I was sure that the Duke of Windsor was a man of religious convictions',[6] his unsolicited approach led to a swift response from A. G. Allen, the duke's solicitor. After ascertaining that Jardine was sincere in his desire and not an agent of the newspapers (or, worse, the royal family), Allen asked him to conduct the wedding at the Château de Candé in France, home of the Franco-American industrialist Charles Bedaux.

Jardine did not know that Edward's lawyer and fixer, Sir Walter Monckton, had already attempted to recruit a pliable vicar to perform the ceremony. One man, W. F. Geikie-Cobb of Farnham Common, responded that 'it would be presumptuous for me as an ordinary humble parson to consider myself suitable for the honour of marrying the Duke', but agreed in principle to do so if the Bishop of London would authorise him to perform the ceremony. He did not. Another clergyman, C. E. Douglas, who knew Monckton slightly, suggested that there was no sacramental objection to the ceremony itself,* and wrote, 'if there is any difficulty about finding a priest to administer the sacramental oath in this case, I feel so strongly about the principle that I should personally be willing to "defy authority" . . . by officiating'.[7] But he ultimately found himself unable to offer such defiance.

Either Geikie-Cobb or Douglas would have been a preferable choice. But cometh the hour, and so Jardine made his way to France, weighed down by both responsibility and the consequences for his career. But he was resolute in his belief that God 'had foreseen, provided and chosen a man to fill the breach created by hypocrisy, cant and un-Christ like action on the part of Parliament and prelate'.

Edward had left Britain on the night of 11 December 1936† with a sense of unfinished business. Less than a fortnight had elapsed between Blunt's sermon and the abdication, and most of that time was consumed with political intrigue and constitutional wrangling.

---

* Wallis's status as a divorced woman left this issue in doubt.
† 'In darkness he left these shores', Lang would later crow in an ill-judged and vitriolic valedictory sermon he preached after the former king's departure.

A few exhausted men, including the future king, attempted to come to terms with what his unlooked-for reign would involve. Edward was calm, unlike most of those working for him, but his serenity was disturbed by two concerns: recognition for Wallis, and a desire that appropriate financial support should be provided for them both.

The duke therefore wrote to his brother on 17 January 1937 that 'The events of December are past history and you and I have now only the future to look forward to - you have your life as King and you know how hard I have tried to make your succession as easy as possible - and I will throughout your reign (which I hope will be a long and a grand one) and for the rest of my life do all in my power to help and support you to the best of my ability', and suggested that 'for the first time in my life I shall be very happy'.

But trouble lurked, even as Edward was quick to remind his brother that 'Wallis and I have committed no crime.' He asserted that 'you and you alone can dispel and contradict any of the doubts and rumours that are abroad to the effect that you and Mama disapprove of us and that any one who does stick to us as friends will have a bad mark against their name in your "book" or with the "new regime" as they call it!' He mixed man-of-the-world wisdom ('You know how charming and charitable people are and I doubt your ever having heard that such gossip and rumours are being spread indiscriminately. But believe me they are Bertie, and it hurts like the dickens') with straightforward pleading: 'A lot of people are kicking us for the moment and you can stop it all - please do so quickly for our sakes and for our happiness and usefulness in the future - you can and you must do that.'[8]

Tension soon rose between the brothers. As Monckton recounted, 'there were some difficulties to smooth over between the King and his brother who was troubling him a great deal on the telephone, and I was told to go out and persuade him to discontinue this'.[9] The king was preparing for his coronation, amidst rumours that he suffered from epileptic fits and was unable to face the responsibilities of ruling. Hardinge later wrote of him that 'he had no training for the task now thrust upon him . . . his health, together with the impediment in his speech, had placed him under a severe physical handicap'.[10]

The contrast with his elder brother, as well as his younger siblings, the Duke of Kent and the Duke of Gloucester, was unflattering. The king may not have been beset by 'fainting fits', as gossip magazines such as *Cavalcade* suggested, but he was a chronic stammerer, given to nerves at the prospect of any appearance in public and miserable at the burden that had been thrust upon him with inadequate preparation for the challenges he faced. Hardinge's wife Helen called him 'completely unambitious' and stated that 'he and his wife were appalled by the position in which they found themselves'.[11] Likewise, his elder brother's sleeve-tugging when it came to money was irksome. That the recently married Duke of Kent was exciting public attention due to his dalliance with the society model Paula Gellibrand ('the next Mrs Simpson?') was merely the rotten cherry upon a stale cake.

Socially, the king deferred to his wife, who combined charm with recognition of when her husband was uncomfortable. She had written to the socialite – and Hardinge's mother-in-law – Viscountess Milner* during the abdication crisis to say, 'we can only pray & hope that we may both have the health & willpower to do our job for this dear country <u>whatever</u> happens'.[12] The fate that her husband had dreaded was upon them. She was determined they would both succeed.

Nicolson, who attended a dinner with the two of them on 17 March, was impressed by her bearing. He wrote of how 'She wears upon her face a faint smile indicative of how much she would have liked her dinner party were it not for the fact that she was Queen of England.' He praised her 'charm and dignity', and contrasted it with that of Wallis, remarking, 'I cannot help feeling what a mess poor Mrs Simpson would have made of such an occasion . . . it

---

* Channon, no admirer of her son-in-law, called her 'a most dangerous, domineering old harridan'.

demonstrated to us more than anything else how wholly impossible that marriage would have been'.[13]

When George inherited the throne in December 1936, he thought of continuity, rather than revolution. It did not help that, as Hardinge later wrote, 'the scene on to which King George stepped . . . was not a happy one . . . the international situation was growing daily more precarious as the German and Italian dictators proceeded on their brutal and aggressive courses'.[14] His first act as sovereign was to knight Walter Monckton in his house in Piccadilly, remarking afterwards, 'Well, Walter, we didn't manage that very well, but neither of us has done it before.'[15] He stressed to Monckton, who had agreed to remain as his attorney general, that he wished him to be a counsellor and friend, as well as a go-between between him and the Duke of Windsor.

This soon presented the lawyer with a predicament. He wrote to the king shortly afterwards to acknowledge that 'It is a comfort that you understand what a delicate position I am in: it is in one way quite impossible to hunt with the hounds & run with the hare but I have always determined to deserve the confidence both of you and your brother and to try and be what the Queen called last night "the link" that keeps you both friends. I am sure that link is important from the public as well as the personal point of view.'[16] Maintaining warm relations with both siblings would occupy Monckton in both personal and official capacities for years to come.

Yet the king also cast off the baser elements with whom his brother had associated. Edward's louche friend Emerald Cunard, who had referred to him as 'Majesty Divine', was banished from court. Queen Mary wrote to her cousin Prince Paul of Yugoslavia to say, 'I fear she has done David a great deal of harm . . . I feel none of us, in fact people in society, should meet her.'[17] And Peregrine 'Perry' Brownlow, Edward's loyal lord-in-waiting, was dispensed with. This, however, was not from moral judgement, but because he was a buffoon. He was subsequently known, in a mocking reference to his country seat, as 'the Lincolnshire Handicap'.

*

The Duke of Windsor lingered in Austria, bored by enforced in-dolence. Even his confidant, Edward 'Fruity' Metcalfe, who was by his side, remarked, 'if he's not doing something, he gets very moody & irritable & things are by no means easy'.[18] The duke occu-pied himself by telephoning his younger brother to tell him what to do. Monckton observed that 'this advice often ran counter to the advice which the King was getting from his responsible advisers in the Government'.

The conversations frequently ran into difficulty due to the king's stammer, and Edward seized the advantage of his own fluency. As Monckton noted, 'the Duke of Windsor was particularly quick in understanding and decision and good on the telephone, whereas King George VI had not the same quickness and was troubled by the impediment in his speech'.[19] Edward's intention seemed to be to bully his brother into giving him what he wanted through charm and coercion. Unsurprisingly, the king soon stopped taking the calls. Metcalfe recounted the duke's shock when he was told that his brother could not speak to him until the following evening 'as he was too busy to talk any other time'. He described his face simply as 'pathetic'.[20]

The major discussions were about cash and Wallis's royal status. The agreement between the brothers at the time of the abdication was that the Duke of Windsor would receive an annual allowance of £25,000, a sum paid directly from royal finances rather than by the nation. This would keep it a family matter and remove any danger of taxpayers subsidising Wallis. Yet as Monckton remarked, 'the advice which the King was getting prevented him from making the immediate and unqualified promise which he would have wished and made the Duke suspicious'.[21]

It did not help that the details of the financial agreement had been leaked to the papers, something that made the king 'very disturbed'. He complained to the duke, 'I haven't told anyone that we even signed [an agreement] . . . this is now public property & it is very unfortunate at this moment when the Civil List is just coming up'. He knew who he was dealing with. He suggested that 'There is certain to be enquiry as to what has happened to the savings from the Duchy of Cornwall, before you came of age, & the rumour is that you have saved a very large sum from this source. You must tell me whether this is so, as I understood from you when I signed the paper at the Fort that you were going to be very badly off.'[22]

Edward responded angrily to this, as he always did when questions of finance and probity were concerned. 'You now infer that I misled you at that time as to my private financial situation. While naturally not mentioning what I have been able to save as Prince of Wales, I did tell you that I was badly off, which indeed I am considering the position I shall have to maintain and what I have given up. You now ask me to tell you what my private means are, but I prefer not to do so for two reasons – firstly because the figure of £25,000 which you agreed to pay me in the event of Parliament not voting me this money in the new Civil List was in no way arrived at by reference to my private means, but solely as being the lowest provision that would be appropriate in the circumstances – we all thought at that time that Parliament would make at least that provision, and after all it is through no fault of mine that they are now going to fail us.

'Secondly I am certain that it would be a grave mistake, if the private means of any member of the Royal Family were to be disclosed to the Select Committee and that it would only embarrass you and your advisers if I were to put you in the position of being able to answer questions on this subject.' He suggested, with veiled threat, that 'I have kept my side of the bargain and I am sure you will keep yours . . . I should be very sorry and it seems quite unnecessary that there should be any disagreement between us over this matter – but I must tell you quite frankly that I am relying on you to honour your promise.'[23] He finally offered to rent his brother Sandringham and Balmoral for £25,000: a calculated insult that had the desired effect of angering the new monarch.

Edward remained in thrall to Wallis. She told him on 3 January that 'I am so distressed over the way your brother has behaved from the first and is certainly giving the impression to the world at large that your family ... do not approve of me ... naturally we have to build up a position but how hard it is going to be with no signs of support from your family'. Anticipating the difficulties they would face ('one realises now the impossibility of getting the marriage announced in the Court Circular and of the HRH'), she lamented, 'I loathe being undignified and also of joining the countless titles that roam around Europe meaning nothing.'[24]

If her fiancé had been braver, he might have replied that they could have anticipated this predicament as soon as they left Britain. However, he could only agree with her. By the end of March, she referred to the king as 'your wretched brother' after he had informed the duke that 'you have misunderstood the suggestion that I made to you in my last letter about our agreement ... it is no fault of yours you say, it is likewise no fault of mine, but I do hope you realise that if this agreement comes to light, Parliament will at once say that it is providing for you indirectly. This means that the Civil List will be reduced by that amount, a contingency which will endanger my being able to carry out my part of our agreement.'[25]

Wallis, fearing penury, panicked. She suggested to Edward that 'if he continues to treat you as though you were an outcast from the family and had done something disgraceful and continued to take advice from people who dislike you ... there would be only one course open to you and that would be to let the world know exactly the treatment you were receiving from the people (family) you had placed in their present position'. If it sounded like blackmail, this was borne out by her resolution that her fiancé should screw his courage to the sticking place: 'don't be weak, don't be rude, be firm and make him ashamed of himself'. She concluded, 'I love you and want you here so badly.'[26]

Others attempted to intercede. Winston Churchill, then a backbench MP, had been a supporter and friend of Edward before and during the abdication crisis. He praised the duke on

24 March 1937 for how 'very wise and prudent'[27] his actions since leaving Britain had been. He also revealed that he and David Lloyd George, another partisan, were attempting to use their influence with the prime minister, Neville Chamberlain, to satisfy Edward's requests.

While Churchill hoped that all could be settled 'in an acceptable and agreeable manner', he was less insouciant about the situation to Monckton. On 23 March, he remarked that 'I am concerned about the financial position of the Duke of Windsor', and that 'it is evident that a proper establishment with due formality is required for His Majesty's elder brother, and for one who has occupied the Throne'. Unlike the king, he was under no illusions as to Edward's fortune, which he estimated in a note to Chamberlain as being between £800,000 and £950,000 in capital.* Much of this was settled on Wallis, although since the abdication she had been reduced to an annual allowance of £10,000 a year: barely enough to keep her in the jewels and couture that Edward had lavished on her while he was Prince of Wales. Churchill believed that allowing the duke to retain the capital and receive an annual allowance of £25,000, in exchange for his relinquishing any interest that he might hold in Balmoral and Sandringham, was a satisfactory resolution to the matter.

Others disagreed. At the beginning of April, Clement Attlee, leader of the Labour Party, asked embarrassing questions in Parliament about any financial arrangements that existed regarding Civil List provision for Edward. Churchill suggested to Chamberlain on 8 April that 'the idea of a dispute between the two brothers upon the question of good faith, and still more of legal process, would of course be a disaster of the first order to the monarchy'.[28]

Chamberlain, who regarded Churchill as a 'bandit' and a 'pirate', believed that he was trying to force the king into a compromised

---

* Alec Hardinge, private secretary to both Edward and George VI, estimated that Edward's personal funds were even larger than this, being as much as £1 million in cash, and producing £60,000 a year in income.

position thanks to his 'swindling arrangements' and 'threats to make trouble in Committee',[29] and did not believe such an allowance needed to be formalised. Therefore he refused to acknowledge or endorse any such request, and support for the duke's petition remained fragmented.

To make matters worse, the former king remained without a country. Churchill wrote in a briefing note to Chamberlain that 'it was stated to Parliament by the Attorney-General during the passage of the Abdication Bill that no condition of exile followed a voluntary abdication', and that even if ministers felt that Edward's free return to Britain was undesirable, they should be prevented from passing an Act of Parliament barring him from his former home.

As he remarked, 'it would not be right to take such a step, which would cause much pain and scandal throughout the British Dominions and the world, merely upon grounds of social convention and etiquette'. Instead, he suggested that Edward be allowed to return after several years, when the position of the new king and queen was more established. He argued, 'time is a healer of many things . . . what is important in these intervening years is to make the relations between the Duke and the King, or other members of the Royal Family, those of warm and easy friendship and affection, all doing their utmost for mutual benefit and in the public interest, and trying to help out each other in every way they possibly can'.

Edward had moved on from the Schloss Enzesfeld and was idling in the luxury hotel Landhaus Appesbach, near the resort area of Salzkammergut. Yet leisure was the last thing on his mind. On 16 April, he complained to Churchill that '[the] correspondence that has passed between my brother and myself this week . . . makes the government campaign against me more than easy to see. These last months have been more trying than I can say.' Still, the reunion with Wallis would offer some compensation. He sighed, 'the thought that there are little more than two weeks of our separation left seems too good to be true'.[30] Only the most cynical could have begrudged the pair their happy ending, although it remained ambiguous as to who was the dashing prince and who the swooning maiden.

The king, meanwhile, faced more prosaic difficulties. He did not feel established or confident on the throne, and fretted about the responsibilities of his coronation. His assistant private secretary, Alan 'Tommy' Lascelles, told Sir John Reith, the BBC's director general, in January that 'the King was more fussed about his Coronation Day broadcast than anything else'.[31] He knew his brother's easy popularity with his people would be hard to replicate.

His stiffness was obvious to his social circle. When he hosted Duff Cooper, the Secretary of State for War, and his socialite wife Diana at Windsor Castle in mid April, she moaned to her friend and confidant Conrad Russell that 'it's too dull and dreary and different for words'.[32] Diana had been a good though not uncritical friend to Edward, and had offered similarly sardonic comments to Russell about visits she had paid to Fort Belvedere (in which she mocked the 'pink Venetian blinded, pink-sheeted' bedroom she slept in) and as a guest of the then king on the yacht the *Nahlin* the previous summer. That trip became a notorious international incident due to the lack of discretion with which Edward and the married Wallis comported themselves across Europe.*

There was no such danger with the new king and queen, but no concomitant excitement either. Diana had exchanged cocktails and sexual permissiveness for a 'throttlingly stuffy' bedroom and strict etiquette. As a woman, she was excluded from the male world of 'rumble and talk and drinks', and was instead expected to gossip with her familiars. After bemoaning the impropriety of the dress that she wore ('high cut and modest in design, but I'm not sure that it isn't worse than striptease because for some reason it shows the minutest details of anatomy through its draping'), she acknowledged that the queen had been 'lovely' and that the atmosphere was

---

* See *The Crown in Crisis*, Chapter Four.

'fine',[33] but whenever Edward and Wallis were mentioned, tension hung in the air. She informed Russell that conversation between the queen and Duff Cooper had involved her talking 'of Kingship and herself but not of the crisis'.[34] She mocked the relationship between her husband and the queen, writing, 'It's d'Artagnan - no, Buckingham. It's Boswell, it's Potemkin, it's Stromsee, it's Lancelot', before concluding, 'it's boring'.[35]

Diana remained unimpressed throughout the weekend, despite her admiration for the queen. She described the talk at dinner as 'jabber, jabber, jabber', and told Channon that while Fort Belvedere could be described as an 'operetta', Windsor Castle was merely 'an institution'.[36] This stood in contrast to her emotional farewell letter to Edward the previous December, in which she wrote, 'I shall miss your grace, your "flare", your unusualness and your great goodness to Duff and me quite terribly.'[37]

Yet the king was capable of retaliation. Hosting his friend the writer Osbert Sitwell at Windsor the following week, he described to him 'a person you know very well - a person who has said a number of foolish things in her time'. Referring to her self-described status as a 'rat', or a supporter of his brother, he informed Sitwell that the person was none other than 'DC'. As Sitwell noted, 'all members of the royal family consider initials to be an absolute and impenetrable disguise, absolving the person who employs them from any blame that might be incurred by mentioning a name, but at the same time affording an unmistakeable indication of identity'. This code initially defeated him - 'stupidly, I failed to fit the correct names at once to the initial letters' - before he realised the identity of 'my old friend, Lady Diana Cooper'.[38]

Such moments were light distraction as the coronation loomed before the king like a monolith. The service was scheduled for 5 May 1937, and Queen Mary was involved in the planning of it 'with her characteristic vigour'.[39] Yet the king's stammer seemed an insuperable obstacle to the day's establishment of him as the new sovereign. The ceremony itself did not worry him too much. Reith's suggestion that it should be televised had been dismissed by Lang as sacrilegious, to say nothing of impossible to censor if the king's physical twitches needed to be concealed. It was the subsequent speech on the radio that terrified him. Reith, who had organised his brother's abdication broadcast from Windsor Castle on 11 December, was keen, both for his monarch's sake and for the reputation of the BBC, that the king should 'make a good broadcaster'. He worked with the speech therapist Lionel Logue and the BBC's outside-broadcast engineer to make him feel comfortable enough to perform his speech live.

Thankfully, both the broadcast and the coronation ceremony passed without difficulty. The king's much-rehearsed speech, in which he declared how 'with a very full heart, I speak to you tonight . . . never before has a newly crowned king been able to talk to all his peoples in their own homes on the day of his coronation' and told the nation that 'the queen and I will always keep in our hearts the inspiration of this day', was a success. *Time* magazine praised his 'warm and strong' voice. Millions of his subjects sat at home listening to the broadcast, willing him to succeed while knowing of his stammer and the difficulties that even speaking a few short sentences publicly had caused him. The nation was relieved by the successful delivery of the first ever coronation broadcast.

Inevitably, his presentational difficulties remained. Channon wrote on 7 May 1937 of how, addressing a gathering of the Dominion prime ministers in Westminster Hall, the king was 'faltering, pathetic with his halting speech and resigned kindly smile, and everyone pretending, so much did they hope he would, that he was doing it well'. The diarist remarked that 'It was the thing to praise him, for all realise he is batting on a difficult wicket.'[40]

Yet fortunately for the coronation ceremony, the king's nerves seemed to vanish on the day, aided by his sincere religious faith: another characteristic absent from his brother's life. As he later told Lang, 'he felt throughout that Some One Else was with him'. He confided in the Labour politician Ramsay MacDonald that 'for long periods at the Coronation ceremony, he was unaware of what was happening'.[41]

Although there were minor mishaps,* mainly caused by the fumbling and fussing of the various bishops and prelates, the king remained serene. He was helped by his mother abandoning protocol that dictated that a previous monarch's widow would not attend a subsequent coronation and coming to offer moral support. This also implicitly suggested that it was his reign, rather than Edward VIII's, that continued that of her late husband, George V. His bearing struck many of the onlookers as being, for the first time, regal. Even Churchill was moved to tears as he remarked to his wife, Clementine, 'You were right. I see now the "other one" wouldn't have done. No one could forget that, had it not been for "the other one".'†42

'The other one', in the form of Mrs Simpson, was not at the ceremony, but it is doubtful that she would have attended even if she had been invited. Royal relations had reached a nadir the previous month, when the king had refused to offer Edward any official recognition of his impending wedding. He wrote, 'I am very sorry that I cannot make the arrangements you would like about your marriage. You know that I should like to help you all I can, but the trouble is I can't treat this as just a family matter however much I want to.'43

He begged the headstrong duke to see sense, although this was a doomed endeavour. 'In spite of the affection which of course there still is towards you personally, the vast majority of people in this

---

* There might have been another, in the form of assembled dignitaries being closely packed together within canvas walls and women in danger of fainting, but the resourceful Lascelles drew his dress sword, slashed a door in the wall and helped them escape from harm. The king was especially delighted to hear this anecdote, Lascelles remarked.

† The king wrote to Churchill shortly after the coronation and candidly remarked, 'I know how devoted you have been, & still are, to my dear brother, & I feel touched beyond words by your sympathy & understanding in the very difficult problems that have arisen since he left us in December.' He concluded with his gratitude for '[the] good wishes . . . of one of our great statesmen' in aiding 'the great responsibilities & cares that I have taken on as King'.

country are undoubtedly as strongly as ever opposed to a marriage which caused a King of England to renounce the throne. You know that none of us in the family liked it, & were any of them now, after a few months interval, to come out & help you get married, I know that it would be regarded by everybody as condoning all that has happened.' This, the king feared, 'would place us all in an impossibly false position & would be harmful to the Monarchy, which after all has already had a great shock'. He concluded, 'You will understand how much I loathe having to do this, but with your knowledge of the world, you will appreciate that I cannot do anything else.'[44]

The duke responded in a cold but civil manner, which confirmed the estrangement that now existed between the brothers, less than six months after the abdication. 'I believe you when you say that you loathed writing it . . . I will never understand how you could ever have allowed yourself to be influenced by the present Government and the Church of England in their continued campaign against me ever since I left in December. You have had my personal expressions of loyalty to you both as King and as my brother, in writing as well as in words; surely this must mean something to you. And your ministers being aware of the sincerity of my loyalty need never have had any cause to doubt it. However, if for some reason they ever have, their minds can now be at rest, because after this final insult, I don't imagine that I shall ever have the desire to set foot in Great Britain again.' He ended with a personal attack. 'There is nothing more for me to say except that I shall always be sorry to remember that you did not have the courage to give me the same support at the start of my new life, that I so wholeheartedly gave to you at the beginning of yours.'[45]

Happier times awaited. When the duke arrived in France on 4 May 1937, Sir Eric Phipps, the British ambassador there, reported that he appeared to be 'in excellent health and spirits', not least because Wallis's decree nisi had been made absolute the previous day. There was no longer any impediment to their marriage. Phipps also remarked that 'it looks as though we must be prepared for a fairly prolonged stay in the country, which may, I fear, raise a certain number of problems'.[46] This was heroic in its understatement.

However, Edward's thoughts lay on wedding preparations for the following month, even without knowing who would be allowed to conduct the ceremony. The option remained of a French civil union, but this seemed unbecoming and also raised the possibility that it would not be recognised in his home country. The duke – rightly, as it transpired – simply ignored the issue, assuming, Micawber-like, that 'something would come up', and remained fixated on his family's refusal to grant Wallis a royal title.

Their reunion in early May at the Château de Candé, where they planned to marry, was worthy of a romantic novel. Wallis said, 'Darling, it's been so long, I can hardly believe that it's you, and I'm here.'[47] Their bliss was only marred by listening to the coronation ceremony on the radio. As Wallis later wrote in her memoirs, *The Heart Has Its Reasons*, 'I fought to suppress every thought, but all the while, the mental image of what might have been and should have been kept forming, disintegrating and re-forming in my mind.'[48]

They were soon joined at the chateau by Monckton, although he arrived without the hoped-for gift of a royal title for Wallis. The lawyer's personal preference was for her to be granted such an honour, on the grounds that withholding it looked insulting, but he was powerless to influence those who could have made her an HRH.* Letters patent published on 28 May 1937 declared that 'the Duke of Windsor shall, notwithstanding his act of Abdication, be entitled to hold and enjoy for himself only the title, style or attribute of His Royal Highness, so however that his wife and descendants, if any, shall not hold the said title of attribute'. Wallis was cast out of the inner sphere for ever.

This was not a royal decision. Monckton observed that 'if the King had been left to himself, I feel confident he would not have assented to this course, because he knew the effect it would have

---

* He tried and failed to intercede with Sir John Simon, the Home Secretary, on Edward's behalf.

on his brother'.[49] Instead, responsibility lay with the socially conservative dominions of Australia and Canada. The previous year, they had blocked Monckton's idea for a morganatic or 'left-handed' marriage that would have enabled Edward to remain on the throne and marry Wallis. They now made their disdain clear at the idea that she should ever be awarded the status and consequent respectability she craved.

Although he had been forewarned that Monckton was bringing 'not very good news' from his brother, when he was told of the decision, Edward shouted, 'This is a nice wedding present!'* His first reaction was to abandon his own title altogether, but Monckton talked him out of such a decision. It would have caused offence to his family and would have achieved nothing. The lawyer acknowledged, nonetheless, that 'it was a little hard to be told when he did marry her that she would not have the same status as himself', and told the king, with a politician's tact, that 'Your Majesty, I know, understands perfectly the Duke's natural wish that his wife should be recognised openly & in the family and that in addition the ceremony should be conducted by an . . . established person. But I fully appreciate the reasons why you cannot permit what he wants.'[50]

The duke blamed his mother for this. Shortly before his wedding, he wrote to her criticising her for her coldness and formality. Her letters, he said, read as if the recipient were 'a young man who is stopping for a while in a foreign country to learn the language'. He professed himself 'definitely disgusted' with the king's behaviour, but attacked her too, saying, 'many things that I have heard of your attitude do not encourage me . . . for the first time in my life, I am happy and can honestly say that I look forward to the future'. He signed himself 'your disappointed son, David'.[51]

Churchill remained a go-between, despite his belief that 'the

---

* According to Monckton, the king used almost exactly the same words when he was dispatched with the message - presumably with a sense of regret rather than vengeful mirth.

right one' had been crowned. He wrote to the duke on 17 May and acknowledged that the coronation had been 'a brilliant success', especially the people's 'magnificent displays of loyalty'. He then spoke as a mentor. 'Outside the circle of friends there is a great deal of bitterness from those who are hostile to you, and from those who are hostile because of their disappointment.' His own stance was 'I wish to see the King reign gloriously, and the Duke of Windsor live happily.' He did not dwell on the incompatibility of such a desire.

For the first time, he suggested that Edward's absence from Britain and from his home, Fort Belvedere, should be measured in years rather than months, but that patience would bring about the wished-for result. He talked of 'a general arrangement, covering a period of, say, three years, not only on finance, but on other matters . . . I think time is needed before we can attain the ideal, namely that Your Royal Highness and [his] future wife could live pleasantly in England . . . this is it seems what we have got to work for and I believe patience and perseverance will secure it'. After all, he suggested, 'everything, apart from a proper financial settlement, should be subordinate to this ultimate objective'.[52]

Edward was more concerned with preparing for his wedding than thinking about the future. The finest social adornments were procured for it. Wallis's dress was made by the couturier Main Rosseau Bocher, 'Mainbocher', and the floral arrangements were provided, free of charge, by the London florist Constance Spry. Cecil Beaton, who had a reputation for photographing the royal family and aristocracy, was engaged to take pictures of the duke and duchess, although, being a mere tradesman, he was not invited to the wedding proper on 3 June. He wrote in his diary of Wallis that 'not only has she individuality and personality, but [she] *is* a personality - a strong force'. Even as he praised her intelligence and admiration for the duke, he offered the judgement that '[she] is determined to love him, though I feel she is not in love with him'. He was less impressed by the duke ('like a little boy home for the holidays') and wrote of his 'sad, tragic eyes belied by impertinent tilt of nose' and 'rather common hands - like a little mechanic - weather-beaten and rather scaly'.[53]

As the Reverend Jardine made his way across Britain and France for the matrimonial event of the decade, Monckton remarked that 'it was a strange wedding for one who had been six months before King of England and Emperor of India and Dominions Beyond the Seas'. Very few of the invited guests appeared, and no members of the royal family, under a three-line whip imposed by the king, or his courtiers, fearing embarrassment.* The only royal acknowledgement was a telegram saying, 'We are thinking of you with great affection on this your wedding day and send you every wish for your future happiness' and ending, 'Much love, Elizabeth and Bertie'.

Monckton attended regardless, figuring that as he drew only a nominal amount from the royal purse for his work as attorney general to the Duchy of Cornwall, its loss would make little difference. In the event, the king chose to overlook his disobedience. Yet his loyalty to his former sovereign distinguished him. Only seven guests from England turned up, including Randolph Churchill, Fruity Metcalfe and his wife, Lady 'Baba' Alexandra, and Allen. They were outnumbered by journalists.[†] It was, as Baba described it, a 'sad little service'.

Monckton was unimpressed by Jardine, who he described as 'rather a rebellious priest', although he also acknowledged that 'he seemed a simple man and genuinely anxious to serve and to help the Duke'. However, he bemoaned Jardine's 'marked weakness for self advertisement'.[54] This was mild compared to Cosmo Lang's denunciation of him as 'a seeker of notoriety . . . [how had Edward] so far lost his dignity as to ask a man of this sort to celebrate his marriage?'

---

* The stated reason was that it would be wrong to support a wedding that had not been conducted under the auspices of the Church of England, despite Jardine's renegade presence.

† Uniquely, Randolph Churchill occupied the offices of both guest and writer, moving with alacrity from 'outside' to 'inside' and back again.

By the Fighting Parson's own account, he arrived at the Château de Candé the day before the wedding, to be greeted by Wallis's friend Herman Rogers, who said, 'Thank God you have arrived. Now I shall have something to say to the press.' The priest knew his time had come. 'God always has a man to step into the breach. It may be a Moses, a Daniel, a Wesley – or, don't smile, simply a Jardine.'[55] The 'level-headed Scotchman' was introduced to the duke, clad in shorts, who said, 'Pardon my language, Jardine, but you are the only one who had the guts to do this for me.'[56]

The bridegroom, 'as happy as a schoolboy', sent for his wife-to-be, and Jardine was enraptured. He praised her as 'queenly in her poise and beauty . . . being a student of physiognomy, I saw courage, the power to hold steadfastly on a chosen course and the ability to relinquish that which would hinder soul progress . . . between the eyes lurked discernment; and in the crown of the head, reverence for the Creator'.[57] Wallis's description of the man who married her was pithier. She called him 'a typical country parson in appearance and manner . . . I thought it brave of him to defy his bishop in order to marry us, and David and I gratefully welcomed him as a man of God.'[58]

After a dinner at the Hotel l'Univers in Tours, consisting of 'a very happy group of people', and during which the duke was 'very sparing with his drinks',[59] Jardine was given a pair of gold cufflinks by Wallis, embossed with her and Edward's joint crest. The vicar prepared for the day 'blubbering like a child', after turning down £700 from a reporter for his account of proceedings. ('Admittedly it was a great temptation, but I rejected it.')[60] By now, he had come to believe that he, as divine representative, was the focal point of the day. He cited one newspaper as saying, 'Calm and confident was the man who had stolen all the headlines.' He described the ceremony in detail in his memoirs ('quietness and an atmosphere of spiritual power marked the entire service'), and called the affair 'a fitting climax to a life lived and given unselfishly to the people [the Duke] loved'.[61]

Even at the moment of union, snubs to Wallis were neither

forgotten nor forgiven. The duchess asked Jardine to inscribe her prayer book, and Edward told him to write 'Her Royal Highness', a gesture of defiance with which the vicar was happy to be complicit. He subsequently wrote, 'I cannot understand how an honest, God-fearing nation, that believes in a square deal and talks so much of "playing cricket", can refuse to give the Duchess her rightful title.'[62] The ceremony concluded, he was given a slice of wedding cake and waved off. ('That picture will remain - the smiling face, the wave of the hand, and the voice crying "Goodbye, Jardine."')[63]

Edward and Wallis were grateful for the Fighting Parson's efforts. Shortly after the wedding, the duke wrote to him saying, 'The Duchess and I want to thank you from the bottom of our hearts, for your generous act in offering to come out to France, to marry us.' After praising with just a hint of condescension 'the lovely little service' and hoping that Jardine was not being 'unduly harassed by the Press', Edward offered to give him an altar cross for the church in which he officiated. He ended by saying that he was 'looking forward to seeing you again some day'.[64]

The reunion never occurred. Jardine arrived back in England, ready to officiate at another wedding in Darlington, to discover that he was notorious. The Bishop of Durham ('an ecclesiastical weathercock, as changeable as the wind'),[65] who had denied him a licence to perform the ceremony, was angry at being ignored. He therefore ensured that the priest's career was over. Jardine discovered that his status as 'Rebel no 1', as an admirer addressed him, resulted in ostracisation by his fellow clergy and the mass resignation of his parish council committee in protest at his actions. Unable to find a living in Britain, he travelled to America, but found similar difficulties in being received there. He did not help himself by denouncing the Archbishop of Canterbury as 'an ecclesiastical cad' and the Anglican Church as 'rotten'.

After an unsuccessful attempt to market himself as 'the Duke's Vicar' at speaking and ceremonial events, he threw himself into stunts like a latter-day Harold Davidson, the so-called 'Prostitutes' Padre', who had preached from within lions' cages after being

defrocked.* These included becoming involved with an unpro-
duced Hollywood film titled simply *Indecency* and judging a series
of beauty pageants known as 'Miss Spiritual of America'. This initiative hit the buffers when Miss Spiritual New York was found to be
conducting a three-way sexual relationship with two men.

As Jardine languished in Mexico, his American visa having long
expired, a reporter asked the Duke of Windsor in Palm Beach if
he would be prepared to assist the man who had married him.
Edward's response was dismissive. 'I haven't heard from him in
a long time', he replied. 'But I know of nothing I can do [to help
him].'

This was untrue. On 5 July 1939, Allen suggested that Edward
provide a pay-off of $1,000 to Jardine in exchange for his future
silence and his no longer calling himself 'the Duke's Vicar', saying
that 'the advantage of a positive step of this kind would be to give
you a full answer to any criticisms which might be made against
you in the future'.[66] Unsurprisingly, no such help was forthcoming.
The clergyman had to continue his moneymaking activities thus
unsanctioned.

Jardine died penniless and forgotten in 1950, a victim of collateral damage in the duke's orbit. The wedding cake was long eaten
and the cufflinks lost, or pawned. Yet he had attracted most of the
headlines from the wedding, deflecting attention from another
man who had been present: Charles Bedaux, the chateau's owner.
He and his wife Fern had been generous hosts, ensuring that the
duke and duchess could have a lavish wedding fit for royalty.

Less than seven years later, Bedaux would be in FBI custody,
accused of treason and trading with the enemy. Before then, the
metaphorical bill that Edward would be called upon to settle for his
wedding day would be produced. Bedaux's machinations would
lead the Duke and Duchess of Windsor into the company of none
other than Adolf Hitler.

---

* Coincidentally, Walter Monckton assisted in Davidson's prosecution as a
young lawyer.

Chapter Two

'Germany's No. 1 Gentleman'

Shortly before their wedding, Edward and Wallis received an unwelcome gift. It came in the form of anonymous correspondence entitled 'Public Opinion - The Truth about Mrs Simpson'. Forwarded to the Metropolitan Police by Herman Rogers, the document called Wallis 'a scheming adventuress' and a 'Delilah and a harlot . . . [who has caused] more grievous harm to the British empire than any other foreigner'.[1] Special Branch declined to take any action, on the grounds that, as the assistant commissioner Norman Kendal mused, the allegations were 'rather well done [and] surprisingly accurate'. The most scandalous details, which were treated as fictitious, concerned the apparent Nazi sympathies of both the duke and the duchess, arising from their friendship with a group of German-American social climbers. Had the truth been known, Kendal may have been less sanguine.

Charles Bedaux remains an enigma. Born in Paris in 1886, he emigrated to America in 1906, where he married, had a son and worked in a series of menial jobs. He made his fortune from the development of an efficiency scheme of scientific management adopted by businesses around the world, the so-called 'Bedaux System', which calculated how much work per minute could be achieved by the average person in normal circumstances. By 1927, he was wealthy enough to have purchased the Château de Candé in the Loire, renovating it in 1930. He took no day-to-day part in his organisation, but instead amused himself with financing polar expeditions and hunting big game. The former king and his new wife would be the most impressive specimens to grace his trophy room.

The wedding held at his home in June had few guests, but it brought international attention to his activities. Bedaux relished the publicity.* He knew that his association with the duke and duchess could be advantageous, as he was anxious that the Nazi regime in Germany was unsympathetic to his business interests. Their continued operation had needed a large bribe to be paid to the German state, and for Bedaux to acknowledge that his German work would henceforth take place under the jurisdiction of the Arbeitsfront, the Nazi labour organisation. It seemed likely that this situation would not last.

Bedaux knew that Edward was sympathetic towards the Germans, and so planned a high-profile visit by the duke and duchess to Germany in the autumn of 1937. This would promote Edward's interest in how the Nazis had improved the lot of the ordinary working man - with a view to reporting the intelligence back to Britain - and additionally give Hitler a propaganda triumph. At the same time, Bedaux hoped to strengthen his own connections with a country that he believed would dominate Europe, and the world, over the coming years. He contacted Hitler's adjutant Fritz Wiedemann, who confirmed that the Führer would be amenable to such a trip. Now all he had to do was convince Edward and Wallis.

He was helped by the deflation that both the duke and the duchess felt after their wedding. As with many newly married couples, the excitement of the day had swiftly worn off, and they knew that they remained pariahs as far as British society was concerned. One unwelcome reminder of Edward's brief reign came in the form of a letter from his would-be assassin, George McMahon. After a failed attempt either to warn the former king, or to kill him, in

---

* He wrote to Monckton after the wedding to say, 'We are gratified that many people in England appreciate our gesture. We want you and them to know that if the opportunity presented itself again, we would be even more happy to repeat this gesture than we were the first time we made it.'

July the previous year,* McMahon was newly released from prison and continuing to make protestations of loyalty and affection. He included the detail that he had kept a picture of the duke on his cell wall, where others may have placed an image of a wife or sweetheart. Edward passed on McMahon's unsolicited good wishes to Monckton to be dealt with in the usual fashion.

Other, more important figures were less forthcoming. The duke was furious that his mother had not bothered to send a wedding present, and wrote to say, 'I was bitterly hurt and disappointed that you virtually ignored the most important event of my life', hissing that 'You must realise, by this time, that as there is a limit to what one's feelings can endure, this most unjust and uncalled for treatment can have had but one important result; my complete estrangement from all of you.'[2] She did not reply.

The couple's reputation in England had declined even amongst their intimates. Nicolson wrote in his diary of 14 July that at a dinner thrown by Edward's former mistress, Sibyl Colefax, he sat next to Diana Cooper, who confided that she had turned against Mrs Simpson, saying, 'I am the largest of all the rats.'[3] She also told Nicolson that Wallis had lied to all her friends that there had been no physical relationship between her and Edward prior to their marriage, and that it was likely that they had had sex on their cruise on the *Nahlin* the previous year, given the fact that they had had adjoining cabins.

The duke could no longer count on the loyalty of his former friends. Even as he wrote to Sibyl to thank her for a wedding present of a gilt dish and called their current situation 'a real haven of rest after all we have been through',[4] he knew it was illusory. Exile particularly affected Wallis. Monckton wrote that 'she wanted [Edward] to have his cake and eat it ... she could not easily reconcile herself to the fact that by marrying her he had become a less important person'.[5] She had informed Sibyl earlier in the year

---

* See *The Crown in Crisis,* Chapter Three, for further details of McMahon's actions.

that 'I am neither surprised or disappointed at the way people have behaved . . . it is a cruel world and honesty doesn't seem to be the quality that gets you the longest way'.[6]

The duke reserved his greatest contempt for his own family, egged on by Wallis. She told Sibyl that 'I fail to understand how the Royal Family have allowed one of its members to be so unfairly attacked – it does not increase the prestige of anyone.'[7] The king wrote an anguished letter to his elder brother shortly after the wedding, complaining that the duke had caused their mother 'a great deal of pain'. After claiming that 'whatever I have done has been absolutely necessary for the sake of the country', he bemoaned his own compromised situation. 'How do you think I liked taking on a rocking throne, & trying to make it steady again? It has not been a pleasant job & it is not half finished yet.' Even as he half-heartedly suggested that 'I am only so anxious that we remain the best of friends', he had to delete some of the more contentious passages from his letter, such as the suggestion that 'all the bitterness is on your side'.[8] Any neutral observer would have suggested its distribution was evenly weighed.

Edward was, naturally, infuriated. 'When you informed me that my letter pained Mama and that writing to her makes her absolutely miserable, had you ever stopped to think how unhappy I have been made by the family's treatment of me or how much it has hurt me?' He took exception to his brother's description of the 'tottering' throne, and said, 'I do not think that even my more vindictive enemies would deny that I have done a great deal to preserve the system, over which you now preside.' Once again, he presented himself as a wronged elder statesman whose motive for abdicating was a patriotic one, rather than a selfish dilettante. 'I have always felt that one of the sources of power of the monarchy in Great Britain has been the fact that we were a united family, with no public discords and working together as one for the welfare of our people.'

Finally he issued two threats. Firstly he suggested that 'I therefore have it in mind to discontinue my use of the title of Royal

Highness', which would have been embarrassing if it was mined for publicity; secondly he hinted that unless Wallis was to be sent the same medal commemorating the coronation that he himself had received, he would make his estrangement from his brother public knowledge. As ever, he seemed unconcerned with mere facts, instead adopting the righteous stance of an elder brother to tell the king, 'I am sure that on reading this letter over, you will agree that any weakness to the structure of the throne that may have been caused by my being forced to leave could surely have been equally well repaired, without attacking the dignity of the position of my wife and myself.'[9]

If Edward could not influence his brother, he could at least try and put pressure upon others at court. In July, he wrote to Monckton, who thought him 'better than I have seen him for a long time . . . more peaceful & easy',[10] to thank him for a wedding gift and to say that 'life continues very peaceful and pleasant here'. But he then continued, 'how sore I feel [towards my mother and the king] from their humiliating treatment of me ever since I left England in December'.[11] Even the Duke of Kent, the most sympathetic of the royals, was unable to visit him. Queen Mary announced that she considered it inappropriate for any of her children, or their families, to acknowledge the Duchess of Windsor publicly.

Edward bemoaned the 'incredible information . . . that the Duchess of Kent should not meet my Duchess'. He wrote to his mother, 'I unfortunately know from George that you and Elizabeth instigated the sordid and much publicised episode of the failure of the Kents to visit us', and declared, 'it is a great sorrow and disappointment to me to have my mother thus cast out her eldest son'. He also put pressure 'in no unmeasured tones' on the king for this restriction to be lifted, which it was. The Duke of Kent was therefore allowed to come for a visit in September ('not that we cared one way or the other'), and Edward believed that he had seen into the psyche of George VI. 'It is interesting to observe a definite change of policy, and it was only brought about by taking a firm line with Kent, and telling him that if his wife could not come, then there was no point in his coming alone.'[12]

Edward took a minor concession to be a major victory, which was symptomatic of the war he waged against the king and a ruling class that had refused to accept or acknowledge Wallis. But in fact, his youngest brother had not especially wanted to visit, not least because he foresaw the possibility of a row developing if he and his wife were expected to meet Wallis. As he wrote to the king on 13 August from a yacht in Constantinople, '[David] telephoned on arrival & he asked us both to come over - I told him Marina couldn't as she wanted to see her family. I could come alone - he said no - they wanted us both to come, as we were going away would we come in September - I told him I'd let him know. The next day he called up, said he'd been thinking our conversation over - and wanted me to be frank. Was Marina not wanting to come or wasn't she allowed to - I told him the truth therefore - that she didn't much want to meet [Wallis], & also that it was settled by both Marina & [Queen Elizabeth] that she shouldn't.'

Edward was, inevitably, 'very upset' but informed Kent that although their friendship remained unaffected, he would be unable to see him alone, as to do so would be tantamount to an insult to Wallis. Kent telephoned him in an attempt to repair relations, but his wife remained resolute - 'she thinks she'll be very much criticised & that it is the thin edge of the wedge for W meeting her - and also that it looks as if we were giving in to him'. He therefore turned to the king as arbiter. 'I had asked your advice and you had given it . . . we must do what you wanted, but I told Marina that I would write to you and explain the circumstances to you and see what you thought when you had read this letter. D said he would much like to see me as he had lots of things to discuss - but I don't know of anything important.'[13] Marina's refusal to meet Edward's wife created, as Monckton wrote, 'bad feeling between the two families . . . from that moment on'.[14]

The duke had no idea of the diplomatic or social problems that his bull-in-a-china-shop attitude had created. Before his wedding,

Sir Robert Vansittart, the Permanent Under-Secretary of State for Foreign Affairs, had written to Hardinge and described the issue of how the exiled couple should be handled as 'bristling with every conceivable sort of problem'. He reported Foreign Secretary Anthony Eden's belief that the two should be treated abroad by ambassadors and dignitaries 'rather as they would a member of the Royal Family on a holiday', and decided, 'I think that in any case we shall need instructions or confirmation from the King'.[15] These were seldom forthcoming, even as the monarch attempted to maintain some civility. But the question of Wallis's title dominated all.

Shortly after the wedding, Monckton wrote to his fellow guest Allen to say that he was 'disturbed at the course which HRH proposes to adopt', apropos Wallis demanding the title of Her Royal Highness. He stated that the British public still thought of their former ruler with 'courtesy and goodwill', but believed that 'a great number of people would regard a challenge of the Letters Patent* as a challenge to the King in whose name they were issued'.[16]

He was convinced this would be a catastrophe. 'Nothing should be done now to raise a controversy ... [Edward's] patience and forbearance in very difficult circumstances are having their effect and I am sure the tide is beginning slowly to turn in his favour.' He knew his former monarch's inclinations. 'If he wants eventually to make his home in this country it is essential to do nothing to spoil this result ... [otherwise he] will be accused of having put [the king] into a position he never wanted and then increased his troubles.' Monckton added, 'He was determined to be married at all costs – and the cost goes on mounting up. This present trouble is one of the items in it but I do think it has got to be paid.'[17]

Bedaux, meanwhile, asked his own substantial price, but Edward and Wallis were happy to pay it. When the idea of an industrial

---

* Wallis described these in a July letter to Sibyl Colefax as 'completely fallacious' and noted, 'we are getting hundreds of letters protesting [the government's] treatment of their former King ... but one wants no arguments at present'.

tour of formerly depressed areas of Germany was proposed to the
duke, followed by a longer visit to America, he responded with
alacrity. He was pleased both by the prospect of a holiday in his
wife's home country and by the chance to spend time in a land that
he had great fondness for, thanks to his family connections there.

His warm relationship with members of the German embassy
to Britain, not least the ambassador, Joachim von Ribbentrop, was
still remembered. He believed that he would be treated with more
respect and dignity within Germany than he had been in his home
country since the abdication. He also believed that he could be the
instrument of peace and harmony between the two countries, and
show his family how they had underrated his abilities.

The self-appointed ambassador was not given any counsel
against the visit, although word had reached his brother. 'Are the
rumours true?' he asked Monckton, who answered that he did not
know. 'I do not think it wise,'[18] the king said. In late 1937, Anglo-
German relations were still theoretically cordial, but by then
few were under any illusions as to the scale of Hitler's ambition.
Monckton shared the king's disquiet both at Edward being used as
propaganda by the Nazis, and at the damage to his reputation in
Britain. But there was nothing he could do.

Monckton had worked hard to bring about better relations between the duke and his family, and saw that a visit to Germany,
whatever its motivation, could be disastrous. One problem was
that Edward was not offered any formal advice, because anyone
doing so could expect anger from the sovereign and his courtiers.
Monckton lamented that 'Kings not only live in glass-houses but
have constant access to the best advice in every sphere . . . responsible advisers never went near [the duke] and instead he was surrounded by friends who, for one reason or another, lived abroad
largely divorced from English society and interests'.[19] Even the
lawyer was not allowed the chance to remonstrate with him. The
duke cancelled a planned meeting with him in Paris, fearing that
his counsellor would seek to change his mind about his German
visit.

Like many thoughtless men, Edward acted impulsively and then presented his decisions as a fait accompli. It was left to smaller people to clear up the chaos left in his wake. He refused to listen to Monckton or Churchill, who remained both sympathetic and unable to check the worst of his impulses. This made him prey for false comforters and manipulators alike. The actions that he now undertook would affect his reputation until the day he died, and beyond.

Although the king was not told about his brother's plans to visit Germany until 3 October, the press rumours were ubiquitous. Wallis wrote to her aunt Bessie on 13 September to confirm them, saying, 'We are actually planning on going there to look at [workers'] housing and conditions as the Duke is thinking of taking up some kind of work in that direction.' She described Bedaux as 'Germany's No. 1 gentleman' and hoped that the visit would be interesting. Yet even as she warned her aunt, 'it is a secret so say nothing',[20] she knew that when the news broke, it would be received in England with horror.

The press release that appeared on 3 October was inevitably provocative. It stated that 'in accordance with the Duke of Windsor's message to the press last June that he would release any information of interest regarding his plans or movements, His Royal Highness makes it known that he and the Duchess are visiting Germany and the United States in the near future for the purpose of studying housing and working conditions in these two countries'. Investigations were made into the credentials of the organisers, and the Nazi politician Robert Ley, the head of the Arbeitsfront* and the man that Bedaux was desperate to impress, was denigrated by the security services as 'a drunkard who used to live in a Cologne brothel'.[21]

Edward's actions were viewed by the king and the queen, as well

---

* The Arbeitsfront was the Nazi-organised labour movement at the time, which replaced the individual trade union movements.

as their courtiers, as a challenge to royal authority, especially the planned visit to America. This was the prerogative of the monarch, and strengthened fears that the duke was attempting to establish himself as king over the water. George VI described the news to Monckton as 'a bombshell & a bad one too', and did what he could to frustrate at least the American leg of the trip. He informed his mother, 'I have told my ambassadors that the embassy staff cannot help him in any official sense . . . the world is in a very troubled state, & there is plenty to worry about', and lamented that 'D seems to loom ever larger on the horizon.'[22]

Phipps was sent to see Edward and to dissuade him from being himself. He wrote in his report, 'I warned His Royal Highness that the Germans are past-masters in the art of propaganda and that they would be quick to turn anything he might say or do to suit their own purposes.' Yet the duke was nonchalant. 'He assured me he was well aware of this, that he would be very careful, and would not make any speeches.' Even if this was true, there was dread in Phipps's final line, that 'the Duchess told a member of my staff last night that when in Germany they would be entertained by Herr Hitler'.[23]

The question of who Bedaux was, and what he wanted, now became pressing. On 17 October, Sir George Ogilvie-Forbes, counsellor to the British embassy in Berlin, informed Vansittart that Prentiss Gilbert, his American equivalent, believed that Bedaux's actions were dictated by his wishing to obtain recognition from the United States government when the duke visited. This would therefore allow Wallis to be treated with all the dignity that an HRH would usually receive. Gilbert remarked that 'the American Press correspondents who had hitherto painted in vivid colours the trivialities in the life of a married couple which had stirred the enjoyers of the vulgar, had now decided that HRH had entered the arena of politics and that they would now develop that aspect'.

Gilbert was also scathing about Bedaux's motivations, which he believed stemmed from his desire to sell his efficiency system to the German government. He told Ogilvie-Forbes, 'it was clear that this individual was "running" HRH and probably paying his expenses for the tour outside Germany'. Alluding to future planned trips, including one to Sweden during which the duke would be introduced to a millionaire with plans for bringing about world peace through labour reconciliation,* Gilbert reported that '[Bedaux] even went so far as to express the opinion that HRH might in due course be the "saviour" of the monarchy!' Ogilvie-Forbes noted of the 'painful reading' that 'it would be as well to keep an eye on Mr Bedaux's activities'.[24]

The king and queen felt 'extreme nervousness' about Edward's antics, according to Sir Ronald Lindsay, British ambassador to the United States. Lindsay believed that 'his theatrical appeals to popularity and these visits of inspection [are] perfunctory and no doubt pretty insincere, but none the less evidence of his readiness to bid for popularity'.[25] He argued that the duke should be treated with the courtesy and dignity that he would usually merit, but the king, Hardinge and Lascelles laid into Edward, describing him as an international embarrassment who sought the company of Nazi sympathisers in an attempt to bring about a comeback.

Yet Lindsay was more affected by the queen, who, rather than blustering with indignation, spoke 'in terms of acute pain and distress, ingenuously expressed and deeply felt'. She remarked that she felt grief more than anger, and remained, despite everything, affectionate towards 'David'. She added, 'He's so changed now, and he used to be so kind to us.' Lindsay wrote that 'with all her charity she had not a word to say for "that woman" . . . I found myself being deeply moved by her'.[26]

Lindsay's opinion of the king, less than a year into his reign, was that 'he is like the medieval monarch who has a hated rival claimant living in exile'. Although the analogy had its limitations – 'I don't think George wanted the throne any more than Edward, and if he is there it is owing to a sense of duty which Edward lacked and not owing to a love of power which one sometimes thinks

---

* Axel Wenner-Gren, who was believed to have Nazi sympathies, and who became a more important figure in Edward and Wallis's lives in due course.

Edward may have after all' - he remarked that the circumstances in which George VI found himself had parallels with his forebears. The king felt 'uneasiness as to what is coming next - sensitiveness - suspicion', and wondered what Edward and Wallis really wanted, concluding that she wielded the power in the relationship. He remained 'violently prejudiced'[27] against her.

Yet for all his anger, the king could do nothing to prevent his brother from visiting Germany. Despite international tensions, the two countries were at peace, and Edward's intentions for his visit were worthwhile, if naïve. The trip was arranged for 11 to 23 October, under the auspices of Bedaux and Ley. The highlight would come on the penultimate day, when Edward and Wallis would be received at Berchtesgaden. The Führer had his holiday home in the mountains there, and was keen to meet them both.

While Edward was still king, Adolf Hitler had tried to bring him round to the Nazi cause, courtesy of the ambassador to Britain, Joachim von Ribbentrop.* Although this had been unsuccessful, Hitler continued to admire a man he described as 'a kind of English national socialist'. He had supported him in his desire to marry Wallis, whom he praised as 'a girl of the people', and believed that his intentions had been frustrated by 'plutocrats and Marxists'.

Back in 1935, political gossip suggested that Edward had been radicalised by the Nazi sympathiser Emerald Cunard, not least when he made what Channon called 'an extraordinary speech' to the British Legion suggesting friendship with Germany. When he was forced off the throne, a secret civil service memorandum stated that Hitler was 'very distressed at the turn that affairs had taken in this country, since he had looked upon the late King as a man after his own heart, and one who understood the Führerprinzip,† and was ready to introduce it into this country'.[28] Now, at last, he had his chance to make his acquaintance.

---

* See *The Crown in Crisis*, Prologue, for more details.

† The 'Führerprinzip', or 'Führer principle', referred to Hitler's belief that his word carried greater importance than any law.

'I am sure that, with him, we could have achieved permanent cordial relations with England,' Hitler sighed to his Minister of Armaments, Albert Speer. 'With him, everything would have been different.'[29] Wiedemann, who had made the necessary introductions, knew that his superior 'had always had a certain weakness for the Duke of Windsor',[30] but also wanted to make sure that there would be adequate press coverage of the meeting with the distinguished visitor. Despite the relationship between Ribbentrop and Edward, little had been achieved towards the end of 1936, so this represented a chance to redress matters.

Before their encounter with the Führer, the tour had gone well. Hardinge attempted to prevent anyone from formally receiving the duke and duchess upon their arrival, on the grounds that to do so might be seen as condoning their actions. A document stated that 'His Royal Highness and the Duchess must not be treated by His Majesty's representatives as having any official status during the visit, and the Embassy must scrupulously avoid in any way giving the appearance that His Majesty the King and His Majesty's Government countenance the proposed tour.'

Yet Ogilvie-Forbes refused to accede to the demand, as he considered it 'extremely embarrassing and painful' to snub Edward. The duke was grateful when Ogilvie-Forbes called upon him, in defiance of the Foreign Office's order that 'you and your staff should refrain from entertaining His Royal Highness or the Duchess'.[31] The diplomat commented in 1940, of attempts to frustrate his 'very pleasant evening'* with Edward, that 'it was a series of similarly gauche blunders committed by the Foreign Office that is greatly responsible for the appalling mess that the world is in today'.[32]

Edward enjoyed his visit to Germany, because it represented a change of scene and an opportunity to be feted, rather than merely tolerated, on the international stage. Beaverbrook's *Daily Express*

---

* It was grudgingly accepted that 'if His Royal Highness himself were to invite either [Ogilvie-Forbes] or any members of his staff to visit him in an informal capacity, they should not decline'.

reported that the duke had visited a beer hall in Munich, not unlike
the one from which Hitler had attempted to launch his *coup d'état*
in 1923, and had drunk pints of beer while wearing a false mous-
tache before gushing about how much he was enjoying his visit to
the city. Yet such frivolity was exceptional. Wallis was pleased that
Nazi officials called her 'Her Royal Highness' at all times, and told
Aunt Bessie on 18 October that 'no words can express how interesting this trip is, but very strenuous',[33] as they marched around
factories and housing settlements, looking to be impressed and
photographed.

They met several leading Nazis, including Rudolf Hess, Joseph
Goebbels (who affectionately called the duke 'a tender seedling
of reason') and Göring, as well as renewing their acquaintance
with Ribbentrop, still ambassador to Britain, at a dinner in Berlin.
There, they were also introduced to leading film stars including
Marianne Hoppe and Gustav Gründgens. The meeting with Göring
was good-humoured, as both he and the duke enjoyed playing
with a toy aeroplane that dropped wooden bombs onto a convoy
of trains below. It was believed that Edward restrained himself
from offering any Nazi salutes during his visit, but recently un-
earthed photographic evidence of his giving a salute while visiting
a coal mine in the North Rhine-Westphalia district suggests otherwise.* This would not have been an isolated occurrence during
his travels.[34]

And then it was time to ascend into the mountains and meet the
man Channon had called 'some semi-divine creature'. Whether or
not Edward saluted Hitler during their reception on 22 October,
it proved to be both an auspicious encounter and a fruitless one.
The Führer kept the duke waiting for an hour, but once he greeted
him - Wallis was not granted access to their interview - he was

---

* As revealed by Valentine Low in *The Times* on 22 July 2015. Edward, of course,
had form in delivering Nazi salutes at inappropriate moments, as another story
from the same month in *The Sun* revealed: film existed of Edward, the Queen
Mother and Princess Elizabeth all performing Nazi salutes in 1933. Buckingham
Palace denounced the footage as 'misleading and dishonest'.

friendly and warm, as if seeking to compensate for the treatment that Edward had received in England. He did, however, place distance between the two men by insisting on speaking through the interpreter Paul Schmidt rather than directly, despite the duke's fluent German.

This meant that there was a witness to the conversation, but according to Schmidt, nothing important was discussed. 'Hitler was evidently making an effort to be as amiable as possible towards the Duke, who he regarded as Germany's friend, having especially in mind a speech the Duke had made some years before, extending the hand of friendship to Germany's ex-servicemen's associations.' He noted that Edward was apolitical: '[there was] nothing whatever to indicate whether the Duke of Windsor really sympathised with the ideology and practices of the Third Reich', although Hitler assumed that he did. Edward offered some 'appreciative words' for what Germany had achieved in terms of social welfare and housing, as contrasted with the slums of Britain that he had visited, aghast, while king.*

Hitler and the duke parted on amicable terms, pleased that they had managed to meet.† They were then photographed alongside Wallis, both formally and informally. In the staged pictures, the three of them stood alongside one another, Wallis on the left, Hitler on the right and Edward in the centre. The duke had a half-smile on his face, which could be interpreted either as amusement or regret at the situation that he had placed himself in. Wallis gazed directly at the camera with an enigmatic look that hinted at concern for how the photograph would be received. And Hitler wore a grim expression of determination, as if anxious to get back to subjugation and conquest but tolerating this for a moment. He was warmer in the casual photographs, in which he was seen smiling

---

* The duke's equerry, Dudley Forwood, claimed that Edward made some remarks less complimentary about the Nazi regime, which Schmidt refused to translate. This led the duke to say, *'Falschübersetzt'*, or 'wrongly translated'.
† According to the historian Jonathan Petropoulos, the duke now offered Hitler a Nazi salute.

and laughing with the duke and duchess, both of whom seemed amused by his conversation.

'What did you talk about?' Wallis asked afterwards.

'What Hitler's trying to do for Germany and to combat Bolshevism,' the duke replied.

'And what did he say about Bolshevism?'

'He's against it.'[35]

Then it was time to head to Munich, to be feted once again at a gala dinner at the Vier Jahreszeiten hotel, before returning to France. Edward and Wallis were sure they had performed a valuable diplomatic service, and looked forward to their American trip later in the year.

The visit was a propaganda coup for the Nazis. After the disappointment of the abdication, it showed that the duke could still be a useful tool for influencing British opinion. One German ambassador crowed that it had indicated Edward's 'special sympathy and understanding of Germany', and that as a representative of 'liberalism', or pro-German feeling, in Britain, 'the Duke of Windsor is by no means finished in his work'.[36] Edward himself wrote of his trip as 'intensely interesting', and portrayed himself as 'an independent observer studying housing and industrial conditions'. He remarked that he was glad that the 'apolitical' visit had not caused offence.

The time that he spent with Hitler had left a favourable impression on the Duke. On 23 October, he wrote the Führer a formal letter of thanks in German, saying that 'the Duchess of Windsor and I would like to thank you sincerely for the great hospitality you have shown us, and for the many options you gave us to witness all that has been done for the working people of Germany. Our trip through Germany has made a great impression on us, and we won't forget the attentiveness you surrounded us with and the warm welcome we received everywhere.'[37] He concluded with heartfelt thanks for the wonderful time* that he and Wallis had enjoyed at Hitler's retreat.

---

* In German, the literal translation is 'beautiful hours'.

Had the letter been made public, it would undoubtedly have caused horror. But, despite the fears of the king, Hardinge* and various diplomats, the trip was well enough received in England. Churchill wrote to Edward shortly afterwards that 'I am told when scenes of [your tour] were produced in the news reels in the cinemas here, your Royal Highness' pictures were always very loudly cheered.' While acknowledging that 'I was rather afraid beforehand that your tour in Germany would offend the great numbers of anti-Nazis in this country, many of whom are your friends and admirers', he professed himself glad that 'it all passed off with so much distinction and success'.[38]

Before complaining that 'politics here are horribly dull . . . there are no quarrels, no vehement debates, no stormy scenes',[39] Churchill advised Edward to travel aboard the *Normandie* to America rather than the *Bremen*, thereby avoiding antagonising public opinion by making connections with his recent visit to Germany. This advice was ignored, and Edward and Wallis prepared to embark on the *Bremen*. Chamberlain received a note from the Foreign Office accepting the inevitability of the trip: 'it is embarrassing that HRH should contemplate embarking on a second such visit, but I imagine that there is nothing to be done'.[40]

Yet even as Churchill assured the duke that 'the American journey I feel sure will be prosperous and you will get a reception from that vast public which no Englishman has ever had before', he showed tone-deafness as to how Edward's German embassy had been received in the United States.

The American reaction to the duke and duchess's wedding had previously been warm, and critical of the royal family's actions. The *New York Herald Tribune* wrote in an editorial of 29 May that 'we wish to remark upon the contrast, steadily growing more marked, between the dignity and rightness of the conduct of the

---

* Who had expressed a hope to Monckton earlier in the year that Edward and Wallis would settle permanently in Austria. 'It would have the double advantage of giving him an interest in life . . . and of anchoring him somewhere not too near this country.'

Duke of Windsor and the course being pursued by the powers that rule England', and suggested 'there can be no question of the duke's stature . . . he has grown, not diminished, in the eyes of the world since he made his dismaying decision'. They called the royal boycott of the wedding 'as unwise as it is unworthy' and referred to Edward as 'now still the object of wide affection and sympathy'.

The visit to Germany destroyed this affection and sympathy. The response of the *New York Times* to the publicity was typical. It remarked that 'The Duke's decision to see for himself the Third Reich's industries and social institutions and his gestures and re-marks during the last two weeks have demonstrated adequately that the abdication did indeed rob Germany of a firm friend, if not indeed a devoted admirer, on the British throne.' It even suggested that he had lent himself 'unconsciously but easily' to Nazi propa-ganda, and that 'there can be no doubt that his tour has strength-ened the regime's hold on the working classes'.[41]

Bedaux planned on taking a leading role in the duke and duch-ess's American tour, and had arrived in New York on 1 November to begin making the necessary arrangements. He was surprised firstly to be presented with bills for unpaid income tax, and then by the inquisition of a hundred journalists. All of them seemed opposed to both the trip and Bedaux's involvement within it.

If Wallis had hoped to visit her home city of Baltimore and be received rapturously, she would have been disappointed to learn that the Baltimore Federation of Labour condemned her and her husband's visit to Germany for giving succour to 'the world's most notorious foe of democracy and freedom of conscience'. The Federation also stated that for all of Edward and Wallis's public concern for life in Germany, similar conditions in Baltimore 'are to be studied by one who while resident here in no way showed the slightest concern nor sympathy for the problems of labour or the poor or needy'.

Bedaux, shocked by the collapse of his ambitions, retreated from America and telephoned the duke's secretary to tell him that the trip was off. He sent a telegram the following day absolving himself from any involvement in the visit: 'I am compelled in honesty and friendship to advise you that because of mistaken attacks on me here I am convinced that your proposed study tour would be difficult under my guidance . . . I respectfully suggest and implore that you relieve me completely of all duties in connection with your American tour.'[42]

Edward contacted Lindsay in Washington for advice as to whether to proceed with the visit, and was told that, given the hostile publicity, it seemed inadvisable to travel at great expense to a nation that no longer seemed keen to receive him. He issued a press statement cancelling his much-anticipated trip owing to the 'grave misconceptions which have arisen . . . regarding the motives and purposes of his industrial tour'.[43] He claimed to be nothing more than an apolitical observer, but it was too late.

The duke and duchess reacted stoically to the disappointment. She remarked to her aunt Bessie that 'we feel we made a wise decision about the US', and he wrote to Bedaux on 9 November to say, 'my decision was the only one possible'. But they had been shown that they remained pariahs. Their actions, whether knocking back steins of lager in Munich beer halls or fraternising with Nazis, ensured that respectability and acceptance remained distant. Never mind, they thought. Time to dust themselves off, resume hostilities with George VI and try and get what they could out of him.

Unfortunately, a pressing matter was shortly to occupy the king's, and Britain's, attention.

Chapter Three

'A Vague Sense of Fear'

Any king - indeed, any man - would have been fortunate to have
had a private detective as devoted as David Storrier. He first joined
Edward's service in 1936, when he was still on the throne, and accompanied him into exile at the end of the year. He became known
as his 'guardian shadow', so closely did he follow his master's every
movement. After Storrier's death in 1969, the duke wrote to his
family to convey his sorrow, calling the former policeman 'our
most loyal efficient and devoted bodyguard who we held in the
highest esteem'. During his service, he had even unbent so far as to
describe Storrier as 'one of the family'.

Had he known that the loyal, efficient and devoted retainer was
passing on details of his every action to MI5, the duke might have
regarded him differently.*

Storrier was a patriot, and his communications with the security services were detailed and informative. He informed MI5 in
August 1937, while Edward and Wallis were in the Austrian town
of Wasserleonburg, that the duke 'is now appreciating greater
difficulty in agreeably occupying his time', and was consequently
'more easily irritated by minor details such as the non-arrival on
time of things he may have ordered or a temporary breakdown
of the weather'.[1] On another occasion, a trip to Venice led Storrier

---

* It has been suggested that Edward and Wallis were aware of Storrier's actions
but remained indifferent to them. There was no complicity between the three,
however.

to write that 'Americans were very much in evidence and in their curiosity, armed with cameras, caused such obstruction and inconvenience on the beach that, after remarks by HRH, uniform police were called in for duty.'[2]

Although the response to the presence of Edward and Wallis was enthusiastic, they still created a furore everywhere they travelled. The curious regarded the spectacle of the former monarch and his wife as a Madame Tussauds display brought to life for their amusement. It was little wonder that Storrier noted the duke's contemptuous attitude towards unflattering press coverage. Elsewhere, the bodyguard wrote, of the need for his continued employment, that 'Threatening letters have practically ceased but numerous insulting letters are still received, although these are, in general, anonymous and unworthy of notice.'[3]

In the aftermath of their abortive visit to America, and the trip to Germany, there seemed little point or purpose to the exploits of the duke and duchess. Even clergymen had taken against them.* The English vicar of St George's church in Paris, Canon Dart, told journalists before Remembrance Sunday that 'I would rather the Duke of Windsor did not attend the service . . . I say emphatically that I will not meet him, speak to him or touch his hand . . . I would feel that I was betraying all my political and ecclesiastical ideals.' He added, 'I consider indeed that the Duke of Windsor has committed a sin more grave than any other person who is likely to be in my church tomorrow.'[4]

Storrier acknowledged this on 19 December when he filed his report from Paris, saying, 'No definite decisions [as to the future] appear to have yet been made . . . recent events have naturally changed the general outlook and called for complete alteration of plans'. Although the duke mentioned at the beginning of 1938 that he would like to 'search for a little sunshine', which Storrier thought alluded to a desired visit to Cuba, he and Wallis were bored.

The detective had attempted to influence the duke's actions

---

* *Plus ça change*, perhaps, given the actions of Cosmo Lang and Bishop Blunt.

previously, but had been ignored.* Regard for Storrier was generally related to whether he was saying something Edward and Wallis wished to hear. He reported to the Metropolitan Police commissioner Sir Philip Game about the abortive American trip that 'Reviewing recent events, which certainly came as a shock, permit me to say, sir, that I foresaw the consequences in each case and placed my opinion in the quarter concerned', before noting that '[this] opinion, I may add, was not in the first instance favourably received'. He later asserted that 'the correctness of [this], by force of circumstances, had to be later admitted by those most concerned'.

Edward and Wallis now realised how detached they were from events and opinion. Even the cessation of the threatening letters was a snub of sorts. They had passed from vitriol into disinterest, even as they were reminded how poorly they were regarded in the United States ('Recent incidents have led to an increase in the number of abusive communications, particularly from USA').[5] Storrier remarked, 'Time hangs heavy . . . difficulty is expected as regards the best course in arrangements for the immediate future and in finding suitable means of entertainment'.[6]

Still, Edward had some unlikely supporters. An Arthur Herts called at the Foreign Office on 7 January, claiming that he had been approached by an American Jewish syndicate with a view to helping restore the duke to the throne. Herts said that a fund was being subscribed to in New York under the auspices of influential Jews including, allegedly, the lawyer and civic leader Samuel Untermyer. The Foreign Office believed that Herts hoped to be recruited as

---

* He was dismissed late in 1938, ostensibly because there was no more money available to pay him, but perhaps because Edward and Wallis had tired of his double-dealing. He wrote a pained letter to Monckton on 4 January 1939, begging the lawyer to intercede and saying, 'the position I find myself in is due entirely to some misunderstanding so far, from my side, unexplained'. Monckton was obliged to check that there could be no possibility of blackmail, leading an outraged Storrier to respond indignantly that 'my heart is still with HRH'. And, he might have added, his longed-for salary.

an agent provocateur, and that his intentions were financial rather than patriotic. The file noted that he 'appears to live very comfortably "on his wits"' and the information he gave to the Foreign Office may have been prompted by 'a desire to leave this country forthwith . . . in order to avoid the possibility of further imprisonment'.[7] If any fund of the kind that Herts described existed, it never achieved fruition, but his claim at least demonstrated that Edward was not entirely irrelevant, even if he was an unwitting party to attempted fraud.

In France, Wallis continued to take the primary role in the relationship. The diplomat Ronald Campbell informed Vansittart that Prince Paul of Yugoslavia had lunched with the duke and duchess in Belgrade, and that although Edward seemed well enough, he was 'in a highly nervous condition' and had to jump up and leave the room on occasion, only for Wallis to sigh, 'Don't be surprised; he has to do that to calm his nerves.' It seemed to Paul that she was out for revenge against the royal family, and that 'she might prompt the Duke to do something deliberately malicious . . . out of pure spite and vindictiveness'.[8]

They remained *persona non grata* in the circles in which they wished to move, which caused them both 'acute pain'.[9] Phipps remarked to Hardinge that in view of their recent actions, the Duke and Duchess of Windsor were 'of course' not invited to a gala dinner in January 1938 in Paris. He asked the private secretary* to find out from the king whether their presence at the evening reception would be acceptable, saying, 'I shall not invite them until hearing from you.'[10] Although they were occasionally visited by politicians – Lloyd George and Churchill had been their dinner guests in Cannes between 21 December 1937 and 9 January 1938, an otherwise 'uneventful' time – the couple did not receive the sycophancy they expected. Churchill acknowledged this with

---

* The previous year, Hardinge had suggested that 'in my view, a reconciliation [between the king and Edward] is bound to take place' but qualified this by saying it would take place in the future – 'perhaps a somewhat distant future'.

the observation that the 'strange' party '[consisted] entirely of *ci-devant** . . . ex-kings, ex-prime-ministers, ex-politicians. It is like Voltaire.'[11]

Irrelevance vexed them. Edward wrote angrily to Neville Chamberlain at the end of 1937 to demand a date by which they could return to England for a visit. 'I never intended, nor would I ever have agreed, to renounce my native land or my right to return to it for all time.'[12] In response to his brother's request that he give his word not to return to his home country without royal consent, the duke huffed, 'I should have thought that my record as Prince of Wales and as King was sufficient to convince anyone that I am a man of my word and that there was no necessity to impose financial sanctions on me.' He stated that he had no intention of residing in Britain again, and that he would 'scrupulously avoid doing anything which might in any way cause embarrassment to him or the Government'.[13]

His German visit of the previous year – to say nothing of the events around the abdication – was not alluded to, but it gave the lie to the duke's outrage at his treatment. In any case, he was more concerned about the delayed provision of his allowance, a situation he called 'unfair and intolerable, as it would be tantamount to my accepting payment for remaining in exile'. Its long-awaited appearance might have led the unkind to compare it to Billy Bunter's mythical postal order, which the Fat Owl is forever expecting from one of his 'titled relations'.

Money fermented discord. A document drawn up on behalf of the king on 22 November 1937 agreed to the provision of a payment, but stated that 'there has been some discussion, and indeed some differences of recollection, about what passed when you left this country at the time of the Abdication as to an assurance that you would not return here'. The king wrote, 'you will realise that the return of an ex-monarch to the country where he used to be King would necessarily be a public matter with which my constitutional

---

* Meaning 'from an earlier time'.

advisers must be concerned . . . I feel, and my Ministers confirm me in this, that I should not be justified in continuing the voluntary allowance if the above constitutional position was not maintained.' He concluded, 'I sincerely hope you will see the reasonable-ness of my attitude.'[14]

A subsequent memorandum Hardinge drafted suggested that in order to ensure that the duke was kept out of Britain, government ministers would first tell the king that Edward should not return to the country. If the duke chose to disregard his brother's request – 'which all concerned agree is most unlikely' – his wallet would suffer the consequences. 'This would very likely bring about a disclosure of financial arrangements in which public money would be thought to be concerned, directly or indirectly.' Hardinge stressed that constitutional monarchy depended on the government's permission, rather than simply royal inclination. 'Ministers might well feel that there was a risk that His Majesty would become involved in public controversy if he continued to make the payment, and, in order to prevent that, they would then doubtless feel obliged to advise His Majesty to suspend it.'

Chamberlain attempted to build bridges between the government and the feuding siblings. He wrote to Edward on 7 January 1938, 'I am extremely sorry to learn that any advice which the Government have thought it their duty to tender to His Majesty has caused you pain . . . there has been misunderstanding of what we have had in mind'. He added that 'it is the earnest desire of the Government to see an end to the discussions . . . in a manner which will remove all feelings of bitterness or resentment' and he hoped 'I shall have removed from your mind any idea that the Government is actuated by motives unfriendly to Your Royal Highness'.[15] Edward replied, 'I now feel that it will be possible to bring the discussions between the King and myself to an early and satisfactory conclusion.'[16]

Yet all Chamberlain had done was to offer platitudes. Wallis was not to be granted her longed-for HRH status, and the pair remained in exile. She attempted to make the best of the situation, writing to her aunt Bessie on 26 January to say, 'We have tried to work out a 2 year plan which doesn't involve putting too much money into a place we may not like', but expressed her irritation at the 'fantastic rumours' about her in the US press ('I can't think of any two people except the Lindberghs* that have had such press persecution'). She remarked that her husband remained 'furious' with his family, even as she conceded that 'if they read and believe some of the things written I suppose they have a right to disapprove of the marriage', before concluding, incorrectly, 'time will be useful in adjusting it all'.[17]

The duke and duchess directed especial anger towards George VI and Queen Elizabeth, whom they denigrated as 'Mr and Mrs Temple'.[†] Yet the king attempted to be their advocate at court, even as Phipps reported the duke's comment, made during an interview with the *Daily Herald*, that he would be prepared to return to his country as president of the English republic, should the Labour Party wish it. This was dismissed as mere troublemaking. But there was one proviso to the king's support. He was opposed to any situation arising where Edward and Wallis could return to England on their own terms rather than his.[‡]

This came about from pragmatism. The duke and duchess were still popular figures in Britain, events of the previous autumn notwithstanding, and their return might have confused public opinion as to who was the 'real' monarch, despite Edward's professed support for his brother. But the king was also jealous. His elder

---

* Charles Lindbergh, the aviator, was also a noted Nazi sympathiser, fond of stating maxims such as 'Racial strength is vital; politics, a luxury.'
† The most insulting allusion was to their elder daughter, Princess Elizabeth, whom they sneeringly referred to as 'Shirley Temple'.
‡ Money remained the greatest hold the government had over the duke. One official note to Chamberlain fretted that 'every effort ought to be made to dissuade him from coming, at least in the near future . . . [but] it is difficult to see how Ministers can seek to impose a condition, the effect of which is thought by the Duke to mean that he is to go into exile and to continue in exile "for ever" . . . unless he is prepared to sacrifice this part of his income'.

brother had always been popular, able to make public appearances and speeches with aplomb, and Bertie had spent his life watching his glamorous sibling from the sidelines. Although he had never sought the role of monarch, he was determined to perform it to the best of his ability. The last thing he desired was a back-seat driver informing him, and anyone else who would listen, how the new king was getting it wrong and how much better the last one would have done the job.

The queen, meanwhile, feared for her husband. He had been approached by a lunatic at the Cenotaph on Remembrance Sunday the previous year,* and although he had remained calm and no disturbance had occurred, it was another reminder how unsettled his reign remained. She remarked to the diplomat D'Arcy Osborne on 5 January that 'Now young people have rather given up religion in any form, they look more & more to individual leadership, or rather leadership by an individual, and that is going to be very difficult to find.' George VI was not that man - 'it is almost impossible for the King to be that sort of leader' - and she reflected, 'For many years, there was a Prince of Wales, who did all the wise & silly & new things that kept people amused & interested & yet, because he did not, or would not realise that they did not want that sort of thing from their King - well he had to go.' She knew that 'it seems impossible to mix King and ordinary vulgar leadership . . . we don't want [Oswald] Mosleys', but presciently told Osborne, 'now there seems to be a vague sense of fear'.[18]

Her husband, meanwhile, felt isolated from national and international events alike, over a year into his reign. He chafed against this, fearing that it demonstrated his impotence. When Eden resigned as Foreign Secretary on 20 February, due to his frustration with Chamberlain's attitude of appeasement towards Italy, the king only discovered the news from the Sunday newspapers.

---

* A reminder, perhaps, of the abortive assassination attempt of George McMahon on his brother on 17 July 1936; see *The Crown in Crisis*, Chapter Three, for details.

This oversight led him to demand that Hardinge involve him more closely in the political developments of the day. His anger with Eden was balanced by his admiration for Chamberlain, whom he regarded as a paternalistic and candid figure whose advice was sound.

Even as the king told Eden, while formally accepting his resignation, that 'he had great sympathy for his point of view and did not think it would be long before he saw him again as one of his senior ministers',[19] he was relieved that it would be Lord Halifax, a supporter of Chamberlain's foreign policy, who would succeed him. Halifax was not overburdened by passion for his new position - one biographer said of him, 'he did not find the study of foreign affairs a matter of absorbing interest'[20] - but the so-called 'Holy Fox', to use Churchill's dismissive nickname for him, retained the languid charm and assurance bestowed on him by his Etonian schooldays. The king was relieved to be assured by older, more experienced men that everything would be fine so long as he listened to them and did not bother himself too much with irrelevant details. After all, the implication was, his brother had become over-invested in trivialities during his reign, and look what became of him.

One means of demonstrating Britain's soft power was to organise a European tour. Edward's only such foray had taken place aboard the *Nahlin* in the summer of 1936. It had been a diplomatic success despite its having been intended primarily as a holiday for him, Wallis and selected friends. The new king had initially hoped to travel to India early in his reign to visit the outposts of the Empire there, but apprehensive of the strain that it would cause, he postponed his tour indefinitely. It was instead decided that he would make his first official state visit to France in the summer of 1938, to develop and strengthen the alliance with his country's most significant neighbour.

When the Duke and Duchess of Windsor, who were staying in Versailles for three months, learnt the news through the papers, they were curious as to whether this trip represented an attempt at a rapprochement with them, or simply a further provocation. It would have been a snub for George VI to have visited France and not made any attempt to meet his brother, for the first time since the abdication crisis.

Edward asked his solicitor, Allen, to discover from Monckton what was going on. The lawyer wrote on 12 February that 'the Duke is naturally anxious that their Majesties' stay in Paris shall be a great success; and while he would, of course, be willing to fall in with any plans which may be made for the visit, he is, at the same time, very hopeful that the King and Queen may take the opportunity which this visit will afford of paying a call on the Duke and Duchess'. Allen had not earned his high professional reputation as a meticulous lawyer for nothing; he suggested that '[The duke] feels that such an invitation would serve the general interest since it would become known to everyone that the estrangement which has existed in their past is now ended.'[21]

Horace Wilson, Chamberlain's *éminence grise*, vetoed any such plan. He suggested to Monckton that 'Allen's letter goes a good deal beyond what I gather was put to you in Paris', especially the idea of an official reception for Edward and Wallis, and complained that '[it] raises so many complications that I should have thought it was better to drop it'. He acknowledged that Chamberlain believed that 'if the King and Queen felt disposed to agree to call, he would be inclined to think that it might be a good thing', but equivocated that 'there do not seem to be any particularly strong reasons why their Majesties should be persuaded to go if their inclination is otherwise'.[22]

Monckton therefore resumed his role as go-between. He was not optimistic about the result of the interview – 'I am afraid that this will seem a more definite and obvious estrangement with inconvenient consequences'[23] – though he accepted his burden with the commitment he had demonstrated since the abdication crisis.

Wilson responded that 'I feel sure you will have difficulty when you go out there . . . it is just a little early to try to get anything done'. Remarking that 'some of the memories [of the abdication crisis are] rather too fresh', he wished Monckton good fortune 'in another difficult task'.[24] Monckton might have been forgiven for telling him to go to hell, although knowing Wilson's Machiavellian flair, he would undoubtedly have made himself indispensable to Lucifer once there.

Monckton made one final attempt to resolve the situation by begging the king to reconsider. He wrote that 'the Duke is very sore with me for not having obtained a decision to communicate to him before this' and suggested that Edward's anger stemmed from being kept waiting for a decision until the last possible moment. He informed his monarch that 'a prompt decision on the question now will do much good'.[25]

The king, thus chivvied, made his move. He would not see his brother, and called the state visit 'a most unsuitable moment for meeting'. His animosity was dictated by how 'their behaviour has not been polite to us', and he stressed that it was 'much better for them to go away while [our] visit is on'.[26] He left it to Monckton to tell the duke the news, before receiving the French prime minister, Édouard Daladier, who was in England in April to elicit support for a united front in support of Czechoslovakia against Hitler. His efforts were in vain, as Chamberlain and Halifax were adamant that they could not risk war over such a matter. A disappointed Daladier was unimpressed with the king and queen, describing him as 'a moron' and her as 'an excessively ambitious woman who would be ready to sacrifice every other country in the world in order that she might remain Queen Elizabeth of England'.[27]

When informed of the royal affront, Edward seethed. He and Wallis had been shunned by the French society they had hoped would welcome them. Channon noted sympathetically that 'they dine alone night after night, ignored, snubbed by the French and neglected by the English . . . he is so lonely, so bored'. Wallis complained to her aunt, 'What snobs the world produces and what treatment can be handed out once power has gone.'[28] Yet

as Channon observed, the duke remained 'very pro-German'. He
believed that had Edward still been sovereign, no Austrian coup*
would have taken place, as the monarch would have been able to
appeal personally to Hitler. The duke shared Channon's high opinion of his abilities.

A public rapprochement with the king, whatever their private
opinions of one another, would have been an important step in
Edward's rehabilitation. But he was denied this olive branch too.
So, in a nod to conciliation, the king agreed to a financial settlement of £25,000 a year, and Edward professed himself satisfied
with this. Accordingly, he wrote to 'Dear Bertie' on 30 April from
Versailles to say, 'Wallis and I have . . . done our best to understand
the reasons which have prompted the conclusion you have arrived
at', and agreed to depart from France as requested.

Yet his resentment remained clear. He hissed, 'We would be less
than human if we did not feel deeply all that has been done to us
in the past sixteen months, and we naturally hoped for an end to
such treatment. Surely the time has come for some form of official
gesture towards us on the Continent where we are residing, out
of deference to you alone, to show that you, as King, require us
to be . . . "treated with proper attention and respect", so that there
may be a termination of the indignities to which we are constantly
open, and which are as much a reflection on the Royal Family as a
whole, as upon us personally.'

He demanded 'some proper recognition of our position as your
brother and sister-in-law', before concluding that 'We do frankly
feel that a formal reception given for us by your diplomatic representative in Paris is distinctly overdue to say the least. Had it ever
been considered that such a proposal could be in any way injurious
or prejudicial to your status, it would not have been suggested. On
the contrary, I am convinced that, properly handled as it would be,
the atmosphere of your State Visit may well be enhanced.'[29] Wallis

---

* Hitler marched his troops into Austria on 12 March 1938, effectively taking
control of the country.

was more candid. She told her aunt on 9 May, 'the King thinks it would make him too nervous to see the Duke, charming little cad that he has shown himself', and that 'once again the Duke makes life easier'.[30]

A compromise was reached. Phipps agreed to invite Edward and Wallis to the embassy as dinner guests, Halifax ensured that decorated and decorous high-profile members of the French government would be present, and Monckton told the king, 'I feel that a real step will have been taken towards appeasement which may go a long way to relieve His Majesty's anxiety in the matter.'[31] The duke and duchess were advised by Monckton against a planned summer visit to Hammamet near Tunis - 'that place has an extremely unsavoury reputation'[32] - and left instead for Antibes at the start of June. The king wrote blandly to Edward, 'I trust that the Embassy dinner party will be the sort that you will like . . . I am so pleased that you agree with me that our State Visit to Paris would not be a suitable moment for us to meet after all that has passed. But I hope that we shall be able to arrange a meeting at some future date under quieter conditions', before stating that 'I am very satisfied with the outcome of our financial settlement. It took a long time but there was so much to manage.' He could afford to be magnanimous. After all, he had won, and his embarrassing brother had been pushed aside.

The Duke and Duchess of Windsor remained out of sight, out of mind and out of reach, and a return to England seemed as unlikely as it had ever been. Had the duke recalled his mother's words on the day of the abdication - 'To give up all that for this' - he may even have agreed with her.

Meanwhile, the king and queen prepared for their visit to France. The trip was postponed after the death of the queen's mother, Lady Strathmore, on 23 June, which devastated her. The duke offered formal condolences, and the queen was relieved that they came only from him, and not from Wallis, her *bête noire*. Her concession to public mourning was to wear not conventional black attire, which would have seemed too dowdy for Paris, but an all-white ensemble designed by the couturier Norman Hartnell, something that gave her an atypical dash of glamour.

They left for France on 19 July, amidst tight security. Scotland Yard had intelligence of an eclectic range of plots against the royal couple, with participants rumoured to include anyone from the Gestapo to a band of Catalan anarchists calling themselves 'the Dwarfs'. A more serious concern was that some individual with a grudge, unfounded or otherwise, would act spontaneously and violently. The full resources of the French police force were therefore poured into Paris to greet the king and queen.

There were more pleasant aspects to their visit, such as 10,000 pigeons being released at the Bois de Boulogne station to greet them. The press coverage was warm. The magazine *L'Illustration* wrote that 'Nobody has a more simple, natural and easy style of approach than the King of England . . . The handshake which he gives one, frank, energetic with *je ne sais quoi* of spontaneity and sympathy, puts you at your ease, however modest your social station might be.'[33] Had the king known of the comments, he might have been reminded of similar things that had been said about his elder brother two years before. He may even have enjoyed the comparison.

The state visit was successful, but overtones of conflict could not be escaped. The king laid a wreath at the tomb of the Unknown Soldier, visited a military hospital and unveiled a memorial to the dead of the Great War. It was no coincidence that his speech on the first night's welcome banquet at the Elysée Palace talked of British sympathy and solidarity with their host country, even as he declared, in a sop to Hitler and Mussolini, that 'our entente has nothing exclusive about it . . . our friendship is not directed at any other power'. Halifax and Chamberlain attempted to play a game of brinksmanship, stressing England's affection towards France but also remaining committed to wider appeasement. If the king believed there was anything improper about his being used as a pawn, he did not make his reservations public.

Diana Cooper attended the party along with Churchill. She

described the royal banquet to Conrad Russell as consisting of mediocre food but 'gay noise, a band, lashings of wine and a general spectacle'. She sat next to the king at dinner, 'remembered not to talk him down - succeeded partially', and was drawn into gossip about the aristocracy. When she remarked of Diana Mitford, 'Oh, now she lives in sin with [Oswald] Mosley', the king replied, 'They say her sister lives in sin with Hitler, but I don't believe it', adding with just the hint of an innuendo, 'He doesn't do anything like that, does he?' Lady Diana professed herself unimpressed with the queen's outfit - 'the Queen's figure better, I really think, but an unfortunate dress, hooped in the wrong place, made of silver' - while her husband, Duff, was subjected to an assault of royal flattery. 'She has told him all the things about himself he most liked to hear, and discussing it after we both feared that she behaves so to all gentlemen, in fact that she has kissed the Blarney stone to some tune.'

Protocol and etiquette were an ever-present feature of these trips. Diana remarked how she paid 'a deep curtsey to the King on rising, remembering criticisms last year, I don't know if it was right. I followed the Queen out, & suddenly was hurt by what felt like a grappling iron jerking my arm out of its socket. It was the hand of [royal courtier] Sir Hill Child obstructing my obstructing of the King's exit.' She grumbled, 'One ought to be told. One can't guess that he goes out before the women and that the men go out after the women.' However, her mood was ameliorated by a long talk after dinner with the queen, whom she pronounced 'very easy and happy'. One of her ladies-in-waiting, a Mrs Bowlby, explained 'how they knew by an expression, not a look or a gesture, when the Queen wanted a change of companion'.[34] Diana considered herself fortunate not to have been so supplanted.

Yet the badinage had its darker side. Even as the king acknowledged the hospitality that he had received in a speech to the country's President Lebrun, saying, 'Nor . . . shall we ever forget the warm and affectionate welcome given to us by the men and women of your country, for it has touched us deeply and we are truly grateful', and the queen described the whole trip as 'a marvellous experience', the rise of Hitler and fascism led to disquiet.

Diana left one state banquet early to immerse herself in a throng of 10,000 French, all cheering the king and queen, who stood on the balcony of the foreign ministry. She eschewed her customary waspishness to say, 'I can never forget it. To the French, the Royal Visit seemed a safeguard against the dreaded war. That at least is what they told me, but I could see nothing to allay my fears.'[35] And witnessing a fly-past of military aircraft at Versailles led her to confess her apprehension at the 'sinister reminder of reality' that dominated, 'like a deathly hand, when the fog of peace dispersed'.[36]

The royal couple had overcome personal tragedy and the king's withdrawn and reserved manner to make their French expedition a triumph. Hardinge suggested to Monckton, who was heading to meet the duke and duchess, that 'it might be a good thing to rub in the great success of the Paris visit both at home and abroad, especially [the queen's] personal triumph', and crowed, 'That will get home, I think!'[37]

Yet what Churchill would term 'the gathering storm' lay on the horizon. Even as the prime minister and his Cabinet sought to avert the inevitable, it was clear that the spectre of another European war was upon them. And another, more intimate conflict continued to cause difficulty.

Chapter Four

'Humiliation Is Better Than War'

Stanley Baldwin, the prime minister who steered his monarch and country through the abdication crisis, once described himself, not without pride, as 'a remnant of the old Victorians'. His successor, Neville Chamberlain, was scarcely more modern as a premier, with the appearance and personality of the exasperated headmaster of a troubled minor public school, but he might have cavilled at calling himself Victorian. He saw himself as Edwardian in terms of outlook, as he sowed division in the House of Commons and displayed antipathy to the 'sob-stuff' sentimentality that he believed Attlee's Labour Party specialised in.

He came from a distinguished political family, which gave him a firm, even entitled belief in his right to rule. His father, Joseph, was a ruthless Liberal parliamentarian who was said to have originated the phrase 'you cannot teach old dogs new tricks'. Joseph gloried in imperialism, and announced, 'The day of small nations has long passed away. The day of Empires has come.' This was an edict that Neville remembered, and which coloured his political approach. Meanwhile, his elder brother Austen, one-time Chancellor of the Exchequer and leader of the Conservative Party, demonstrated a confidence in his own intellectual abilities that his sibling did his best to emulate. Had he not been mired in the most notorious bait-and-switch of the twentieth century, he might even have surpassed them.

By no means universally popular by the time he became prime minister, even with his own side - Nicolson spat that he was 'anything but a gentleman' and 'a bourgeois shit' - Chamberlain was nonetheless regarded highly by many. His friend Channon praised him for his elegance, bearing and 'charm of manner', and announced in February 1938 that 'I determined to support him always . . . I feel loyal about him as I never did about Farmer Baldwin.'[1] He was sufficiently cognisant of the relationship between his predecessor and Edward VIII to decide that he would be a different premier, taking a paternalistic and, when necessary, interventionist approach towards his king.

It helped that he had a fondness towards the king and queen that he had never felt towards Edward. He described Elizabeth, while she was still Duchess of York, as 'the only royalty I enjoy talking to' and praised her as 'always natural'. He even wrote in his diary in April 1937 that '[people] fervently thanked heaven that [the Duke of Windsor] was out of the way and replaced by Sovereigns whom everyone could respect'.[2] He wished to show a private warmth towards the king that few of his peers saw - 'I am not really an alarming person',[3] he wrote to his sister Hilda, as if expecting contradiction. He succeeded. By August 1937, the relatively new prime minister* was able to write, after a trip to Balmoral, 'my relations with yourself and the Queen will henceforth be on a new footing . . . I need hardly say how greatly I value this approach to intimacy and how helpful it will be to me as head of Your Majesty's Government.'[4]

At sixty-eight, he was not especially elderly by the political standards of the day (Winston Churchill was sixty-one in 1937), but he could not remain prime minister indefinitely. It was instead expected that he would make way for a younger and more dynamic successor after a calmer period of government than Baldwin had overseen. Unfortunately, Hitler's belligerence meant that Chamberlain's longed-for status as a patrician elder statesman was endangered from the beginning of his premiership. A less arrogant man might have surrounded himself with younger, even ideologically

* He became PM on 28 May 1937.

opposed figures, such as Eden and Cooper, and encouraged, rather than tolerated, their opinions. But Chamberlain believed that he had the support of Parliament and the Conservative Party - and more importantly, the king - in pursuing a policy of appeasement towards Hitler and Mussolini. Even Eden's resignation in February 1938 could not shake his belief that he was following the right - indeed, the only - path for his country's well-being and future.

Neither Chamberlain nor Halifax believed that Hitler and his lieutenants presented an existential threat to Britain. The Foreign Secretary described Hermann Göring, whom he met on a visit to Berlin in 1937, as 'like a great schoolboy, full of life and pride in what he was doing . . . a modern Robin Hood . . . a composite impression of film-star, gangster, great landowner interested in his property, Prime Minister, party manager [and] head gamekeeper at Chatsworth'.[5]

Although Halifax's German embassy was a lower-profile visit than the Duke of Windsor's shortly before, it was similarly ill-fated. The Foreign Secretary was unconcerned about Hitler's intentions, as he continued to believe that the Führer was an essentially reasonable, if ridiculous, man. At one crucial meeting at Berchtesgaden, he even mistook the unassuming-looking Hitler for a servant and was only disabused of his error by Konstantin von Neurath, his German counterpart, hissing in his ear, 'Der Führer, der Führer.'

Therefore, when Hitler annexed Austria in March 1938, neither Halifax nor Chamberlain was alarmed by his actions, which they saw as essentially a European domestic matter and not one that concerned Britain. Even as the Führer's imperial ambitions became clearer throughout the rest of the year, with the conquest of Czechoslovakia an inevitability, Chamberlain concentrated on maintaining the status quo at home. A vote of censure was moved against him by Labour and the Liberals in the Commons on 4 April, but without success. The warmth and amity with which the king and queen were greeted in France in July 1938 reflected well on Chamberlain and his government, and the international situation was felt to be sufficiently calm for the monarch to head to Cowes, on the Isle of Wight, for a holiday aboard the royal yacht, *Victoria and Albert*.

At this stage, the king, guided by Halifax and Chamberlain, supported appeasement unconditionally. Channon wrote in his diary on 22 June that 'the King is sound, and against Anthony Eden', who, he noted, 'in two years caused more trouble than any Foreign Secretary since Palmerston'.[6] However, the monarch's outlook stemmed from the influence of the two father figures. They kept telling him that war would be an outrage and that every step must be taken to prevent it, not least because the country was neither financially nor militarily prepared for conflict. Those who would have given him different advice, including Cooper and Churchill, were not allowed to offer their heretical opinions.*

At the Battle of Copenhagen in 1801, Lord Nelson, when ordered to end a potentially catastrophic action, placed a telescope to his sightless eye and famously (and apocryphally) said, 'Ships? I see no ships.'[†] On that occasion, Nelson's tactical acumen ensured victory. Chamberlain was no Nelson, however, and his refusal to countenance what was upon Britain and Europe made him look delusional. When his visit to a wet, cold Balmoral was interrupted by an emergency Cabinet meeting in London on 26 August, he sat silently as Halifax remarked that 'the only deterrent which would be likely to be effective would be an announcement that if Germany invaded Czechoslovakia we should declare war upon her'.[7]

However, once this course of action was mentioned, Sir Nevile Henderson, the British ambassador to Germany, immediately raised objections to it. Henderson, who should have known better by then, suggested that Hitler was interested in peace rather than war, and that any attempts to escalate the situation would 'strengthen the position of the extremists rather than the moderates'.[8] Leaving aside the fact that Hitler himself was the extremist, Chamberlain

---

* Hardinge was also anti-appeasement, but it would appear that he did not attempt to influence the king's opinion.

† The actual, slightly less pithy, quote is 'Foley, you know that I have lost an eye, and have a right to be blind sometimes. I really do not see the signal.'

ensured that the Cabinet, without the absent Duff Cooper, unanimously agreed that they would not issue any threat or ultimatum. He returned to Balmoral to reassure the king and queen that any rumours of imminent war that they had read in the press or heard from courtiers were baseless.

Yet even as Lord Beaverbrook's *Daily Express*, briefed thanks to a leak from the Cabinet meeting,* could declare on 1 September 1938, 'THERE WILL BE NO WAR', and praise Hitler as 'a man of exceptional astuteness', and Chamberlain reassured the king on the 6th that 'developments seem very slow', the Führer had set his plans to invade Czechoslovakia in train. On the 12th, he prepared to address his people at Nuremberg, telling them with the fervour of an evangelical preacher that the Sudeten Germans† wished to be self-determining, but that they were being threatened by the despotic Czechs, who wanted nothing less than the 'annihilation' of the peaceful Germans. In this way he framed his actions less as an act of belligerence and more as a regrettable but inevitable step. The crowd adored it, and repeatedly shouted, 'We will follow our leader.' Some of the English attending were less convinced by his rhetoric. The politician and former Colonial Secretary Leo Amery called the 'raving tone' and 'fierce cheers of the crowd' terrifying, and said, '[we must] leave [the Germans] in no doubt where we stand'.[9]

Chamberlain was now compelled to act, and so headed to Germany for his first face-to-face meeting with Hitler, which took place on 14 September. He told the Führer that 'in view of the increasingly critical situation, [I intend] to come over at once and see you with a view to trying to find a peaceful solution'. Hitler was delighted at this, crowing, 'I fell from Heaven!'[10] Yet Chamberlain still had public opinion in Britain behind him. Channon called this 'one of the finest, most inspiring acts of all ... history must be

* Probably from the Home Secretary, Sir Samuel Hoare, who had been taking Beaverbrook's cash for years in exchange for such information.
† The ethnic Germans who were living in Czechoslovakia at the time.

ransacked to seek such a parallel'. He added, 'Of course a way will be found now. Neville by his imagination, his practical sense, has saved the world. I am staggered.'[11]

As Chamberlain left, the king, concerned by the speed of developments, returned from Balmoral to Buckingham Palace. In lieu of being able to take more constructive action, he informed Halifax that he had written to Hitler 'from one ex-serviceman to another', asking him to do what he could to avert another war: an idea of Hardinge's. Halifax, knowing that the Führer would only be amused by such a missive, suggested that it might be best for the king to wait until his prime minister's return and to seek his counsel then. Instead, the monarch sent Chamberlain a letter in which he praised his 'courage and wisdom' while hoping for a peaceful outcome.

It was soon clear that Chamberlain, and by extension Britain, had been outplayed. Channon may have written on 16 September that 'the Chamberlain-Hitler meeting seems to have been a huge success',[12] but this was wishful thinking. Like Halifax, the prime minister was unimpressed by the Führer's appearance, calling him 'entirely undistinguished' and 'the commonest little dog he had ever seen',[13] but Hitler worked himself up into a frenzy of excitement over his righteous actions.

Chamberlain was compelled to acknowledge that Germany had the right to self-determine the Sudeten lands in Czechoslovakia. Eventually the two men parted in a state of mutual satisfaction, promising that they would meet again soon in Cologne. Chamberlain decided, despite his earlier misgivings, that Hitler was trustworthy, calling him 'a man who could be relied upon when he had given his word'. The Führer meanwhile sneered that he had 'manoeuvred this dried-up civilian into a corner'.[14]

The king received his premier on the evening of 16 September, after writing to him to say, 'I am naturally anxious to hear the result of your talk, and be assured that there is a prospect of a peaceful solution on terms which admit of general acceptance.' Chamberlain was able to do no more than repeat what he had said to the

Cabinet, namely that he believed that Hitler, whatever his personal failings, was sincere and wished for peace. For the first time, the monarch began to believe that his prime minister was mired in obfuscation. His feelings can be discerned by a letter he wrote to Lascelles the next day, in which he bemoaned how 'everything is in a maze' and said that 'if [the French] won't stand up to Hitler, how can we, & the world must be told it is their fault and not ours'.[15]

The most vivid account of the crisis came from Hardinge, who wrote a series of letters to his wife Helen between 16 and 28 September detailing his first-hand experience of events. Undoubtedly he would have conveyed the same sentiments to the king during this period. 'What deplorable times we live in', he groaned. Although he praised the prime minister's trip for 'providing the true ray of hope . . . it seems to have come off well', he feared that the international situation had passed a point of no return. 'The Czechs will have every justification for saying that, in spite of a series of concessions, they have been abandoned by their powerful friends, and thus evoke a great deal of sympathy.' He did not trust Hitler – 'With him, however, it is always take, and no give' – but noted with relief a change in the national mood. 'There is evidence of a substantial change in the country from the defeatism and 'peace at any price' attitude of recent times.'[16]

Over the next days, Hardinge remained gloomy. After speaking with both Eden and the king, he told his wife that 'The outlook is far from good, in fact it could not be worse.' He blamed the situation on the government's foreign policy – 'carried on by amateurs in disregard of all expert advice' – and predicted that 'We are properly in the soup now, in spite of our wonderful PM.'[17] He wrote to the queen on 19 September and outlined the dangers of Hitler's policy of annexing Czechoslovakia, stating, 'I find it difficult to say what view the country will take – they are torn between the humiliation of impotence and the attraction of "peace at any price".'*[18] And he

---

* Helen wrote caustically on the envelope on 12 October that 'it's a pity Alec's literary gift is wasted on such an unliterary family'.

remarked to his wife that 'Oliver [Stanley]* and one or two others are not at all happy, but the PM has promised to do his best and get some *quid pro quo* from Hitler, but I doubt if he will succeed. Oliver says that he will then resign - but I have my doubts.' The American ambassador Joe Kennedy, meanwhile, was said to be 'horrified' by the situation, but Hardinge mused that 'humiliation is maybe better than war ... I attribute our plight mainly to the feeble resistance to the dictators shown by the Government since [Eden] went, for which they rightly deduced that we are a "peace at any price" lot.'[19]

Subsequently, he blamed the 'hateful time' on the humiliations wrought by the failings of British diplomacy earlier in 1938, and stated, 'I feel it however to be vital that our foreign policy should be altered - and that we should tell the dictators straight out that we shall be visiting force against any further acts of aggression against weaker forces, whether our vital interests are affected or not. I feel we must either stand up to the dictators, or clutch our hands ... and reject all entanglements in the continent.'[20] Unlike many around him, he was no supporter of appeasement, believing it an appalling idea. He remarked to his wife on 21 September that 'it makes it almost worse that I have disapproved so strongly of the conduct of our foreign policy since [Eden] resigned. I do not say that he would have prevented this happening, but he would have seen that we were in a better position, so that if we were not going to stand up, we should not be humiliated', and asked, 'Do we join in again and tacitly condone the complete dismemberment of Czechoslovakia which is obviously Hitler's objective? Or do we fight?'[21]

Public dissatisfaction now became a noticeable issue. Hardinge observed the next day that 'Feeling is running high against the Government. Apparently a Paramount newsreel giving speeches by Wickham Steed† and others attacking the Government has been

---

* A Conservative MP and President of the Board of Trade.
† A journalist, historian and former editor of *The Times* who was notable for being one of the first British public figures to warn against the danger posed by Hitler and his regime.

received with enthusiasm in London cinemas.'[22] He subsequently remarked that 'The feeling against the PM is pretty strong – and the country is bellicose – but I think nevertheless that the wicket is a bad one.'[23] The same day, he wrote a memorandum for the king that laid out the situation in unsentimental terms: 'Public opinion considers the surrender to have been complete, even if unavoidable, already. The anticipation by a few weeks of the occupation of the Sudeten areas by German troops would add little to it, nor would this aggravation be sufficient to achieve unanimity for the prosecution of a war. The Government should therefore make the best arrangement possible with Hitler now, even if it involves some revision of the frontier of Czechoslovakia with Poland and Hungary.'

Hardinge then looked to the future. 'It would be vital to make it clear that the country must never be put to such humiliation again, and that further aggression by the dictators would be forcibly resisted. The Government should propose therefore to put industry on a new footing, so as to make as many aeroplanes as Germany possessed, coûte que coûte,* and to impose a limited form of compulsory national service solely for purposes of defence and precaution against air attack.'

Presciently, he also addressed the political make-up of a wartime Cabinet. 'The Government would at the same time be reconstructed, so as to include those who have previously advocated resistance to the designs of the dictators, the opposition Liberals, and, if possible, some new blood from outside. The Labour opposition would probably prefer not to join the Government, but they would no doubt be willing to cooperate in the strengthening of democracy against dictatorship.' Noting Chamberlain's perceived weakness, he remarked, 'They might, of course, be reluctant to extend [their cooperation] to the present Prime Minister.'[24]

Worse was soon to come. By 25 September, Hardinge reported that Stanley was on the verge of resignation, on the grounds that

---

* Meaning 'at all costs'.

'people are rather taking the view that no more concessions can be made . . . as Hitler has given nothing in exchange for the "Anglo French plan", it cannot be looked upon as a contribution to European peace, which was the only basis on which it could be commended to the people of the country'.[25]

Patriotism was not enough to combat the threat. Duff Cooper rejected Chamberlain's assurances of Hitler's integrity at Cabinet and called Nazi Germany 'probably the most formidable power that had ever dominated Europe'.[26] This was not a crisis that could be handled merely with fine words and stirring invocations. On 22 September, the prime minister again headed to Germany to meet with the Führer, only to be told that Hitler now wanted the disputed territory to be evacuated by the Czechs by the 28th. It seemed as if Chamberlain was being pulled this way and that as if he were a marionette on a string, but he attempted to find a path towards peace even as he became aware of the manner of man his adversary truly was.

When he confessed his humiliation to the king at lunch at Buckingham Palace on 25 September, he described Hitler more harshly than before, calling him a warmonger who was making unreasonable and unfulfillable demands, and warning the sovereign that conflict was increasingly inevitable. Halifax now no longer believed that appeasement was an option, and insisted that Chamberlain issue the ultimatum that unless Hitler agreed to settle the affair through negotiation, Britain and France would unite in aiding Czechoslovakia. This would bring about a state of war.

Conflict seemed a fait accompli, and Hardinge could only say, dolefully, on 26 September that 'This is the blackest day of all. Feeling, both in this country and in France, has stiffened enormously against the German demands . . . It looks as if we shall have to see it through now. Certainly life this last year has been made unbearable by fear and threats of war, and, as you know, I have always held the view that as long as dictatorships last, a life of peace and prosperity would be impossible for humanity.' He described Hitler as 'completely mad . . . the one thing that will certainly go bust if a war comes is Nazidom'.[27]

Despite this, the monarch continued to believe that a personal appeal to the Führer would carry regal weight. Chamberlain disabused him of this idea, leading the king to tell Queen Mary on 27 September of the suggested compromise, namely that Germany should occupy a designated area of Czechoslovakia and the rest be allowed to self-govern. He remarked that 'If Hitler refuses to do this, then we shall know at once & for all that he is a *madman* . . . It is all so worrying this awful waiting for the worst to happen.'[28] Hardinge, meanwhile, was sceptical of this compromise. He argued that 'If we manage to get through without a showdown – and it seems incredible that a world war should be fought on so small a margin of difference – the danger will be that we shall all sit back saying how peaceful-minded the Germans are, and that it is not in the least necessary to rearm', before concluding, 'Our pro-German friends will have to be carefully watched.'[29]

War, which everyone had tried to avoid for the past two decades, seemed at last to be upon them. Trenches were dug in Hyde Park, gas masks were handed out to schoolchildren, and a weary Chamberlain broadcast to the nation, calling the situation 'horrible, fantastic [and] incredible'. As Queen Elizabeth launched a vessel in her name on the River Clyde that day, she attempted to cheer her people, saying, 'I have a message for you from the King. He bids the people of this country to be of good cheer, in spite of the dark clouds hanging over them . . . He knows well that, as ever before in critical times, they will keep cool heads and brave hearts.'[30] The message, written by Hardinge, was not poetic. But it reminded the nation that whatever the compromises and obfuscations reached by politicians, the royal family would continue to be a shining beacon of hope, decency and integrity throughout the country and the world.

'The more I think of it, the more I am convinced that a visit to Germany would be disastrous in its effect on public opinion both in England, which was on the brink of war with Germany a week ago, and in the United States, where it would revive the legend of his Nazi sympathies which I worked so hard to dissipate last autumn.'[31] So Phipps wrote to Monckton on 21 September, aghast at the suggestion that the Duke of Windsor planned another visit to Germany to offer his services as an agent of peace. As his former country stood on the precipice of conflict, the man who had done more than most to damage its international standing lingered in France.

'We do not mean to spend our lives in exile', Wallis had upbraided Nicolson when the politician asked why the duke and duchess had not considered purchasing a property in France. Their goods, which had once graced Edward's beloved Fort Belvedere, were mainly stored at Frogmore, a villa in the grounds of Windsor Castle. They instead furnished their rented houses with French *bijouterie* that Wallis had spied in various Parisian antique markets and boutiques.

The cages were gilded, but they remained cages. Edward's eye 'twitches in pain'[32] when Nicolson mentioned his imminent return to England. Other visitors noted that he talked incessantly about when it would be his time to go home. Their friends were sympathetic but unable to help. When Churchill sent the duke the gift of a book about Marlborough on 12 September, he added, 'Sir, things are going very badly, and I fear they are going to get much worse.'[33]

When Monckton visited the duke and duchess in August 1938 at the Château de la Croë in Antibes, he wrote that Edward, 'anxiously considering a return to England', would drag him up to his study and ask for his assistance in drafting letters to the king, Queen Mary, Chamberlain and others. When he was not writing angry epistles, Monckton observed the duke at play, frequenting the local casino and heading to the golf course. He noted that he saw Kennedy playing behind Edward, and that the ambassador 'was very careful to keep away from the Duke'.[34]

The letter that the two of them constructed for the king was a fantasia on well-worn themes. 'One of the uppermost thoughts in my mind since I left England over twenty months ago has been to determine the most suitable opportunity for Wallis' and my first visit to our country after our marriage . . . I have purposely remained abroad since December 1936, at great personal inconvenience, in order to leave the field clear for you. As there can be no doubt that your position on the throne is by now consolidated, and that consequently my presence in England can no longer embarrass you, we propose to come over on a visit next November.'[35] Edward referred to 'important private business', which remained indeterminate, and a desire to visit friends, before asking that a house in Windsor should be placed at their disposal.

It was a provocation, but it could not be ignored. Upon his return to England in September, Monckton, conscious that the duke was capable of either making mischief or having it made for him, went to Balmoral to discuss the situation with Chamberlain and the king and queen. The visit alternated between formality and jocularity. One lunchtime, Monckton, inappropriately attired in trousers rather than breeches, talked with the young Princess Margaret, who took pleasure in asking him whether he shot, fished or played golf. When he answered in the negative, Margaret enquired, 'What *do* you do?', at which point the king took pity on him and 'extraordinarily deftly' replied, 'Something you know nothing about, Margaret. He works!' Monckton professed himself grateful for his sovereign's ready wit and social nuance in this situation.*

Chamberlain, the king and the queen each took a different approach towards the duke's long-term future. The prime minister, distracted by Germany and Czechoslovakia, suggested that he might eventually resume his place in the royal family as if he were

---

* The princesses' nanny, Marion 'Crawfie' Crawford, wrote presciently of Margaret that 'Old men were often [frightened of her] . . . she had too witty a tongue and too sharp a way with her, and I think they one and all felt that they would probably be the next on her list of caricatures . . . this misunderstanding of her light-hearted fun and frolics was often to get her in trouble long after schoolroom days were done'. Crawfie concluded that 'she could be extremely tiresome'.

a trusted younger brother, able to officiate at functions in the king's stead. The king equivocated, suggesting that he was not against the idea, but that he had no wish for a return to take place as early as the duke's hoped-for date of November 1938.

The queen, however, was adamant that Edward should not return or be given any significant role. In Monckton's estimation, 'I felt then, as always, that she naturally thought that she must be on her guard because the Duke of Windsor, to whom the other brothers had always looked up, was an attractive, vital creature, who might be the rallying point for any who might be critical of the new King who was less superficially endowed with the arts and graces that please.'[36]

It was therefore decided that it was impossible politically or socially for the duke to be given any encouragement to return to Britain, now or in the future. The only concession that Chamberlain could wring from the king and queen was that the Duke and Duchess of Gloucester would be allowed to visit him in Paris in November. It was Monckton's 'difficult task' to inform the duke what had been decided, especially that his brother and sister-in-law considered it 'inadvisable' that he return to England so soon.[37]

It was not what Edward had expected. He had written to Chamberlain in August saying, 'I need hardly tell you as an Englishman how distasteful voluntary residence in a foreign country without a defined object can be.' His attitude was that he had kept his side of the bargain, so why should his exile persist? A letter from the king did not assuage his anger or disappointment. It stated that opposition to a visit (or eventual return) did not stem from personal grounds, but instead was done in 'the national interest', that catch-all term that could be drawn upon to present anything disagreeable as a necessary sacrifice. The duke might have been forgiven for scepticism at his brother's assurance that 'I naturally want your first visit to be a success, & one which would be devoid of any untoward incidents towards either of you ... every month that passes lessens the chances of any bitterness that may remain from rising to the surface to cause you annoyance'. The only hint at any timetable was the king's suggestion that 'I agree with the Prime Minister that the spring or early summer of next year would be a better moment.'[38]

The letter had been considerably toned down. An angry draft that still exists in the Royal Archives spoke of how 'during the last twenty months, while you, as you desired, have been enjoying the leisured life of a rich private individual, I have been endeavouring, to the best of my ability, to restore the Monarchy to the position that it held when you succeeded, and to make good the damage done to it by the circumstances of your abdication . . . all I ask therefore, on purely public grounds, is that if you do pay your proposed visit you will help me by not giving any encouragement to those forces which I know are only too ready to make use of you in their attempts to embarrass the Government, thereby indirectly bringing discredit on the Crown and our family'. There was even a dig at Wallis. 'The risk that [the duchess] might be insulted, either in public or private, does, I am afraid, exist, and it is of course for you to decide whether such a risk is worth taking.'[39]

Yet whether from diplomacy or cowardice, the king sent his brother a blander version. The duke still regarded this as unacceptable, but he could not summon the energy to berate the sovereign once again. Instead he decided to offer his services to world peace.

Back in England, war now seemed inevitable. But on the night of 27 September, the once-unthinkable happened: Hitler appeared to blink. He sent a message to Chamberlain, who was 'wobbling about all over the place',[40] saying that he was prepared to convene a conference, to which he would also invite Mussolini and Daladier, with the aim of averting conflict. When Mussolini accepted these terms on 28 September, naming Munich as his desired location for a summit, Chamberlain was able to surprise his colleagues in the House of Commons: 'Herr Hitler has just agreed to postpone mobilisation for twenty-four hours and to meet me in conference.'

This was received extremely well. Even his nemesis Churchill made a point of shaking his hand and wishing him 'God speed'.

Queen Mary, who had been watching from the Ladies' Gallery, called it 'dramatic' and 'wonderful',[41] and told the king that she had been too emotional to speak.

The previous evening, Chamberlain had made a listless broadcast to the nation, calling himself 'a man of peace to the depths of my soul', which Cooper dismissed as 'a most depressing utterance'. Hardinge, however, told Chamberlain that the king had been pleased by his words, saying that it was 'marvellous, exactly what was wanted'.[42] And the king continued to be impressed by his premier, especially when he arrived back in England at 5.30 p.m. on 28 September, triumphantly holding 'a piece of paper', the Munich Agreement. War had been averted, for the moment at least.

Chamberlain's achievements were symbolic. When Hitler was upbraided by Ribbentrop for having given ground, he laughed, 'Oh, don't take it all so seriously. That piece of paper is of no significance whatsoever.'[43] The Führer was now able to achieve his desired objective of annexing 11,000 square miles of Czechoslovakia, and to do so with the assent of Britain and France. He had achieved his victory.

And yet the feeling of relief in Britain was so great that the prime minister, for the first and last time in his premiership, was given an ecstatic reception. He appeared on the Buckingham Palace balcony alongside the king, graciously acknowledging the applause of the masses, before heading to Downing Street. Here, he made a hubristic speech that would forever haunt him thereafter, in which he said, 'This is the second time in our history* that there has come back from Germany to Downing Street peace with honour. I believe it is peace for our time.'

Many were unconvinced. Cooper resigned immediately, and after an audience with the king described his monarch as 'frank and charming . . . he said he could not agree with me, but he respected those who had the courage of their convictions'.[44] Churchill, appalled by the perceived betrayal of the Czech people, called it 'only

---

* The first being Disraeli returning from the Congress of Berlin in 1878.

the beginning of the reckoning', and railed against 'the abandon-
ment and ruin of Czechoslovakia'. His reward was to be sneered at
by The Times as making 'Jeremiah* appear an optimist'. But the king
described the result as 'a great day'. He wrote to Queen Mary that
'the Prime Minister was delighted with the result of his mission,
as we all are, & he had a great ovation when he came here'.[45] Nor
was Halifax's loyalty forgotten. The king praised him, saying, 'The
responsibility resting on the Foreign Secretary at a time like this is
indeed overwhelming, and the wisdom & courage with which you
have borne it have earned for you the admiration and gratitude of
the whole Empire.'[46]

The contrast with other politicians was implicit but clear. Queen
Mary, meanwhile, was infuriated by Churchill and Cooper's ingratitude. She complained to her son, 'I am sure you feel as angry as I
do at people croaking at the PM's action', and cited Lady Oxford's
remark, 'He brought them peace, why can't they be grateful?'[47]

Chamberlain was smug about his personal success. 'At times,'
he remarked to the king, 'the old diplomacy fails, and personal interviews with dictators are called for.' His wife, Anne, meanwhile,
received a warm letter from the queen, in which she wrote, 'you
must feel so proud and glad that through sheer courage & great
wisdom [Chamberlain] has been able to achieve so much for us
& for the world', and declared that 'our gratitude is beyond words
. . . our prayers that he might be sustained & helped through these
frightful days have been very real'.[48]

Others saw the situation in less idealistic terms. Hardinge remarked to Viscountess Milner that 'The unfortunate PM was forced
into a frightful dilemma. Either contract the best terms he could
from a man standing at the frontier with 1½ million bayonets - or
bring about a world war with unpredictable consequences.' While
he allowed that 'I think the lesser evil was the right course . . . in
the circumstances I cannot see what else there was to be done', he

---

* The so-called 'weeping prophet' of the Old Testament was not noted for his
sunny and cheery disposition.

grimly announced that 'we must not let ourselves get into that sort
of position again', and expressed his fear that the much-desired
peace was illusory. 'It is possible that we may before long be faced
with a similar situation', he noted, before qualifying his statement:
'in much less favourable circumstances'.[49] Hitler and his actions
remained a terrifying threat beyond everyone's comprehension.

The only member of the royal family with first-hand experience of
the Führer was now in a belligerent mood. The Duke of Windsor
wrote to Monckton on 31 October from Paris, defending himself
against the king's 'quite stupid and rather impertinent suggestion
that I am "a publicity seeker"', a statement undercut by his then
asking his counsellor's advice about the most effective way of
presenting his and Wallis's meeting with the Duke and Duchess
of Gloucester to the media. He suggested that 'careful consideration [must be] of course given to "timing" . . . if [a statement] were
handed out too soon beforehand, the visit would look like a stunt
and loose [sic] the normal aspect it is so important to preserve'.
The recent events in his former country appeared to have made
little impact on him, as he exhorted Monckton that '"Attack, attack,
attack" must be our motto.'[50]

   To this end, the duke contacted Chamberlain on 23 October to
see if the prime minister might be recruited to his side. He had
already attempted to establish a relationship with him, expressing
his admiration for 'the courageous manner in which you threw
convention and precedent to the winds by seeking a personal meeting with Herr Hitler and flying to Germany'. He made an explicit
comparison between the premier's deeds and his own approach by
calling Chamberlain's action 'a bold step to take, but, if I may say
so, one after my own heart, as I have always believed in personal
contact as the best policy in "a tight corner"'.

   Edward denigrated the Cabinet as cowards ('it would not surprise me if there were, among your colleagues, some who debated
the wisdom of such dramatic last hour tactics') but reiterated his
admiration for the prime minister himself. 'You followed the

dictates of your conscience in the same fearless way in which you have faced up to all the complex phases of foreign politics that have confronted you in the last year.'[51] He had already praised Chamberlain to the king, saying, 'I agree with you wholeheartedly that the Prime Minister's personal contact with Hitler was the only thing that saved the World from war last month. The strain for him must have been appalling, and I am in the front rank for taking off my hat to him.'[52] The snare had been laid. Now to catch the woodcock.

Acknowledging the controversy engendered by his abdication, the duke claimed that 'the flame of those strong feelings was to a large extent fanned by wild and inaccurate statements in the newspapers of the world, and by false rumours and gossip . . . concerning both of us'. He then asked the prime minister to aid him and Wallis with a public relations campaign. If he would do so, he would thereby be 'counteracting a great wrong done to us', and ensure that any return to Britain would not be dominated by 'mischief makers exploiting our first visit in one way or the other for sensational purposes'.

Suggesting April 1939 as his preferred date, Edward wrote that 'if our visit is to be the success which you obviously desire, it must be of the first importance that there should be no possible suggestion of discord in our family'. He then restated his request that Wallis should receive the title of Her Royal Highness. He justified his reprise of the old tune by claiming that 'it would not only remove the embarrassments which the present situation involves for all both at home and abroad, but would go far to satisfy public opinion that good relations exist between us and the other members of the Royal Family'.[53]

Chamberlain turned his attention from one power-hungry European resident to another. His response was confident. He refused to offer any support for Wallis's title ('it is essential that Your Royal Highness' first visit should not become the subject of controversy')[54] and instead suggested that it was the king's responsibility to deal with the matter. The duke privately called Chamberlain's

letter 'fatuous' and bemoaned his 'futile observations', before replying that any favourable publicity that could be arranged would
counteract 'the unjust impressions that were allowed to be created
in the minds of the British people concerning ourselves, at the time
of the Abdication'.

He concluded, in an attempt to be conciliatory, 'I agree with you
that subtler methods could be more effectively employed nearer
the time, thus ensuring that any possible note of controversy,
from which we are all so anxious to protect the visit, be avoided.'[55]
These 'subtler methods' included the much-anticipated meeting
between the Gloucesters and the Windsors in Paris that month,
which Chamberlain saw as a means of testing public opinion about
a return for Edward and Wallis to Britain. The day was pleasant
enough, with lunch at Le Meurice hotel and a walk around the city,
but Edward still smarted at the king's request that he should not
court publicity for the visit, which he described as both 'a purely
private matter between us' and 'an excellent opportunity & a very
natural way of "breaking the ice" as we might call it'.[56]

The duke sneered to his brother that 'I have every reason to be
just as anxious as you are that the private nature and normalcy of
this family meeting be preserved, and that my one concern since
hearing from [Gloucester] has been as to how possible inaccurate
and sensational reporting can best be avoided ... The Kents unfortunately failed to "break the ice" in Austria last year; had they
come to see us as I understand you told them to, the process of
"breaking it" would not be the same special interest to the newspaper world.'[57]

Although Wallis made a special effort to ensure that things were
harmonious, and the Duchess of Gloucester called them both 'more
than kind', the meeting's success would be measured by its reception. Unfortunately for the Windsors' hopes of a British return, the
reaction was not warm. The Gloucesters received over a hundred
'extremely rude' letters complaining about the visit. It would fall to
Chamberlain to break the news to the duke.

The two had met on 24 November in Paris, and the prime

minister kept a record of the encounter. He reported Edward's distress at the 'mendacious and disgraceful' stories that had been spread about Wallis, which he blamed for her not receiving her rightful title. Chamberlain replied that 'it would be a mistake to imagine that the question of the title was merely one between you and the other members of the Royal Family. The feelings of resentment and bitterness which had been aroused at the time of the abdication had not died away as rapidly as I had hoped they would, and it had been sufficient for the papers to mention visits of the Duke and Duchess of Gloucester and the possibility that [you and Wallis] might visit England for some revival of these old feelings.' When Edward suggested that he had seen unfair speculation that should he return to England he would engage in 'disloyal agitation' against the king, the prime minister was able to correct him. 'I said that I had never heard of or seen any such suggestion, and that the remarks in the letters which I had seen were directed against the Duchess and not against himself.'

He ended by asking, 'I suppose, sir, you would not care to come alone for the first visit?' But if he had expected the uxorious duke to consent, and save endless bother, he would have been disappointed. Edward replied, 'No, I certainly could not do that: married people ought not to be divided.'[58] Nonetheless, the continued unpopularity of Wallis compelled Chamberlain to break the news to the duke that the wounds caused by their departure were still too raw and would be reopened by a comeback. He subsequently wrote that their encounter had 'given rise to considerable comment . . . by far the greater part of it being of an unfavourable character', and warned the duke that his projected visit to Britain would lead to 'strong protest and controversy'.

Alluding to the more than 150 letters of protest that he had received ('my wife has had over 30'), Chamberlain let Edward know that all classes stood against him. In addition to the British not wanting him to return, residents of Canada, New Zealand and America wished him to remain in exile. He concluded, 'Your Royal Highness agreed with me that it is essential that your first visit should not become the subject of controversy . . . bearing in mind how important it is that the Royal Family should unify opinion and not divide it, I cannot escape the conclusion that it is my duty to advise Your Royal Highness to abandon the idea of the visit in March'.[59]

The duke ignored the king's injunction not to be a publicity-seeker and promptly put out a press statement in response: 'The Duchess and I have been receiving so many enquiries from our friends as to when we intend to return to England, that I feel it would only lead to misunderstanding if we continue to leave such questions unanswered.' Sugar-coating the messages that Chamberlain had alluded to ('I want to say how touched we are by the many expressions of goodwill that have reached us lately from all parts of the world'), he chose to make public what many would have preferred he kept to himself. 'We had looked forward to making a short private visit to England in the spring, and should have done so had we not been informed that such a visit would not yet be welcome, either to the Government or the Royal Family.'[60] It had no effect, and connoted little more than the frustrations of an impotent figure.

The king, meanwhile, made his own feelings clear to the prime minister on 14 December. 'There is a strong feeling amongst all classes that my brother should not return here for a short visit with the Duchess of Windsor . . . this is the moment for you to write & tell him that it would not be at all wise for them to contemplate such a visit'. He added, 'I think you know that neither the Queen nor Queen Mary have any desire to meet the Duchess of Windsor & therefore any visit made for the purpose of introducing her . . . obviously becomes impossible.' He trusted in his prime minister to do the right thing. 'As this matter is one of such an intimate nature . . . perhaps my brother would take this decision in a more kindly manner from you than from me.'*[61]

---

* An earlier letter from the king to Chamberlain on 2 December 1938 noted, 'the more I think about his coming here on a visit, the less I like the idea, especially as some sections of the Press are behaving so stupidly about it'.

As Chamberlain was feted as a peacemaker and politician of substance, with the king and queen beside him, the Duke and Duchess
of Windsor seemed destined to slide into irrelevance. Yet as he had
boasted, Edward believed that he flourished in a tight corner. He
would try something different. If he could not achieve what he
wanted by playing along with his brother and the prime minister,
he would go his own way and the consequences be damned.

Chapter Five

'Freedom Is Worth Dying For'

Despite the international euphoria at the Munich Agreement,* the sceptics made their opinions known in the months afterwards. Some, like Churchill and Duff Cooper, were disappointed at the concessions to Hitler, but others, who were even keener on appeasement than Chamberlain, believed that the agreement did not go far enough. In his 1941 novel *Hangover Square*, Patrick Hamilton expressed this ambiguity through the book's antagonist, the manipulative and cynical Netta Longdon.

He wrote of her and her friends that 'They went raving mad, they weren't sober for a whole week after Munich - it was just in their line.' This was because, as Hamilton described it, 'they *liked* Hitler, really . . . it was their cup of tea all right, was Munich'.[1] His protagonist, George Harvey Bone, is more clear-sighted, despite his perpetual drunkenness. Bone calls the deal a 'phoney business' and reflects, 'He still couldn't get over the feeling that there was something indecent about it - Adolf, and Musso and Neville all grinning together.'[2]

Whether one believed that Chamberlain had achieved 'peace for our time', or, like Hardinge, simply that he had postponed the inevitable, the beginning of 1939 marked the end of the 'low, dishonest decade' that Auden alluded to in 'September 1, 1939'. It was a ripe time for charlatans and liars, where half-truths and

---

* President Roosevelt sent Chamberlain a telegram simply saying, 'You're a great man.'

outright lies gained traction over principle and honesty. It presented a chance for the unscrupulous and amoral alike to seize the initiative, and present their actions not as opportunism but as patriotism.

The Duke of Windsor was no amateur when it came to preening and posturing. He believed that his one-time regal status meant that his former subjects should regard him with respect and gravitas. Unfortunately for his ego, this seldom manifested itself in the fashion he wished for.

A typical complaint to the long-suffering Monckton on 28 November 1938 talked of 'the packet of anonymous "tripe" that we have received from Great Britain, Canada and America'. One correspondent, 'a well-known Trade Union leader', summed up public opinion by calling the Duke of Windsor 'the world's greatest quitter' and describing Wallis as 'of low American origin, bearing the worst of immoral reputations'.[3] Edward was dismissive – 'these badly typed and expressed . . . letters are of no concern to us' – but his truer feelings might be discerned from his statement that 'the "Nazi spy" story was one of the most harmful . . . and the most often referred to in disagreeable letters'.[4]

Unfortunately, this was not an opinion restricted to abusive correspondents. A Special Branch memorandum of 5 January 1939 by the Chief Constable, assessing the political undercurrents in Britain, noted the widespread contempt displayed for both Edward and Wallis. The memorandum stated that the belief that the duke only wished to return to make 'a personal effort to raise the social status of his wife' had led to 'a great measure of disapproval'. However, various other parties awaited any return with interest.

The communists took an attitude of 'wait and see' – 'the presence of the Duke and Duchess of Windsor would be a political embarrassment . . . the situation thus created might easily serve the communists' purpose' – but the British Union of Fascists, led by Oswald Mosley, were said to anticipate Edward's homecoming with enthusiasm. The memorandum noted that 'some form of welcome and support will be forthcoming should the proposed visit take place . . . although outwardly proclaiming loyalty to King George VI, [the Fascists] have made no real secret of their support for the Duke of Windsor and for any move to secure his return to the country and, if possible, the Throne'.

At the beginning of 1939, such support was scattered but genuine. While the so-called Society of Octavians, which campaigned for the duke's return and reinstatement, was insignificant in its membership numbers* and, the Chief Constable wrote, 'the activities of this Society have been, generally speaking, innocuous . . . their existence as an organised body might very easily provide the means to start demonstrations which might quickly develop and cause conflict between supporters and opponents of the Duke of Windsor, should he come to England'.

Hardinge was dismissive but amused. He informed Monckton on 12 December 1938 that the leader of the Octavians, Robert Wish, had been described by Scotland Yard as 'mentally unbalanced and has four convictions for fraud', and suggested, 'perhaps you might have an opportunity of letting the Duke know what sort of man he is'. He joked, 'I am now investigating the history of Mr Wish and his Octavians . . . it sounds rather like a jazz band!'[5]

Edward – a great connoisseur of jazz, especially if it was playing to his tune – was frustrated that neither his brother nor the prime minister listened to him. He was not above contacting sympathetic news publishers, such as Lord Beaverbrook, and Associated Newspapers' Esmond Harmsworth, to argue his case. The Chief Constable observed that 'it is openly stated in circles connected with the Press that the Duke of Windsor has been in touch with certain newspaper proprietors with the object of starting a publicity campaign in this country, in order to create an atmosphere favourable to the return of himself and the Duchess of Windsor'.[6]

As the duke contented himself with telling Chamberlain that

---

* It numbered no more than a few hundred members. None had any public prominence save the writer Compton Mackenzie, who had published a sympathetic biography of Edward the previous year.

news of his extended exile had caused him 'great disappointment',[7] and asking that 'any date now determined [for a visit] is definite and final',[8] Monckton once again had to intercede on his behalf. Claiming that Edward's intention was a short private visit, not 'ostentatious joy-making', he acknowledged that the earliest practical date for his return was October 1939: 'If I have correctly understood . . . the Prime Minister's views on the matter, he would wish to get it out of the way until the autumn from everyone's point of view.'

Monckton knew that unpopularity and scandal would dog Edward and Wallis for months, if not years, to come – 'it is not possible to name in advance a precise date by which such controversy and division will have died down to enable the Prime Minister to advise that the visit can take place without objection'[9] – but he took the attitude, *pace* Shakespeare, that 'if it were done when 'tis done, then 'twere well it was done gradually'.

The duke now decided that it would improve his popularity if he could take a proactive role in the international situation, as a free agent. Believing not only in his personal bond with Hitler but also that he understood the workings of the world, he now aspired to be an international statesman. He would not be bound by party politics or royal responsibilities, but was instead able to rise above such trivialities and bring about lasting peace. The gratitude that his actions would merit would, he believed, see him restored to favour in his home country, and who knew what else might follow subsequently.

It was left to Monckton to temper his grandiloquence with unexciting fact. A tactful letter of 22 March stated that 'it is, of course, not going to be easy for anybody to intervene effectively without some degree of authority to speak or listen on behalf of one of the interested governments'. Knowing that Edward's freelance diplomacy would be resented, as well as there being 'a real risk of accidentally running counter to the Government's policy', Monckton advised that 'no step could well be taken [without] the knowledge and approval of the Government'.[10]

He promised that he would consult Wilson, but he knew that nobody in government had any time for Edward and his plans, given what had happened since the beginning of the year. Hitler's expansionist actions, which had included occupying Prague and turning large parts of Czechoslovakia into a German protectorate, had led Chamberlain to take a more pugnacious approach than before. He was forced into this by politicians such as Bob Boothby, who described appeasement as 'a desperate gamble, out of weakness, on the good faith of the dictators' and despaired that 'our present situation is grimly reminiscent of last September . . . only the stakes are higher . . . weakness or indecision this time will be fatal'.[11]

In a well-received speech in Birmingham on 17 March, the prime minister warned Hitler that if this approach was to be continued, it would lead to war. He followed this up with a statement to the House of Commons on 31 March that Britain and France would, if Poland was attacked, come to its aid and lend it 'all support in its power'. The pieces were assembling, at last, on the chessboard. The only question now was who was the grandmaster, and who was merely a pawn.

As Hardinge remarked that 'The last few days have been very strenuous, but it is quieter to-day . . . I don't imagine Hitler's speech will interfere with the week-end. I sincerely hope not', his wife spoke to the queen and, later that evening, the king. She subsequently wrote a detailed account of the conversation because '[it] has rather disturbed me ever since'. As an account of royal table talk as well as a candid and unvarnished insight into their characters and beliefs as war approached, the never-before-seen document is invaluable.*

---

* I discovered the document in late 2021 during my research into the Hardinge papers, which are currently kept at the Kent Archives; an invaluable resource for any historian of the period, in that it contains the widest record of the private papers of both Alec and Helen Hardinge, which were previously in the collection of Hardinge's grandson, Lord Hardinge. They were kept under embargo until 2021, but will now be available for other historians to consult.

Helen noted that 'HM's judgement & common sense are so right', as the queen remarked that the 'peoples of the world', as she termed them, were 'terrific' as long as one could see past 'their bandit leaders'. Politically, she defined the queen as 'a diehard Tory' who was deeply sceptical about the possibility of a Labour government. She was greatly surprised to learn that the royal couple only read *The Times*; she described it as 'that very misinformed paper'. When it came to discussing the situation in Spain, the queen said, 'We went wrong there surely? And inexcusably?'

The conversation initially revolved around national service, which the queen professed herself against, on the grounds that 'she did not like the idea of compulsory service at all - especially as a gesture to foreign powers - which is what she considered NS to be'. Instead, she and the king favoured youth training in camps ('the King's great crusade'), and when Helen demurred, on the grounds that such an endeavour would take a long time to set up, the queen 'tho' angelic' professed herself impatient with this argument, saying that two years of military training was entirely adequate. She then stated that she did not believe that the country needed a large army, or that the spirit of the English was compatible with the present-day state of scaremongering and rumour.

She then advanced her own worldview, which was essentially isolationist in nature. 'She thinks it is not right to [build an army] to defend other people's frontiers & that it will mean we shall be left "carrying the baby" (as usual!).' Helen, bearing in mind her husband's view of the threat of fascism, disagreed. 'We are not an aggressive nation & not likely to abhor our nationalism. The position abroad has created a great will to serve in this country & National Service would be the right dedication of this will & would make for the security of world peace. Our combined wealth & weakness are a temptation to the predatory.' Yet the queen continued to argue that there was too much 'technical training' in the country, and that it did not help with the discipline and character in the young that she considered all-important. Finally, she stated that 'there is already enough opportunity for service in the Voluntary System' and drove the conversation on to a related issue: that of foreign policy.

Helen recounted that 'HM cannot see where we have been wrong' and that 'her whole judgement is based on what it is right or wrong to do, not on its consequences, which is what makes this aspect so strong'. It was at this point that the conversation became 'much more involved', as the queen argued that diplomacy should control French actions, even as Helen suggested that 'our diplomacy weakens French action, which is usually more logical than ours'. Helen noted that 'HM resents the blame which has been attached to England over Czechoslovakia for she says the French deserted their allies', and even as she argued that 'the French were doing everything at this moment to repair the fault', she stated, 'I do not want to give the impression HM [is] anti-French - she repeatedly said she liked them - which I know is the case but she thinks our diplomacy superior to theirs.'

She went on to say that there was great danger in Britain not wholeheartedly supporting France at that moment, and that 'the German propaganda in France to the effect that "the English will fight to the last French man" is doing great damage'. The queen replied, 'But what can France do?' Helen answered that she believed it might effectively become a protectorate of Germany, something the queen thought 'incredible'. Helen wrote in her notes that 'I'm not sure she's not right . . . I did not answer that France is surrounded on three sides & a country will do a great deal for peace - as we have seen - because this is also what the Germans are saying.'

When the king arrived, he was treated to a précis of the discussion. Helen wrote that 'He did not seem worried at the idea of compulsory service or conscription. We had a discussion on the words "compulsion" or "conscription" which are disagreeable and foreign sounding, but I think that it ceases to be "compulsion" if it is what the large majority want, as I believe is the case.' The king spoke of his disdain for the so-called 'reserved occupations' ('it has been very exaggeratedly drawn up & that there is great weakness in any system which did not well absorb unemployment') and talked evangelically about his plans for training camps for young people to meet the future in war and peace. The queen appeared to disagree, but the general hubbub made it difficult to follow her line of argument.

One point, however, was made explicitly. The trade unions were discussed, and Helen said that she believed they could be talked round to cooperating with such a scheme. When the king asked, 'Who by?', the queen replied, 'You'll have to do it of course darling.' The conversation then broke up as the queen reiterated her distaste for national service. 'Abroad, it means military training & that was what would be expected of us & it would mislead people if we had our own form.'[12] That conflict would turn these issues into mere chatter was not remarked upon by any of the participants.

The document is considerably more interesting than mere gossip, because it demonstrates both the queen's reluctant attitude towards conflict and her laissez-faire position regarding compulsory national service. Even after the near-miss of late 1938, the idea of war remained a serious threat, but judging by Helen Hardinge's report, neither of the royal couple believed that conscription or an accelerated national service programme would be effective. Some might call such an attitude cautious, others complacent. But before long, its wisdom would be called into question.

Shortly afterwards, the king and queen faced another state visit, but this one was uncharted territory for any monarch. Throughout 1938, they had enjoyed warm relations with Joe Kennedy. The ambassador had sought to explain his country's policy of non-aggression in terms of the consequences of the last war, which he claimed had led to 'dictatorships, quarrels and miseries', but the queen had demurred. 'If we had the United States actively on our side,' she said, 'working with us, think how that would strengthen our position with the dictators.'[13]

Although Kennedy was unwilling to commit his country to a formal alliance, he suggested that the royal couple should head to America. This put a plan in train that would be formalised by President Roosevelt's invitation of the king and queen to the United States and Canada in 1939. They accepted, and on 6 May set sail on the *Empress of Australia* for a six-week visit. Roosevelt suggested a private meeting between the royal couple and himself, saying, 'if you could stay with us at Hyde Park for two or three days, the simplicity and naturalness of such a visit would produce a great effect'. This was agreed upon for June, after a wider tour of the continent.

The intention was nominally to allow the royal couple to see something of a modern, progressive nation, but all involved knew that it was diplomatically essential that the visit should show them, and by extension Britain, at their best. They had to win over a suspicious, even hostile country, where the actions of the former colonialist King George III were still fresh in recent memory and they had to do so against the backdrop of impending war at home.

One article by Josef Israels in *Scribner's*, 'Selling George VI to the United States', was particularly scathing. It began, 'If a public relations counsel had the power to choose from scratch which British personalities he would drop into the American scene for the greatest British profit, they would not have been King George and Queen Elizabeth.' Israels went on to lambast the king as a 'colourless, weak personality', given to epileptic fits and offering 'an impression of poorer royal timber than has occupied England's throne in many decades', and sneered that he was married to someone 'far too plump [and] too dowdy in dress' to be a convincing queen. He suggested that 'the difference between apathetic acceptance of the product and its enthusiastic purchase by the American people will be the difference between success and failure of British–American relations during the next critical international period'.[14]

Courtiers were alarmed by Israels' message, not least because, despite its exaggerations and unpleasant tone, it encapsulated many

of the concerns that had been raised about the king since he had reluctantly acceded to the throne just over two years earlier. He was a
decent man, but he lacked both the authority of his father and the
charisma of his brother, and he showed no signs of growing into
his role. That he was more approachable than either of them mat-
tered little. The royal family, and Britain, needed a greater advocate
than a likeable, if shy, fellow that one could have imagined having
a drink with at one's club.

It did not help his cause that the last member of the royal family
to have successfully visited America was Edward, while he was still
Prince of Wales. Indeed, had the king thought about his brother
as he set sail aboard the *Empress*, he might have mused that he had
been unusually quiet of late. There had been fewer splenetic and
accusatory letters, and even the questions of Wallis's recognition
and the royal handouts were not being pushed with as much vigour
as they had been. Was the duke at last behaving himself?

Leopards do not change their spots, however, and angry former
kings do not simply fold up their tents and retreat from the field
of combat. Instead, the duke had planned an intervention that
would take his relationship with his king and country in new and
even more difficult directions. And he had come up with it all
by himself.

'For two and a half years, I have deliberately kept out of public
affairs, and I still propose to do so. I speak for no-one but myself,
without the previous knowledge of any government. I speak
simply as a soldier of the last war, whose most earnest prayer is
that such a cruel and destructive madness shall never again over-
take mankind . . .' As the Duke of Windsor addressed the world
once again, from a hotel room in Verdun on 8 May, he may have
been forgiven for feeling a sense of exhilaration, like a schoolboy
who has slipped the leash of a feared teacher on an outing and
run amok.

He had spent the previous two years straining against his
bonds. The ruin of his planned American visit had frustrated him

from reappearing on the public stage in late 1937, and no other opportunity had presented itself. Now, he was able to speak his mind – his truth – and by so doing reintroduce himself to the world in dramatic circumstances.

The impetus to broadcast came after Edward had written a letter to the *Catholic Herald* in support of its editorial urging its readers to secure peace. As this was the first time he had put his name to a public statement of this nature, it caused a stir. The broadcaster Fred Bate, head of the European arm of NBC and a friend of Edward and Wallis, saw an opportunity. Since the abdication, Bate had been anxious that NBC should secure the coup that would be the duke's first public broadcast. That he should ostensibly ask for peace from the city famous for the longest and most intense conflict of the Great War did not escape the attention of those attuned to this kind of symbolism.

When the broadcast was announced on Saturday 6 May, it caused uproar in Britain. Although NBC offered every interested country in the world the opportunity to relay the speech, the BBC refused to do so,* after a five-hour meeting to debate its implications. Two and a half years before, the first director general of the BBC, Sir John Reith, had been the man who introduced Edward's abdication transmission. Now, his successor, Frederick Ogilvie, mindful of the anger in the morning newspapers at the proposed broadcast, decided not to air it. Unsurprisingly, now that they had been given what they wanted, the evening editions of the papers attacked the BBC for being a mouthpiece of the government, just as their sister editions had pre-emptively criticised it for even contemplating such an action. *O tempora, o mores.*

In any event, the duke's former subjects could have heard the broadcast on NBC's short-wave transmission, and so many waited expectantly in their homes at 10 p.m. on the evening of 8 May.

---

* The recording in the BBC archives explicitly is marked 'not for broadcast', indicating that the activities of the Duke remained off-limits as far as the national broadcaster was concerned.

Would Edward seize the opportunity to make a grand political statement, perhaps even to announce his return to Britain? Or would he make a resounding declaration of support for his brother and Chamberlain? Either way, his speech would overshadow the coverage of the king's visit to Canada and the United States, showing his flair for backing into the limelight.

In the event, his broadcast was neither seditious nor especially helpful. He did not mention Chamberlain or his brother by name, but instead referred to how 'peace is a matter far too vital for our happiness to be treated as a political question', and stated that 'in modern warfare, victory will lie only with the powers of evil'. Quite who 'the powers of evil' were as far as the duke was concerned was ambiguous, as he praised the Germans in the same breath as the British, Americans and French, saying, 'there is no land whose people want war . . . international understanding does not always spring up simultaneously of itself'.

In the second half of his speech, he began to advance his credo, perhaps for the first time in public. He expressed a desire for world peace, with the implication that he could be a roving ambassador, bringing harmony where discord existed. As he did so, he made veiled references to his own situation, although so subtly that only someone intimately familiar with his travails would have known what he alluded to. He talked of how 'the problems that concern us at the moment are only the reproductions on a larger scale of the jealousies and suspicions of everyday life', and that 'in our personal contacts, we all strive to live in harmony with our fellow men'.

He was scathing about 'heads of government' and their 'public utterances . . . in declaring that war would be disastrous to the well-being of their people'. And he stated angrily that 'harmful propaganda', by which he might have meant any media coverage he found personally unfavourable, 'tends to poison the minds of the peoples of the world'. He noted righteously, 'I personally deplore . . . the use of such terms as "encirclement" and "aggression" . . . they can only arouse just those dangerous political passions that it should be the aim of us all to subdue'. That Hitler displayed both 'encirclement' and 'aggression' was not remarked upon.

In his peroration, the duke presented himself, Cassandra-like, as one who had seen the horrors of conflict but who also proposed to bring peace. 'In the name of those who fell in the last war, I urge all political leaders to be resolute ... the world has not yet recovered from the effects of the last carnage ... the greatest success that any government could achieve for its own national policy would be nothing in comparison with the triumph of having contributed to save humanity from the terrible fate that threatens it today'. Even as he displayed the rhetorical technique of litotes* to say, 'it is not for me to put forward concrete proposals ... that must be left to those who have the power to guide their nations towards closer understanding',[15] he had made a dramatic and timely return to public life.†

After the furore, the broadcast was generally well received by those who heard it. Bate wrote to the duke to say, 'you have never spoken better ... it was a great combination of words, time, place and situation – moving and beyond criticism'.[16] Edward received thousands of letters of support, including messages from the eclectic likes of Lord Alfred 'Bosie' Douglas, the Republican political figure John Foster Dulles, and the women's rights campaigner Marie Stopes. A Gallup poll suggested that 61 per cent of the population were now keen for the Windsors to return to Britain, with 23 per cent undecided. Only 16 per cent were against the idea.

The broadcast was not universally popular, however. Some regarded it as an attempt to divert attention from the king and

* As famously displayed in Marc Antony's speech in *Julius Caesar*.
† It remains unclear as to who, if anyone, helped Edward compose the broadcast. There is no record of his asking Monckton or Churchill for any assistance with it, and his authorised biographer, Philip Ziegler, suggests that he wrote it entirely by himself. If so, it can be regarded as his own unfiltered thoughts.

queen's trip - Channon called it 'a fine performance' but 'ill-timed' and 'extraordinarily tactless'[17] - which was for once unfair. Edward had not been aware of the dates of their journey when he agreed to Bate's request, and by the time he realised that they would co-incide, it was too late to cancel. Nonetheless, the previously loyal *Daily Express* called his actions a mistake, and suggested that he had strayed into an area that was the monarch's purview, not his. The Duke of Kent was blunter. He wrote to the king on 16 May to say of their brother, 'What a fool he is, and how badly advised; and everyone is furious he should have done it just after you left.' Kent noted the omission of any statement about the sovereign - 'if he had mentioned you in it, it wouldn't have been so bad' - and questioned the speech's very purpose, saying, 'why he broadcast such a peace talk only to America, where they have no intention of fighting, I don't know'.[18]

While Edward may have been either naïve or unfortunate in his timing, those in Britain who regarded the unchecked former monarch as dangerous were not reassured by his return to international prominence. Hardinge was angered by the broadcast, and suggested that 'the idea that it can possibly do the slightest good [is] simply ludicrous'.

Yet whatever his statements, the duke had issued a public reminder to those who had thwarted him that he would not - could not - simply languish in exile and be denied the opportunity to contribute his thoughts on the international situation. This arrogance made him both unpredictable and, with the outbreak of war drawing closer, dangerous. At a time when it was crucial that the loyalties of prominent public figures were transparent, his inclinations remained opaque.

The king and queen, meanwhile, disembarked the *Empress of Australia* on 17 May at Wolfe's Cove, Quebec. Their journey had been delayed a few days by fog in the middle of the Atlantic, but Lascelles referred to the party being cheered by the 'hilarious spirits' of the sailors. He wrote of the enforced pause that 'it has done the King a power of good - it is the only really idle and irresponsible spell he has had since he acceded'.[19] The monarch needed the rest. Edward's broadcast had raised expectations of his visit, and so it was vital that no fault could be found with the king or the queen on either a political or personal level.

Thankfully, the tour proved to be a successful, even joyful one. The novelist John Buchan, now Lord Tweedsmuir, governor general of Canada, was informed that the crowds that welcomed the royal visitors were 'as impressive as those at the Coronation'. Tweedsmuir himself summoned up his creative ability to describe the scene to the absent Hardinge:* 'It was a wonderful example of what a people's king means, and it would have been impossible anywhere else in the world. One old man shouted to me "Ay, man, if Hitler could see this" . . . the capacity of Their Majesties for getting in touch with the people amounts to genius. It is the small unscheduled things that count most, and for those they have an infallible instinct.'[20]

'Papa and I have had a wonderful welcome everywhere we have been', the queen wrote to her elder daughter, Princess 'Lilibet' Elizabeth. She was thrilled by how 'wonderfully loyal' the inhabitants of Quebec and Ottawa had been, and by the fact that they could take 'an opportunity to show how British they are'.[21] This was mirrored by one Canadian officer, who wrote to Monckton of his surprise at the 'amazing success' of the trip, 'probably far exceeding anything they themselves anticipated, certainly exceeding what was expected out here', and praised the 'radiant, gracious, chic, understanding, wonderfully tactful and lovely' queen. They had anticipated someone 'dowdy, plump and uninteresting'. He hoped

---

* In his absence, the king and queen were accompanied by Lascelles, the assistant private secretary. He conducted his duties with such admirable efficiency that the king knighted him, apparently spontaneously, as he had Monckton. Lascelles wrote, 'The King, giggling in a most disarming fashion, knighted me in the train tonight, as the train was approaching Buffalo. I think I can fairly claim to be the first man to be dubbed in a train, and also the first Englishman to be so treated by his Sovereign on American soil; so the episode has, at any rate, some historic interest.'

that 'if war in spite of everything does come, it may quite possibly mean tens of thousands [of] earlier volunteers from Canada and a sympathetic USA, which won't stay out nearly as long as the last time'.[22]

This was the objective, but both the king and queen knew that America would be a tougher prospect. The queen wrote to her daughter that 'the next fortnight will be very hard work, but it is worthwhile, for one feels how important it is that people here should see their King, & not have him only as a symbol'.[23] To her mother-in-law, recovering from a car accident,* she was more candid but no less effusive. 'We get very bored & tired, but both feel very well and so encouraged to feel the strength of feeling for the Empire here. More & more one feels that the hope of the world lies in the unity, sanity & strength for good in the British Empire – freedom is worth dying for.'[24]

They arrived at Washington Union Station on 8 June, in the midst of a heatwave, to be personally greeted by the president and his wife, Eleanor: a mark of both honour and respect. Roosevelt had been re-elected to office in 1936 with a landslide, thanks to the success of his New Deal programme, and was well regarded and popular. Both he and the king knew something of overcoming a personal affliction with courage and good humour. The president had suffered from polio in 1921, turning him from a dashing and charismatic figure into one confined to a wheelchair. Yet he refused to let his disability daunt him, instead dealing with every affliction or opportunity he encountered with a mixture of warmth and calculation. Like the addressee of Kipling's 'If', neither foes nor loving friends could hurt him, and all men counted with him – but none too much.

There were other similarities between Roosevelt and the king.

---

* Queen Mary's car collided with a heavy goods lorry in Wandsworth on 25 May 1939, and the car ended up on its side, necessitating the production of a ladder to help her escape. It was said that 'she walked down the rescuers' ladder as composed as if she had been descending the State staircase at Buckingham Palace'.

Both had served in the navy, and had seen warfare, which united them in a determination that further conflict should be avoided at all practical costs. They met in the early summer of 1939 with the aim of building a personal bond that would be mirrored in warmer relations between their two countries. The term 'special relationship' had not yet been invented, and America had fought Britain as often as it had fought alongside it. Therefore as the two men shook hands in Washington, with a thousand photographers jostling one another to capture the historic moment of a British sovereign's first official state visit to their country, there was a sense of momentum and potential, but also of a supplicant meeting a ruler. Which one of them was the supplicant and which the ruler remained unclear.

The royal couple's stay at the White House was enjoyable, once issues of protocol had been dealt with. The only British newspapers that were considered acceptable for the king and queen were the *Times*, *Telegraph* and *Daily Sketch*, while those regarded as *infra dig* included the *Daily Express*, *News of the World* and *Daily Mail*: the Beaverbrook and Rothermere titles were still viewed as unacceptable due to their support for Edward during the abdication crisis. Royal expectations of American hospitality were modest. The king had brought his own supply of spirits and wine with him, in case a country only six years out of Prohibition should frown on His Majesty toping at his host's expense.

'We didn't know what sort of attention we would have, but they were tremendously welcoming',[25] the queen wrote subsequently. The relationship between the king and the president was, as hoped for, warm and sincere from the outset, helped by careful preparation on both sides for months beforehand. A friendship also developed between the queen and Eleanor, who was by no means a royal aficionado. She said of Elizabeth, when faced with a crowd, that she dealt with the thousands of well-wishers with sincerity and real charm, 'actually looking at people in the crowd so I am sure many of them felt her bow was really for them personally'.[26] This was especially impressive as the queen was suffering from sunburn and exhaustion. She wrote to Queen Mary that 'it really was ghastly . . . very damp heat and one could hardly breathe', even as she praised how 'everybody was very very kind & welcoming & made us feel quite "at home"'.[27]

The royal couple were interested in everything they were shown, from lavish diplomatic receptions and White House garden parties to cadet corps camps that may have led them to question the attitudes they had expressed to Helen Hardinge. Their open-minded attitudes towards the country were noticed and lauded. The *New York World Telegram* declared, '[The king and queen] are greeted by the American people not merely as representatives of another great democracy, or as royalty, but as two great human beings who have won that distinction in their own right.' The newspaper encapsulated public opinion in its statement that 'We like them. And we hope they like us.'

Yet to borrow an expression from the country's vernacular, 'talking turkey' was what the king and the president were primarily expected to do. The visit had a crucial diplomatic purpose that needed to be achieved if it could be called a success. These candid conversations would take place at the president's country house, Hyde Park. Its name reflected a certain Anglophilia in both its trappings and its staff. It even boasted a snobbish English butler, James, who, aghast at the proposed presence of two black staff from the White House, took his annual holiday during the royal visit, saying, 'I cannot be a party to the degradation of the British monarchy.'[28]

Roosevelt enjoyed playing 'mine host' with the king, and the warmth of the weather was mirrored by the welcome that the exhausted couple received. When a cocktail was offered to them as they arrived, the president quipped, 'My mother thinks you should have a cup of tea; she doesn't approve of cocktails.' As his guest took one with the relief of a drowning man spying land, he replied, 'Neither does my mother.'[29] And then, thus refreshed, it was down to business. The major obstacle to Roosevelt offering Britain any explicit assistance was the existence of the Neutrality Act, which had been put before Congress in 1937 and sought to limit American involvement in any future world wars. The Republican party believed that if Roosevelt should veer away from this agreement, they would be able to win the 1940 election easily, bringing his political career to an end.

Before his visit, the king had been briefed about the situation in America, thanks to a Foreign Office document entitled 'Vade Mecum* 1939'. This instructed him about Roosevelt's strengths and weaknesses - both personal and political - and the level of anti-British feeling in the country. It was believed that while many Americans had a residual grudge against Britain because of historical grievances, they would nonetheless fall into line and join the struggle against fascism if it became a binary choice, as 'a Nazi world would not be worth living in'.

Roosevelt was described as an Anglophile who distrusted Germany and Hitler. He was willing to circumvent the Neutrality Act as far as he could without actually breaking it, specifically in shipping vital aeroplane parts from America to Canada, where they could be assembled and then sent across the Atlantic. He could not promise that the United States would come in behind Britain at the precise time that its leaders might wish it to, but stated that his country's opinion was 'on the right tack'. A more experienced interlocutor might have said this was not good enough when Britain faced the deaths of millions and the potential loss of democracy in Europe.

Although he may not have achieved the breakthrough that he might have hoped for, the king enjoyed his conversations with Roosevelt. He was emboldened enough to write in his diary of his belief that 'if London was bombed, the USA would come in'.[30] The president was alternately paternalistic - always a fruitful stance to adopt with the sovereign - and philosophical. He played the role of wise sage towards the younger man, and at one point even suggested that it was time for the exhausted king to go to bed.

The monarch was impressed by FDR. He told the Canadian

---

* Meaning 'a guide that should be kept at hand'.

prime minister, Mackenzie King, that 'he found it easier to carry on a conversation with [Roosevelt] than with almost anyone, and that he had appreciated the open way in which [he] had talked over many matters', as well as stressing that 'his admiration could not have been greater'.[31] The two drank beer and ate hot dogs together, and a genuine friendship grew up between them. At the time, this was a pleasant and welcome development. Later, it would prove vital.

As the king and queen finally departed from Halifax on the *Empress of Britain* on 15 June, both felt deeply moved. There had been tears during the king's farewell speech, and Roosevelt had wished them 'all the luck in the world' as they left. The king's good opinion of the president was reciprocated, and Roosevelt was impressed by the way in which the royal couple, 'very delightful and understanding people', were well briefed not only on foreign affairs, but also on the social legislation of his country. The press too gave the visit a good report, with the *New York Times* commenting that the king and queen had 'not put a foot wrong . . . [and] have left a better impression than ever their optimistic advisers could have expected'.

They arrived back in Britain to a reception fit for conquering heroes. Enormous and raucous crowds, delighted by the success of the historic state visit, sang 'Land of Hope and Glory' and 'God Save the King' outside Buckingham Palace. Relieved MPs forgot their usual pose of superiority and sang and waved flags with the rest of their constituents. Nicolson wrote in his diary on 23 June that 'we all lost our dignity and yelled and yelled. The King wore a happy schoolboy grin. The Queen was superb . . . she is in truth one of the most amazing Queens since Cleopatra.'[32] The *Daily Mail*, no uncritical supporter of George VI, called it 'the greatest of all homecomings, the closing scene of the greatest royal day since the Coronation'.

The following day, the king addressed his people at the Guildhall in London. He spoke with a confidence he had never displayed publicly before, partly due to the adrenaline of the previous day's celebrations still surging within him, but also because the previous two months had taught him several vital lessons. From this point forth, he would no longer regard himself as 'the accidental monarch', forced into a role he had never wanted because of his elder brother's selfishness and caprice. Conflict lay at hand, both internationally and at home. How he dealt with enemies without and within would dictate both his destiny and that of the nation. Cometh the hour, cometh the king.

Or so those around him hoped.

Chapter Six

'Not Only Alive, But Very Much So'

Everyone alive in Britain on 3 September 1939 could remember exactly where they were at 11 a.m. when the radio announcer interrupted the scheduled broadcast to bring the country the lugubrious voice of Neville Chamberlain. The prime minister, who was suffering from a bad cold, announced that as the deadline set for the withdrawal of German troops from Poland had expired, 'consequently this country is at war with Germany'.* Munich had been a mirage, and the piece of paper Chamberlain had held was now worthless. Immediately after he finished his speech, sirens wailed, sounding an air raid warning. On this occasion it was a test, but it would soon become a familiar, and unwelcome, accompaniment to everyday life.

The king had anticipated the news by beginning a diary the previous day. The first entry was 'The die was cast. We were at war with Hitler & his regime, & all that it stands for.' Yet he also confessed to 'a certain feeling of relief that those ten anxious days of intensive negotiations with Germany over Poland, which at moments looked favourable, with Mussolini working for peace as well, were over'. At the outbreak of the previous war, he had been an eighteen-year-old midshipman on HMS *Collingwood*. Now he was an unanticipated monarch. He reflected stoically on what lay ahead. 'For the last year, ever since the Munich agreement,

---

* The news was a surprise to Hitler, who remarked to von Ribbentrop, 'What shall we do now?'

Germany . . . [has] caused us incessant worry in crises of different magnitudes . . . so today, when the crisis is over, & the result of the breakdown of negotiations is war, the country is calm, firm and united behind its leaders, resolved to fight until liberty & justice are once again safe in the world.'[1]

He made his own broadcast that day, as he sought to inspire a nation. He asked that 'my people at home and my peoples across the seas . . . stand calm, firm and united in this time of trial'. Speaking with conviction and determination, he said, 'The task will be hard. There may be dark days ahead and war can no longer be confined to the battlefield. But we can only do the right as we see the right and reverently commit our cause to God.'

These words gave succour to his subjects and allies across the world. Yet when the Duke of Windsor was told by Sir Ronald Campbell, British ambassador to France, that his country was at war, his response was rather different. 'I'm afraid in the end this may open the way for world communism',[2] he sighed, before shrugging and diving into the pool for a refreshing swim.* Some things, after all, were more important than a global conflict, even as he remained ambiguous about his preferred side.

He could at least claim that he had done his best for international diplomacy, albeit on a self-important basis. As war drew near, he had sent Hitler a telegram on 27th August asking if there was any way conflict might be avoided. He wrote, 'Remembering your courtesy and our meeting two years ago, I address to you my entirely personal simple though very earnest appeal for your utmost influence towards the peaceful solution of the present problem.' If he had believed his personal intervention would make any difference, he was delusional. Hitler's reply of 2 September, 'Assure you that attitude towards England remains the same and my wish to avoid a new war between our two countries remains', was qualified

---

* Showing his knack for perspicacity, he dismissed *The Times*'s news that Germany had invaded Poland on 1 September as 'just another sensational report'.

by his remark that 'It depends however on England whether relations between Germany and England can find the correct channel.'

Opinions differ as to whether Edward was attempting, in a blundering way, to do the right thing, or capable of considered, even treacherous actions. Attempting to open back-channel discussions with the most dangerous man in Europe, without consultation with the king, prime minister or any other interested parties, was an act of arrogant folly. But the duke believed that he had a good personal rapport with Hitler, after their meeting in September 1937, and the dictator was quixotic enough to have listened to him while ignoring more senior and knowledgeable men. Or perhaps Hitler, and those around him, had already identified Edward as a figure who might be of use to them if developments went their way. He was therefore humoured with a tolerance that they would not have extended to others, including his brother.

If the king had hoped that his triumphant visit to the United States and Canada would lead to a period of restful acclaim, he was disappointed. On 23 August, while at Balmoral, he was told that the Nazis had signed the German-Soviet Pact, which guaranteed a decade of peace between the two nations and therefore allowed Hitler to invade Poland without any fear of retaliation by Stalin. After sending a well-intentioned but useless message of friendship to the Emperor of Japan ('dealing with Orientals, direct communication between Heads of State may be helpful'),[3] the king left Balmoral for Buckingham Palace, to be in constant touch with Chamberlain and others.

With his offer to write directly to Hitler tactfully refused, the monarch still hoped that peace could be salvaged at the last minute, as it had been in 1938. He remarked to Sir Miles Lampson, the British ambassador to Egypt, that he was annoyed that the crisis had spoilt the grouse season at Balmoral ('1,600 brace in six days . . . never had so many grouse up there this year') and that it was 'utterly damnable that the villain Hitler had upset everything'. He trusted that the Führer's actions were a show of strength that had little intent behind it. 'HM now thought that there would be peace and that this time Hitler's bluff had been called.'⁴

Others still believed that peace was possible. Hardinge wrote to his wife of the 'unpleasant time of waiting' that 'it is impossible to foretell what the outcome will be. I think a great deal of the recent German bluster - including the Soviet pact - is intimidation, and if it is only a question of Danzig,* I feel that a solution can still be reached. If on the other hand Hitler is determined to smash Poland, and is encouraged to do so by his temporary immobilisation of Russia then there can be only one answer. It is impossible to tell you which of the two is the real motive.' Nonetheless, he reassured her that military preparations were going smoothly, and suggested that 'I suppose that within the next 48 hours we shall know where we are.'⁵

Behind the scenes, confidence gave way to panic. The duke could not be allowed to remain at large in France if war broke out, and so Monckton asked Wilson whether the government would be prepared to repatriate him. Wilson initially expressed little interest in helping his former sovereign, suggesting that Edward should make his own arrangements, but the king intervened, seeing the possibility of disaster if his brother were to be captured by the Germans. As Monckton later wrote, 'though the situation was difficult and dangerous it was not "sans espoir"'.†⁶

On 29 August, he informed Wilson that the king would send a plane to France to collect Edward and Wallis in the event of the outbreak of war. Upon their return to Britain, they would stay with the duke's best man, Fruity Metcalfe, and his wife in Sussex. Monckton also raised the possibility of what the former monarch would be expected to do during the war. He suggested, 'the King has in mind the possibility of the Duke being a Deputy Commissioner

* The so-called 'Free City of Danzig' was a city state with disputed territorial ownership by both the Poles and the Germans. On 1 September, the Germans shelled it, and invaded a few days later.
† Meaning 'hopeless'.

for an area . . . I have not had a chance to say anything about this to the Duke.'[7]

Monckton soon discovered that Edward was less receptive to the idea of an immediate return to his home country than he had repeatedly claimed earlier in the year. He had wasted a vast amount of government time on the question of when he would be allowed back to Britain, and now, told that he could come home, he equivocated. The hill he chose for his stand was that he would not return unless he was billeted in either Windsor or one of the other royal castles. Therefore, with a pilot standing by, Monckton wrote, with understandable irritation, that 'after a midnight conversation with Alec Hardinge, I was compelled to cancel the flight and war was declared with the Duke still at Antibes'.[8]

To watch from one's swimming pool as Europe prepared to fight and then to refuse a lifeline because the standards of accommodation being offered did not live up to one's regal standards shows a peerless level of narcissism. It would be almost admirable were it not for the duke's failure to comprehend that there were more pressing concerns at hand than the level of comfort he was expected to endure. It was typical of him that after refusing the chance to return to Britain, he asked that the plane be made available to him anyway, for whatever purpose he wished. Germany was not very far away, after all.

Unsurprisingly, his reaction was met with anger by both the king and Chamberlain.* It was decided that he could now only return at public expense if he was prepared to take one of two minor roles, either deputy regional commissioner in Wales under the air marshal Lord Portal, or an army liaison officer. Both were proposed as punishment for his hubris, and Monckton was dispatched to France to ascertain whether he would accept such a

---

* Metcalfe, perhaps insulted at the implication that his home wasn't good enough for his former king, responded, 'You have just behaved as two spoiled children. You *only* think of yourselves. You don't realise that there is at this moment a war going on, that women and children are being bombed and killed while *you* talk of your PRIDE.'

demotion. As he handed him the task, the king remarked wryly, 'You should write a book on "Odd Jobs I Have Done".'⁹

Liaising with the duke proved to be an especially odd job. After Monckton landed in France, he and his flying officer were arrested on suspicion of being German spies. They were only released after a local clergyman threw up his hands in horror at their atrocious attempts at the language and said, 'No one but an Englishman could speak such French!' When they eventually arrived in Antibes, they were greeted by Metcalfe, still angry at the duke's behaviour, and Monckton found that an apparently penitent Edward was prepared to accept one of the demeaning posts he was offered. He stated that he would rather serve as a liaison officer, which at least nodded to the military experience he had accrued in the previous war.

When he was told that he was being brought to Britain, however, he now demurred at flying, asking instead if he could travel by destroyer, as befitted his status. If this was intended as a means of frustrating his journey, it was unsuccessful. The HMS *Kelly*, captained by his friend Louis Mountbatten, was placed at his disposal, and the once unthinkable happened. Nearly three years after the abdication, the Duke and Duchess of Windsor returned to Britain.

If Edward had expected that he and his wife would be greeted with regal fanfare, he was disappointed. As she remarked to him when they arrived in Portsmouth, 'I don't know how this will work out. War should bring families together, even a Royal Family. But I don't know.'¹⁰ Their welcome party was deliberately inauspicious, with only Monckton, Lady Metcalfe and the local naval commander present to mark their arrival, as a Royal Marines band parped out 'God Save the King'. But if the Windsors had assumed that this was because of indifference on the king and queen's part, they would have been mistaken. The queen fretted to Queen Mary on 31 August, 'What are we going to do about Mrs S? Personally I do not wish to receive her, tho' it must depend on circumstances; what do you feel about it, Mama?'¹¹ Wallis was regarded with hostility by Queen Mary,* and the rest of the royal family, many of whom blamed her for Edward's actions over the previous few years. Although this was unfair, it was easier to heap discredit upon the head of a wanton American rather than acknowledge that the former king had brought his difficulties on himself.†

Not everyone regarded Edward's return with horror. Churchill wrote from Chartwell, his country home, to welcome him back, saying, 'Your Royal Highness well knows how I have looked forward to this day.' Making his excuses for not greeting him personally but instead being represented by his son, Randolph, he wrote that 'We are plunged in a long and grievous struggle. But all will come right if we work together to the end.'[12] His warm words concealed a pointed instruction as to the duke's expected behaviour now that he had returned home.

The duke and duchess stayed with the Metcalfes while what Monckton referred to as 'long and rather boring discussions' took place about how Edward would be received by his brother, if at all, and what Wallis's status should be. The lawyer eventually resolved the issue by excluding women from any meeting, explaining to Hardinge that 'it would save trouble if it were a stag party'. The queen, with some relief, left London. Finally a solution was decided upon. On 14 September, nearly a fortnight after the outbreak of war, the king would receive the Duke of Windsor at Buckingham Palace. It would be the first time the two men had been together since 11 December 1936.

*

---

* It was entirely mutual. The historian James Pope-Hennessy wrote that he visited the duchess and observed 'one further facial contortion, reserved for speaking of the Queen Mother, which is very unpleasant to behold and seemed to *me* akin to frenzy'.
† The antipathy between the King and the Duke of Windsor was well known in court and political circles. Channon wrote on 1 August that 'I have heard before that the King has become rather violent against his predecessor', and damned the Royals as 'a violent, disloyal family; [they] always argue about one another.'

The country that Edward had returned to was already very different from the one he had left nearly three years before. Hardinge
commented to his wife that 'This is a very strange life that we lead
here, particularly at night. Everything is hermetically sealed (as regards illumination) from sundown onwards. No street lights, and
even the side-lights are covered with newspaper. If we go out on
foot – taxis are not easy to come by – one has to take a torch as
well as one's respirator! In the day time is more normal, except
that one must never be parted from one's respirator, and of course
uniforms are about everywhere. The nights are rather depressing –
and when the days become short, and we revert to ordinary time,
the duration of the gloom will be very great.'

While Hardinge acknowledged that public feeling was 'admirable' – 'no hysterical people outside the Palace etc., and apparently
not an atom of doubt about the propriety and justice of our cause'
– he nevertheless said that 'It has been a v nerve-wracking time,
especially on this Saturday night when the House of Commons
was in an uproar – the Cabinet in revolt, the French looking as
if they might run out, the Poles in despair and showing signs of
breaking, and Turkey holding back from signing her treaty with
us . . . Everyone's nerves have been on edge and I sometimes feel
quite exhausted by it.'[13] It was into this febrile atmosphere that
the former monarch returned, with all his attendant potential for
mischief-making and general trouble.

Neither the king nor his brother wanted to see each other. When
Churchill, now created First Lord of the Admiralty, visited the king
on 5 September, he suggested that the duke's return would be a
good thing, only for the monarch to correct him: 'Not for long.'[14]
Relations between them had been cold, and both found the idea of
a reunion distressing. Yet the duke could no longer be allowed to
remain on his own terms in France. Something had to be found
for him to do, and for the first time in many years, he could make
himself useful. And the former sovereign took the opportunity of
a face-to-face meeting to remind his younger brother that despite
everything, he still considered himself *primus inter pares*.

The two men's accounts of the eventual encounter differed, but they concurred that it had been better than might have been expected, given what had passed. The king told the Duke of Kent afterwards that the meeting had been reasonable but 'very unbrotherly', and that Edward had been 'in a very good mood, his usual swaggering one, laying down the law about everything'.[15] He wrote in his diary that 'there were no recriminations on either side', and that the 'very confident' duke 'looked very well and had lost the deep lines under his eyes'. As usual, Edward 'seemed only to be thinking of himself', taking care to ask about his younger brothers but pointedly making no reference to their mother, younger sister or any other female member of the family. The king was struck by his determined aversion to discussing the past: '[he] had quite forgotten what he had done to his country in 1936'.[16]

Monckton, who had been waiting nearby for 'an anxious hour', was told by the king, 'I think it went all right', which Edward, 'with a wary eye', picked him up about later, saying that 'it had been all right because, on [your] advice, [I] kept off all contentious subjects'.[17] The duke referred to the meeting simply as 'cordial enough'.[18]

The conversation stayed determinedly on the present. Edward presented himself as a committed patriot, and said that he would now prefer to remain in Britain in the role of deputy regional commissioner than head back to France. His brother gave his verbal assent to this, with the proviso that he would have to secure his ministers' permission. According to the king, the duke then announced that he would go to Wales but wanted to have a month's holiday in England first, flaunting Wallis to various Home Command army departments. As the monarch reported it, 'I told him he would not get a good reception if he did.'[19]

Public reaction to the duke's return had in fact been favourable, belying the fears of the prime minister and king. An editorial in *The Times* suggested that 'It has always been tacitly assumed that war would sweep away the difficulties there may have been in the hour of the Duke's earlier return' and that '[events] relieve his

homecoming of all possible traces of controversy or embarrassment'. It added, in a coded message to all parties, 'No-one could
dream of the Duke's absence from England at a time in which absence would become intolerable exile, or suppose for a moment
that anything would be lacking on the Government's part to speed
the fulfilment of his dearest and most urgent wish.'[20]

The duke knew that his return was conditional, at best. He was
not received by any other member of his family - Queen Mary
told the king at lunch that 'she had no intention of seeing him
if she could avoid it'*[21] - and Wallis remained *persona non grata*.
Although a meeting with Churchill on 15 September was warm,
there was still tension between them, best expressed by Churchill's
question, 'We are all in this together, aren't we?'[22] Edward was able
to reassure him of his bona fides, but a subsequent interview with
Chamberlain was less happy, as the 'broken, nervous' prime minister reminded the duke of his unpopularity with many politicians
and statesmen.

Including, it soon transpired, the Secretary of State for War,
Leslie Hore-Belisha. The two had been broadly on the same side
during the abdication crisis, but now Hore-Belisha had the distasteful task of informing Edward that he was not wanted in Britain after all, and that the Welsh post had been withdrawn. Instead
he was expected to head to the Howard-Vyse mission† in France,
where he would serve as an acting major general, a role far below
his honorary rank of field marshal.

This was done under royal instructions. Hore-Belisha wrote in
his diary that the king seemed in a 'distressed' and 'very disturbed'
state after his interview with his brother and said that 'the Duke
never had any discipline in his life'. The monarch complained
that every previous ruler had succeeded to the throne after their

* This contradicts Channon's sentimental diary entry of 11 October that 'Queen
Mary cries and cries because her eldest son did not call upon her; but he
refused to go unless accompanied by his wife: impasse.'
† Howard-Vyse was the Head of the British Military Mission to the French
High Command.

predecessor had died, but 'mine is not only alive, but very much so'.²³ He informed Chamberlain that 'the sooner [the duke] went to France the better for all concerned. He is not wanted here',²⁴ and wrote in his diary that 'I did not want D attached to any unit of the British Army ... in the British Military Mission in France, D would get access to the secret plans of the French, [and] would pass them on to his wife'. Nonetheless, he reflected that 'there was nothing for him to do in England, & that they were better out of it'.²⁵

Edward was therefore told that he would not be able to take a tour of his former country, on the grounds that soldiers were not allowed to assume their new postings when it suited them, and that his roving around a nation in a state of war would attract unnecessary attention. To his credit, he did not remonstrate or argue at this humiliating demotion, but instead asked whether he might have some time with Wallis in England first. In Hore-Belisha's tactful words, he 'appreciated all the arguments and expressed agreement'.

The duke and Wallis remained with the Metcalfes for nearly a fortnight while he received his formal instructions and was measured for his uniform. It was in such attire that Nicolson saw him at a social engagement. The politician remarked, 'he is dressed in khaki with all his decorations and looks grotesquely young ... I have seldom seen the Duke in such cheerful spirits and it was rather touching to witness their delight at being back in England.'²⁶ Edward was cheered in the streets, received thousands of complimentary letters* and generally enjoyed a hero's welcome that belied the doubts that had been displayed by so many.

Seasoned observers of the duke may have wondered at the conciliatory attitude he had displayed since his return to Britain. He had been snubbed, patronised and treated without the dignity

---

* When Chamberlain, to make a point, showed him the abusive letters that he had received since the Windsors had returned, Edward handed them back unread, saying airily that he was used to getting them by now.

he might have expected.* Rather than arguing or remonstrating, however, he took chastening blows without demur. Those who knew him of old may have wondered what his agenda was.

Hardinge was unimpressed by the prodigal duke. The two men had cordially loathed one another when they had been monarch and private secretary in 1936, and their reunion was an unhappy one. Hardinge wrote to his wife on 17 September apologising for his 'rather crotchety' temper and giving Edward's presence as its reason. 'My nerves have been so completely exhausted – and I am trying to restore them with more [Duke of Windsor] – but altogether without success.' He went on to outline Edward's wish to roam the country before heading to Paris. Some government figures were sympathetic ('Horace Wilson and Hore-Belisha were very ready to acquiesce'), but Hardinge wrote with relief that 'luckily Ironside[†] would have none of it, and said that he would send the Duke his orders to go to his job in Paris before the end of this week!' The private secretary continued to distrust his former master, and the duchess. 'He (the Duke) is not going to be told any secrets because of her known unreliability. I think this is quite a good solution.'[27] Even in absentia, as she tarried with the Metcalfes, the Duchess of Windsor continued to horrify the highest echelons of British society.

On 29 September, Edward and Wallis returned to France, with the duke ready to report for duty at Vincennes to Major General Sir Richard Howard-Vyse, aka 'the Wombat'. He wrote to Monckton in good spirits on 2 October, saying that apart from a 'filthy rough crossing', he was pleased to be back in France and that he wished to remain in Paris. He commented that 'I shall have to be away a certain amount touring various areas . . . besides we have an excellent cellar'.

He kept any political discussion to a minimum, other than to

---

* A letter from Hardinge to Howard-Vyse ended with the handwritten postscript, 'The King is so sorry for landing you with him, but has complete confidence in your tact and power of control.'
† General Edmund Ironside, Chief of the Imperial General Staff.

comment that 'I did not like the tone of [Churchill's] broadcast of yesterday.* I have no idea what force the Nazi-Soviet peace over-tures will take or how they will be presented, but it seems to me sheer folly and a betrayal of the people to follow Winston's line and not at least make a pretence of examining them.' He also expressed his hopes to see Monckton again soon, as 'while great caution must be exercised, there is much to say that I cannot possibly write'.[28]

The duke may have expected that his role would be little more than a sinecure, an opportunity to be photographed looking seri-ous in uniform. Yet the Wombat and those around him had other intentions. Hardinge had indicated that Edward was only to be used sparingly, writing to Howard-Vyse that any occasional visits to be made to the GHQ 'would only be done for some special purpose and that [Edward] would have instructions to return as soon as his task had been accomplished, and not be allowed to go drifting about at his pleasure'.[29]

It has been suggested† that Howard-Vyse's department was an informal espionage organisation, intended to spy on their French allies. The British distrusted their comrades-in-arms, whom they found secretive and obstructive, from the commander-in-chief, General Gamelin, downwards. The high-profile presence of the Duke of Windsor made it harder for the French to obstruct their allies' fact-finding forays into their lines without causing a diplo-matic furore. Brigadier Davy, the mission's chief of staff, described it as nothing less than 'a heaven-sent opportunity of visiting the French front'.[30]

Edward began October 1939 energetically. He and Metcalfe trav-elled 800 miles together along the Maginot Line, France's major de-fence fortifications, and the duke compiled reports for Ironside. He noted both how poor the defences were, making a mockery of the oft-repeated claims of French excellence and insuperability, and

---

* Churchill had described Russia's intentions as 'a riddle wrapped in a mystery inside an enigma'.

† Most notably by Michael Bloch in his book *The Secret File of the Duke of Windsor*.

how low morale was. The forces were obsessed with feuding with one another and seemed entirely unprepared for war. Describing Gamelin evocatively as a 'weak sister' - his knowledge of family rows gave him experience of this - Edward decided there was no serious possibility that the French could resist a full German assault. The War Office received his reports and ignored them, believing them to be dictated by a desire to make trouble. This would prove to be a mistake, but the duke was regarded so poorly that his useful counsel was regarded with suspicion.

Nonetheless, believing that he was making a difference, he was in the best spirits he had been in since the abdication. Metcalfe praised his 'splendid form' and called him 'absolutely delightful company', with the proviso that when bills had to be settled, the duke's old closeness about money caused him to become 'frightful'.[31] Yet even minor transgressions became redolent of his untrustworthiness. He had a chance encounter with the Duke of Gloucester, who was serving as a liaison officer to Lord Gort,* and it made for an awkward meeting. Edward was seen wearing the uniform of marshal of the RAF, which he was not entitled to in his major general role. And eventually, when he took a salute from the men that was intended for Gort, he was formally reprimanded and removed from his duties. By way of reprisal, he referred to his superior as 'Fat-boy Gort'.[32]

One does not have to like the duke to see that he was treated dismally over this period by everyone from the king downwards. He had been sent to France to keep him out of trouble in Britain, but the necessity of finding something for him to do that would not lead to embarrassment proved beyond the beleaguered British forces. There was also resentment towards him from the other officers, epitomised by the comment by Henry Pownall, Gort's chief of staff, that 'If Master W thinks he can stage a come-back he's mighty wrong.'[33] The duke was seen as an attention-seeker who wished to hog the limelight, and was treated as such, to his

---

* The commander-in-chief of the British Expeditionary Force.

anger and distress. Hardinge wrote a tart memorandum in which he summarised the matter: 'The Duke of Windsor is supposed to be serving in France as a Major-General on the Staff, and not as a member of the Royal Family enjoying special privileges. If it is not HRH's desire to give his services under the same conditions as any other soldier, different arrangements will have to be made, and the reason publicly explained, if necessary.'[34]

Edward remained unpopular with his family. The queen re-marked to Hardinge on 30 October that 'On the BBC news this afternoon there was an account of the Duke of Windsor looking younger (& I suppose more beautiful) than ever, making a tour of the Maginot Line & chatting to Tommies ... & saying how glad he was to find such true friendship between them etc.' She was unimpressed. 'I don't want to be super critical, but it sounds so like the old stuff, & never a mention of the poor Duke of Gloucester or Duke of Kent ... I am sure that we must be on the look-out for these advertisements.' Absence had not made her impressions of her brother-in-law any warmer. She told the receptive Hardinge, 'I do not trust him one inch.'[35]

When the duke became aware of this 'back-door intrigue', he re-acted decisively. In early November, he returned briefly to London, staying at Claridge's hotel. He demanded to see the king to discuss his military appointment, which he told Monckton was now un-tenable and intolerable, due to 'the recent exposure of a network of intrigue against me'. He asked the lawyer, who was now working in the propaganda office, to arrange a meeting, and described the nature of this campaign of intrigue as 'so virrulent [sic] that I wish to seek both your and Winston's advice before seeing the King, only of course he is not to know this'.[36]

He wrote angrily to Churchill on 12 November, seeking the counsel of the politician he explicitly described as a father figure. 'The situation is neither new nor surprising, being merely fresh evidence of my brother's continued efforts to humiliate me by every means in his and his courtiers' power.' He bemoaned the king's in-volvement in attempts to ban him from entering British-occupied areas in France, and stated that 'I must confront my brother with all this and protest, firstly against the order itself as undermining . . . my position as a major general in the army . . . and secondly, against the underhand way in which the order was given, and in which it was to be applied.'[37]

For the duke to have presented his brother with allegations of underhand behaviour would have been disastrous, especially if such an encounter had become public knowledge. Monckton explained that it would be impossible for a formal meeting of this nature to take place without the presence of both General Ironside and the Wombat, and that since Howard-Vyse was still in France, 'I do not think . . . the King would be willing to discuss the matter with you.'[38] He suggested that the visit would be abortive, something echoed by Churchill, who wrote, 'It seems to me very probable . . . that the King would refuse to see you.' He also noted that, humiliatingly, 'an order might be given by the War Office for your immediate return, which you would have to set an example in obeying'.

Instead, Churchill told the duke to take his uncomfortable treatment with equanimity. 'In my opinion it would be utterly impossible to make head against the Royal and military authority under which you now lie; and any protests would only expose you to rebuff and vexation.' The First Lord appealed to Edward's pride by saying that he should naturally 'treat all minor questions of ceremony and precedence as entirely beneath your interest and dignity', and that if he did not allow himself to be riled, 'your Royal Highness would place yourself in an unassailable position, and clothe yourself in impenetrable armour'.[39] It was excellent advice, but Edward was too proud to take it with the humility it merited. After all, who was he if not the former king-emperor?

Denied an opportunity to see the king, he instead occupied himself by dining with Monckton. He vented spleen about his brother, his family and how much better the country would be doing if he was still in charge. On one occasion, they were joined by Beaverbrook, and they had what Monckton called 'a very frank talk' about the war. Appeasement had given way to a realisation that 'there was nothing to be done but fight it'. Still, as Monckton put it, 'it was like walking further and further into a thick wood knowing that whichever way you went there was a pit which you could not avoid at the other end'.

Between dinners, Edward wrote to Monckton to sneer that his brother was 'scared of a tête à tête' and that 'he won't face me alone' but insisted on being accompanied by Howard-Vyse. If this happened, the duke wished for Monckton to be present too, on the grounds that 'I hope that the meeting may well prove to be the best and anyway . . . the last round of the series of contests in which you and I have been engaged for the last three years.'[40] In the event, this mano-a-mano combat never took place.

The duke hoped to recruit Ironside, a 'forceful personality', to his cause and to ask him to put his case to the king. He observed that 'the second line of defence in Queen Elizabeth is of Maginot proportions, so that Ironside, like Hitler, may be up against a tougher proposition than he knows'. Even as he claimed not to wish to drag the general into 'a private family feud',[41] his earlier stance of cooperation and amiability had disappeared. In its place was a determination to settle old scores.

A compromise was ultimately reached. The duke was allowed to visit British troops as long as there was a specific reason for his visit and with approval from his superiors. He boasted to Monckton, 'I have won my point', but conceded that 'the edge has naturally been taken off the keenness in the job, and I am only really carrying on because it's the [role] that suits the Duchess and myself the best'. Self-absorption dominated all, even now.

When the king visited France in early December, his brother was advised to remain a tactful distance away. Wallis described this to her aunt as 'all very childish . . . competition still exists in the English mind - so one must hide so there is no rivalry'.[42] During his trip, the king, encouraged by Hardinge, decided that Hore-Belisha should be fired on the grounds of incompetence. This was no hardship, as the monarch disliked the Secretary of State for War. He had written in his diary on 11 October that 'Hore-Belisha must always steal a march on his expert advisers if he can. He likes the limelight & personal kudos.'[43]

Hore-Belisha's involvement in the so-called 'pillbox affair', in which he made the criticism that too few pillbox defences were being constructed for the British Expeditionary Force, proved to be his downfall, not least because of latent (and overt) anti-Semitism. That he was later proved to be correct did not help his cause. Hardinge wrote cryptically to his wife on 5 December that 'H[RH] has been terribly upset over the incident of which you know, but today he seems to be happier. I do not think we have heard the last of it, as the feeling on all sides out there is so strong against the individual in question, that I wish his position is almost impossible.'[44]

In January 1940, Hore-Belisha was dismissed, amidst disquiet about his performance.* The ease with which this was accomplished indicated both that Hardinge remained the most political of private secretaries and also that the king, apparently in thrall to him, was happy to facilitate his desires. As Channon put it, 'the King himself insisted on Leslie's resignation . . . egged on by both the Queen and the Duke of Gloucester'.[45] Although the diarist was a friend of Hore-Belisha and loathed Hardinge, to whom he referred as the 'Black Rat',† there is no reason to doubt the veracity of his account. Once, this action would have been seen as epochal, but now it was clear that at a time of war, the monarch's power was in the ascendant. Major personnel decisions could be taken quickly and unilaterally.

One man who suffered from these developments was the Duke of Windsor. For all his faults, there was some truth in his statement

---

* Few mourned his departure, save Channon. Pownall described him as 'an obscure, shallow-brained, charlatan, political Jewboy', contrasting him unfavourably with the 'great gentleman' Gort.

† Channon hissed on 6 May that 'the "Black Rat" is increasingly dangerous and sees himself as ruling the country'.

that he was 'banished from the hearts of the citizens', and that he and Wallis were treated like 'rats in a trap until the end of the war'.[46] He had behaved in a conciliatory fashion, but the hostility he received left him in no doubt that he would never be accepted or welcomed back by the elite, even as the public offered him a warmer reception.

The couple were easy prey for someone who would show them the attention and respect they craved. It was unsurprising, then, that the German ambassador to the Hague could tell his masters in Berlin, at the beginning of 1940, that he was the proud possessor of 'a line leading to the Duke of Windsor'.[47]

Chapter Seven

'The Darkest Day in English History'

For the king to have one Lord Steward of the Household with fascist sympathies might be considered a misfortune; to have two can only be described as carelessness. Yet for many of the leading figures at court in the late thirties, admiration and appreciation for Hitler and fascism was almost the norm. Some hid behind the fig leaf of appeasement to frame their feelings in a politically expedient manner, and argued that they were only taking the same path that the prime minister, foreign minister and king had all followed in the run-up to war.

Yet there were others who were far more vocal in their views. These included everyone from the Mitford sisters, Unity and Diana,* to the novelist Henry Williamson, to say nothing of aristocrats such as Patrick Boyle, Earl of Glasgow; Harold Harmsworth, Viscount Rothermere, the *Daily Mail* proprietor (who wrote an editorial for the paper headlined 'Hurrah for the Blackshirts!' in 1934); and Josslyn Hay, Earl of Erroll. These men and women were influential in the grandest salons of the day, and were responsible for the unease that many had felt about going to war with Germany until the belligerence of Hitler's actions made it

---

* Their sister Nancy, never one to ignore the comic possibilities of real-life material, had satirised the British Union of Fascists and Diana's then lover Oswald Mosley in her 1935 novel *Wigs on the Green*.

inevitable.* Erroll, for instance, had been present at the coronation in 1937, despite his open support for the British Union of Fascists. Still, if every aristocrat who had ever espoused unacceptable views had been excluded, there would barely have been enough people attending to fill Westminster Abbey's Lady Chapel.

It was unsurprising, then, that the ceremonial post of Lord Steward of the Household should attract trouble. It was a symbolic but significant role, which had existed since the early fifteenth century, its holder nominally in charge of the royal household's everyday expenditure. Included amongst its incumbents were Elizabeth I's favourite Robert Dudley, and Thomas Percy, Earl of Worcester, who had been responsible for an uprising against Henry IV. By 1940, it was a coveted aristocratic position, and had been held by Walter Montagu Douglas Scott, Duke of Buccleuch, since 1937. His presence in Buckingham Palace was unremarkable. A war veteran of impeccable standing, Britain's largest landowner and the brother-in-law of the Duke of Gloucester, he moved in the highest circles, and did so initially untainted by whispers of unfortunate associations.

Unfortunately, due diligence did not exist for such appointments, otherwise a courtier such as Hardinge or Lascelles might have whispered in the king's ear that Buccleuch was likely to bring embarrassment, or worse, to the royal household. Hardinge had even written to his wife in September 1938, in the context of 'pro-German friends', that 'I saw Walter in the Lobby yesterday and had a talk with him, but avoided the controversial aspect of the matter.'[1] His tact did him credit, but eventually the issue would have to be raised.

Like many others, Buccleuch was keen on appeasement on the grounds that another conflict would be catastrophic for Britain and

---

* They were dubbed the 'Cliveden set', because Cliveden's owners, Lord and Lady Astor, were thought to be at the centre of pro-fascist plots, but as Claude Cockburn, editor of *The Week* and the man who invented the designation, admitted, '[They] would not have known a plot if you handed it to them on a skewer.'

the world. However, he went several steps further than most of his peers. He made a number of private visits to Germany with a view to cultivating friendly relations with Hitler and other leading Nazis. He wrote to Cooper on 2 October 1938 to say, 'Can any of us prove or judge in advance that it is impossible under any circumstances to trust Hitler or Germany?' Stating that his own travels were of vital international value ('Hitler has perhaps never met a gentleman and statesman before'), he announced that Chamberlain had made 'a very good start' with the Führer and, telling Cooper 'don't be too bellicose', suggested that 'Hitler may well profit and learn by further talks.'[2]

Buccleuch believed that the Munich Agreement showed a willingness on Germany's part to compromise, and even as Hitler's territorial expansions became more threatening, he continued to think that war had to be avoided at all costs. As he confided to the pro-appeasement Conservative politician Rab Butler in April 1939, 'neither Hitler nor Ribbentrop are likely to be quite as inhuman as feared'.*[3]

He was so committed to his self-appointed task that he visited Germany that month and twice saw Ribbentrop, who assured him that war was not in anyone's interests. He had planned to attend Hitler's fiftieth birthday party, but was tactfully informed by Ogilvie-Forbes that the optics of 'a high official of the King's court' attending such an event might lead to 'not being all square with the present feeling of the King's Government'. He was advised to find that he was occupied in metaphorically washing his hair back in Britain that evening instead. His visit rebounded embarrassingly on his brother-in-law, whom *The Week* suggested was 'in the hands of the Germans'.[4] Gloucester sternly instructed the would-be peacemaker not to visit Germany again, both while he was Lord Steward and while the international situation remained tense.

---

* In the same letter, he optimistically suggested that Unity Mitford could be used as a kind of go-between, saying, 'Miss Mitford's frequent meetings with the Führer should not be underestimated.'

Nonetheless, Buccleuch, writing a report of his visit, felt able to say that there was 'a desire for improvement in Anglo-German relations', as he complained to Butler about the 'West-End gossip and anti-German bias' prevalent in Britain. He singled out Churchill, along with Eden,* as examples of those who 'have really scorned all along the possibility of compromise or consideration of any argument which the other side might advance, and thus bring war much closer'.[5]

Hardinge was furious at this unhelpful 'intervention'. Channon reported with relish on 3 May that '[Walter has] been seriously "ticked off" by Alec Hardinge . . . they nearly came to blows', but saw this as a demonstration of the limits of Hardinge's influence. 'Evidently [he] is not as popular or as omnipotent as I thought.'[6] Buccleuch subsequently enjoyed a thirty-five-minute interview with the king on 5 May, and Channon reported triumphantly that '[he] listened intently to all Walter said and was impressed thereby, so sucks to that shit Hardinge. Walter now hates him and proposes to say so to the Kents, with whom he is lunching.'[7]

One man spared Buccleuch's (and Channon's) contempt was Chamberlain. The prime minister wrote to Buccleuch in August 1939 that 'We are living through difficult hours, but I hope we may yet be successful in avoiding the worst',[8] and expressed a desire to go grouse shooting with him if conflict was averted. The grouse were spared. Four days later, war was declared.

It was provocative on Buccleuch's part, nine days after the outbreak of hostilities, to attend a meeting at the Duke of Westminster's house in the company of such known fascist sympathisers as Lord Mottistone and Sir Philip Gibbs. The agenda was the immediate cessation of hostilities between two such simpatico nations as Britain and Germany. It was equally bold of the Lord Steward to write to Churchill in early 1940 and suggest Göring as an

---

* About whom the king was initially disparaging. He wrote in his diary on 11 September 1939 that 'I find [Eden] is difficult to talk to and he does not give me confidence.'

ambassador for peace between their two countries. He bemoaned the fact that a war against Hitler himself had become transmogrified into a war against Germany. Yet he was not alone in believing that the country had blundered into a destructive and unwinnable conflict through little more than carelessness and a desire to protect a nation to which it had no historic or ancestral links.

If Buccleuch had been uncomplicatedly loyal to the king and to Britain, there would have been no question of a conflict of interest. However, his allegiances appeared to lie elsewhere. He wrote an extraordinary letter to the monarch on 12 December 1939, which had it been made public may well have resulted in accusations of treason. Acknowledging that the way he had behaved over the previous year was 'probably not correct for the Lord Steward of Your Majesty's Household', he suggested that his resignation was now inevitable, as 'I find it difficult to keep strictly within the rules & customs binding one in my position.'

He was then explicit about why he found this so taxing. 'I can hardly presume to put before Your Majesty too many of my own opinions, but they are shared by a large and growing number of Your Majesty's most loyal subjects, & among them many wise & distinguished citizens. I and others have felt keen disappointment that there were not efforts of a rather different nature and greater perseverance to establish a closer contact with the German leaders in the early part of last summer, & some discussion on a basis of equality as was begged for from Berlin, to forestall & avoid the destruction of Poland and the calamity of this war, instead of waiting til the last minute when discussion was hopeless.'

He lamented that 'the great attempts of our Prime Minister were so largely counteracted by some of our own press & public men as well as by actions directed from Berlin', and expressed his regret that 'it was not seen fit to further and take greater advantage of the Dutch-Belgian mediation offer to encourage definite proposals from London & Berlin that might have resulted in a satisfactory peace for Europe'. He was then explicit about his desires, which amounted to ever closer union with Germany and the Nazis. 'It is a tragedy that so much bitterness & hostility & the present state of affairs is a result of suspicion & misunderstanding on both sides, inflamed by press campaigns, rumours, insults & propaganda, quite apart from certain features of the internal & external policies of the present rulers in Germany. The trump card was played by those convinced of the necessity of war, & some even wanting it when they persuaded Lord Halifax and others that Hitler and the Nazis were determined on world domination & the subjection of Britain & must be fought at once. However much this may be a normal ambition to many Germans, there was definitely no immediately or rapidly approaching danger, and ordinary diplomacy, backed by some strength and helped by some cooperation with Germany on a basis of equality, as so definitely wanted & preferred by Hitler, would have prevented the danger from becoming a closer real-ity. It was at most only half a truth to say that our freedom was threatened.'

Instead, he suggested, the machinations of politicians and the press had blinded them to their true common enemy. 'How much better to have allowed Germany to come up against Soviet Russia instead of pushing them into that alliance. Though at the start of war we were said to be fighting Hitlerism, now it may be more a life & death struggle for both, the vast majority of the nation including moderates previously opposed to him, & all those known to me, are united in defence of their country, and they may well hold out for a long time unless providence removes Hitler, or we take ad-vantage of strange developments to change our front altogether.'

He described the war as 'absolute madness', and said, 'Til France, Britain and Germany can cooperate, whatever our governments & politics, there can be no settlement in Europe . . . However great the evil on the other side, and the justice on ours, I cannot feel that the French or ourselves have always acted justly towards that country, and I am afraid we have been seriously guilty of misrep-resentation as well as they during the last eight months, and that this spoils our case in spite of constant vile perpetrations on the other side, always becoming worse since war began.'

Urging that 'neutral mediators or arbiters' should help settle the matter, he acknowledged that 'I have endeavoured to be discreet in public, and am loyally resolved as others to help dutifully in every way, though with no enthusiasm for the waging of this war', though his true feelings were made clear by his statement that 'from continuous evidence I do not feel the nation is as united for war as is frequently stated, but naturally one does not wish to disclose any disunity'. He concluded, 'I fear your Majesty will hardly read through this, nor can I expect that your Majesty will have time to grant me a few minutes if any further explanation is needed, but I have felt obliged to write, and it is perhaps natural that many high and low have begged me to do so.'[9]

In its own way, it was as explosive a letter as the one Alec Hardinge had written to Edward VIII three years before, in which he had urged the king to banish Wallis from the country or risk constitutional chaos.* Hardinge at least wrote from a position of propriety. Buccleuch's mixture of implicit threat, high-handed advice and hints at a whole cabal of like-minded fellow travellers working against both the government and, potentially, the monarchy was a chilling reminder of the prevalence of forces in the country for whom appeasement was only the beginning of what could have evolved into a mutually rewarding relationship with Germany.

The king initially ignored the letter, and made no record of its receipt in his diary. He did, however, do his best to avoid Buccleuch. Channon (who said of the Lord Steward, 'he is slow, shy but sure and I am devoted to him') ascribed blame to Hardinge, whom he called 'that green-eyed monster of treachery', even if Buccleuch assured him that 'AH, though still all-powerful at the Palace, is not really liked or trusted by the Sovereigns [sic].'[10]

However, by May 1940, it was clear that Buccleuch's offer to resign had to be acted upon: his comments had gone too far. The king therefore replied calmly and without rancour, but also with

---

* See *The Crown in Crisis*, Chapter Six, for more details.

a considered rebuttal of the Lord Steward's arguments. 'I did not answer your letter of December last at once, because I felt that as the war went on, you might possibly change your mind over the certain matters of which you wrote, and also I did not desire any gossip about your retirement . . . [but] I feel this would be an opportune moment for you to resign, without too much unfavourable comment.'

Six months into the 'phoney war', it was still uncertain what lay ahead, but the king now knew that the likes of Buccleuch could be neither humoured nor tolerated. 'I assure you that we feel the tragedy & futility of war as deeply as yourself, and can only trust that a true peace may emerge from this conflict. I know that your reasoning is patriotic, & based solely on a wish to help this country, but I, & the bulk of my people, feel that the Nazi regime is an evil one, & one which has so far spread nothing but misery and cruelty in the little peaceful countries which have the misfortune to be neighbours to Germany.'* He accepted the Lord Steward's resignation 'with, I may say, great regret', and finished with his own elegantly phrased warning. 'The Queen & I know that you will do all in your power to help this country in her great need, and we do feel so sorry that your opinions preclude you from standing by us at this moment.'[11]

The Lord Steward's departure was now inevitable,† and the king accordingly wrote in his diary on 26 June that 'Walter Buccleuch came to say good bye. He has resigned. It was a rather painful interview as he has been "dubbed" as being pro-German in his attitude towards the War & has said stupid things, but we parted amicably.'[12]

---

* In a phrase deleted from the draft reply that survives, the king wrote, 'Once again the Germans have made the great mistake of thinking that because as a nation we hate war & love peace, that we are not only hypocrites but decadent as well.'

† Channon sighed in his diary on 28 May that '[Walter] tried to prevent the catastrophe of the war, the horrors and humiliations which we are now to endure, and his only reward was to be reviled by the unthinking.'

The same mistake could not be made again. It was important that Buccleuch's successor should be both loyal and patriotic, so the new choice seemed ideal. Douglas Douglas-Hamilton, the 14th Duke of Hamilton, was a dashing pilot and one of the first men to have flown over Mount Everest. Square-jawed and handsome, he seemed to fulfil the role admirably. It was then a pity for the king that his new appointment as Lord Steward should have his own connections with the Nazi Party. These stretched back as far as 1936, when he had attended the Olympic Games in Berlin as a guest of Ribbentrop. Douglas-Hamilton might have argued, as Buccleuch did, that his presence in the country did not connote approval of the nation's actions, but then another high-profile visitor to Germany the following year, the Duke of Windsor, had attracted opprobrium when he and his wife were photographed standing next to Hitler.

There was a growing sense, thanks to the presence of Buccleuch and Douglas-Hamilton at court, that German influence had penetrated British society at the highest levels. Should it find a charismatic and willing outlet, the consequences could be regrettable.

If that man was out for revenge against his country, and above all, his brother, matters could only worsen.

The Duke of Windsor began 1940 in poor humour. He returned to London again in January, and had an interview with Beaverbrook, who suggested that the war should be ended by a brokered peace with Germany. Should this happen, the duke would find himself a popular figure. Beaverbrook's advice was that Edward should consequently 'stump the country*, in which case . . . [you] would have a tremendous success'.[13]

Whether this was meant as a serious proposition or simply a piece of flattery, it indicated that there were still influential figures who believed that Edward's status as 'king over the water' could be used to beneficial effect. George VI was still seen as an uncertain

* Meaning 'canvassing public opinion throughout Britain.'

figure, who described his obligatory recent Christmas broadcast to his empire as 'always an ordeal',[14] and many longed for the return of his more charismatic and able brother. It was left to Monckton, knowing that such a conversation bordered on treason, to interject that the glories of such a return would be marred by the necessity of paying income tax as a British citizen.

The relationship between Edward and Monckton had, for the first time, soured. This was partly because the lawyer, busy with his work as director general of the Press and Information Bureau, was no longer available to act as go-between, agony uncle and facilitator - roles that he was expected to perform with neither complaint nor recompense - but also because his working relationship with the king meant that the duke was now less able to trust him. Edward growled to the historian Philip Guedalla that 'We can sense in our old friend a certain wariness where I am concerned',[15] and the cheery and candid personal letters between the two were gradually replaced by more formal correspondence.

If Monckton had any regrets at the turn their relationship had taken, he did not make them public. He acknowledged in his memoirs that 'from time to time, [the duke or duchess] began to show signs of mistrust', but wrote that 'we surmounted these difficulties and our friendship remained unbroken and closer'.[16] In any case, more important considerations were at hand. For the first few months after the declaration of war, an autumnal stillness hung in the air, as preparations were made for conflict but nothing seemed to happen. The so-called 'phoney war' lasted until 9 April, when Germany invaded Norway and occupied Denmark, making it clear to the complacent that action was imminent on all fronts.

Chamberlain, suffering from the bowel cancer that would eventually kill him, was flailing in his job. The king suggested on 25 March that 'I cannot help feeling a little apprehensive of the criticism which might arise if there not a leavening of younger men in [your] War Cabinet . . . I felt it would be a pity if it were to have a damaging effect in the reconstituted Government.'[17] More candidly, he noted in his diary on 17 March that 'I am very worried over the general situation, as anything we do or try to do appears to be wrong, and gets us nowhere',[18] showing the frustration that both he and the country felt.

The duke felt similar peevishness. When he returned to France, he was angry at the treatment he had received, and therefore prey to the appeals of those who would flatter him. One of these figures was Julius 'Zech' von Zech-Burkersroda, the German ambassador to The Hague and a well-informed observer of Edward's movements. He was able to report in late January of the duke's anger at the way in which he had been frozen out of greater responsibilities. By February, he had a considerable scoop on his hands. The duke had attended an Allied War Council meeting, and had apparently argued that the neutral country of Belgium should not be occupied by the Allies in any circumstances, even in the event of German invasion. While this proved to be inaccurate information, Zech ensured that the news passed firstly to Edward's former friend Ribbentrop, and then, inevitably, to Hitler. The hopes of the Nazi high command that they had a senior figure they could do business with appeared to be justified.

Back in Britain, the escalation of war was imminent. 'Things over here are taking on a more exciting and active aspect',[19] Monckton informed Edward on 15 April. It seemed inevitable that Chamberlain would have to make way for a younger leader, but Monckton did not anticipate a major change in the government for a few months. He wrote, 'At present the position of the Government is strong, particularly that of Winston and the PM', although he suggested that his tip for the next premier was Lord Halifax, saying, 'under the surface, it may well be that Halifax is stronger than either of them in the long run'.[20]

In fact, Monckton was wrong, unless he was deliberately feeding the duke misinformation. After an attempt by the Allies to send troops to Norway to assist there failed, there was a challenge to Chamberlain's authority as prime minister. Attlee and others now refused to serve in a national government as long as Chamberlain remained premier, but made it clear that they were open to working with another leader. This culminated in the Conservative MP Leo Amery echoing Oliver Cromwell in a debate on 7 May, as he told the prime minister, 'You have sat here too long for any good you have been doing. Depart, I say, and let us have done with you', before denouncing him with the damning words 'In the name of God, go!' A vote of no confidence followed the next day, and although Chamberlain won it, the majority of 81 was insufficient for him to remain in office with any security. On 10 May, he resigned, something that Channon hyperbolically called 'perhaps the darkest day in English history'.*²¹

The king, who liked and admired his prime minister, was dismayed at his departure being forced in such circumstances. He told Chamberlain that 'the great triumvirate' of him, Churchill and Halifax could not be bettered, and also that he deserved more than the innuendo and back-stabbing that he faced from press and politicians alike. He wrote in his diary on 9 May, 'It is most unfair on Chamberlain to be treated like this after all his good work . . . Conservative rebels like Duff Cooper ought to be ashamed of themselves for deserting him at this moment.'†²² But it was undeniable that 'the Old Umbrella', as the prime minister was derisorily nicknamed, had folded. A new broom was needed in his place, someone who would sweep the country in a vigorous and forward direction.

Naturally the man of the hour seemed to be Lord Halifax. He was a unifying figure amongst both Conservative and Labour

---

* As Channon morosely drowned his sorrows at the Savoy Grill that night, he was surprised to see Hardinge and Monckton drinking champagne together, apparently in celebration. The two had been contemporaries at Harrow, and continued to enjoy friendly relations during the abdication crisis and beyond.

† This appreciation was shared by Queen Elizabeth, who wrote warmly and emotionally to Chamberlain on 17 May 1940, 'I can never tell you in words how much we owe you. During these last desperate and unhappy years, you have been a great support and comfort to us both, and we felt so safe with the knowledge that your wisdom and high purpose were at our hand.'

MPs, to say nothing of the Liberals. He was also popular with the king and would undoubtedly have been Chamberlain's choice to continue his legacy. The 'Holy Fox' was said to be a man without enemies, and so seemed the obvious choice to take on the mantle of the premiership at such a tempestuous time.

Yet he demurred, to the king's disappointment. The sovereign wrote in his diary that 'H was not enthusiastic, as being in the Lords he could only act as a shadow or a ghost in the Commons, where the real work took place.' Although the king believed Halifax to be 'the obvious man', and wondered if his peerage could be suspended for the duration of the war, the German invasion of the Low Countries on 10 May, bringing destruction and chaos in its wake, meant that there was no time for vacillation.

There was another man who could serve as prime minister. He was not necessarily a popular choice. He had angered and offended many in his party, not least by his defection to the Liberals between 1904 and 1924, and his support of Edward VIII during the abdication crisis had trodden a fine line between upholding a monarch's constitutional right to rule and pure provocation. As recently as 1939, many had believed him to be an anachronistic figure, warning from the sidelines about the dangers of Hitler and appeasement. Now he represented the only chance Britain had. It was therefore not without wariness that the king wrote, 'I knew that there was only one person whom I could send for to form a Government who had the confidence of the country, and that was Winston. I asked Chamberlain his advice, and he told me Winston was the man to send for.'[23]

Their first official meeting at Buckingham Palace began warmly enough. The king remarked, 'I suppose you don't know why I have sent for you.' Churchill teased him gently by replying, 'Sir, I simply could not imagine why.'[24] The monarch was impressed by the new prime minister's 'fire and determination' to carry out his duties. But once this amiability was established, the two men found themselves at odds almost immediately. The king wrote to Churchill after their first encounter to veto one of his suggestions for his Cabinet, Lord Beaverbrook, whom the new prime minister proposed to make Minister for Aircraft Production. The monarch suggested that Beaverbrook would be unpopular in Canada, despite or perhaps because of his Canadian heritage, and added, 'I wonder if you would not reconsider your intention of selecting [him] for this post . . . I fear that this appointment might be misconstrued.'

His rationale for such advice was that 'I want to be a help to you in the very important & onerous office which you have just accepted at my hands',[25] but it also suggested that, far from the relationship he had enjoyed with Chamberlain, Halifax and even Roosevelt, all of which had been paternalistic in nature, he was determined to stamp his own authority on the situation and bring his potentially rebellious premier into line. If this was his intention, it failed. Beaverbrook was appointed, and subsequently made a success of his role.* The king, meanwhile, wrote in his diary that 'I cannot yet think of Winston as PM', and admitted that 'I met Halifax in the garden and told him I was sorry not to have *him* as PM.'[26]

The new prime minister informed his Cabinet on 13 May that 'I have nothing to offer but blood, toil, tears and sweat', a phrase he liked so much he used it in the Commons again later that day while asking for a vote of confidence in the new government.

Events in Europe were escalating, after the inaction of the previous few months of the war, and they affected foreign royalty as well as their people. Queen Wilhelmina of the Netherlands fled to Britain, escaping the Germans by moments. She was greeted at

---

* After the Battle of Britain, Lord Dowding, head of Fighter Command, wrote, 'We had the organisation, we had the men, we had the spirit which could bring us victory in the air but we had not the supply of machines necessary to withstand the drain of continuous battle. Lord Beaverbrook gave us those machines, and I do not believe that I exaggerate when I say that no other man in England could have done so.' This was considerably higher praise than that from Channon, who glumly described Beaverbrook as looking like 'the town tart who has married the mayor'.

Liverpool Street station by the king, who noted that she carried no personal effects bar her jewellery and a tin hat. This displacement of a fellow monarch without warning was a stark reminder of the world they now inhabited.

Within days, the Duke of Gloucester saw that deadly force was everywhere and could strike at anyone, regardless of birth or title. He had been loitering in France, which he had come to loathe,* when Belgium was invaded. He set out to see if there was any assistance he could offer to his cousin King Leopold. However, before he could accomplish anything, the news that everyone had dreaded arrived. France had fallen to the Germans with unbelievable speed, as Hitler's dreams of conquering Europe in a fashion that nobody had dared contemplate since Napoleon came to fruition. It was little wonder that when Gloucester finally encountered Leopold, the Belgian king was said to be 'very depressed' about the fate of his army and his country.

Gloucester realised that there was nothing he could accomplish, and knowing that the capture of a high-ranking member of the royal family - and an army officer to boot - would be disastrous for British morale, and another victory for German propaganda, he tried to withdraw to the relative safety of the Belgian headquarters in Brussels. But before he could reach them, his car was caught in a bombing attack outside the city of Tournai. He and his driver were forced out of the vehicle and into a nearby alley, where tiles and rubble landed on their prone bodies. Such was the force and ferocity of the bombing, they both felt the earth vibrate beneath them as they cowered in terror, covered in blood and dirt.

Gloucester's enthusiasm had nearly seen him killed. Even as he made light of his experience in a letter to his wife - 'Motoring about is not nice as many villages are being bombed'[27] - he was sent back home, as the German advance meant that he was an obvious target.

---

* He wrote to his wife in February to say, 'I think I hate this country and war more than ever. It is such an awful waste of everything.'

It was also feared that he was a Jonah who brought bad luck. As he said to his mother, Queen Mary, '[everywhere] I went, or had been, I was bombed'.[28] The Duchess of Gloucester lamented, 'How dreadful everything is ... I do hope and pray the tide may turn soon in our favour.' But things were about to get worse.

Chapter Eight

'Anything Except the Right Thing'

In her memoir, *The Heart Has Its Reasons*, Wallis Simpson described her and her husband's involvement in what would become one of the defining scandals of the war. 'David and I left Madrid early in July and motored across Spain, taking two days for the trip. We had known the British Ambassador to Portugal, Sir Walford Selby, and his wife in Vienna. He had arranged for us to be put up at the house of a Portuguese banker, Dr Ricardo de Espiritu Santa e Silva.'[1] While the original intention was that the duke and duchess would only remain there overnight, Edward told Selby that he would not be leaving the house until he knew where his future lay and what was in store for him. He did not add that he might have been unsure as to which side he would take in the conflict engulfing the world.

The events that befell Edward and Wallis between the German invasion of France on 10 May and their departure for the Bahamas on 1 August 1940 have been shrouded in confusion and mystery, despite the best efforts of historians and biographers to separate exciting rumour and gossip from facts. Yet the reason the events of those three months continue to fascinate people is because they cut to the heart of the central question about the Duke of Windsor: was he really a Nazi, or was he simply a naïve dilettante?

For Philip Ziegler, Edward's official biographer, the answer is clear. As he told me, 'Edward wasn't a Nazi. They buttered him up, and he was an authoritarian by nature, but if he had known about Belsen, he would have been horrified. But then nobody else knew, either. A large number of right-wing (if not fascist) people thought that the Germans had cleaned up their mess.' Nonetheless, Ziegler added, 'I'd be surprised if we could ever find proof of what the Duke and Duchess got up to; if any letters had ever existed, they would have been destroyed.'[2]

Yet the duke's actions and behaviour over the course of a febrile time were considered to be sufficiently worrying for Churchill to draft a letter to the Commonwealth prime ministers in early July 1940 that stated, 'The activities of the Duke of Windsor on the continent in recent months have been causing HM and myself grave uneasiness as his inclinations are well known to be pro-Nazi, and he may become a centre of intrigue.' The letter continued, 'We regard it as a real danger that he should move freely on the continent', and 'even if he were willing to return to this country, his presence here would be most embarrassing both to HM and the Government'.[3]

These incendiary sentiments were toned down. Churchill's eventual letter stated that 'though his loyalties are impeccable, there is always a backlash of Nazi intrigue which seeks to make trouble about him'.[4] The extent to which this intrigue spread, even going so far as a German operation that would have seen the duke placed back on the British throne with Wallis at his side, has been an endless source of controversy ever since. That the Nazis attempted to take unprecedented action over the course of the summer of 1940 is a matter of historical fact. Had they succeeded, the consequences can only be speculated about.

Yet what is debated is whether Edward and Wallis really were the innocent, even frightened victims they chose to present themselves as, and how far they were complicit in a plot that would have been, in many ways, the most desirable outcome for them both, with the duke's former country being damned in the process. MI5 and royal files that might offer a definitive answer have long since been either destroyed or removed from any public view. But the extraordinary events of that summer have left their own fascinating legacy.

*

'I would much prefer that HRH did not come back for the present',[5] Howard-Vyse announced on 20 May. As France fell to the Germans, it was unclear what the duke should now be doing. Acting either out of a sense of duty, or simply a desire to be at the centre of events, he returned to Paris on 22 May anyway. There, he behaved provocatively, even by his standards. He announced that he would return to his house in Antibes 'to settle the Duchess in', and took little notice of the inconvenient conflict that he had found himself at the heart of. Even Metcalfe complained that 'I am very uneasy about him. He might do anything – anything except the right thing ... I do not know what will happen. W is like a magnet ... it is terrible'.

The duke combined dedication to Wallis with a desire to save his own skin. By 29 May, he was back with her in the South of France. This may not have technically been the desertion of duty it was taken for. Churchill alluded to there being 'a great deal of doubt as to the circumstances in which Your Royal Highness left Paris',[6] but it is likely that Howard-Vyse was aware of the duke's actions, even if he called him 'not [one] at all for running into danger'.[7]

However, it still looked as if Edward was pursuing his own ends at the expense of those around him. Metcalfe commented angrily, 'Re my late Master', that 'he has run like two rabbits' and that 'After twenty years I am through ... utterly I despise him.' He told his wife, who shared his fury at the betrayal, 'He deserted his job in 1936; well, he's deserted his country now, at a time when every office boy and cripple is trying to do what he can.' As he prepared to leave Edward's service for good, he said, 'It is the end.'

It is possible to defend the duke from Metcalfe's allegations, which were made furiously and without complete knowledge of the facts,* but the contrast between the increasingly Boschian scene that was overwhelming Europe and the calm lives that

---

* Metcalfe was subsequently overheard shouting at a members' club that 'he had no patience with a man who was always pining for his wife and rushed from the front to join her'. Nevertheless, he and the duke managed to resume their friendship after the war.

a reunited duke and duchess wished to lead is striking. Even as Edward mused that 'Europe is lost . . . this is the finish',[8] rumours began to circulate as far away as America that there had been contact between Wallis and the Nazis. An FBI memo stated that MI5 'ascertained that the Duchess had informed von Ribbentrop of her itinerary, schedule etc. prior to her departure'.[9]

The duke and duchess headed to the Château de la Croë, where they entertained guests and relaxed by the sea. In the north of the country, hundreds of thousands of stranded soldiers were transported from Dunkirk, and Churchill announced that 'We shall fight on the beaches, we shall fight on the landing grounds, we shall fight in the fields and in the streets, we shall fight in the hills.' Yet as the prime minister vowed, 'we shall never surrender', the once unthinkable now seemed not just possible but likely. As the king wrote in his diary on 12 June, 'the invasion of this country comes next'.[10]

It seemed clear that Edward and Wallis should return to where they could be observed, though that they might make themselves useful seemed a step too far. Yet the duke and duchess had other plans. After Marshal Pétain announced that 'the fighting must cease' and that he would make terms with the Germans, they decided that France was no longer a hospitable destination for them, and so fled to Spain on 19 June. Halifax sent urgent telegrams the same day to British consulates in France asking for information about Edward's whereabouts, with the intention of summoning him back to Britain. But the duke and duchess, with a small entourage, arrived in Barcelona on 20 June. The next day, Edward telegrammed Churchill: 'Having received no instructions have arrived in Spain to avoid capture. Proceeding to Madrid. Edward.'[11]

Although Spain, under the leadership of General Franco, was nominally a neutral country and therefore safe for refugees fleeing Hitler, the duke and duchess were no ordinary fugitives. From the moment of their arrival in the country, they faced stories in the Spanish press that claimed they were there with a view to negotiating an Anglo-German peace, and that Churchill had demanded that the duke be imprisoned if he dared to return to England. While this was untrue, their presence in Spain had attracted the attention of various parties, including the German ambassador, Eberhard von Stohrer. Dr von Stohrer wrote to his superior, Ribbentrop,* on 23 June to say, 'we might perhaps be interested in detaining the Duke of Windsor here and eventually establishing contact with him'.[12]

Ribbentrop, when he learnt of these developments, was said to be ecstatic. Over the course of a disastrous ambassadorship to Britain between October 1936 and February 1938, he had established a good relationship with both Edward and Wallis. He had promised Hitler that he could intercede on Germany's behalf to frustrate the mooted abdication, and, if need be, to keep the king on the throne with German backing. This had ended in humiliation, as nothing of the kind occurred, but Hitler continued to have faith in his underling. Ribbentrop in turn sought another opportunity to impress his Führer. Now it seemed to have arrived. He sent Stohrer a telegram asking if the duke and duchess could be detained in Spain for a couple of weeks, and was delighted when the Spanish foreign minister, Colonel Juan Beigbeder y Atienza, acceded to this request. The great work could at last begin.

When it became clear that Edward and Wallis were at large in Spain, it was initially hoped they could be repatriated to Britain. The king discussed the matter with Halifax on 23 June, but noted caustically that 'she as usual was the stumbling block'.[13] The recently appointed British ambassador to the country, Sir Samuel 'Soapy Sam' Hoare, was reasonably disposed towards the duke, having offered him a degree of support during the abdication crisis, but he was alarmed at the idea of Edward now becoming his responsibility. When the duke arrived in Madrid, where he was staying at the Ritz, Hoare was charged with ensuring that he and Wallis behaved themselves. However, Edward's loquaciousness led him to say to an American

---

* Whom he detested: he referred to 'Herr Brickendrop' with contempt as 'that cold-blooded cad'.

ambassadorial functionary that 'the most important thing now to be done was to end the war before thousands more were killed or maimed'.[14]

Initially, verbal slips aside, their stay seemed destined to be both uneventful and brief, as the duke and duchess were asked to head to Lisbon on 24 June, and thence to Britain. Yet this would clash with a visit to the city by the Duke of Kent, and it was 'inconvenient and undesirable' for the two brothers to be there at the same time. A reluctant Hoare invited Edward* to linger in Madrid for another week or so, but his longer-term intentions remained opaque. Churchill instructed him to head back to Britain on 22 June, but Edward replied, 'I cannot agree to returning until everything has been considered and I know the result ... In the light of past experience my wife and myself must not risk finding ourselves once more regarded by the British public in a different status to other members of my family.'[15] He had previously suggested that his return would be 'an embarrassment to all concerned, myself included',[16] and now he seemed to be toying with the idea of exile, this time on his own terms.

Churchill was unimpressed. He had already suggested to the king that '[the duke] can have no following here ... we must guard against his becoming champion of the disgruntled',[17] and now his former monarch was displaying active signs of sedition. The prime minister wrote by hand on the telegram, 'Your Royal Highness has taken active military rank and refusal to obey direct orders would create a serious situation. I hope it will not be necessary for such orders to be sent. I most strongly urge immediate compliance with [the] wishes of the Government.'[18] When the duke received it, he was said to reel as if he had received a blow. Churchill's warning

---

* The duke's charms clearly worked on Soapy Sam again. The ambassador wrote to Churchill on 27 June to plead his case, saying, 'Could you not give him a naval command of some kind? I do feel strongly that this is the moment to get them both back to England and to clear up the situation ... [otherwise] there will be a prince over the water who will be a nuisance and possibly an embarrassment.'

was not even a veiled threat, indicating how far apart the former friends had now grown, but it played into German hands. Stohrer now reported that 'Windsor has expressed himself in strong terms against Churchill and this war.'[19]

Edward angrily replied that 'I used to have your support until you reached the supreme power of PM, since when you have subscribed to the court's hostile attitude towards me ... you [have] threatened me with what amounted to arrest, thus descending to dictator* methods in your treatment of your old friend and former King'.[20]

As rumours spread that the duke was actively hostile to his own country, it was unfortunate timing that Edward should now contact the German and Italian embassies and ask them to ensure that his houses in Paris and Antibes should be given protection for what promised to be a long absence. The request was innocuous enough, and Ribbentrop's response was to authorise 'unofficial and discreet measures for an unobtrusive watch on the Duke's residence'.[21] A favour had been done. Its repayment would be called upon before too long.

Ribbentrop's primary objective was to keep Edward in Spain. As long as he was there, he was within reach of ostensibly neutral but in fact fascist-supporting ambassadorial staff, who were happy to act as go-betweens between the former king and the Nazis. Yet they bided their time before making any explicit offer of support, instead observing his actions and indiscreet statements. During his stay, the duke received his cousin Infante Alfonso, who spoke about the apparent invincibility of the German forces. Edward remained impartial in his opinions, only commenting that the Channel might present an obstacle to an invasion of Britain by sea and land, if not by air. With attempted aerial attacks an imminent prospect, his remarks could have been interpreted in any number of fashions.

---

* Edward originally wrote 'gangster methods', but Wallis changed it to the more timely 'dictator methods'.

Indiscretion seemed to be his means of entertainment. Word of his proclamations, in Hoare's assessment, 'stimulated pro-German propaganda', even as Soapy Sam insisted with the loyalty of an old friend that 'they have both been very discreet and have made a good impression on the Spaniards'.[22] For the sake of peacekeeping, Hoare begged that if the duke and duchess did return to Britain, they should be guaranteed a formal reception with the king and queen, which would be promoted in the Court Circular. He wrote to Churchill that 'this is the moment to end the trouble, and if it is not ended now, the rift between them and the rest of the Family will become deeper and possibly more dangerous'.[23]

The prime minister disagreed. The duke had become an embarrassment to his family and his country, and Churchill knew the rumours of back-channel communication between Edward and Wallis and the Germans. Diana Cooper reported to Channon that 'the Windsors genuinely believe that they will be restored to the throne under German influence: he will become a sort of Gauleiter* and Wallis a queen'. The duke remained unpopular with courtiers who had neither forgotten nor forgiven his behaviour around the abdication crisis. Nor had he helped his cause by sending telegrams to the king in which he suggested that he would only return to Britain if his status and financial position were to be guaranteed. As the monarch remarked, 'the PM & I told him to obey orders', and with the knowledge of a lifetime of this behaviour, 'he is going to be very difficult, I can see'.[24] Hardinge wrote to Churchill's private secretary, Edward Seal, remarking that 'there [are] widespread expressions of hope that the Duke and Duchess would not return to this country', and suggested his own animosity towards his former king when he said, 'I cannot see how it is possible for him, as an ex-King, to perform any useful service in this country.'[25]

Rather than have the duke and duchess back in Britain at a

---

* A leading member of the Nazi Party, responsible for the control of an individual region: Goebbels and Adolf Wagner served as Gauleiters in Berlin and Munich respectively. Perhaps Edward aspired to be Gauleiter for Mayfair.

time of national crisis, it seemed better to look further afield –
considerably further afield, in fact. Britain still had some colonies
that operated under the auspices of the Crown, and what more
apposite way of rewarding one of them for their continued loyalty
than sending them their country's former ruler as their governor?
An idea that would in other circumstances have seemed both out-
landish and disrespectful now had the virtue of convenience and
poetic justice. Churchill put it to the Cabinet and the king, who
both approved of the plan. The monarch remarked to the sceptical
Queen Mary that it would be better than having Edward at home,
and wrote in his diary that 'there were plenty of snags but it was a
war expediency'.*26

Yet before it could be discussed with the duke, he and Wallis
had left Spain for Lisbon. It was unclear as to what they hoped
to achieve by their move, which seemed to play for time in the
hope that a superior offer from Britain might yet present itself.
When Ribbentrop learnt of their departure, he was furious, and
berated his ambassadors for failing to convince the Spanish to
detain Edward and Wallis as enemy aliens. Then he decided to take
action. If the duke and duchess could not be wooed by suggestion,
they would have to be seized by force.

On 7 July, Sir Alexander Cadogan, the under-secretary at the
Foreign Office, received a telegram that he greeted with horror.
On it, he wrote, 'PM to see', and made it clear that it should also be
passed to the king. It drew upon a source who was in touch with
Konstantin von Neurath, the Reich Protector of Czechoslovakia,
and suggested that 'Germans expect assistance from Duke and
Duchess of Windsor, latter desiring at any price to become Queen.
Germans have been negotiating with her since June 27th. Status
quo in England except undertaking to form anti-Russian alliance.
Germans propose to form Opposition Government under Duke of

---

* He was, however, irritated that Churchill offered Edward the post without
further consultation, complaining, '[it] is all wrong & most annoying as the
matter has not been thought out'.

Windsor having first changed public opinion by propaganda. Germans think King George will abdicate during attack on London.'[27]

When not railing against the failings of Churchill and the government, Edward demonstrated a hitherto unsuspected talent for prophecy. He informed Marcus Cheke, the junior secretary to the British embassy in Lisbon, that after the inevitable decline of the current administration and its replacement by Labour, a negotiated peace with the Germans would follow, followed by the king's enforced departure. Modesty did not allow him to make explicit what he clearly believed, but the throne, like nature, abhorred a vacuum. Who could be better placed to fill it than someone with previous experience of such a role?

Yet it was also feared that his treachery stemmed from his submissive attitude towards Wallis. The king and Churchill both knew of Wallis's obsession with being given her 'fitting' title, and of the duke's attempts to see her thus beatified. Yet the idea that a man who had once ruled Britain would be driven to collaborate with the Nazis in order to achieve these aims seemed unthinkable. They agreed that Edward and Wallis should not be allowed to return to Britain, but would instead be dispatched to the Bahamas, where the duke would be ordered to assume the post of governor and commander-in-chief. Halifax said that the prospect made him feel sorry for the Bahamas, and the king replied, 'I don't think the Bahaman ladies will be best pleased.'[28]

The duke learnt of his new role from Churchill on 4 July, while staying at the villa of the banker Ricardo Espírito Santo. The telegram suggested that 'if you accept, it may be possible to take you and the Duchess there direct from Lisbon', and asked that he confirm the offer without delay. The only personal touch was Churchill's conclusion that 'I feel sure that it is the best open [sic] in the grievous situation in which we all stand. At any rate I have done my best.'*[29]

---

* Wallis wrote more candidly to her aunt that 'Naturally it is the family who are scared of him . . . all the foreigners have [seen through this] including the Germans, who will use it as propaganda'.

Edward and Wallis were both appalled at the instruction, which they considered demeaning. Wallis later complained to Lady Metcalfe that it was 'anything but welcomed and was in fact most heart-breaking for both of us'.[30] It was especially hurtful as the duke had unconditionally agreed to return to England only moments before. Yet for the time being, they could relax and enjoy Signor Santo's hospitality. Had they known the name of his estate – 'Boca do Inferno', or 'the jaws of hell' – it might have jolted them out of their complacency.

Santo, an intimate friend of the Portuguese prime minister António Salazar, was one of the wealthiest men in the country, and famous for his charm, good looks and collection of *objets d'art*. Many years later, the duke said of him that 'he was a pleasant enough host, with a fine collection of Lowestoft china'.[31] He was not a Nazi, but MI5 believed that his inclinations were pro-German, or at least not pro-British, despite the hospitality he extended towards their citizens. One of these was the British ambassador, Sir Walford Selby, who had a warm relationship with both Santo and the duke and duchess, and so his presence at a reception for the pair was welcome.

Yet Selby now relied upon his right-hand man, David Eccles, who was delegated such tasks as informing Edward of his Bahamian appointment. He was possessed of sufficient charm to perform a public relations operation, telling the duke that the job would be both safe and patriotic in its requirements. He also hinted that, if performed diligently, it would do him no harm in the eyes of his countrymen after the war when it came to finding him a more desirable appointment. Musing aloud, Edward said, 'The Bahamas are one of the few parts of the Empire which I missed on my travels. Well, Winston said he was sorry, but it was the best he could do, and I shall keep my side of the bargain.'[32] He accepted the job, much to Eccles' relief. He later informed his wife that the duke was 'pretty fifth column', and that Wallis was 'a poor creature',[33] but also told Selby that 'this won't be the end of it'.

Following a conversation with Edward, he remarked, 'when I

asked HRH why he thought the French were right to stop fighting, he said "because they would have got worse terms if they had gone on"'. 'Do you believe the Germans will keep any terms that have been made?' a surprised Eccles responded. The duke refused to answer, and Eccles pressed him again, only for Edward to shrug and say, 'Why not?'[34] Such conversations did little to assuage growing doubts as to his loyalties.

As the Battle of Britain began, Ribbentrop was pleased to hear that Edward, now temporarily resident in Portugal, continued to air views that were at best pro-appeasement and at worst helpful to the German cause. The German ambassador to Portugal, Oswald von Hoyningen-Huene, was a friend of Santo's, and was therefore able to tell the minister that the duke 'is convinced that if he had remained on the throne war could have been avoided, and characterises himself as a firm supporter of a peaceful arrangement with Germany'.*[35] He was also able to present Edward's Bahamas posting as a further exile dictated by a desperate and near-defeated country.

Ribbentrop, delighted to hear that the duke was still in play, asked Stohrer if Edward and Wallis might be persuaded to return to Spain and, once there, be convinced that Germany's intentions were peaceful.† After all, who could serve as a better ambassador for such aims than the former king of England? If they were uncooperative, he suggested, the duke could be arrested as a deserting military refugee, but if Edward was prepared to go along with such plans, his life would be much easier. Ribbentrop wrote with dry humour, 'we would . . . be prepared to assure him and his wife an existence which would enable him, either as a private citizen or in some other position, to lead a life suitable for a king'.[36]

He also suggested, in order to capitalise on the duke's poor relationship with his home country, that the story be put about

---

* When the duke was shown this document in 1953, he emphatically wrote 'NO' beside it.

† Hitler appealed to 'reason and common sense in Great Britain' on 19 July in a public address, saying, 'I see no reason why this war should go on . . . Mr Churchill no doubt will already be in Canada.'

that the Bahamas posting was an attempt by the security services to assassinate him once he was out of Europe. Such an idea was preposterous,* but in Edward's paranoid state, it might have seemed believable.

Ribbentrop therefore decided that the couple must return to Spain, as only there could German influence be successfully brought to bear. It did not help his cause that Edward was being watched by the Portuguese secret police, who were attentive both to his welfare and to the possibility that their guest might say or do something outrageous that would inflame the political situation. Yet Ribbentrop had always believed that he had some privileged insights into the mind and opinions of the duke, ever since he was Prince of Wales. If he was correct, it would take little to convince the former king to betray his country. As Stohrer wrote in his memoirs, 'Ribbentrop evidently believed that he could play the Duke off against the new King and the existing British Government.'[37]

Ironically, it was not the Nazis that represented the greatest threat to British national security in this situation, but the duke's own arrogance and inability to gauge the environment. As he and Wallis lounged around in 'the jaws of hell', arguing with the government about which servants they would be allowed to take to the Bahamas and whether they could go shopping in New York en route to their new appointment, they chafed at their constraints. Santo ensured that they were comfortable, as well as assuring them that he could transport their personal possessions from war-torn France to the Bahamas. They did not question him too closely as to how this could be accomplished, instead being content that someone, at least, was acting in their interests, as Edward bemoaned the 'wretched mess' of 'the mire of this infernal war'[38] to Allen.

The British government did not view Santo as a benevolent and generous host. A memo of 19 July suggested that he was 'very pro-German and a centre of peace propaganda', that he liaised directly

---

* Edward's previous entanglements with MI5-affiliated assassins notwithstanding.

with the German embassy, and that under his guidance the duke 'manifested extreme defeatist and pacifist sympathies'. His wealth and possessions were believed to be of dubious origin - 'politically he is a crook'[39] - and it was noted that he laundered stolen money for the Germans, with whom he was in close and constant touch. He had even had a three-hour interview with Hoyningen-Huene on 15 July. And this man now had habeas corpus of the Duke and Duchess of Windsor.

This was a potentially disastrous situation. Yet the time for skulduggery and underhand secrecy was soon to pass. As the date on which Edward and Wallis were to leave for the Bahamas drew near, Ribbentrop decided to seize the initiative. A plan was put in place that, had it been successful, may have changed everything.

And he had just the man in mind to execute it.

Chapter Nine

Operation Willi

Walter Schellenberg, the duke's would-be nemesis, was a young man in a hurry to make his name. He was ambitious, with a hunger driven by his childhood as the son of a piano manufacturer rendered penniless by the Depression. The Nazi Party seemed like the solution. It appeared to be a meritocratic organisation that rewarded young men who would accommodate its tenets without argument, and so he rose through its ranks with speed. He joined the SS in 1933 and by 1940, at the age of thirty, had become a *Brigadeführer*, or major general.

His department was the SD, a secretive and vicious organisation that was responsible for the more unpleasant side of operations. Its talents ranged from espionage and interrogation to torture and assassination, when required. Schellenberg dealt with his responsibilities pragmatically, and came to the attention of Reinhard Heydrich, the so-called 'man with the iron heart', who saw the younger German as a protégé. That Schellenberg later claimed to have become a Nazi merely to obtain a larger government grant to continue his studies did not affect his rise to prominence.

As a reward for his having masterminded the Venlo incident,* Schellenberg was awarded the Iron Cross. He was also put in charge of the plans for what would happen in the event of Operation Sea

---

* An operation in November 1939 that saw two British spies, Captain Sigismund Payne Best and Major Richard Stevens, captured, and which subsequently served as a pretext for the German invasion of the Netherlands in May 1940.

Lion, the proposed invasion of Britain. Showing his youth and inexperience, he miscalculated various aspects of the British character, belittling the enemy as nothing more than a country run by 'Freemasons, Jews, and a small public-school-trained elite'.[1]

Operation Sea Lion came to nothing, but shortly afterwards, Schellenberg was at his desk in Berlin when a telephone call came from none other than Ribbentrop. 'Tell me, my dear fellow,' the foreign minister said, 'could you come over to my office at once?'

'Certainly,' Schellenberg replied, 'but could you tell me what it's about?'

Ribbentrop counselled caution. 'No, no, come at once. It's not a matter I can discuss over the telephone.'

When Schellenberg arrived, Ribbentrop greeted him with folded arms and a serious expression, and asked whether he knew much of the diplomatic workings of Spain and Portugal. Upon receiving a non-committal answer, he started asking more leading questions about the younger man's thoughts and opinions about the Duke of Windsor. Schellenberg replied that he believed that the duke, and the English, had dealt with the issues raised by his abdication in a sensible and reasonable manner.

He was surprised when an 'astonished' Ribbentrop vehemently disagreed with him and immediately began correcting him, based on his own friendship with Edward. Schellenberg reported that he said, 'Since his abdication, the Duke has been under strict surveillance by the British Secret Service. We know what his feelings are: it's almost as if he were their prisoner.' This was because, according to Ribbentrop's intelligence, Edward still harboured 'sympathetic feelings towards Germany', and if given the right opportunity, he would wish to escape to Switzerland or some other neutral country. And he needed a knowledgeable and patriotic German to aid him in the endeavour.

Ribbentrop added that he had spoken to Hitler about the matter, and that Schellenberg had been hand-picked to make 'some sort of exploratory contact' with the duke. He was to be armed with both carrot and stick. The carrot was the sum of fifty million Swiss francs, which would be paid to Edward if he was prepared to make a public statement disassociating himself from the actions of his family, and by extension his country. And the stick was Ribbentrop's instruction that Hitler himself 'would have no objection to your helping the duke to reach the right decision by coercion – even by threats or force if the circumstances make it advisable'. Schellenberg was to be given an entirely free hand in the matter. It was made clear that even more money would be offered if necessary, but also that he was to take decisive, even violent action against any Secret Service operatives who frustrated his actions.

Schellenberg, who was baffled but intrigued by the assignment, was then given an earpiece so that he could overhear a conversation between Hitler and Ribbentrop. The Führer sounded less enthusiastic about the operation than the foreign minister, but suggested that 'Schellenberg should particularly bear in mind the importance of the Duchess's attitude and try as hard as possible to get her support.' Basing his assessment on both German intelligence and his own impressions from meeting the couple, Hitler accurately advised that 'She has great influence over the Duke.' He then announced that '[Schellenberg] has all the authorisation he needs. Tell him from me I am relying on him.'

With that, Schellenberg was sent back to Heydrich, who regarded the plans as a waste of time but acknowledged that 'once the Führer gets hold of such a notion, it's very difficult to talk him out of it'. He told Schellenberg that he faced a certain amount of danger – 'if I were head of the British Secret Service, I would settle your hash for you'[2] – but dismissed him with his blessing. That both Heydrich and Hitler seemed unconvinced by the plan was unsettling, but Schellenberg had made a success of the operation in Venlo the previous autumn, and the chance to catch and turn the Duke of Windsor was an exciting one for an ambitious man. The relationship between Ribbentrop, Heydrich and Hitler, driven by respect, jealousy and distrust, was an ever-shifting one. Should Schellenberg succeed in his work, perhaps his name would be mentioned in the same breath as theirs.

On 25 July, Schellenberg, along with two hand-picked SD agents, left Berlin for Madrid. He had his orders, and the nickname for his quarry, Willi, gave the operation its code word. He hoped to accomplish his mission quickly and easily, without the need for the force that Ribbentrop had alluded to. The primary objective was that the duke and duchess should be extracted from the country safely and efficiently.

What he had not been briefed about, because nobody had considered it, was that someone else might be attempting to do the same.

Ramón Serrano Suñer, the Spanish Minister of the Interior, was committedly pro-fascist at a time when most of his colleagues remained more guarded in their opinions. To this end, he tried to persuade Franco to bring Spain onto the side of the Axis powers. The general demurred on the grounds that the country, still recovering from a ruinous civil war, could not afford open involvement in the conflict. Suñer, undaunted, played host to Stohrer on 12 July. The two men discussed the most efficient way of dealing with their mutual friend the duke. Both agreed that his removal from Portugal to Spain was desirable, and his Bahamas expedition should be frustrated. Yet neither had a close enough relationship with Edward to be able to approach him with any expectation of success, even if they had committed diplomatic chaos by attempting to conduct German business on Portugal soil. Therefore they needed to put forward someone who had a friendship with the duke and duchess and might stand some chance of success.

Stohrer suggested Miguel Primo de Rivera for this task, to Suñer's surprise. Rivera was, in his estimation, 'a frivolous and irresponsible buffoon who sought posts and honours but never did a stroke of work in his life'.[3] Unlike his sombre father, a former dictator of Spain, he was a playboy who had capitalised on his famous name in order to seduce as many women as he could, and was described by one colleague, with a touch of jealousy, as 'a spoilt youth who went through life with a bottle in each hand and a girl under each arm'. The parallels with the former king were striking. Unsurprisingly, the two had been friends since 1927, when Rivera had hosted and entertained the Prince of Wales on a visit to Spain.

Therefore, when he was tasked with what he called 'a historic mission', Rivera made immediate plans to head to Lisbon, in the spurious role of a secret envoy. His task was to liaise with the duke and see what, if anything, could be done to keep him in Europe. Yet although Rivera was a dilettante, he was not a traitor. He was not informed of German complicity within the plot, so he could approach Edward with the guileless warmth of an old friend rather than the calculation of a Nazi spy.

Much later, the duke described Rivera's attempts to lure him back to Spain as 'distinctly half-hearted', in part because the Spaniard spent as much of his time in Portugal enjoying himself as devoting himself to diplomatic activities. When he finally dined with Edward on 17 July, in the company of Santo, he was privy to a number of candid remarks from the duke, which he later reported, along with notes from a subsequent dinner with both Edward and Wallis on the 20th. In Rivera's words, the duke 'expressed himself most freely', claiming to be 'almost a prisoner' and 'surrounded by spies', and openly announced that he had 'moved further and further away from the King and from the present English Government'.

He was derogatory about his 'utterly stupid' brother, and contemptuous about the 'clever Queen, who is said to intrigue constantly against the Duke and particularly against the Duchess'. As a result of this, Rivera reported the extraordinary news that 'The Duke is toying with the idea of disassociating himself from the present tendency of British policy by a public declaration and breaking with his brother.' Had he done so, he would have fulfilled one of Ribbentrop's wishes without any need for further prompting, or payment.

Initially at least, the duke and duchess seemed open to the idea of returning to Spain and taking up residence there, so long as they were not interred as enemy aliens.* Yet when this was made more explicit, with the suggestion that they should not go to the Bahamas but prepare themselves to return to Britain, and the throne, they backed away. Rivera reported in another dispatch of 25 July that 'both the Duke and Duchess seemed astonished' at his idea; 'completely enmeshed in conventional ways of thinking . . . they replied that under the English constitution this would not be possible after the Abdication'. His suggestion that the war might alter the constitution led the duchess to become 'very thoughtful',⁴ but he achieved little, other than the chance to dine with an old friend and his wife. Responsibility for luring the duke back to Spain, and elsewhere, therefore passed entirely to Schellenberg, and so Operation Willi commenced.

As Edward sent testy telegrams to England regarding his proposed Bahamas departure, telling Churchill that '[I] have been messed about quite long enough . . . strongly urge you to support arrangements I have made as otherwise will have to reconsider my position',⁵ he attempted to delay sailing from Lisbon until 8 August. The king described these prevarications as 'preposterous propositions he [is] putting up about his journey from Lisbon to the Bahamas . . . I said to [George Lloyd, Secretary of State for the Colonies] D has got to obey orders now. From telegrams I have read D has forgotten that we are at war & that the authorities are busy here with greater problems.'⁶ Nonetheless, he tried to be emollient. He wrote to his brother that 'I am glad that you have accepted the post of Governor of the Bahamas. Winston & I both saw the difficulty of your coming here, & I am sure you realised it as well.' He offered his sympathy for the 'great deal of trouble [you had] in arranging the journey', and mentioned how his own life

---

* When the duke was shown the document with Rivera's statements on it in 1957, he acknowledged that his criticisms of his brother and his wife were correctly expressed, made no comment on the detail that they wished to return to Spain, and denied both his intention of disassociating himself from British policy and Rivera's statement that he wished to ask the Spanish interior minister to assist them in a return to the country.

was 'very strenuous & full of anxieties'.[7] The duke did not reply, to the king's chagrin.

Simultaneously, alarming intelligence reached Britain, via Eccles, that the duke had decided to inform the Spanish ambassador to Lisbon, Nicolás Franco y Bahamonde, that he was keen to return to Spain, regardless of fears that his doing so voluntarily would place him in the hands of the Germans. Yet they had no inkling how significant the danger at hand was.

The man with the greatest interest in his quarry's movements arrived in Madrid on 25 July, where Stohrer briefed him on Edward's sympathies and movements. Schellenberg was informed that the duke was planning a hunting trip to a destination on the border between Spain and Portugal, which would allow an opportunity to approach him. He therefore decided that 'the chief requisite is to obtain willingness to leave by psychologically adroit influence upon the profoundly English mentality of the Duke'.[8] It was uncertain as to whether Edward would be willing to come freely with Schellenberg, or if he would have to be cajoled into the journey, but the operative was prepared to find out. He left for Lisbon the following day, intent upon his task.

Through a mixture of existing contacts and bribery, Schellenberg now prepared to mastermind either an approach towards or an extraction of both the duke and duchess. He had a network of Portuguese agents at his disposal, whom he tasked with minor but threatening acts of intimidation, such as throwing stones at the windows of the Windsors' villa during the night. He called these 'scare-manoeuvres'. The idea was to attempt to convince them through servants' gossip that MI5 was responsible for these actions, so that the frightened pair would be more pliant. The plan succeeded, but only insofar as they decided to leave Santo's hospitality in favour of the Hotel Aviz in Lisbon. This was well known as a haunt of the British who happened to be lingering in the city, not least representatives of the intelligence service.

This was anathema to Schellenberg. He organised another scare-manoeuvre by asking one of his agents, posing as a concerned member of the Portuguese police, to visit the couple and explain that the Aviz, far from being a safe haven, was riddled with those who were ill-disposed towards Edward and Wallis. He even hinted that their lives would be endangered by such a move. His ploy was successful, helped by a letter sent from Rivera that talked of 'something of extreme gravity which directly affects the personal safety of Your Highness and that of the Duchess, should you manifest an opinion or act in some way contrary to a decision of the British Government'.

They accordingly cancelled their stay at the Aviz. Rivera then made plans for them to head to Spain, 'equipped with guns or fishing apparel so as to better disguise [themselves]', and then explicitly stated the Germans' intentions for them. 'If Spain should enter the war, Your Highness could choose between remaining in Spain as a prisoner of honour or leaving for England or any neutral country, for instance Switzerland.'[9] The reception that Edward would have received in his home country after such associations with the Nazis could only be speculated at.

Rivera's letter did not make the desired impact on the duke, who was said to be 'very worried' as he read it before describing it as 'sehr gut'.* But he was where Schellenberg and the Nazis needed him to be: vulnerable and alone. There was nobody other than Wallis he could trust, as his friends seemed to have their own agendas and the British government seemed to be alternately frightened and angry by his remaining in Europe rather than heading to the Bahamas.

Yet even as he wished for a comrade-in-arms to discuss the situation with, an old ally appeared. His task was to undertake what he described with typical understatement as another 'very odd job'.[10]

'Today, as announced, there arrived to stay with the Duke the English Minister who calls himself Sir Walter Turner Monckstone [sic], lawyer from Kent. The Portuguese confidential agent assumes, as I do, that a cover name is involved.'[11] So Schellenberg

---

* Or 'very good', presumably meant sardonically.

incredulously reported the arrival of Monckton in Lisbon on 28 July. It seemed unbelievable to him that the British secret service would not send out their best agent if they knew of the existence of a plot involving the Duke of Windsor. Yet for all his cunning, Schellenberg was unaware of the manoeuvres and contortions that Monckton had undertaken nearly four years before in order to assure the passage of Edward VIII's abdication. The lawyer had built his reputation on being able to untie the most intricate of knots, but this challenge seemed beyond even his expertise.

Monckton had left England under orders from Churchill, who had 'some doubt . . . whether [Edward] would go [to the Bahamas] and in what frame of mind'. He bore a letter from the prime minister that stated, 'I am very glad to be able to arrange for your Royal Highness and the Duchess a suitable sphere of activity and public service during this terrible time when the whole world is lapped in danger and confusion.' Churchill went on to say that he hoped 'that your Royal Highness and the Duchess will lend a distinction and dignity to the Governorship which will be to the best interests of the island'.

Like Schellenberg, the prime minister mixed flattery with veiled threat. While he presented himself as Edward's friend and adviser, he also ventured 'a word of serious counsel'. Alluding to the openness with which the duke offered his opinions, Churchill wrote, 'It will be necessary for the Governor of the Bahamas to express views about the war and the general situation which are not out of harmony with those of His Majesty's Government', and added, 'The freedom of expression which is natural to anyone in an unofficial position . . . is not possible in any direct representative of the Crown.' Referring to 'sharp and unfriendly ears' and 'malicious tongues', he informed the duke that 'conversations have been reported by telegraph through various channels which might have been used to your Royal Highness' disadvantage', and ended with the injunction that 'We are all passing through times of immense stress and dire peril, and every step has to be watched with care',[12] making it clear to the duke that his careless talk had to cease.

Monckton, meanwhile, wrote of his Portuguese embassy that 'it was an astonishing contrast to London ... the lights [were] on, [there were] gay dinners at the Exhibition in Lisbon, gayer parties still at Estoril and a country house to live in'. He praised those around him as 'most helpful and friendly'.[13] Yet he was not in the country for a jolly, but on a mission of grave delicacy. As he recorded, 'I got very worried with an attempt made by the Phalangists [sic],* no doubt under Axis influence.' He knew of the existence of a purported plot against Edward and Wallis, which he described as 'fantastic'. The duchess later recorded in her memoir, with a touch of exaggeration, that the 'very serious' Monckton told them, 'British intelligence had picked up information that German secret agents were plotting to kidnap us ... Winston is convinced that Hitler is crazy enough to be tempted, in the event of a successful invasion of Britain, to try to put the Duke back on the throne in the belief that this would divide and confuse the people and weaken their will to resist further.'

Wallis presented Monckton as a proud patriot, who said of Churchill, '[he] is always ingenious and imaginative. He overlooks no possibilities - however unlikely.'[14] Even allowing for her dramatic licence, Monckton believed that the major risk to the duke and duchess remaining in Europe was that in the event of a Nazi invasion of Britain they could be used as collateral, whether in an attempted restoration to the throne or simply as hostages.

Although Monckton was not so unbending as not to enjoy his time in Lisbon, being photographed in the pool and drinking cocktails - his biographer Lord Birkenhead described his 'astonishing and almost guilty sense of liberation'[15] - he was there to work. He sought out Rivera, whose loyalties he doubted, and the two had what Monckton called 'an amusing conversation'. What he did not know was that Rivera's unexpected return to Lisbon was due

---

* 'Falangist' was a name given to a supporter of the Spanish political movement Falange, a right-wing nationalist organisation that Franco assumed jurisdiction over in 1937.

to the Germans attempting to use his influence with the duke to persuade him to remain in Portugal, away from the entreaties and commands of the British government.

Both men knew Edward well, and they were able to talk with a candour that did not obscure their individual objectives. The lawyer stated that he saw no reason, without *prima facie* evidence, why Edward and Wallis should not leave for the Bahamas. When Rivera replied, 'I thought that you were devoted to the Duke, and wanted to save him from danger', Monckton said, 'No doubt about that, but I have a duty to my country and to its government.' Rivera suggested that if Monckton could wait another ten days, he would be able to supply the details of the danger the duke and duchess were in that were so urgently required. The lawyer demurred, and suggested instead that they head off as planned to the Bahamas on 1 August. Should a plot be revealed, 'I will stop him in Bermuda if, by the time that he was due to leave that island, evidence was forthcoming to justify such a step.'

Rivera was dissatisfied. Whether or not he communicated directly with the Germans, Schellenberg soon learnt of the dawning failure of his plans. As he wrote in his memoirs, 'The Duke of Windsor no longer intended to accept the hunting invitation . . . He obviously had no intention of going to live either in a neutral or an enemy country.'[16] While Edward clearly did not relish the prospect of his Bahamas posting, he was also less amenable to German entreaties than had been supposed. On 29 July, Schellenberg lamented, 'The Spanish plan [has] collapsed completely . . . Willi won't play.'[17] It seemed as if all was up with the plot, and that the duke and duchess would depart on 1 August as planned. Edward even made an impromptu speech at the British embassy on 30 July saying how much they had appreciated Portuguese hospitality and expressing their happiness at having had 'three weeks of peace and quiet at this difficult time'.

Schellenberg had to report the failure of his mission to Ribbentrop. The diplomacy and skulduggery he had engaged in with his agents in both Lisbon and Spain had been for nothing. With two days to go before the duke and duchess left, there seemed to be no hope of any diplomatic solution. It was time, he thought, for a final throw of the dice. He placed his faith in Ribbentrop and Hitler, explicitly asking for instructions as to the measures he should take to prevent Edward and Wallis leaving for the Bahamas.

In Schellenberg's recollection of events, the telegram he now received was unprecedented in its implications. Ribbentrop wrote simply, 'The Führer orders that an abduction is to be organised at once.'[18]

It has often been debated whether Schellenberg's account was true, or if he was exaggerating to make his memoir more compelling. There is some evidence in German files that 'protective measures' would be provided by Nazi agents on the Spanish border if such a crossing could be effected, although another memorandum suggests that a forced abduction will be 'ill-advised'. In Schellenberg's own account, he described the last-minute change to Operation Willi as 'madness' and 'ultimate folly', and suggested that he was prepared to disobey a direct order from Hitler rather than bring about a situation that could have led to both the duke and duchess being killed.

This is probably exculpation rather than pragmatism. Despite the assistance that Schellenberg had received from pro-German elements in both Portugal and Spain, there was no practical means of abducting one of the most famous men in the world. He toyed with firing gunshots at the windows of the duke and duchess's residence, or even placing a time bomb on board the *Excalibur*, the ship they were due to board for the Bahamas on 1 August, which would be discovered and halt the departure. He rejected both ideas on the grounds that such actions might make 'Willi' even keener to depart rather than remain in Portugal for another month.

Edward, meanwhile, knew nothing of such plans, but could detect that something was not right. One contemporary Portuguese secret report stated that 'the Duke and Duchess were strongly impressed by the reports of English intrigues being carried out against them ... they no longer feel secure'.[19] Their intention of leaving for the Bahamas consequently strengthened, especially as Monckton secured the presence of Detective Sergeant Harold Holder, a detective from Scotland Yard, who would go with them on their voyage. He wrote that Holder's presence 'made the whole difference to the Duke'.[20]

Operation Willi stood on the brink of failure. As Edward and Wallis hosted an eve-of-departure dinner at the Hotel Aviz, Schellenberg tried in vain to think of stratagems that might prevent their leaving Europe. He attempted to delay the passage of their luggage from Paris to Lisbon, with the reluctant complicity of Wallis's maid, Jeanne-Marguerite Moulichon, but such antics amounted to little more than rearranging the deckchairs on the *Excalibur*. He enlisted Santo to persuade Prime Minister Salazar to influence the duke and duchess to remain in his country for longer, but by now his manoeuvres were symbolic, designed to indicate to Ribbentrop and Hitler that he was still making an effort, even as the odds of success shrank.*

Yet the scheme had already succeeded more admirably than those involved in it had realised. The duke wrote a graceless letter to Churchill on the eve of his departure – 'I naturally do not consider my appointment as one of first class importance, nor would you expect me to . . . since it is evident that the King and Queen do not wish to bring our family differences to an end, without which I could not accept a post in Great Britain, it is at least a temporary solution to the problem of my employment in the time of war'[21] – and left Europe defeated and diminished, no longer king across the water but a relic of another era. There would be no more talk of his replacing his brother.

---

* It has transpired that Edward, in the words of the MI5 deputy director Guy Liddell, 'fixed up some kind of code with . . . Santo Silva in order that he might fly back to Portugal from Florida if his intervention was required'. He then asked as early as August if this was a possibility. Although some biographers have seized upon this as a 'smoking gun' of Nazi complicity, it is more likely that the duke, already bored of his Bahamas sojourn, was desperate to return to Europe by any means possible. In any event, his offer was not called upon.

Outmanoeuvred and humiliated by Churchill, and guided by his old friend Monckton, Edward was now bound for an exile even less salubrious than the one he had been thrust into in late 1936, with his departure unlamented by his former subjects. For all his attempts to reintroduce himself and Wallis onto the international stage, he seemed to be nothing more than an anachronism: a silent-picture actor in a world that had moved on to the talkies long ago.

Schellenberg watched the *Excalibur* sail away from port on 1 August, with Edward, Wallis and Monckton safely on board. Despite his talk about some dramatic last-minute solution that would achieve his goals, there was no way of frustrating the forces of British bureaucracy that now resumed possession of the duke and duchess.

As he stood in the tower room of the German embassy, his prize disappearing, he could console himself with what had been achieved. The duke, emboldened by believing himself to be amongst friends, had talked repeatedly, openly and indiscreetly about the failings of the British government, and had denigrated his brother the king. He did not need to stand up and perform a Nazi salute, or pledge his troth to Hitler, for his comments to be a propaganda victory for the Germans. Likewise, his loyalties were now believed so questionable by his erstwhile friend Churchill that he had been threatened with disciplinary action – even arrest – if he did not obey a direct order.

The king, meanwhile, was given a sanitised account of what had happened by Monckton. He wrote in his diary on 6 August that 'D had wished to remain in Lisbon til the 14th as a Spaniard, a son in law of Primo de Rivera the last PM of Royalist Spain, had told [D] a wonderful story of a plot to kill him in the Bahamas at the behest of the government here. And D believed it as being possible. [Monckton] saw the Spaniard and said that he could not possibly report such a story to the government at home. Of course the Spaniard being a Falangist wanted to use D and keep him in Europe. Walter told me D had different ideas about the war to what we had, & that he would be quite ready to make peace.' The king's conclusion was that 'D's attitude was a selfish one, as all he had to live for now was his private & comfortable life.'[22] That his brother could have been actively treacherous was too much to be considered, let alone written down, even in the privacy of a diary.

Monckton was able to offer Churchill greater candour. He supplied details of the fantastical plot and of Rivera's actions, and suggested that the greatest danger had been that the Germans might have made an attempt on the duke's life and claimed that it was the work of a British agent. However, he announced that 'I ought to telegraph the Duke at Bermuda saying that the matter of the alleged plot has been brought to the notice of all the relevant Government Departments here and that the heads of these Departments are satisfied that there is no foundation for the allegation and that accordingly he should proceed to the Bahamas in accordance with arrangements which they have already made.'[23] The prime minister replied, 'It was very lucky you were on the spot to dissipate strange suspicions.'[24] Just as he had brought about a successful resolution of the abdication crisis in December 1936, so Monckton had once again saved the day, although he could barely expect gratitude for his actions. There was, after all, a war on.

Despite the accounts of Schellenberg, Wallis, Monckton and others, all of whom took care to present themselves and their actions in the best of lights, there remain some inevitable lacunae in the day-to-day details of what, if anything, the duke said when he was a few glasses of wine and whisky down. It seems a reasonable assumption that, pressed for details of his former life as king, he was happy to reminisce about his brief period on the throne. If an interlocutor, such as his dining companion Infante Alfonso, had managed to draw some details out of him about his circumstances in Buckingham Palace, specifically where his private quarters were, what their relationship was to the rest of the building and how they might be accessed, his conversation could have been of vital strategic importance to the German war effort, especially with the proposed invasion of Great Britain being Hitler's intended aim that year.

Therefore, when his brother and sister-in-law nearly lost their lives in the Buckingham Palace bombing on 13 September 1940, it is fair to wonder whether the well-planned attack had its origins in a warm summer evening's conversation in a Portuguese villa called, appropriately enough, 'the jaws of hell'.

We may, on balance, excuse the duke and duchess of the most sensational claims of full collaboration with the Nazi regime. But the evidence against them suggests that, whether through carelessness or ambivalence towards the country that Edward once ruled, their actions in Spain and Portugal should be regarded as little less than treason. As they sailed towards the Bahamas, bound for their undesirable sinecure, they could take some comfort that they were headed for a life of dull security rather than the confines of a prison cell.

But a pressing situation awaited at home. And though the isolated, exhausted nation hoped for a miracle, it showed few signs of materialising.

Chapter Ten

Team Man or Bloody Buccaneer

'I feel quite exhausted after seeing and hearing so much sadness, sorrow, heroism and magnificent spirit. The destruction is so awful and the people too <u>wonderful</u> - they <u>deserve</u> a better world.'[1] So Queen Elizabeth wrote to Queen Mary on 19 October. After the skulduggery and intrigue that had surrounded the Duke and Duchess of Windsor, the couple were now far away in the Bahamas. The question of Edward's loyalties was therefore less pressing than it had been when he was at large in Europe. Yet after the king and queen had narrowly survived the bombing of Buckingham Palace the previous month, it was clear that the war, for so long an abstract thing, had now arrived in earnest, and was tearing apart everything the British held sacrosanct.

The king and queen had sequestered themselves in Windsor Castle after a series of bombings and attacks, only returning to London during the middle of the week. A landmine had exploded in St James's Park, blowing out the windows in the front and quadrangle of Buckingham Palace, and another one had to be defused, leading to an anxious wait. The queen wrote to her sister, May Elphinstone, on 25 October that 'we have been attacked here 2 nights running', but counselled caution, knowing that letters might be intercepted: 'We don't want the Germans to know anything that might help them aim!'

She was able to express herself to May with greater candour than she had to her mother-in-law, showing the stress and misery that the previous year had placed her and her family under - to say nothing of their country. 'It makes me <u>furious</u> seeing the wanton destruction of so much. Sometimes it really makes me feel almost <u>ill</u>. I can't tell you how much I <u>loathe</u> going round these bombed places, I am a beastly coward, & it breaks one's heart to see such misery & sadness.' Even as she allowed that 'the spirit of the people is so wonderful' and that 'one feels ashamed to mind so much for them',[2] it seemed as if the whole edifice seemed to be collapsing, with Europe falling to the Nazis and Britain forced into a defensive retreat. Before long, it would not simply be the windows of Buckingham Palace that were destroyed.

Britain in late 1940 was a miserable but stoic place. Monckton informed the Duke of Windsor in October, 'You would find life very different here. Very few people dine out, no evening theatres or cinemas.' However, the much-celebrated 'Blitz spirit' could still be found. Monckton remarked, 'Nobody seems to mind ... The bits of London that get knocked down are in most cases very quickly put right, and one gets used to such changes as remain to be seen.' He later mentioned to Wallis that 'the loss of life is remarkably small in comparison to the damage done to houses and shops, churches and hospitals'.[3] As he observed how 'uncomfortably close'[4] the king and queen had been to death, the contrast between the duke's new life in the Bahamas and the responsibilities his brother faced was a striking one.

Other developments were more welcome. On 13 October, the fourteen-year-old Princess Elizabeth made her first public broadcast, during the BBC's *Children's Hour* programme, addressing the children who had been evacuated from their homes and billeted with strangers in the country. Although the content was unexceptional - 'We are trying to do all we can to help our gallant sailors, soldiers, and airmen, and we are trying, too, to bear our own share of the danger and sadness of war. We know, every one of us, that in the end all will be well' - rehearsing and delivering the speech was nerve-racking. Her nanny, Crawfie, wrote that 'it was a long and tedious business for a little girl ... [but] Lilibet herself put in several phrases that were quite her own'. The speech was a success, and demonstrated that the princess could, if required, step up and embrace responsibility, even at her young age.

The king, meanwhile, found his own confidence in adversity. As he toured the East End after yet another bombing, one local politician responsible for civil defence described how 'the King was evidently most interested and talked to all and sundry. He insisted on carrying out the programme to the full', adding, 'it is almost impossible to believe that he is the same man who took the oath before the Privy Council less than 4 years ago'.[5] *Time* magazine claimed, 'Never in British history has a monarch seen and talked to so many of his subjects, or so fully shared their life', and the sovereign wrote in his diary, 'I feel that our tours of bombed areas in London are helping the people who have lost their relations & homes & we have both found a new bond with them as Buckingham Palace has been bombed as well as their homes.'[6]

He did what he could in the circumstances. In a broadcast on 23 September 1940, he announced the creation of a medal for acts of conspicuous gallantry, the George Cross, and, with his stammer in abeyance, offered what would become his credo for the remainder of the war. 'The walls of London may be battered,' he declared, 'but the spirit of the Londoner stands resolute and undismayed.' Even as the city, and the country, feared that invasion and conquest was imminent, the monarch declared, with more faith than genuine optimism, 'There will always be an England to stand before the world.'

However, he expressed his true feelings when he wrote in his diary on 5 October, 'something I am sure is brewing up for the near future'.[7] The bombing had intensified. A bewildered Cosmo Lang, Archbishop of Canterbury, was forced out of Lambeth Palace when it was hit by a rocket, indicating that even men of God could not expect special treatment when it came to the reckoning the Luftwaffe had in store for the British. There was now an existential threat not just to the fabric of the city and society that the royal family had spent their lives as part of, but to its very purpose. For all his uplifting words, the king knew he could not lead his people in any more than a symbolic fashion. He had instead to place his faith and trust in Churchill, a prime minister he neither trusted yet nor especially admired.*

It was therefore a personal as well as symbolic loss when on 9 November, Chamberlain died of bowel cancer. His friend Channon declared, 'the world has lost its best friend'.[8] Chamberlain had known that he was ill by June, and had been operated on for a constricted bowel in late July. Although he initially believed he could resume some sort of life, albeit as 'a partially crippled man', he knew his political career was over. He wrote in his diary on 9 September that 'any ideas which may have been in my mind about possibilities of further political activity, and even a possibility of another Premiership after the war, have gone'.[9]

By the end of September, his condition had worsened, and he was compelled to resign from his position as Lord President of the Council and a member of the War Cabinet. He was also, by a quirk of the political process, still leader of the Conservative Party, as Churchill was prime minister of a national government rather than a purely Conservative one. Yet it was clear that he could not carry on any of these responsibilities with his health in an increasingly poor state.

He wrote a valedictory letter to the king on 30 September: 'I cannot contemplate the termination of my relations with you, Sir, as a Minister, without a good deal of emotion. Broadly speaking, I was your first Prime Minister and I shall always recall with gratitude the confidence with which [sic] you have been good enough to give me, and the increasing intimacy of our conversations which were so encouraging and helpful to me during some of the most anxious and difficult periods which have ever faced a Minister in all our long history.'

He knew he had not succeeded as premier - 'it has been my

---

* Nonetheless, when Churchill made an emotive speech to the French people in which he called Hitler 'this evil man, this monstrous abortion of hatred and deceit', the king both congratulated him on it and wrote in his diary, 'I am getting to know Winston better and he is telling me more of his ideas.'

fate to see the failure of all my efforts to preserve peace, and the destruction of all the hopes which I had entertained that I might be able to steer this country into calmer waters' - and feared that posterity would judge him harshly.* Yet casting aside the diplomacy with which he had dealt with Hitler two years before, he described the Führer's behaviour as 'the insatiate and inhuman actions of a fanatic'.[10] He told Baldwin on 17 October that 'I regret nothing in the past', as he remarked, with typical understatement, 'I accept what I can't help and hope I shan't cumber the earth too long.'

The king was saddened by his former premier's impending demise. He recalled his pleasure at their audiences, and attempted to play down Chamberlain's failures. He wrote that 'I have sympathised with you very much in seeing your hopes shattered by the lust and violence of a single man, and yet . . . your efforts to preserve peace were not in vain, for they established, in the eyes of the civilised world, our entire innocence of the crime which Hitler was determined to commit. For this alone, the country owes you a debt of gratitude.'[11]

In a mark of his appreciation, the king, along with the queen,[†] visited the former prime minister on his deathbed at his home on 14 October, something Chamberlain described with pride as 'a characteristic act of human kindness and sympathy'. The three of them spent around half an hour together, and the ebbing politician remained philosophical in the presence of his monarch. As he subsequently remarked to Halifax, 'approaching dissolution brings relief'. The king wrote in his diary that 'he does not look at all

---

* As, of course, it has. Chamberlain's reputation was not helped by the publication of *Guilty Men* in July 1940, a scathing and pseudonymously written polemic that denounced him (along with Baldwin, Wilson, Halifax and others) for being insufficiently prepared for inevitable conflict with Germany.
† She shared her husband's high opinion of Chamberlain, and had written to him earlier in the summer upon his resignation to say, 'You did all in your power to stave off such agony, and you were right. We can now only do all in our power to defeat this wickedness and cruelty', before concluding, 'it is going to be very hard'.

well, but it was a good day for him, and he was very cheerful, & talked in his usual way'.[12] But later he wrote to Queen Mary that 'I am very sad about poor Mr Chamberlain and I know that I have lost a trusted friend.'[13] He noted that their meetings had featured an unusual degree of candour, and indeed had continued beyond Chamberlain's premiership while he was Lord President of the Council.

The king had looked to his former prime minister as a mentor, despite his faults. After Chamberlain died, he was forced to turn to Churchill, who was preoccupied with fears of imminent invasion following the Battle of Britain. In one exchange, on 10 September, the monarch asked Churchill whether the mass bombing of Britain's ports and coastal defences meant that the prospect of invasion by sea was now a possibility, even a probability. Churchill replied, 'Our preparations are all ready for any eventuality', but the two remained unable to build a warm personal relationship as the pressure mounted on them both.

It may have been coincidence, or a grim joke on the part of the Nazi high command, but within a few hours of Chamberlain's funeral at Westminster Abbey on 14 November, Operation Moonlight Sonata began, orchestrated by Goebbels. As the king, queen and their children watched in horror from Windsor, hundreds of German planes headed north towards Coventry, each armed with tons of bombs. When they reached their target, they reduced the medieval city centre to rubble, destroying the cathedral and killing and injuring nearly 1,500 people. So successful was the attack that the Nazis coined the term 'Coventrated' to denote an orgy of destruction.

The king visited the damage two days later, travelling by car because the ruins were impassable by train. The smouldering remnants of the hundreds of fires caused by the high-explosive and incendiary bombs were still emitting smoke and ash, and the landscape was desolate. The city had ceased to exist in any recognisable form. He was appalled by what he saw, writing that 'I was horrified . . . [the people were] quite dazed after what they had been through, [and] the shock to them was very great'.[14] The only analogy he could produce, in a letter to his mother, was that it was 'just like Ypres after the last war'.[15] That had been believed to be a once-in-a-lifetime vision of hell. Now, just over two decades later, a comparable inferno had arrived in Britain.

The king regarded his actions in terms of duty. He wrote on 17 November that 'My visit to Coventry was appreciated I hear, and did help to alleviate their sadness at the loss of their personal belongings and their town. I feel that this kind of visit does do good at such a moment, and it is one of my main jobs in life to help others when I can be useful to them.'[16] But although he was praised for his dignity and compassion, he was beset by terror. He suffered from social anxiety that manifested itself either in the display of such neurological conditions as vertigo and agoraphobia, or in his stammer.

As a younger man, he had tried to avoid public events as far as he could, for fear of humiliating himself, but he now knew that such responsibilities were integral to his role as father to the nation. He refused to shirk his tasks, however challenging they might have been. One courtier reported how he walked up a steep flight of spiral steps to the top of a lighthouse, an experience that left him sweating with anxiety. As they remarked, 'He could have got out of doing that because he was the King, but just because he was the King, he went ahead and did it. He never ducked doing anything unpleasant.'[17]

'The Windsors seem so happy . . . they look as though [they are] just married', said the crew of the *Excalibur*, which took the couple to Bermuda before their final destination of the Bahamas. So the *Daily Mirror* reported on 11 August, when the Duke and Duchess of Windsor arrived there. The relationship between the two of them was said to be 'bubbling with enthusiasm', and their cabin steward, when asked if they were content, answered, 'Oh boy, they were happy.'

The duke repeatedly called Wallis 'darling' and 'dear', and looked at her with love shining in his eyes. A sign of their mutual adoration, according to the no doubt handsomely paid steward, was that both favoured pink nightwear: the duke, quite literally, wore pink pyjamas for his nocturnal activities. When he was out of his cabin, he was greeted informally by the ship's crew with 'Hiya, Duke, how ya doing?', and he responded with smiling pleasantries. Only the portrait of his mother hanging in the dining room reminded him of the country he had left behind.

They were bound for Government House, their designated residence in Nassau; a desired diversion via New York had not been permitted. Shortly after they arrived, Monckton wrote to the duke to assure him about the necessary provisions that had been made for his security, and also to suggest that should he fulfil his role as expected, it would represent an opportunity to present himself as a trusted elder statesman to the public once again. He told the duke, 'I can confidently say that . . . [the press] are all sympathetically interested in your Royal Highness' new appointment . . . [and] are not regarding it, as some American papers seem to regard it, as a mere holiday command.'[18]

Edward was, however, unconvinced by this, and began agitating almost immediately to be allowed to visit his ranch in Canada. He and Wallis were dismayed by Nassau and the cramped conditions they found themselves in. He decided that it was too hot and that Government House was in an unbecoming condition for a man who had once been king-emperor. Although £2,000 had been allotted for its refurbishment, he immediately asked for a further £5,000 for it to be brought up to his accustomed standards, describing its current state as 'quite unacceptable'. Churchill was 'very grieved' to hear of this, and authorised Monckton to inform Edward that '[Winston] hoped that, when people here were having to put up with so much, you would be willing to put up with this discomfort and remain at your post until weather conditions made things less unpleasant.'

Monckton remarked to Godfrey Thomas, who had been Edward's assistant private secretary, that 'it would . . . be worse than useless for me to do the heavy father', but he stressed the need to avoid 'giving any opportunities for unkind critics to suggest extravagance on their part'.[19] As before, he brought up money to make his point, reminding the duke that his solicitor, A. G. Allen, had suggested that 'another and most important part of the problem'[20] was that any unauthorised visit Edward and Wallis made to Canada or the USA could jeopardise his financial settlement.

The duke wrote to Churchill* around October. His letter typified the resentment and boredom he felt. He stated that 'I would generally regard it as a man's duty to accept without complaint whatever the appointment he was given', especially in wartime, but immediately added the qualification that 'There are, however, even in moments of national danger, always exceptional cases where a man would be doing a disservice to his country's cause were he not honest enough to bring to the notice of the Government the fact that he is "a square peg in a round hole", or sufficiently frank in giving his reasons for such a state of affairs.'

He was not blind to the potentially compromising instances of his work - 'the most disagreeable feature of all in this place is the fact that I am open to being exploited in all manner of ways' - and after bemoaning the island's reduced tourist trade, he raged that he and Wallis were now the major draw for curious pleasure-seekers, and that enquiries had already come from American tourist agencies as to whether they might promise their clients the opportunity to gaze on the exiled king-emperor and his scandalous wife on a cruise.

He went on to announce that 'the truth of the matter is that the place is far too small to carry anyone who has been the subject of so vast an amount of publicity, good and bad, that I have', and that, while his own experience was merely 'very unpleasant', he feared for the well-being of the Bahamians. He added, 'they will never,

* Edward's biographer Michael Bloch suggests that the undated letter, which does not exist in Churchill's archive, may never have been sent, and therefore should be viewed more as an expression of Edward's psychological state than a serious attempt to liaise with his Prime Minister.

poor people, be able to take the fierce glare of the spotlights that quite accidentally have been suddenly switched on to them'.[21] His implication was clear: return us to our old lives, quickly, or face the consequences.

In early November, Churchill and the king discussed the situation. Both were candid about the chaos - or worse - that would have ensued had Edward still been sovereign. Churchill openly said that 'D's ideas and his pro-Nazi leanings would have been impossible during the crisis of the last three years', and the king wrote in his diary that 'D was certainly dictatorial and obstinate if he could not get his way, and felt frustrated in many ways under Papa's regime.'[22] The former monarch's sympathies and inclinations were now an open secret, at best. But even thousands of miles away, he and his wife remained as troublesome and dangerous as ever.

'I hate this place more each day', Wallis complained on 16 September to her aunt Bessie. She went on to clarify that 'We both hate it . . . the locals are petty-minded [and] the visitors common and uninteresting.'[23] After the pageantry of their arrival, which was declared a public holiday, disillusionment and boredom set in. With the previous governor, Charles Dundas, complaining, 'I don't know why I should be pushed out to make way for *him*',[24] Edward and Wallis took an attitude of contempt towards their new posting, and the duke's lack of discretion ensured that this was soon common knowledge. Philip Kerr, the Marquess of Lothian and the British ambassador to the United States, remarked to Alexander Cadogan that 'it is most important from the point of view of opinion in this country to avoid the impression that the Duke of Windsor is not taking his new duties in the Bahamas entirely seriously'.[25]

The many demands of the role, once dubbed 'the worst post in the British Empire', were beyond Edward's intellectual and organisational capabilities. The position of governor, as Dundas knew, was not the sinecure that Churchill may have believed it to be, but a complex administrative job requiring an energetic figure who was able to handle the island's diplomatic relations with America.

It was just as well, then, for both the Bahamas and the wider world, that the new governor's powers were limited by the Executive Council, which vetoed any wild decisions. However, it may not have caused Edward much pain to be responsible, along with the rest of the Council, for telling the British government that due to the decline of the tourist trade that the island depended on, they would not be able to lend the beleaguered country more than the £250,000 that had been agreed before the duke's appointment. He wrote triumphantly on one Cabinet Office document that 'I won't let those pinkos push me around.'[26]

As 1940 wore on, a frustrated Wallis moaned about her predicament to anyone who would listen. Unlike her husband, who at least had been tasked with responsibilities, she was doomed to be decorative. She was expected to sit and applaud when he made speeches about social change and progress,* and to smile at local dignitaries. She hated it, just as she was angered to find a telegram on her arrival that made it clear that 'you are no doubt aware that a lady when presented to HRH the Duke of Windsor should make a half-curtsey ... the Duchess of Windsor is not entitled to this'.[27] If she had needed proof that she was regarded as a second-class citizen, she now had it.

She occupied herself by writing angrily to her friends. Monckton replied on 16 November, 'I am afraid from your letter that you are both finding the job very irksome and limited, and you can be sure that Whitehall let it be known discreetly that the Duke cannot possibly be satisfied indefinitely with so restricted a sphere.' Yet there was no possibility of a return, to Britain or elsewhere, while war continued. Monckton flattered Wallis ('I know that both of you would willingly be here to share our dangers if other things were equal and there were no embarrassments'), but also

---

* Which did not include the Bahamas' substantial black community. The duke said of Etienne Dupuch, the editor of the newspaper *Nassau Daily Tribune*, that 'it must be remembered that Dupuch is more than half Negro, and due to the peculiar mentality of this race, they seem unable to rise to prominence without losing their equilibrium'.

made it clear that 'it is some comfort to your friends that you are out of it'.

As he praised Churchill ('Winston is in remarkable form . . . he sees himself as a reincarnation of the Duke of Marlborough . . . he brings to our present troubles all the atmosphere of the eighteenth century and, mercifully, its language') and complained that Edward and Wallis's old supporter Beaverbrook was 'no team man but a bloody buccaneer',[28] Monckton reminded the duchess of her irrelevance. A few years ago, she was the most talked-about woman in the world. Now she was the decorative spouse of a minor functionary. She would do to swell a progress, and start a scene or two, but this particular attendant lady chafed at the restrictions she faced. She remained anything but an easy tool, deferential or glad to be of use. Instead, she reacted poorly to Monckton's attempts at cheering her. She said that she was 'buried alive', and remarked to her friend Betty Lawson-Johnston that 'one must obey the dictate of this Churchill or be beheaded'.[29] Both the duke and the duchess were by now practised at insincere smiles that concealed the anger and despair they felt. They could grin, and howl inwardly.

There were, nonetheless, consolations amidst the boredom and snubs. As a member of the local aristocracy, the 'Bay Street Boys',* put it, '[the Duke] will learn if he hasn't learnt already that the best way to govern the Bahamas is not to govern the Bahamas at all. If he sticks to golf, he will be a good Governor and they'll put up statues to him. But if he tries to carry out reforms or make any serious decisions or help the n—s, he will just stir up trouble and make himself unpopular.'[30] Edward was incapable merely of sticking to golf, but this was not simply from reforming zeal.

Instead, the duke and duchess cottoned on to a new *raison d'être* for their unwanted presence. Although there was considerable social unease and poverty in the Bahamas, the islands were also home to plutocrats and magnates who were delighted that their

---

* The ruling (and exclusively white) oligarchy of the Bahamas, who controlled the islands' financial and political structure.

wealth could not be touched by any taxman. These included Sir Harry Oakes, an American-born British citizen and gold-mine owner who owned around a third of the main island, New Providence, and Axel Wenner-Gren, a Swedish entrepreneur.

Wenner-Gren was the founder of Electrolux and the so-called 'Rockefeller of Sweden', who inhabited a luxurious home known as Shangri-La. His presence in the islands arose partly from his belief that he could parlay his friendship with Göring into becoming the go-between in a new peace accord between the Germans and the Americans, as he had previously brought about good relations between the Russians and the Finns. When unsuccessful in this endeavour, he retired *hors de combat* to Shangri-La.

The duke and duchess had always enjoyed the company of two types of people: the wealthy, and Nazi sympathisers. In Wenner-Gren, they encountered both. Although he was not a paid-up fascist, he, like Charles Bedaux, had extensive business interests in Germany, where he had built a munitions factory. He had seen Göring as recently as March 1940, and had come to the attention of the FBI because of his suspected involvement in the sinking of the SS *Athenia* in September 1939.

Although the attack was ascribed to a German submarine, American intelligence questioned the veracity of this.* Instead, it noted the nearby presence of Wenner-Gren's yacht, the *Southern Cross*, which helped to collect survivors. His suspected motive for staging an attack of this nature was simple. The sinking, which caused the deaths of both British and American citizens, not only hardened the resolve of the British to pursue the war, but also brought America a step further towards belligerence. As the FBI report observed, 'From [the attack] would result more profits for interested neutrals ... therefore it would have been to the advantage of an interested neutral to sink the *Athenia*.' Wenner-Gren was under suspicion as

---

* Not least because the German Admiralty denied that it was responsible for the attack, while fully, even proudly, accepting responsibility for similar acts of war.

'the most interested Scandinavian neutral . . . [and] apparently the only Scandinavian neutral financially able to take such action'.[31]

Wenner-Gren was an influential friend for the duke and duchess to have, and would have been a formidable foe for any individual or country. He was said to speak a dozen languages, and the FBI investigation called him 'a tall, vigorous, pink-cheeked extrovert'. Early in 1940, J. Edgar Hoover, the director of the FBI, authorised an investigation into him, based both on his association with Göring and his suspected involvement with the attack on the *Athenia*. As Sumner Welles, the Assistant Secretary of State, put it in the summer of 1940, after trying and failing to talk with Wenner-Gren on a cruise between New York and Naples, 'I have not a shred of evidence, but I have a very strong feeling that this man acts as a spy for the German government.'[32]

The British government, aware of Wenner-Gren's dubious reputation, attempted to divert the new governor and his wife away from his social circle into the seemlier environment of the 'distinguished social leader' Lady Jane Williams Taylor. But the Swedish entrepreneur continued to fascinate Edward and Wallis. The duke dined with him on 25 October, and then again six days later. This time he was joined by Wallis, who formed a friendship with Wenner-Gren's American wife Marguerite.

Subsequently he offered them the loan of the *Southern Cross* for a brief visit to Miami in December 1940, for the duchess to have an infected gum operated on in the local hospital.* Afterwards they took a short cruise, during which Edward confided in his new friend about his fears for the world. His letter of thanks for the 'comfort and privacy' of the yacht also enclosed a signed copy of

---

* Edward and Wallis's absence between 9 and 14 December 1940 was agreed to with suspicious alacrity; it proved convenient to have them away from any potential embarrassment when President Roosevelt, recently re-elected to a third term in office, visited the Bahamas on the 12th and 13th. Predictably, whether out of callousness or carelessness, this information was leaked to the governor, resulting in further anger at his and his wife's perennially second-class status.

his Verdun peace broadcast of the previous year, which, he commented, 'in my humble opinion, makes as much sense now as it did at that time'.[33]

Appealing to Edward's vanity was an easy way of endearing oneself to him. But once he liked someone and believed them to be simpatico, his conversation became unguarded and candid to a point where it could become compromising. Given Wenner-Gren's ambiguous loyalties, the possibility remained that even thousands of miles away from Europe, the Duke of Windsor might remain 'in play' for the Nazis. This led Sir Stewart Menzies, the head of MI6 – code name 'C' – to describe Wenner-Gren as 'friendly to Nazis and associated with the appeasement circles [in America].'[34]

Schellenberg's attempts to persuade or, *in extremis*, abduct the Duke and Duchess from Portugal had been unsuccessful earlier that year. But the Germans were not finished with the couple yet.

Chapter Eleven

'The Friend You Used to Be'

Suppers, especially last ones, occupy an auspicious place in history, but lunches have traditionally been seen as less significant. Yet on 30 January 1941, the arrival at Buckingham Palace of a hard-drinking American in poor health seemed hardly less propitious than if Jesus Christ himself had materialised. As the king and queen awaited their lunch guest, they knew that he was John the Baptist to President Roosevelt's more messianic figure. If the encounter went well, it could change the course of the war. But if it went badly, Britain would remain isolated and beyond further help.

The arrival of Harry Hopkins was therefore both welcome and tense. Hopkins was an ailing figure who had recently been diagnosed with stomach cancer. He was also Roosevelt's trusted foreign policy adviser and, in Churchill's words, 'a natural leader of men [who] burned with the flame of democracy'. He was primarily responsible for making the decision as to whether Britain was likely to be able to withstand a full German attack, and if not, whether it was worth committing the United States to any further assistance. The reports from the pro-appeasement American ambassador Joseph Kennedy had been damning. The king wrote, 'Kennedy is always the hard shrewd business man, & still thinks in terms of dollars as against the terms of human feelings.'[1] In his most notorious comment, the ambassador remarked on 10 November 1940 to the *Boston Globe* that 'Democracy is finished in Britain ... it may be here', which led him to be recalled to America. But Roosevelt was unwilling to take him at his word. Hopkins was therefore tasked with ascertaining whether, in the president's words, 'British morale was really as bad as Kennedy pretended.'[2]

Hopkins was favourably disposed towards the royal couple, believing that their visit to the United States two years before had been an 'astonishing success', and, more crucially, that they had supplanted any memories of the Duke and Duchess of Windsor. Over the course of a pleasant lunch, where even an air raid could not disrupt conversation, he was able to assure his hosts of Roosevelt's continued respect. In turn, they stressed how the continued morale of the British people meant that victory in the long run was inevitable. This may have been rooted in optimism rather than certainty, but that was enough. As Hopkins later reported to the president, 'If ever two people realised that Britain is fighting for its life, it is these two. They realise fully that this conflict is different from the other conflicts in Britain's history and that if Hitler wins they and the British people will be enslaved for years to come.'[3]

There had already been preparation for ever closer unity between Britain and America. 'I want you and your family to know that you have very warm friends in my wife and myself', President Roosevelt wrote to the king on 1 May. The letter stressed how much the royal couple remained in his thoughts. It was a kind gesture, and precipitated the destroyers-for-bases agreement of early September that year, in which the Royal Navy were granted American destroyers in exchange for US bases being established in British colonies such as St Lucia and Jamaica – to say nothing of the Duke of Windsor's new demesne of the Bahamas.* Yet it did not match Roosevelt's hints that America would not stand back and watch Britain be bombed. The president had been re-elected for an unprecedented third term in office on 5 November 1940, defeating

---

* The king regarded this with mixed feelings, saying to Hardinge on 30 December that 'The Americans have got to understand that in leasing the bases the question of sovereignty does not come in. These islands are part of the British Colonial Empire & I am not going to see my West Indian subjects handed over to the US authorities.'

the Republican Wendell Wilkie, but by a less decisive margin than previously. He had to act cautiously and carefully or risk becoming a lame duck before his term ended. But from a British - and international - perspective, something needed to be done before it was too late.

The crucial rapport was that between the monarch and the president, or his representative on earth. Hopkins ended his lunch both charmed and convinced. He told the king and queen of Roosevelt's continued determination to defeat Hitler and commitment to provide aid to Britain to bring such a resolution about. He reported that they were 'deeply moved' by this. The king responded 'how greatly he appreciated the President's speeches and . . . what was deeply embedded in the President's mind', before asking Hopkins to pass on 'his warmest expression of thanks and appreciation and a personal word of friendship'. If the sojourn in Hyde Park had never happened, with its hot dogs and beers, matters could have been different.

An indirect consequence of Hopkins' meeting with the king and queen was the subsequent passage of the Lend-Lease bill through Congress and the Senate, which offered supplies and military equipment in exchange for American leasing of army and naval bases during the duration of the conflict. Although opposed by isolationist Republicans, who did not believe that a European war could affect American interests and feared that such a bill represented 'the longest single step this nation has yet taken toward direct involvement in the war abroad', it was signed into law by Roosevelt on 11 March. It represented a formal end to the policy of neutrality that had existed since the beginning of the war.

There were other high-profile movements afoot, too. Halifax had recently been replaced as Foreign Secretary by Eden and had become ambassador to the US. The king had sold him the role not as a demotion organised by Churchill to remove a potential rival but as a promotion, saying, 'the post of my Ambassador in USA is more important at this moment than the post of Foreign Secretary here'.[4] Halifax was unconvinced. The king wrote in his diary on

24 December that 'He was very unhappy at the thought of leaving here now, and was perplexed at what might happen if anything happened to Winston. The team was not a strong one without a leader, and there were some hot heads among it. I told him he could always be recalled.'[5] This was fanciful.

Yet in a carefully choreographed event, Halifax was greeted personally on his arrival in America on 24 January by Roosevelt, and treated as near-royalty himself; the king called it 'a very friendly gesture on [the president's] part'.[6] This was later reciprocated when the king offered a similar reception to the new American ambassador, John G. Winant, on 1 March, meeting him at Windsor station that day.

Although America's actions were welcome, and provided a practical and propaganda boost, they did not amount to a formal declaration of war on Germany. For all the success wrought by the soft diplomacy practised by the king and queen, it was no match for Hitler's expansionist methods. Achievements over lunch had to be viewed in the wider context of a country being bombed into rubble day after day, night after night.

The king wrote in his final diary entry of 1940 that 'The 1st half year consisted of a series of disasters for us . . . Winston coming in as PM and Labour serving with him in his government stopped the political rot. Poor Neville Chamberlain, whose resignation as PM was hard for me to accept, and whose untimely death robbed me of an adviser and friend . . . [the] civilian defence services & morale of people [are] splendid . . . the second six months have certainly shown the world where we stand . . . Hitler has not had everything his own way.'[7]

He may have been optimistic, but 1941 began grimly. The German occupation of Europe now seemed all but insuperable, and unthinkable damage had been done to Britain, with the prospect of further assaults continuing indefinitely. It was therefore more in hope than expectation that the king wrote to Churchill from Sandringham on 2 January to wish him a happier New Year and to wish, 'may we see the end of this conflict in sight during the coming year'. The monarch's excursions during the previous months had been exhausting. It was with relief that he informed his premier, 'I am already feeling better for my sojourn here, it is doing me good, and the change of scene and outdoor exercise is acting as a good tonic.'

The king knew that his standing amongst his people derived from his being visible in times of trouble, and so he fretted to Churchill that 'I feel that it is wrong for me to be away from my place of duty when everybody else is carrying on.' He hoped to come back refreshed both bodily and mentally, and ready, as he put it, 'for renewed efforts against the enemy'. The once tense relationship between him and his prime minister had now mellowed into a more trusting one. He thanked Churchill for his help with his Christmas broadcast and for the gift of a siren suit,* and wrote, 'I have so much admired all you have done during the last seven months as my Prime Minister and I have so enjoyed our talks together during our weekly luncheons . . . I hope they will continue on my return as I do look forward to them so much.'[8] On 9 February, he was so impressed by Churchill's stirring broadcast to the Americans ('We shall not fail or falter, we shall not weaken or tire . . . give us the tools and we shall finish the job') that he wrote, 'Winston was at his best. Downright, modest & meant every word he said', and concluded, 'I could not have a better prime minister.'[9]

The warmth of the king's words struck a different note to the caution and suspicion of their initial encounters, when Churchill had forced through the appointment of Beaverbrook and his acolyte Brendan Bracken, whom he made a Privy Councillor, against his monarch's wishes.† As far as he could, the sovereign lived up to

---

* An all-in-one garment designed for use in air raid shelters, invented and popularised by Churchill and tailored for him by his shirtmakers, Turnbull & Asser of Jermyn Street.
† The king's suspicions about Bracken were well founded. It has subsequently been suggested that after the war, he set up a fraudulent summer school in Scotland, where he posed as a sixteen-year-old schoolboy named Mike and paid other teenagers to beat him.

his assistant private secretary Jock Colville's approving comment that 'it is clear that the King has a mind of his own'.[10] Despite the horrors the country faced, the monarch felt relief that the worst had indeed happened. As he had written to his mother the previous year, 'personally I feel happier now that we have no allies to be polite to and to pamper'.[11] It was half admiringly and half wonderingly that Halifax remarked on how cheerful the king seemed to be 'when he must feel that all his Empire may be crashing about his ears'.[12]

Much of this geniality was feigned. It was a blow to the king that his friend and ally Prince Paul of Yugoslavia was vilified for his refusal to bring his country in on the Allied side and thereby come to the aid of Greece, but instead to maintain craven neutrality. He begged Paul not to take 'the first and fatal step in the loss of your country's independence and integrity' and stated that Hitler's blandishments were 'never, and least of all now, to be trusted', concluding, 'We count on you',[13] but it proved fruitless. On 27 March, Paul and his wife were forced into exile and denounced by Churchill as war criminals and traitors for their diffidence at a time of crisis.

The king and queen knew better than to remonstrate with the prime minister, although the Duke of Kent attempted to defend their friend. Personal acquaintance, so vital for social intercourse in peacetime, was now little more than an indulgence. Paul's friend Channon wrote in his diary that 'I cannot believe that the Regent, whom I love more than anyone else on earth, could do anything dishonourable or against the interests of England, which he loves as I do.'*[14] As the queen told her mother-in-law of how 'I am still enraged beyond words over the futile and wicked destruction of the City of London . . . I am beginning to really hate the German mentality - the cruelty and arrogance of it', it was clear that the king's hope that 1941 would see the end of the conflict was nothing more than wishful thinking.

---

* Channon's affection for Paul arose in part from their having conducted a love affair.

Instead, as he confided to Queen Mary, it seemed that invasion was increasingly likely, and that it could come as early as 14 March. In his diary, he spelt out the details that he had been briefed by the Foreign Office: three days of intensive air bombing followed by the mass invasion of a million German troops, a quarter of whom would parachute onto the streets of Leeds and Liverpool before making their way south. 'This is all very worrying,' he wrote, 'as anything may happen suddenly.'[15] With friends and allies being scattered to the skies, it was time to look elsewhere for support. And while the royal couple praised the morale of their subjects, there were those who saw the continuing developments not as a tragedy, but as an opportunity.

It was not only the king and queen who were grateful for America and its representatives. From the Bahamas, the Duke of Windsor wrote to Monckton after a recent visit to the United States on 28 January to praise 'that great country', saying 'the atmosphere could not have been more sincerely friendly and the hospitality lavished on us remarkable'. There had been an encounter with Roosevelt ('there is no doubt that the Third Term President can "charm the birds off the trees"'), who assured the duke that the Lend-Lease agreement would not affect any of the British coloured communities in the Caribbean, and told him of the Civilian Conservation Corps, an organisation for reducing unemployment in America. Edward was impressed by it and expressed his hope that something similar might be instituted in the Bahamas.

The governor's life in Nassau, however, was unhappy. He complained about the 'political snags, pit-falls and intrigues' that he was faced with professionally, and commented that 'even my Colonial Secretary, with twenty years of experience, says that this is the most difficult and unique Colony that he has served in'. Modesty forbade the duke from acknowledging that it also boasted the most difficult and unique governor the islands had ever seen.

When Edward was not railing against 'difficult and vindictive coloured men',* elected by bribery for 'purely personal and selfish motives', he decided that the heat and humidity made it impossible to remain in the Bahamas over the summer. He therefore told Monckton that he intended to head to his ranch in Canada, which he had not visited since 1927. He wrote, 'I am not asking you to mention these plans in Whitehall at the present time',[16] but made it clear that he would call upon his former adviser for support if he met with any bureaucratic resistance.

Monckton replied with sangfroid ('It will be important for you to get away for the hottest weather . . . I imagine you will want occasional holidays from the Bahamas'),[17] but Churchill responded angrily to the duke's suggestion. The telegram he sent made it clear that 'Your Highness' proposed visit to United States would not be in the public interest nor indeed your own at the present time . . . I trust therefore that you will be willing to defer it until a less crucial stage in British and American relations has been reached.'

Churchill had been outraged by Edward's association with Wenner-Gren, which he believed to be politically toxic ('the gentleman is . . . regarded as a pro-German international financier, with strong leanings towards appeasement and suspected of being in communication with the enemy'). He wrote witheringly that 'Your Royal Highness may not perhaps realise the intensity of feeling in the United States about people of this kind and the offence which is given to the Administration when any countenance is given to them.' At a delicate negotiating stage in international relations, Britain did not need its former monarch acting in a fashion that was at best insensitive and at worst harmful to its interests.

Edward did not help himself by an interview he had given *Liberty* magazine on his previous visit to America, and which was published on 22 March. Churchill called it 'defeatist and pro-Nazi, and by implication approving of the isolationist aim to keep

---

* Like many men of his background and generation, his attitude towards racial harmony could be described as unenlightened, but there was real anger in his comment that 'the coloured problem [here] is particularly acute and bitter'.

America out of the war'. During his conversation with the journalist Fulton Oursler, the duke stated that while America's assistance to Britain should be unconditional, it should receive suitable acknowledgement in return. He also offered criticism of 'the insufferable snobs who accept your hospitality and then insult you by a fatuous pretence of superiority', whom he claimed should never be allowed to leave England, and then ridiculed British exceptionalism by saying, 'It is just as blatant for an Englishman to believe that he is superior to the rest of mankind as for Hitler to preach racial superiority.'

The duke undoubtedly believed in his own superiority, but this had to be put aside. Instead, he wished to flatter his hosts. He stated that 'When the war is over, many strange things are going to happen – and one of the strangest is that America will no longer be called the New World. It will be the Old World and Europe will be the New World.'[18] Whatever his intention, it was a politically naïve intervention. Churchill commented that the most generous interpretation of the interview was that the duke had been coerced into making various statements. He wrote, more in disappointment than in anger, 'I could wish indeed that Your Royal Highness would seek advice before making public statements of this kind . . . I should always be ready to help as I used to in the past.'[19] The king, meanwhile, wrote that 'D has been saying the wrong thing in interviews to American reporters, & wants to visit USA now, which have incensed Winston. At last W understands what harm he can do.' He partially exculpated his brother, although in the least flattering terms. 'D has no mind of his own, it is all centred in Mrs S his wife.'[20]

Less than five years before, when Churchill was only a backbencher, he had been both mentor and confidant to the then king during the abdication crisis. He had even helped him write his broadcast the day he gave up his throne. But now, relations between the two were cold. Wallis wrote to her aunt Bessie to inform her of the veto to their planned visit: 'We can *not* come to the US in April . . . the Duke is in a rage. I am used to "no" so am calm.' She reflected with frustration that 'Only when the war stops will we regain our independence from HM Govt.'[21]

She also complained to Monckton on 5 March about the 'pitiful and drab' surroundings they lived in, but commented, of potential American involvement in the war, that 'I have faith in the people.' This mirrored Halifax's belief, as expressed to his sister Mary, that 'The feeling of people here is no doubt overwhelmingly in our favour, and a great many of them are genuinely ashamed at not being already in the war.' However, he cautioned that 'there is an immense feeling, I suppose very naturally, against them coming in, and I doubt myself whether they will come in unless they get somehow pushed in by the Germans doing something outrageous to them. And this I suppose they will try and avoid doing.'[22]

Meanwhile, Wallis's impression of feeling in America, based on their visit the previous December, was more acute than her husband's. She warned Monckton that 'some day many voices must be heard above the few powerful ones that exist in every country - it will not be a happy day for most of us - it wasn't in Russia', even as she acknowledged that 'anything new is exciting and we must prepare for a New Deal, but not Mr R's'.*[23] Monckton had the tact not to reply that this populism was what had seen Hitler rise to power.

Edward was angered by Churchill's instructions. He had already suggested, on 19 March, that if 'I am more of a detriment than of assistance to these vital Anglo-American relations I would prefer to resign',[24] and now he pressed his point further. He sent a telegram to the prime minister claiming that repudiation of his apparent comments in the interview would only attract further attention, and stating, in opposition to Halifax's belief that any journey that he and Wallis made to America would become a carnival, 'our visit [last December] was most dignified and no harm was done to British interests'.

---

* Wallis commented to Monckton that the angry telegrams expressing distaste for their new role 'have surpassed those of Lisbon - which raises the standard quite high', before noting, 'when free speech is taken from us, it is alarming'.

He also took direct aim at Britain and the prime minister himself in the same telegram, when he vented his fury at the queen being quoted in *Life* magazine as referring to Wallis merely as 'that woman'. Knowing that any adverse references to the royal family in publications would be censored, he saw this as a sanctioned insult to his wife, and responded intemperately. He described it as 'no encouragement in our efforts to uphold the monarchical system in a British colony', and again complained about 'the chronic anomaly of my wife not having the same official status as myself', which he called 'unpleasant and undignified'.

He sneered that 'it is not necessary for you to remind me of the sacrifices and sufferings by Great Britain . . . had my simple request* conveyed to you by Sam Hoare been granted by my brother I would have been proud to share these sad and critical times with my countrymen'. He ended on a note of personal betrayal. 'I have both valued and enjoyed your friendship in the past, but after your telegram . . . and the tone of your recent messages to me, I find it difficult to believe that you are still the friend you used to be.'[25]

Churchill's response was to forward a copy to the king, but also to investigate whether Wallis had been intentionally traduced. His assistant private secretary Jock Colville assured him that the *Life* article was not written with the queen's knowledge, and that it had in any case been passed by the censors. Yet placating the governor of the Bahamas was not his highest priority. As bombs continued to coventrate Britain, and German invasion remained a vivid possibility, both the prime minister and the king would find themselves faced with a threat close to home.

Thomas Argyll Robertson, nicknamed 'Tar', was an MI5 intelligence officer who had previously involved himself with the royal family when he had been called upon to bug the telephones at

* For Edward to be given an official role befitting his status, and for Wallis to be recognised as Her Royal Highness.

Buckingham Palace during the abdication crisis.* He had accomplished his unsavoury task with skill, and so was promoted to head of the double-cross section of MI5, the so-called 'XX committee', who were, at the outset of the war, responsible for German counter-intelligence.

A figure who had come to his department's attention back in 1937 was thirty-four-year old Albrecht Haushofer, who was described as 'a close associate of Hitler and . . . on personal terms with most of the Nazi hierarchy'. Haushofer was a well-known fixture of London society, without obvious means of financial support. The MI5 report on him suggested that he 'is probably employed in the collection of intelligence in the UK . . . you may consider it advisable to . . . ascertain his contacts and movements'.[26]

There were many German nationals living in Britain in 1937, and although Haushofer remained a person of interest, especially for his association with Hitler's lieutenant Rudolf Hess, he was not seen as a threat to national security. This would change three years later when a letter arrived from him written in the fondest terms, with its recipient informed that 'my attachment to you remains unaltered and unalterable, whatever the circumstances must be'. After offering commiserations about various late relatives, Haushofer mentioned correspondence from the previous year, alluded to his recipient's 'friends in high places' and then suggested another, surreptitious meeting, potentially in Lisbon. He wrote, 'Of course I do not know whether you can make your authorities understand so much, that they give you leave . . . but at least you may be able to answer my question.'[27]

Anyone who intercepted the letter, which was sent via an intermediary in Wembley, would have been alarmed by the familiarity with which a high-ranking German addressed a British subject during times of war. It was therefore especially unfortunate that its recipient was Douglas Douglas-Hamilton, Duke of Hamilton and the king's Lord Steward. Not only had his pre-war activities

---

* See *The Crown in Crisis*, Chapter Ten.

attracted controversy, to say nothing of a letter he had written to *The Times* in October 1939 calling war against Germany 'wrong and meaningless', but the communication indicated that his contacts had persisted over the past few years. After the connection between Hamilton and Haushofer was established, MI5 sought to play down the seriousness of its implications, with an intelligence note suggesting that 'this is probably not a matter of espionage but of peace propaganda or something of that kind'.[28]

Hamilton himself was not made aware of the letter's existence until December 1940, but MI5 stressed that 'there is no reason to regard the Duke with suspicion'. Yet this seemed unsatisfactory. Even as he decided that 'it is a safe bet that AH is engaged either in espionage or some other form of activity detrimental to British interests', Tar still believed that Hamilton should be interviewed, if only to rule out his complicity.

As Hamilton was serving in the RAF, Tar wrote to Group Captain F. G. Stammers, the head of the air force police, describing the case as 'rather tricky', and noting that 'the date of the letter [from Haushofer] is not without interest, as it was about this time that the Blitz on this country had proved a failure, and it seems possible that the writer was anxious to approach Hamilton in order to sound him out with regard to the possibilities of making peace'. After suggesting that Stammers ascertain whether Hamilton knew anything about the Wembley intermediary or the Lisbon rendezvous, he wrote, 'it is quite likely that under cross-examination Hamilton will be able to offer a reasonable explanation for the letter which will clear things up satisfactorily'.[29]

Hamilton was summoned to the Air Ministry on 11 March and an awkward interview took place. To MI5's surprise, the Lord Steward not only admitted knowing Haushofer, having met him during his visit to Germany for the 1936 Olympic Games, but also told his interviewers that he had been introduced by Haushofer to Göring and other high-ranking Nazis. Their acquaintance had been close enough for Hamilton to meet Haushofer's parents in Munich. His father Karl was an academic who originated the

Geopolitik theory that was an important guide for Hitler's expansionist foreign policy ideas.* He was described by MI5 as 'a man of great influence in Nazi circles'.

Hamilton spoke highly of Haushofer, calling him 'a patriotic German' and claiming that he had attempted to be a restraining influence on the Nazi Party, falling out of favour after the Munich Agreement. He admitted that he had hosted Haushofer 'on frequent occasions during short visits to this country'. He offered to meet him 'if it can be of any service to the country', but also suggested that his flying instructor brother David would be a more suitable intermediary, due to his 'considerable intimate knowledge of Germany'.[30]

Hamilton now became a figure of suspicion in his own right. Although he claimed to know nothing about Lisbon and why Haushofer wished to meet there, Tar decided that the Lord Steward, rather than his brother, should be dispatched to a rendezvous, on the grounds that if the German's intentions really were honourable rather than underhand, it would be useful to ascertain them. Perhaps he also wondered, in his official double-cross role, whether there was an opportunity to see if Haushofer might be turned to British advantage.

This assumed, of course, that Hamilton's loyalty to king and country could be counted on. As the official MI5 report concluded, 'Our records do not give us any positive proof of any pro-German or anti-British activities, but it is felt that it would not have been surprising if the Duke had allowed himself to be used as an intermediary for these terms during the blackest period of the war last summer . . . Owing to his prominence in sports and other circles, he had of course many Nazi contacts in this country.'[31]

Hamilton was summoned to meet Tar, who wished to brief him before sending him to Lisbon. As he put it to Air Commodore

---

* This had been defined by Karl Haushofer in 1935 as 'the duty to safeguard the right to the soil, to the land in the widest sense, not only the land within the frontiers of the Reich, but the right to the more extensive Volk and cultural lands'.

Dermot Boyle, 'it will be necessary to prime [Hamilton] very care-fully as to the story he is to tell Haushofer'. It was decided that the reason Hamilton should give for not replying to the original correspondence was that the letter was lost in the post. Although this sounded fanciful as an excuse for nearly a year's delay, war-time circumstances meant that it was more plausible than it might otherwise have been. Suitably briefed, Hamilton left for Lisbon in mid April 1941, bound for a rendezvous with his friend.

Its consequences would be more eventful than either man could have imagined.

There is no record of what happened during Hamilton's in-tended meeting with Haushofer in Lisbon, but if it did occur, there was surely a direct correlation between their conversation and the unexpected arrival of a mysterious pilot on 10 May in Scotland, crash-landing around ten miles south of Glasgow. When a local farmer found the wreckage of the aeroplane, the pilot declared that he was travelling on a 'special mission' of international urgency, and that he must see the Duke of Hamilton. He gave his name as Captain Alfred Horn, and Hamilton, who was serving as a local RAF commanding officer that evening, was summoned.

When he arrived, it was with surprise that he recognised Rudolf Hess, then Hitler's deputy Führer. Hess proceeded to outline the purpose of his journey. He claimed to be on 'a mission of human-ity', one not officially sanctioned but tacitly approved by Hitler, and that he had been aiming for Hamilton's home, Dungavel House in South Lanarkshire. To complicate matters further, he too had a Lisbon connection. During the Duke of Windsor's sojourn there the previous year, Hess had attempted to reach him but had been unable to join the throng of double agents and diplomats who had paid the former king court.

The interview between Hess and the Lord Steward on Sunday 11 May began uncomfortably. Although Hamilton claimed to have no recollection of meeting Hess, the prisoner remembered encoun-tering him at the Olympic Games, and recalled that the duke had lunched at his house. He observed that Haushofer had suggested that Hamilton would understand Hess's point of view. Once previous acquaintance had been established, Hess, who made much of having arrived unarmed and of his own free will, proposed a deal. If the king would offer him unconditional parole, he would serve as a go-between in bringing about peace between Germany and Britain. Otherwise, he stated, 'the Führer was convinced that Germany would win the war, possibly soon, but certainly in one, two or three years . . . he wished to stop the unnecessary slaughter that would otherwise inevitably take place'.[32] Hamilton wrote, 'Hess was able to express himself fairly clearly, but he did not properly understand what I was saying, and I suggested that I should return with an interpreter and have further conversation with him.' Hess asked that his identity should not be disclosed to the press. This request was not honoured.

His unexpected arrival led to bewilderment and hilarity throughout British society. Whatever the truth of his stated reason for his adventure, there was something bizarre about it all, epitomised by Churchill's reaction to the news. 'Hess in Scotland! I thought this was fantastic.'[33] When the news was put out in a press release from Downing Street, there was disbelief that such a high-ranking Nazi had risked life and liberty in such an activity. Yet there was also a belief that Hamilton's involvement, especially after his friendship with Haushofer and previous acquaintance with Hess had been revealed, was no coincidence. As the king wrote in his diary on 13 May, 'I had to ask Walter Buccleuch [Hamilton's] predecessor to leave owing to his sympathy with the Nazis. Perhaps the post of Lord Steward is bewitched or is it Germanised?' He summarised Hess's arrival by saying, 'The Germans said that Hess was mad & had disappeared in an aircraft. This was news as evidently something had happened in the Nazi party & regime to make one of its number fly straight to the enemy country, & not to a neighbouring state' and noted that Churchill 'thought Hess' landing would do us good [as] no one would believe the German story'. He reflected, 'We should be very angry if Beaverbrook or Anthony Eden suddenly left here & flew off to Germany without warning.'[34]

It was possible that Hess had been aiming for a rendezvous with Buccleuch* rather than Hamilton, but this seemed unlikely given the existing connections between Hess, Haushofer and the duke; Hess even had visiting cards from both Haushofer and his father in his possession. Further interrogation produced few answers. Hess stuck to the same line throughout, claiming to be an emissary of peace. Hitler did not wish to continue to fight Britain, he said, but if terms were not agreed, the Führer 'would crush this country so utterly that we should never be able to lift our heads again'. He also suggested that the Germans had no intention of provoking America, on the grounds that 'it would be madness for them to think that they could ever attack the United States'.[35]

On 11 May, John Simon, the Lord High Chancellor, sat down with Hess to ascertain what exactly he had travelled to Britain for. It soon became clear that his embassy was based on a misconception. In his report, Simon observed that 'he showed himself very willing to reveal his ideas to me, saying that he well remembered that we met in Berlin in March 1935'. Once this personal connection had been established, Simon noted that Hess was dejected at the failure of his mission and feared that he had made a fool of himself. 'Hess arrived under the impression that the prospects of success of his "mission" were much greater than he now realises they are. He imagined that there was a strong peace party in this country, and that he would have the opportunity of getting in touch with leading politicians who wanted the war to end now.' Simon added, 'He is profoundly ignorant of our own constitutional system and of the unity of the country' and suggested that Hess was unbalanced – 'his confusion of mind on all this is extreme'.

The Lord High Chancellor believed that Hess's freelance actions were dictated by a desire to return to relevance. 'His position and

---

* Who was still considered a potential threat; Alec Hardinge wrote scornfully in April 1941 of his 'consistently pro-Nazi attitudes, which, from what I hear, he has not even now entirely discarded', and he was regarded as sufficiently *persona non grata* for the visiting King of Norway to have reservations about taking his hospitality.

authority in Germany have declined, and if he could bring off the coup of early peace on Hitler's terms, he would confirm his position as Hitler's chief lieutenant, and render an immense service to his adored Master and to Germany.'* While acknowledging that Hess made 'my flesh creep', Simon ascertained that he had come up with the plan of his own accord, albeit in the belief that it would be sanctioned by Hitler, and that he had limited strategic or military information to impart ('He breaks down as soon as he is asked for more details'). Instead, he claimed that he was attempting to bring about the end of the war before more civilians were killed, even as he threatened that in the event of a prolonged conflict, blockades would mean that the British would starve.

He spoke proudly of his courage and determination in coming to Britain with tidings of peace. Yet this seemed a strange and dangerous way of making such an offer. Churchill therefore decided to let press speculation run rampant and thereby damage the German propaganda machine. He informed Roosevelt that 'There will be deep misgivings in the German armed forces about what he may say.'[36]

However, whatever Hess's intentions, Hamilton's involvement was not coincidental. Simon noted that 'Hess has constantly asked to have a further meeting with the Duke of Hamilton, under the illusion that "der Herzog" . . . would be the means of getting him contact with people of a different view from the "clique" who are holding [him] prisoner.'[37] This meeting was allowed on 14 May,[†] and when Hamilton visited the king on the 16th, in his official sphere as Lord Steward, he conveyed a message from Hess asking for parole, as well as stressing that he had never met Hess in Germany before the war, and that his only connection was with Haushofer. The monarch wrote in his diary, with incredulity, 'All the leading

---

* At this point, Simon noted, 'He shows no liking for Ribbentrop . . . Hess is quite outside the inner circle which directs the war.'

† During which Hess asked to borrow Jerome K. Jerome's *Three Men in a Boat*, hinting at an otherwise under-explored interest in nineteenth-century English humour on the part of the Nazi high command.

Nazis think they are gods everywhere, as well as in Germany . . . a time of detention here may sober him down & teach him to look at things from a more rational angle'.[38] Hess, who now refused to cooperate further, was accordingly detained as a prisoner of war. He was first imprisoned in the Tower of London and then moved to 'Camp Z', Mytchett Place in Surrey. A suggestion that he should be held at Hamilton's residence, Dungavel House, which was temporarily acting as a hospital, was not taken seriously.

The question of what to do with the embarrassing, if not treacherous, Hamilton remained pressing. Should he be questioned further himself, even arrested for suspected espionage, or publicly exonerated? The former would destroy the potential for the incident's propaganda success. He had written to the king on 19 May to say that everything 'the unrepentant' Hess said was 'the usual Nazi claptrap', and that 'his arrival here, uninvited, has been of considerable advantage to us, if only in the difficulties and discredit in which it has involved the German propaganda machine',[39] but suspicions lingered.

Still, the king wrote in his diary on the 20th that 'The Germans can be kept guessing about what Hess has been telling us. Sinclair is going to exonerate Hamilton. From what I can make out, it looks very much as if Hess really wanted to see Walter Buccleuch.'[40]

It was therefore unsurprising that the Secretary of State for Air, Sir Archibald Sinclair, announced in the House of Commons on 22 May that 'the conduct of the Duke of Hamilton has been in every respect honourable and proper'.

It had not been. There was soon further embarrassment when Harry Pollitt, the general secretary of the Communist Party and an enthusiastic supporter of Stalin, stated in a pamphlet that Hamilton was a close friend of Hess, leading the duke to issue a suit for libel. This was a high-risk strategy, not least because Hamilton intended to call Hess as a witness in the case. The consequences, especially as Hess had now been diagnosed with mental illness, were unpredictable, and the Foreign Office were appalled. Cadogan wrote on 20 June, 'it is clear that in no circumstances must this be permitted to happen . . . it is out of the question that Hess should appear in this case . . . we shall have to bring the strongest possible pressure on the Duke to withdraw the action'.[41]

Hamilton was therefore informed on 15 July that not only would the War Office prevent Hess from appearing, but as an added humiliation, the Crown refused to intercede to allow the case to be held 'in camera', despite Churchill's wish that it should do so, meaning that it would take place in open court. Eventually honour was satisfied when the Communist Party, who were not in a financial position to conduct an expensive lawsuit against a wealthy landowner, offered an apology and a withdrawal of the initial accusation, but it was yet another blow for the duke.

Even if Hamilton had not been told by Haushofer of Hess's intentions in April 1941, it seems unlikely, given his German links, that he did not already have some inkling of what various high-ranking Nazis wished for. Their desire to bring war with Britain to a close did not come from altruism or envy at British morale, but from simple expediency. Hitler was planning Operation Barbarossa, an invasion of the Soviet Union, which began on 22 June 1941, and he did not want to fight on more fronts than he needed to. An interrogation of Haushofer by the Gestapo produced little intelligence of value, yet the Führer had not authorised Hess to contact either Hamilton or Buccleuch. A further interrogation of Hess by the Lord High Chancellor led the king to write on 11 June, 'Simon thinks Hess definitely came here on his own initiative & not on Hitler's orders or with his permission. Hess was trying to impress & warn us that we shall be beaten by Germany and that his own peace "plan" is his genuine effort to reproduce Hitler's own mind as expressed by Hitler to him in conversation.'

Unfortunately, Hess's mental health was declining. Although the king noted that 'Hess has no ideas of his own, & breaks down if asked to explain details of his "plan"',[42] he remained sufficiently compos mentis to produce two lengthy statements attesting to his ill-treatment at British hands. The first, dated 5 September, complained of his being given a 'substance which had a strong effect on brain and nerves' that drove him to attempt suicide. His efforts were unsuccessful, as he only broke his thigh, leading to his being bedbound. He claimed that he was all but tortured by the British medical officers, and that when he complained, they replied, 'We are treating you as the Gestapo treats people in Germany.' This led to him to write, 'I hereby protest most sharply to the British Government against the treatment which I have received. The case is the more serious as it involves a minister of the Reich.'[43]

A fortnight later, he attempted to rebut claims that the Germans were systematically ill-treating prisoners ('When I return to Germany, I shall cause an investigation to be made about the facts which are related. I shall investigate from personal interest whether sub-leaders did in fact behave as described without the knowledge and against the will of leaders'). Nonetheless, his incarceration did not change his ideological stance. 'With the exception of common criminals, the persons in concentration camps have spread Communism in Germany and Austria, either directly by word and deed or indirectly by fighting against its antipodes, National-Socialism. Communism, wherever it was in power, established as a principle the most dreadful terror accompanied by the most bestial tortures.'

Describing the horrors of communist rule in Hungary ('Priests' hats were nailed to their heads; their nails were torn off; their eyes were gouged out with the jovial remark "Why should they arrive in the next world with their eyesight?"'), he ascribed these cruelties to the usual scapegoat. 'I am sorry to say Jews were nearly always responsible. When the country was freed from the Bolshevists, and many of them were condemned, an outcry against the white terror went up in the whole world; the real cruelties were almost ignored. Bishop Prohászka* shows that it has always been so as soon as it became necessary to defend oneself against Jews.'

He ended his statement with a pointed, if factually inaccurate, remark about relative morality. 'As British subjects are not

---

* A leading Hungarian clergyman who was notorious for the strength of his anti-semitic opinions.

concerned, I refuse England the right to deal with the question of the treatment of prisoners in Germany. Otherwise I have to ask for the same right for Germany. Germany would then have to make it her business to investigate the English treatment of the Irish in Ireland, of Indians in India or Arabs in Palestine, etc. . . . if, as someone told me, the closing of concentration camps in Germany is one of England's war aims, Germany would have to make one of her war aims a guarantee that England would never again create concentration camps for women and children, which she did a generation ago . . . during the Boer War, 20,000 women and children died on account of conditions which prevailed in concentration camps. Germany has never sent women and children to concentration camps.'[44]

Neither of his statements produced any action, and so Hess was certified by an army psychiatrist as delusional, incorrectly squawking, 'the king of England will never let these things happen'[45] as he was forcibly sedated. Yet he wrote to the king on 13 November in a last-ditch plea for assistance and, possibly, sympathy. 'In an appeal for the protection promised by Your Majesty I turn to you because I do not trust the British government to see that the guilty are punished and my treatment fundamentally altered . . . the Prime Minister has personally made all decisions about my treatment. He has to be asked even about details.' He asked that a royal commission should be set up to investigate his treatment, to be chaired by Hamilton – who he also asked be allowed to visit him, in lieu of any other contact with friends or family – and described his predicament as 'a most sinister scheme for tormenting a man and perhaps damaging his health for the rest of his life without those who are entrusted with his protection either being aware of it or believing it'.

Hess believed that the reason for his continued incarceration was to compel him to seek English peace proposals 'of such a nature that, in the ordinary course, I should never be prepared to transmit'. Nevertheless, he refused to give in to pressure, both for the sake of his own conscience and because he believed that Hitler would refuse to listen to him. Even as he gasped that 'Never would I have thought it possible that in England I could be subjected to the horrors disclosed by the spiritual and physical tortures which I have described in my letter of protest . . . I came to England relying on the fairness of the English',[46] he begged for the king's compassion.

In this regard, he was to be disappointed. Even as he desperately mused in December that 'It is the greatest wonder that I have not yet gone mad, but there is need for haste. I cannot hold out much longer', Hardinge wrote to Cadogan that the king had seen the letter, in his private secretary's own 'hurriedly and . . . more, rather than less, accurately' translated version, and was unmoved by it, believing it to be nothing other than the rantings of a madman. He commented, 'Hess has evidently got the persecution mania, and I do not imagine that there is anything to be done about it.'[47] No further action would be taken to ameliorate his conditions, or to interrogate him.

Due to Churchill's policy of allowing newspapers to print whatever they pleased, the stories about Hess's arrival in Britain and his connections with Hamilton, and by extension the king, have continued to be a source of scandal and gossip for the last eighty years. After being tried at Nuremberg and found guilty of crimes against peace and of conspiracy with other German leaders to commit crimes, Hess was imprisoned by the Soviet Union in Spandau prison in Berlin. He remained incarcerated until he finally succeeded in committing suicide in 1987, at the age of ninety-three. He never clarified what, if anything, his mission had really been, and any further information that his captors extracted from him remains locked away in some modern-day Lubyanka.

Hamilton remained as Lord Steward until 1964, although forever tainted by his German associations. There was an apocryphal story that he attempted to offer his resignation to Churchill, saying, 'Mr Prime Minister, as my name has been associated with Rudolf Hess, I feel it is only right for me to resign my position as Lord Steward of His Majesty's Household', only for the premier to respond

'Come now, my boy, we can't have you do that.' To lose one Lord Steward was an incident; to lose two, disastrous. And that had to be avoided.

Like many of his aristocratic peers, his loyalty to his king and country may have been compromised by his admiration for Germany, but to describe the Duke of Hamilton as a traitor would seem hyperbolic. However, the events of May 1941 did have one unexpected knock-on effect. As Hess lingered in Mytchett Place, and a compromised Hamilton continued to perform his royal duties, the FBI received information from a confidential source many thousands of miles away that suggested that another former Lisbon resident was frightened by the situation, and that British hopes that his removal to the Bahamas had taken him out of harm's way were dashed. It stated, 'the Duke [of Windsor] is very much worried for fear of being kidnapped by the Germans and being traded for the release of Rudolf Hess'.[48]

Yet the duke's fears - if they were reported accurately - were misplaced. Interest in kidnapping him had passed. Instead, he was far more valuable to German intelligence where he was.

Chapter Twelve

'The Hard Sacrifice'

On 10 August 1941, the queen made a radio broadcast to the women of America. She had not made a similar broadcast since the outbreak of war, and took the chance to address her millions of listeners in largely her own words, with only minor changes made by Hardinge and Churchill. Her purpose was twofold: to thank them for their support and to make it clear that Britain, and what remained of Europe, needed American help more than ever.

She spoke with both conviction and anger. She did not conceal the dreadfulness of the situation ('as yet, save in the valour of our people, we have not matched our enemies'), and bemoaned the 'heavy burden' that the British faced. 'In many cities . . . homes lie in ruins, as do many of those ancient buildings which you know and love hardly less than we do ourselves. Women and children have been killed, and even the sufferers in hospital have not been spared.'

Yet she extolled the 'warmth and sympathy of American generosity'. She said it had 'touched beyond measure the hearts of all of us living and fighting in these islands', and expressed her gratitude for how 'canteens, ambulances and medical supplies have come in an unceasing flow from the United States'. She praised her audience woman to woman, saying, 'It gives us strength to know that you have not been content to pass us by on the other side; to us, in our time of our tribulation, you have surely shown that compassion which has for two thousand years been the mark of the Good Neighbour. Believe me - and I am speaking for millions of us, who know the bitter, but also proud, sorrow of war - we are grateful. We shall not forget your sacrifice.'

Her peroration struck a note of solidarity between the two English-speaking nations. 'To you, tyranny is as hateful as it is to us; to you, the things for which we will fight to the death are no less sacred; and - to my mind, at any rate - your generosity is born of your conviction that we fight to save a cause that is yours no less than ours: of your high resolve that, however great the cost and however long the struggle, justice and freedom, human dignity and kindness, shall not perish from the earth.'[1]

Her speech was well received.* Roosevelt wrote to the king after he heard it to say, 'Will you be good enough to tell the Queen that her radio address yesterday was really perfect in every way and that it will do a great amount of good.'[2] Yet although the royal couple's recent lunch with Hopkins had been both amicable and productive, longed-for action had not followed, which was increasingly critical. The country was in a dreadful state. Almost 1,500 British citizens died in one night of bombing on 10 May, and nearly half a million tons of desperately needed provisions and munitions were sunk in the Atlantic over the course of two months. Even Churchill muttered that these were 'the worst days of the war so far'.[3]

Roosevelt was trapped between his own impulses, which were to support Britain for both personal and political reasons, and the influence of isolationists such as Kennedy. The provision of equipment as agreed in the Lend-Lease agreement was welcome, but it was not enough from a British perspective. The king also grumbled to Halifax that 'the Americans wanted too much written & laid down. Everything was done in their interests, no give or take in certain circumstances . . . I do hope that the Americans will not try & bleed us white over the dollar asset question. As it is, they

---

* Channon was less impressed, calling the broadcast 'adequate, full of clichés but will be a success in the USA' and describing the queen as 'a frivolous but friendly fraud . . . she has fooled everyone'. Nonetheless he wrote, 'I cannot help but admire her, although she has not been loyal to me.'

are collecting the remaining gold in the world, which is of no use to them, & they cannot wish to make us bankrupt.'[4]

But the president had drawn fire from his own country. Halifax informed the king on 16 May that 'there is much bitter criticism of him and suspicion cutting across the main issue'.[5] Even as Roosevelt said on 27 May, during one of his 'fireside chats' with his nation, that 'we shall give every possible assistance to Britain and to all who, with Britain, are resisting Hitlerism or its equivalent with force of arms', assistance fell short of his rhetoric.

The king had been dissuaded from writing to Roosevelt before the outbreak of war, but now he decided that the warmth of his relationship with the president justified a personal rather than formal letter. He wrote to him on 3 June with both praise ('your last speech of May 27 has encouraged everybody in this country to carry on, knowing that the immense potential industrial strength of your country is behind us') and sincerity: 'I do thank God it was possible for the Queen & me to come to America in those few months before war broke out in Europe ... We have a very real affection in our hearts for the people of the United States.' He ended by stressing the informal nature of the correspondence. 'As I know you personally I would like to feel that I can write to you direct ... I hope that you will be able to write back to me in this personal way.'

Roosevelt did not reply. The king assumed, to his chagrin, that his letter had been a victim of the unreliable postal service. When it transpired that the president had received it but was unable to respond in the fashion the sovereign had hoped he would, the mild-mannered monarch gave in to anger and frustration. It was a consistent feature throughout his reign that his dealings with elected politicians assumed a more personal dimension than his predecessors (or successor) may have found appropriate. This had the advantage of forming friendships when other rulers might have retreated into protocol, but it also meant that he took matters to heart in a fashion that other, more detached sovereigns did not.

One result of this approach was that after an indifferent start to his relationship with Churchill, a friendship had arisen between the two. It was not the quasi-paternal dynamic that had existed between the king and Chamberlain, but something closer to a partnership, aided by the weekly lunches the two men enjoyed together. Thus the king could describe his premier to Roosevelt in his letter as 'a great man', one who had 'come into his own as leader of his country in this fateful time in her history' and 'indefatigable at his work'.[6] Given that the president was now in regular communication with the prime minister, he formed his own elevated opinion of Churchill, although he still asked his envoy, and former presidential rival, Wendell Wilkie, who had encountered the premier early that year, 'Is he a drunk?'*[7]

By the time Churchill and Roosevelt met at Placentia Bay in August 1941, something the president subsequently described to the king in an implicitly apologetic letter as 'three delightful and useful days', Germany had invaded Russia. Hitler's feared outcome of fighting on two fronts had come to pass. Again there was no formal declaration of war by America on Germany, but then none had been expected.

Instead, the Atlantic Charter offered worthy but vacuous platitudes about war aims, most of which sounded like the kind of things the headmaster of a third-rate school might list as his failing establishment's achievements that year: 'Working together ... making sure that we can be self-sufficient ... collaborating economically ...' None of it was anything near what Britain needed. As the king wrote despairingly to Queen Mary, 'How are we going to carry [the aims] out? Most of the peoples of Europe will have forgotten that they ever had a government of their own when the war is over. America and ourselves will have to feed them in Europe for years and years.'[8]

When Churchill returned, he was able to make his monarch feel more optimistic about Roosevelt's intentions. As the king wrote in

---

* Wilkie responded, 'Mr President, I had as many drinks as Churchill all the time I was with him, and nobody has ever called me a drunk.'

his diary, 'FDR told [Winston] that at the moment he would not declare war, but that he would wage war with us, against Germany, as evidenced by taking over all convoy work to Iceland. W was greatly taken with [FDR] & has come back feeling that he knows him . . . [he] put our position to [Roosevelt] very bluntly. If by the Spring, Russia was down & out, & Germany was renewing her blitzkrieg here, all our hopes of victory & help from USA would be dashed if America had not by then sent us masses of planes etc., or had not entered the war.' There was also some discussion as to whether another front would open, but the king recorded that 'the Atlantic was much better [and Churchill] thought Japan would remain quiet'.*[9]

The prime minister was normally an acute observer of global trends, as befitted a historian and politician of decades' standing. In this instance, he was incorrect. And yet this mistake would benefit, rather than diminish, the world in its parlous state.

It irritated the Duke of Windsor that while any attempts on his part to head to America were met with either distrust or refusal, the Duke of Kent made an official state visit there and to Canada at the end of July. Kent described the experience as 'fantastic' and praised the 'great work' of the country. It was the first time a member of the royal family had headed over to the continent on state business since the king and queen had triumphed two years previously. The acclaim with which he was greeted was familiar but welcome, as he became a star of newsreel footage and the excited crowds. He remained a consummate ambassador for his country, even if, during a visit to Baltimore, the topic of his brother's ever-controversial wife - 'our Wallie' - was studiously avoided.

Kent wrote to his friend Betty Lawson-Johnston, who was resident in America, to apologise for not having time in his hectic

* Churchill also stated for the first time that 'he thought that Germany might at some time crumple from within'. The king noted, 'I have always thought that possible as the German mentality has always been to follow the leader blindly and never to think for himself.'

schedule to see her, and to comment on his experiences. He had 'endless conversations' with Roosevelt, whom he described as 'really pleasant', and bemoaned the 'terrible collection of people' at the Press Club in Washington. His judgement on the Americans was less warm than they might have hoped for. He remarked that 'they don't know there is a war on & want to keep out of it and not give up their comfortable lives, but they <u>must</u> do more'. He complained of the country - and by extension its president - that 'there is too much talk and they don't listen and they don't listen enough to us as to what they should make and how they should make it after we have had the fighting experience'. He concluded, 'I am feeling rather exhausted as I really have worked hard and I hope done some good over here.'[10]

This had the patrician quality of his eldest brother expecting that the American people would do what they were told, but the king shared his frustration. He even wrote in his diary on 20 October that 'For some little time now I have been depressed about the future. If Russia is contained by Germany, the latter has so many divisions with which to fight in Spain, North Africa, Turkey, the Caucasus and here in the Spring.'[11] Gloomily he predicted that the German air force would resume bombardment in the winter.

Yet there was nothing more that could be done. Roosevelt's hands were pinioned behind his back, and without further developments, American official neutrality would remain the status quo. And so the Duke and Duchess of Windsor were granted permission to visit the United States for a tour in September and October, with the proviso that they would behave themselves and not cause a diplomatic ruckus.

The duke wrote to Monckton in July to comment that 'such a trip, although purely an unofficial one, would nevertheless require a reasonable amount of time for preparation and laying good "ground bait" as far as the press is concerned'. What might have disturbed the king and Churchill was his belief that 'I am so convinced that the British have been and are still often working along the wrong lines with regard to America's position in this war and obtaining the maximum assistance and good will from that great country and her people.'[12]

The trip began well. A lunch with Roosevelt at the White House on 3 October was pleasant, and Halifax informed Churchill that 'the President spoke well to me yesterday on the Windsors . . . he reported the Duke as being very robust on war and victory and his attitude generally showed a great improvement on the impression the President had formed when he met him a year ago in the Bahamas'.[13] Although Wallis's reported shopping extravagances were covered with appropriate gravity in the newspapers, anticipated dangers were largely avoided. Halifax told Churchill on 19 October, with relief, '[The Duke's] visit seems to have gone off all right, and not attracted too much publicity, and on the whole the Press, with the exception of one or two rags, have behaved all right.'

It was the duke himself who gave Halifax concern. The two met privately during the visit, and the ambassador described him speaking freely about his reduced status in life. 'He feels pretty bitter about being marooned in the Bahamas, which he says is a foul climate, and where there is nobody except casual American visitors whom he can see as a friend.' Wenner-Gren was not alluded to, but Halifax expressed sympathy for the duke's predicament, saying 'it certainly sounds pretty grim'.

A consistent facet of Edward's character was that when faced with a man he regarded as being from the same social or economic class as himself, he opened up and became candid. He informed Halifax that 'he had done his best to play the game and avoid making difficulties, but that his family had not responded, and he never wanted to see them again'. Although he accepted that he would remain in the Bahamas for the duration of the war, he looked to the future ('France didn't look as if it would be very good') and suggested that settling in America was a possibility, as he no longer believed himself to be welcome in Britain. In this, at least, he was correct.

Halifax noted the duke's ongoing absence of any self-awareness – 'he has very little appreciation of the difficulties that are inherent in his position' - and interceded as best he could, telling the former monarch that 'he ought to remember the danger of excessive publicity resurrecting old feelings and criticisms'. This was ignored, as Edward believed it to be 'wholly unreasonable'. Yet the ambassador could put an upbeat spin on his encounter.

Informing Churchill that the duke spoke 'very nicely' of him - a *volte-face* from the anger expressed in their correspondence earlier that year - Halifax described Edward's domestic situation as a settled one. 'He said he was completely happy with the most wonderful wife in the world, and certainly looked very well himself - much less nervous and much less on edge.' The ambassador concluded that it would be 'cruelty to animals' to disallow future visits by the couple to America, but also told Churchill that his account of his conversation with the duke had been bowdlerised and softened in his official report to the king, warning, 'Don't show him this letter!'

Halifax also mused on American feeling, following the sinking of a United States destroyer by a German submarine. 'I should guess it will have some effect on all opinion except the hard core of isolationism, and may get things to move faster in several directions. But I should doubt whether it would alter the general policy in the sense of bringing them to anything like an open declaration of war.'[14] Roosevelt's refusal to further his country's belligerent aims frustrated both Halifax and Churchill, but it seemed as if matters were stagnant, more than two years into the conflict.

Although the duke may have believed that his visit to America had passed off without incident, save for a minor contretemps about his changing his travel plans to incorporate a proposed visit to the Chrysler motor plant in Detroit on 29 October,* newspaper

---

* Halifax wrote to Churchill to say how 'it is tiresome that he should have thus varied his programme and confront me with a situation of "fait half accompli"', especially given that he believed such a visit might be 'embarrassing'. The ambassador was treated considerably worse when he visited the city himself, being pelted with eggs and tomatoes by protesters who held up signs saying, 'Down with England'.

coverage was not wholly favourable. The Labour MP Alexander 'Sanny' Sloan therefore stood up in Parliament on 25 November and asked George Hall, the Under-Secretary of State for the Colonies, 'Is my honourable Friend aware of the bitter comment that is being made in United States newspapers and elsewhere regarding this visit, especially in regard to the ostentatious display of jewellery and finery, at a period when the people of this country are strictly rationed; and, if so, will he make representations to his right hon. friend the Prime Minister to have this gentleman and his wife recalled, since their visit is doing a certain amount of harm and certainly no good?'

Although Roundell Palmer, Minister for Economic Warfare, remonstrated, saying, 'Is the hon. gentleman aware that the press reports which have been referred to are by no means representative of the general welcome given in the United States to the Duke and Duchess?', Sloan, a former coal miner and stalwart of the miners' union, persisted. 'Is the hon. gentleman not aware that there are literally scores of thousands of these press cuttings, not filtering into the country but flooding the country? If his noble friend is not aware of this, then I am sure that he cannot be paying attention to the press cuttings.'[15]

The attack was reported comprehensively in the papers. An embarrassed Churchill telegraphed the duke to assure him that he regretted the incident and that Sloan had acted without any great support in the House of Commons. Noting that the press had largely ignored the incident after the initial report, his conclusion was to leave the matter alone. Yet it reminded Edward that his reputation in his home country remained uncertain. Returning to Britain seemed unlikely, even after the end of the war. And a conclusion to conflict appeared impossible. The king lamented on 24 November that 'It is very depressing and one feels so hopeless & helpless. Just one bit of good news to cheer one up would be very refreshing.'[16]

His wish would be granted, after a fashion, a fortnight later.

*

The events of Pearl Harbor barely need retelling. The Japanese surprise attack on the American naval base in the early hours of 7 December 1941 was a brutally efficient coordinated assault, killing and injuring thousands and resulting in the destruction of a significant number of battleships, aircraft and other military equipment. At the same time, the Japanese launched another assault on various British-held territories in Singapore, Hong Kong and Malaya, and sank two British battleships, the *Prince of Wales* and the *Repulse*. As a result of this, Britain declared war on Japan, fulfilling a pledge that Churchill had made to issue such a declaration 'within the hour' should the Japanese attack American soil. Owing to the time difference between the two countries, Britain's declaration was made before a furious Roosevelt could deliver his famous speech about 'a date which will live in infamy' and Congress issued its own declaration of war against the Axis powers.

At last America had joined the conflict. It was everything the king and Churchill had hoped for, although the circumstances of such an action were not what either had anticipated. When they met, the mood was sombre, not least because of the loss of the British ships. The king wrote in his diary on 9 December that '[Churchill] gave me the latest news from America which was dreadful . . . USA has already lost control of the sea in the Pacific. In Pearl Harbour 3 US battleships were sunk & 3 seriously damaged. There are now only 2 effective US ships in the Pacific. A very serious situation for our ships P of W & Repulse who are out there . . . fancy the US fleet being in harbour when the authorities must have known that Japan was already on a war footing'.[17]

He had told Churchill that 'I thought I was getting immune to bad news, but this has affected me deeply, as I am sure it has you . . . there is something particularly "alive" about the big ship, which gives one a sense of personal loss apart from consideration of loss of power'.[18] He wrote a formal note of commiseration to Roosevelt, in which he offered the president his thoughts and prayers at this 'solemn moment', concluding, 'We are proud indeed to be fighting at your side against the common enemy.'

Churchill, however, saw matters differently. As a former First Lord of the Admiralty and naval man, he was personally shocked by what had happened, but as prime minister, he felt a sense of deliverance. After the hopelessness of a few months before, aid had now appeared. It was with this in mind that he replied to the king on 12 December. Acknowledging that 'I realised how deeply Your Majesty would feel about the loss of your two splendid ships', he was not blind to the military disaster that the Japanese attack had engendered. 'Quite apart from personal sorrow it is a very heavy blow, and our combinations formed in the Far East with so much difficulty from limited resources are disrupted.' Yet he also saw the upside of the events. He concluded, 'Taking it altogether, I am enormously relieved at the extraordinary changes of the last few days.'[19]

Churchill knew that he risked accusations of opportunism, and the letter was not included in his official history of the events of the war. But faced with the unstoppable rise of what the king described as 'the most fearful, organised army which has ever been seen or heard of in the world', it was a blessing to know that Britain no longer stood alone. Only a madman would have wished for the not-so-splendid isolation to continue.

The queen was more caustic, remarking of the Americans to Queen Mary that 'they have persistently closed their eyes to such evident danger . . . they are a very young and untried nation'.[20] And Halifax mused that 'the Japanese have certainly hit both the Americans and ourselves very hard . . . it makes the position in the Pacific pretty uncomfortable', but after noting that the United States was unified, 'a bit hysterical' and furious at the attack, he allowed himself a touch of *Schadenfreude*. 'They will be a good deal more ready than they have been hitherto to learn from us.'[21]

That Christmas, both Churchill and the king addressed the Allied nations. The prime minister's speech was delivered from the White House, where he had gone to visit Roosevelt shortly after the Pearl Harbor attack. He announced, 'I spend this anniversary and festival far from my country, far from my family, yet I cannot truthfully say that I feel far from home.' Stressing his American heritage on his mother's side, to say nothing of the two countries being united by the same language and religion, he continued, 'I cannot feel myself a stranger here in the centre and at the summit of the United States. I feel a sense of unity and fraternal association which, added to the kindliness of your welcome, convinces me that I have a right to sit at your fireside and share your Christmas joys.' He spoke on 'a strange Christmas Eve', with 'almost the whole world . . . locked in deadly struggle, and, with the most terrible weapons which science can devise, the nations advance upon each other'. Yet he looked forward to the 'stern task and the formidable years that lie before us' with greater equanimity than he had before, bolstered by the presence of his ally by his side.

The king's address to the British mingled optimism and caution. He did not possess Churchill's rhetorical flair,* but his quiet determination was equally effective. He spoke of those fighting, but also those who had suffered - 'the wounded, the bereaved, the anxious, the prisoners of war' - and used the language of prayer to emphasise the enormity of what his nation faced. 'All these separations are part of the hard sacrifice which this war demands. It may well be that it will call for even greater sacrifices. If this is to be, let us face them cheerfully together. I think of you, my peoples, as one great family, for it is how we are learning to live. We all belong to each other. We all need each other. It is in serving each other and in sacrificing for our common good that we are finding our true life. In that spirit we shall win the war, and in that same spirit we shall win for the world after the war a true and lasting peace. The greatness of any nation is in the spirit of its people. So it has always been since history began; so it shall be with us.'

He acknowledged that they were in 'a stern and solemn time', but suggested that recent events might lead to something that could have been considered impossible: the victorious conclusion of the

---

* Halifax remarked to his sister on 31 December of his former rival, 'How I envy [Winston] his facility and power of phrase-coining.'

war. In his peroration, he bade his subjects 'Be strong and of a good courage', and exhorted them, again with Biblical language, to 'Go forward into this coming year with a good heart. Lift up your hearts with thankfulness for deliverance from dangers in the past. Lift up your hearts in confident hope that strength will be given us to overcome whatever perils may lie ahead until the victory is won. If the skies before us are still dark and threatening, there are stars to guide us on our way.'

He concluded, 'Never did heroism shine more brightly than it does now, nor fortitude, nor sacrifice, nor sympathy, nor neighbourly kindness, and with them - brightest of all stars - is our faith in God. These stars will we follow with His help until the light shall shine and the darkness shall collapse.'

He could only pray that he was right.

King George VI during a fake 'D-Day' visit, 1944. World War II transformed the public reputation of the monarch, from an uncertain and even hapless figure into a decisive, popular king who took an active role in military and political operations.

The Duke and Duchess of Windsor in the Bahamas, 1942. Exiled and ostracised by his country and family alike, the former Edward VIII was compelled to become Governor-General of the Bahamas because his presence in Europe was seen as a political risk.

Neville Chamberlain, 1938. The Prime Minister at the beginning of the war was a strong supporter of appeasement, and was later much criticised for meeting Hitler and agreeing to his terms in a vain attempt to avoid conflict.

Adolf Hitler, 1940. The Führer of Germany was known to have a warm personal relationship with the Duke of Windsor, much to the horror of the Duke's family and public opinion alike.

Sir Walter Monckton, 1945. The lawyer who masterminded the practicalities of Edward VIII's abdication continued to be a friend and counsellor both to the former king and to George VI throughout World War II.

Sir Alan Lascelles, 1940. George VI's assistant private secretary (subsequently private secretary) had a tempestuous relationship with his colleague Sir Alec Hardinge, and kept candid diaries of his time serving the king.

Lord Halifax, 1944. The pro-appeasement Foreign Secretary eventually became Ambassador to the United States, where he found dealing with the Duke of Windsor an increasingly tiresome business.

Franklin D Roosevelt, 1944. The President of the United States was a staunch supporter of Britain during the war, even if his desire to please his own countrymen over the United Kingdom infuriated both Churchill and the king.

Rudolf Hess, 1939. The unexpected arrival of Hitler's deputy in Scotland in 1941, ostensibly on a freelance mission to seek peace terms, remains one of the most shadowy incidents of the war, not least because many pro-appeasement figures were involved.

Clement Attlee, 1941. The leader of the Labour Party worked harmoniously with Churchill in the wartime coalition government as Deputy Prime Minister, before winning a landslide majority at the 1945 election.

Walter Schellenberg. The German mastermind behind a 1940 plot either to compel the Duke and Duchess of Windsor to turn traitors or to kidnap them was unsuccessful in his attempts, but his actions did alert British intelligence to the Duke's pro-fascist leanings.

British War Cabinet, 1941. After Chamberlain was forced to resign and Churchill took over as Prime Minister, he assembled a wartime cabinet of the most able men in the country, which included Lord Beaverbrook, the press magnate, and Attlee.

Walter Scott, Duke of Buccleuch. The holder of the post of Lord Steward was forced to resign his position once it became clear that he held pro-Hitler and pro-Nazi views that he explained at length in an incendiary letter to George VI.

Douglas Douglas-Hamilton, Duke of Hamilton, 1942. The subsequent Lord Steward was also embroiled in similar controversy, which led the exasperated king to complain 'Perhaps the post of Lord Steward is bewitched or is it Germanised?'

Charles and Fern Bedaux, 1942. The fabulously wealthy industrialist who hosted the Duke and Duchess's wedding at his home in 1937 was also a Nazi collaborator who eventually committed suicide before he could stand trial.

Axel Wenner-Gren. The Swedish entrepreneur was one of the Duke's few friends on the Bahamas, but his perceived fascist sympathies meant that he was placed on an economic blacklist by the United States.

The Duke and Duchess of Windsor's wedding, 1937. The sparsely attended ceremony led Monckton to say 'it was a strange wedding for one who had been six months before King of England and Emperor of India and Dominions Beyond the Seas.'

Princess Elizabeth and Princess Margaret, 1941. The young princesses were confined to Windsor Castle for the duration of the war, but Princess Elizabeth briefly served in the Auxiliary Territorial Service in 1945.

King George VI & Queen Elizabeth, 1940. A well-planned and daringly executed attack on Buckingham Palace on 13 September 1940 nearly resulted in the deaths of both the king and queen, leading to suspicions that it was accomplished with insider information.

The Royal Family and Winston Churchill on VE Day, 8 May 1945. The triumphant conclusion to the war in Europe, which saw the Royal Family and Prime Minister repeatedly take to the balcony of Buckingham Palace, did not obscure the grave national problems that Britain now faced, which would, in part, result in Churchill's ejection at the next General Election.

Chapter Thirteen

'If We Can't Bloody Well Fight, We'd Better Pray'

The traditional view of Churchill during World War II is of a patriotic, energetic man who combined tactical acumen with the ability to make rousing and poetic speeches that inspired his people. Even allowing for exaggeration and distortion by propaganda, there is much truth in this perception of the man regularly voted the greatest Briton who ever lived.

However, at the start of 1942, the situation was the most difficult it had been since he became prime minister in May 1940. He had suffered a mild heart attack while in the US after addressing Congress, and ignored the advice of his doctor to take several weeks' rest. Instead he returned to Britain to face discontent from both politicians and the press. He dealt with the former with typical defiance, but the latter proved harder to conquer, even though as a former war correspondent himself, he knew the importance of presenting a clear and simple story in an accessible fashion. He may have informed the king that he was confident of ultimate victory now that the USA had entered on their side - in his words, the UK and USA were now 'married' after a long period of 'walking out'[1] - but after months of unconditional support, the newspapers had wearied of praise, and as the war entered its third year, deference gave way to anger.

'It is a fact that we can lose the war. It is a fact that today we are losing it.' So the *Daily Mirror* stated on 16 February. In its editorial, it railed against 'over-confident, old-fashioned minds [muddling on]', and announced, 'it is the Government that needs warning'.* The *Daily Mail* was even more trenchant. It attacked Churchill personally, contrasting the prime minister who inspired and led the nation through Dunkirk and other European disasters with the figure who stood before them now. It even asked, with angry whimsy, whether there were in fact two Churchills, and stated that 'with the second Mr Churchill, the nation is perplexed'.

The reason for the discontent expressed by the newspapers was the fall of Singapore on 15 February, when 85,000 British soldiers surrendered to a smaller Japanese force. It was a humiliating sequel to the events of Pearl Harbor; Churchill himself described it as 'the greatest military disaster in recent history'. The king wrote in his diary, upon hearing the news, that he was 'very depressed about everything . . . perhaps our way of living has been too comfortable of late years, there was no thought of war in it anyhow',[2] and elaborated on this in a letter to his mother. 'I am very depressed about the loss of Singapore and the fact that we were not able to prevent the 5 German ships from getting through the Channel†.' He concluded that 'We are going through a bad phase at the moment, and it will take all our energies to stop adverse comment and criticism from the Press and others.'[3]

If there were any further doubts on the king's part that his prime minister was the appropriate man for the job, they were dispelled by Hardinge. Although the private secretary had had his differences with Churchill around the time of the abdication, when they had found themselves on opposite sides, Hardinge was able to reassure his monarch that he had spoken with Eden and others, and that

---

* The king wrote in his diary on 18 March that 'The Press is being warned not to put articles into their papers conducive to undermining the morale of the Army & the people, & so helping the enemy', and singled out the *Daily Mirror* as the worst offender.
† The so-called 'Channel Dash' was a German attempt to move their warships from Brest to Germany; they succeeded and British attempts to stop them were lambasted as a failure.

their unanimous verdict was 'Winston is the right, and indeed the only, person to lead the country through the war.'[4]

He suggested, however, that combining the offices of prime minister and minister of defence was too onerous for one man, and the king broached this with Churchill at lunch on 17 February. His premier responded bullishly. He was embarrassed by the attack he faced from the hitherto loyal press, and the king wrote in his diary that '[Winston] is very angry about all this, & compares it to hunting the tiger with angry wasps about him.' He reported Churchill saying, 'I do wish that people would get on with the job & not criticise all the time', but told the prime minister that he would have to watch his health.[5]

Yet both men knew that even in times of war, the purpose of the press was to sell newspapers. Without good news to report, they would turn on the prime minister as the most prominent scapegoat. The queen complained to Helen Hardinge that 'perhaps we ought to clean up our journalists before we start on our task of reforming the world ... they judge everyone by their own very low standard, and make it difficult for the ordinary man or woman to quite trust them as prophets or leaders of thought', and half jokingly suggested that 'I long to start scholarships for those intending to become journalists, and perhaps we might raise the standard a little, if the owners (who are to blame) would agree',[6] but the press could not simply be ignored.

It was no coincidence that Churchill agreed to reshuffle his government, ceding his leadership of the House of Commons to Anthony Eden and bringing the Labour politician Stafford Cripps into his War Cabinet. A further nod to the opposition came in his appointment of the Labour leader Clement Attlee as deputy prime minister. Had Churchill's heart attack a couple of months before been more widely known about, Attlee may have expected to assume office sooner than he did.

The greater presence of Labour politicians in the Cabinet led to another change in personnel. Beaverbrook had served within the

War Cabinet since Churchill's appointment in May 1940, and his roles had included Minister of Aircraft Production, and Minister of Supply. In February 1942, he was appointed to the new role of Minister of War Production. The title sounded impressive, but he came up against the Labour politician Ernest Bevin, Minister of Labour and National Service, who mistrusted Beaverbrook and denied him the chance to have any autonomous influence on his department. The media magnate resigned in a fit of pique after a mere twelve days in his post.

The king, who had remained opposed to Beaverbrook, was sanguine about his departure. He wrote in his diary on 19 February, 'I am glad Winston has been prevailed upon to make [the changes] before and not after the debate [of confidence in the government]. The House of Commons wants Winston to lead them; but they don't like the way he treats them. He likes getting his own way with no interference from anybody and nobody will stand for that sort of treatment in this country. Everybody wants to help him with his job, & they understand his responsibilities in leading them in this total war.'[7] He was more explicit to Halifax, referring to the 'worrying time' that he had faced due to the criticism of Churchill in the papers. He complained, 'if only the press would play fair and give them a chance to get results'. The unspoken rejoinder was that Churchill had had nearly two years in power. Although he had proved himself a master of rhetoric, what the country now needed was military success.

Even the prime minister felt uncertain as to what would now happen. Atypically, the king reported him as being 'gloomy about the future, as he cannot see how we can reinforce any part of the world sufficiently', and asked 'can we stick together in the face of all this adversity? We must somehow.'[8] Churchill was not in good health, and even as the monarch counselled rest for his premier, he once again professed himself disheartened by the situation. 'Anything can happen, & it will be wonderful if we can be lucky anywhere.'[9] There was even the previously unthinkable suggestion that with France under Pétain, Britain would find itself at war with its neighbour for the first time since 1815.

The Americans had joined the war, as desired, but it would take some time for their physical presence to be felt, and even longer for it to make any real difference. As Churchill unsuccessfully urged military commanders in South East Asia to fight to the last man and to refuse to surrender, citing the bravery of the Soviets who were battling Hitler, he seemed a diminished presence. Chips Channon, admittedly no partisan, described him in his diary on 25 February as speaking with a scowl, and concluded that '[Winston] has lost the house.'[10]

Channon was not the only one who pronounced him doomed. Appeasement had been becalmed since 1940, but whispers that a negotiated peace with Germany might still be the best option could be heard again in members' clubs and Mayfair houses. If the talk did not move beyond whispers, that was only because, with Chamberlain dead and Halifax in America, there was no champion for such a path in the War Cabinet. But the status quo seemed untenable too. As Cosmo Lang prepared to retire as Archbishop of Canterbury, he suggested that 29 March - Palm Sunday - should be designated a national day of prayer. The king liked the idea, but Churchill was unimpressed. He snorted, 'If we can't bloody well fight, we'd better pray.'[11]

There were some minor things that could be done for public relations purposes. Princess Elizabeth was appointed colonel of the Grenadier Guards on her sixteenth birthday on 21 April, and she took the role characteristically seriously, conducting an inspection of the regiment at Windsor Castle that day: it was her first official public engagement. She conducted herself with confidence, perhaps too much so; one officer remarked to Crawfie, after the princess made some criticisms of the Grenadiers in slightly too loud a voice, that 'the first requisite of a really good officer is to be able to temper justice with mercy'.[12]

Churchill, meanwhile, suggested to the king in January that he should visit Northern Ireland to meet the American troops who were arriving there, with a view to distributing films of the occasion via newsreels, which he believed would be useful for both American and European propaganda purposes. And the Duke of Gloucester, who had recently become a father for the first time, was dispatched in April on a long military tour of places in Africa, India and the Middle East. The aim was to remind the Commonwealth and its troops that they had not been forgotten by the royal family, nor by the country itself. As the duke, whom his eldest brother had caustically nicknamed 'the Unknown Soldier', put it in unassuming fashion, 'It might do more good than harm.'[13] Once on his travels, he was kept away from the dangers of the German advance, and instead spent much of his time drinking whisky in official residences and offering deathless insights. He reported to a no doubt astonished king that 'the desert is a very healthy place, except during an actual battle'.[14]

Yet it said much for the febrile atmosphere that while Gloucester was gazing at the sands, one Conservative MP, Sir John Wardlaw-Milne, attempted to force Churchill's dismissal via a vote of no confidence. The prime minister had been a less confident performer in the Commons in the early months of 1942, leading Channon to describe him as 'uneasy, halting, almost inarticulate'[15] on 12 April. As the so-called Baedeker raids wreaked havoc on Britain's historic cities, including Norwich, Exeter and Bath, the prime minister's reputation showed few signs of recovery.

Hardinge had suggested to Monckton in March that 'we have had a thoroughly dreary time here lately. One set-back after another gave the disgruntled in Parliament and the press . . . the chance of excessive criticism . . . the result of such an abuse of our freedom of the press has been a temporary loss of confidence among the people in the competence of their leaders'. He hinted at an authoritarian attitude when he complained that 'a large section of the press seems unable to see that their "freedom", if carried to excess, ceases to be a healthy symbol of democracy and becomes a deadly boomerang by creating doubts and thereby undermining morale', before hoping that 'this unpleasant phase is now passing'.*[16]

Despite Hardinge and the queen being united against a free press, the papers were nevertheless fulfilling their democratic function by allowing dissatisfaction with politicians to be voiced. Had the complaints gathered momentum, they might have caused damage to the government and to Churchill himself. Yet Wardlaw-Milne had pitched his tent in the wrong camp. He announced that in order to restore public faith in the conduct of the war, it was time for a new commander-in-chief of the British forces. His nominee was none other than the Duke of Gloucester.

The suggestion was risible. Channon wrote of the 'disrespectful laughter' that the proposal engendered, and noted, 'I at once saw Winston's face light up, as if a lamp had been lit within him, and he smiled genially. He knew now that he had been saved.'[17] Only a matter of a few days before, Churchill's friend and confidant Bob Boothby had had a tense meeting with him. Boothby later commented that 'It was the only time in the whole of the war that I saw [Churchill] looking really anxious, because the only thing in the world he feared was Parliament.' Now his fears were extinguished.

If Wardlaw-Milne had been a stooge, his suggestion, delivered without the knowledge or approval of Gloucester,† could not have served Churchill better. The proposal was defeated by 475 votes to 25, and the prime minister's reputation, at its lowest point in his premiership, was saved. Churchill's own assessment of the

---

* Hardinge's poor temper could partially be explained by his son George being temporarily lost at sea, which led to 'two or three anxious and worrying days'. Hardinge was pleased that the destroyer that collected him was the *Kipling*, given its associations with a man who was then regarded as one of the great Englishmen. The queen wrote sympathetically to Helen that 'waiting is such anguish, and tho' I know how brave you are, the strain must have been almost unbearable'.

† He was displeased when he discovered his mooted involvement, complaining to his wife, 'What impertinence on the part of Wardlaw-Milne, without asking anybody and me in particular.'

scheme was that 'the combination of a Supreme War Commander with almost unlimited powers and his association with a Royal Duke seemed to have some flavour of dictatorship about it'.[18] It also returned the press to his side. The *New Statesman* described Wardlaw-Milne's scheme as 'fantastic and preposterous', and noted that nobody 'at this grave crisis in our history [could think that] the appointment as Commander-in-Chief of a Royal Duke is a suitable remedy'.[19] The implication was clear. Churchill had been warned, but without any better candidate for prime minister, he would not face another challenge. There would be no further vote of no confidence in him for the remainder of the war. By 28 April, the king was able to report with relief that 'Winston was happier about things in general', as he noted, 'German civilian morale is not too good.'[20]

It was a rare moment of relief. Throughout the spring and early summer of 1942, Churchill and Roosevelt were engaged in planning for the foundation of an American-backed second front in Europe, hoping to relieve some of the pressure from the Soviets. Churchill had quipped to Colville that 'if Hitler invaded hell I would make at least a favourable reference to the devil in the House of Commons', but now he was obliged to bring Stalin and Roosevelt into operations, if not in person: the two men were hardly natural allies. And the king was kept involved too. He shook off any resentment he had felt towards the president to tell him on 11 March, 'Though it will take time & great effort on all our parts to prepare, the final issue i.e. victory is without any doubt to be with us.'[21]

In April, the king was reunited with Hopkins, who continued to serve as Roosevelt's representative on earth, or at least in Britain. At one lunch with Churchill, Hopkins and Sir Alan Brooke, the prime minister's military adviser and chief of the Imperial General Staff, there was a discussion of German strategy. Brooke suggested that Hitler was likely to attack Cyprus and Syria and concentrate his efforts against the eastern Mediterranean, meaning that for the first time since the war began, the theatre of conflict would shift away from Europe and towards Africa. This meant that an Anglo-American invasion of Europe, which Stalin was pressing for, would not happen in 1942 or 1943. Instead, by July, the Allied powers had decided that North Africa would become the scene for Operation Torch, which would take place that autumn.

Churchill, recognising that Stalin would be angered by this development, decided to head to Moscow himself to discuss military matters. Before his departure, the king wrote to him with his usual warmth, as a comrade-in-arms. Saluting his 'epoch-making' mission, he said, 'I shall follow your journey with the greatest interest & shall be more than delighted when you are safely home again. As I have told you before, your welfare means a great deal not only to the United Nations, but to me personally.' He signed himself 'your very sincere and grateful friend', prompting Churchill to write to him by hand to thank him: 'Always sir you are [very] good to me . . . I trust indeed and pray that this journey of mine will be fruitful.'*22

The monarch had written to Monckton earlier in the year to discuss the departure of the Egyptian King Farouk, which the lawyer had assisted in facilitating. The king speculated, 'I don't suppose it has ever fallen to the lot of one man to have had to prepare two instruments of abdication in his life time.' As he acknowledged that 'your job of propaganda must be getting harder and harder to put into overseeing the position we have got into in the Far East', he declared, 'we cannot be fighting battles everywhere at once'. He affirmed his solidarity with the prime minister ('Winston has had a bad time with all the misplaced criticism he has had to put up with . . . he has the country solidly behind him') and acknowledged his

---

* The talks went well, and a relieved king was able to write to Churchill on 17 August that 'your task was a very disagreeable one, but I congratulate you heartily on the skill with which you accomplished it . . . the personal relationship which you have established with Stalin should be valuable in the days to come'. Churchill described Stalin to the monarch as 'a cold, uncouth man, but with an understanding mind . . . he knows nothing of the rest of the world'.

own fears. 'I have been very worried over this & other events of late, but one has to steel oneself against getting depressed.' There was also a lighter moment for both men. The king told Monckton that 'I gave the Queen your "love and duty", at which she was both surprised and pleased. I wonder if you did not mean "loyal duty"! Anyhow it made us laugh.'[23] The relief was much needed.

Meanwhile, the king's assistant private secretary, Tommy Lascelles, decided to resume writing a diary. It began on 2 June, as he sat in Buckingham Palace listening to the construction of a new air raid shelter and looking at the cellophane that had replaced the glass blown out of the windows in the previous year's attacks. Despite the less than tranquil surroundings, he felt philosophical. 'Today is the first [day] this year that can be compared to a summer's day – it is indeed a perfect one; coming as it does with a spell of good news,* it makes one wonder if the almost unalleviated sombreness and anxiety of the past two and a half years may not be beginning to lift.'

There were few rational grounds for Lascelles' optimism. Hitler was still dominant throughout Europe, Churchill was beleaguered and large parts of Britain had been reduced to rubble. The notable military engagements of the past two years had been defeats, and now that America had finally entered the war, there were no further *dei ex machina* that might lead to victory. In late October, the king summarised the events of the past three years in downbeat fashion. 'Much has happened since I started this volume 8 months ago . . . most of its contents are very depressing reading as very few of our military expeditions were successful . . . I hope that the next volume will contain some more exhilarating news of a success or two.'[24]

Thankfully, it would. Lascelles epitomised the spirit many felt. The country had been bombed, brutalised and battered. But

---

* He was alluding to the success of two bombing raids on Essen and Cologne, coordinated by Arthur 'Bomber' Harris. He wrote in the same entry, 'Fourteen months ago . . . as we listened to that sinister drone of the wings of the Angel of Death over England, we said "Here they come." Now it is "There they go."'

it had not been beaten. The glass had been blown away, and the usual trappings and formality of Buckingham Palace replaced by the noisy banging of workmen. Yet still it stood, the symbolic representation of Britain, undaunted by everything that had battered it over the previous thirty-three months.

Had Lascelles known that in a further thirty-three months the war would be all but over, he might have allowed himself triumphalism, assuming that he did not have to ask 'Which side won?'

Thousands of miles away, a similar question occupied the thoughts of the Duke and Duchess of Windsor. While Wallis was relieved that America had finally entered the war, writing to her aunt Bessie to say, '[it] is better than being on the outside . . . just think what a real fight it is going to be after the peace',[25] the duke moaned to Allen that 'with Japan's unparalleled treachery and the entry of the United States into the war, the Bahamas winter tourist season dies a natural death'.[26] Although he acknowledged that 'these are only local hardships and easy to bear as compared to the lot of most other countries', it demonstrated the regal detachment with which he viewed a conflict that he believed his country should never have entered into.

He occupied himself with local matters, which he executed with a mixture of weariness and occasional interest. Yet America's entry into the war had an unwelcome side effect, and that was the renewed scrutiny that Axel Wenner-Gren would now be placed under.

FBI surveillance of Wenner-Gren had continued, but although there were fears that he had visited Peru the previous summer with a view to investing his millions in South American projects, potentially backed by German money, there was no hard evidence against him. He was seen as dubious, but while America remained ostensibly neutral, he could hardly be described as an enemy alien. Edward had even attempted to intercede to support his proposed purchase of a large section of the Bahamas. This led Halifax to comment on the 'awkward repercussions' of the duke's involvement, given that MI5 and the Admiralty believed that Wenner-Gren possessed 'doubtful political proclivities'. The Foreign Office responded that the matter was 'of some delicacy' because of Edward and Wenner-Gren's friendship, and noted that 'the Duke is well aware that Wenner-Gren is regarded with some suspicion both here and in the United States of America but he does not himself share those suspicions'.[27] Washington, meanwhile, described the idea as 'thoroughly undesirable', not least because Wenner-Gren continued to make remarks suggesting that the war was a tragedy and that he could intercede and bring peace to the world. The press caustically referred to him as 'Göring's pal'.

Matters changed after Pearl Harbor. On 14 January 1942, Wenner-Gren was placed on a 'Proclaimed List of Blocked Nationals' by the American State Department. This made suspicion against him official, and prevented him from entering America, being allowed to do any business with the country's citizens or being able to make use of his Electrolux assets there. The British government, under diplomatic pressure from their allies, issued a similar edict. Wenner-Gren was now castigated as a Nazi sympathiser and a collaborator, and his reputation was destroyed. It was rumoured that Roosevelt had been personally responsible for placing him on the blacklist.

This left the duke in a quandary. He was loyal to his friends, and Wenner-Gren had been one of the few people in the Bahamas with whom he was able to consort on equal terms. It helped that Wenner-Gren's financial expertise had been available to prop up his governorship. But Edward was now deprived of both friend and cash. Given persistent rumours in America of his own ambiguous sympathies,* he was unable to offer the support to Wenner-Gren that he may have wished. The closest he could do was to issue a

---

* Commander C. A. Perkins of US Naval Special Intelligence reported the 'utterly fantastic' news on 11 February 1942 that his officials had heard that the duke 'may be one of the most important Nazi agents based in the Western Hemisphere'.

statement in his role as governor denying the suggestion that the industrialist's home at Hog Island was a clandestine hotbed of fascism. It stated, 'As a result of continuous rumours to the effect that there are various forms of secret facilities available to the enemy on the Wenner-Gren estate on Hog Island . . . a most thorough search . . . has failed to reveal the existence of anything of a suspicious nature.'[28]

But as he had discovered during the abdication crisis, 'nor can weak truth your reputation save'. As Wallis wrote to her aunt to complain about how the saga was giving the duke 'no end of trouble with all [Wenner-Gren's] enterprises closing down' and the proliferation of 'wild stories' about his activities, the couple were concerned about being linked to the scandal. Wallis observed that 'the real news value of *l'affaire* Wenner-Gren was that he was "Windsor's pal" etc. and one article went so far as to say that he was chiefly known in the world not as one of the great international financiers but as the friend of the Duke and Duchess of Windsor'.[29] The threat was clear: if they did not drop Wenner-Gren as both friend and business associate and end contact with him, their own standing would be damaged. It might even be that questions would be asked once again about their activities in Lisbon, and the taint of collaboration - or worse - with the enemy placed upon them.

It is to Edward's personal credit that he did not wish to break off association with Wenner-Gren, whom he believed had been convicted in the court of public opinion without any evidence. He may have felt that it reflected his own fate. Yet he also had to consider his and Wallis's future. They had enjoyed their trip to America in late 1941, and hoped to visit the country again later that year. Should they be associated with a disgraced and pro-German figure, they would be added to the list of blocked nationals. This would both jeopardise their chances of being able to leave the Bahamas and have far-reaching consequences for what would become of them after the war. Therefore, despite the duke writing to Wenner-Gren to assure him that he believed in his innocence, he and Wallis considered themselves warned off. They never saw him again, and Wenner-Gren died in 1962, his loyalties still ambiguous.

Thus shriven from bad influence, Edward set about making Nassau and his headquarters at Government House safe from U-boat attacks, as he and Wallis looked on scornfully at the recent influx of Americans to the island. Their opinions could be discerned by a letter Wallis wrote to her aunt on 30 March, in which she called the Americans 'awful people . . . it is as though you associated with the shop-owners of Washington', and moaned, 'I really do wish we could move somewhere inhabited at least by our own class.'[30]

A more respectable figure was John Dauglish, Bishop of Nassau, who was leaving the island to return to England. The duchess bore such affection for him that she offered to write a letter of introduction on his behalf to her mother-in-law. Despite the animosity that Wallis and Queen Mary bore one another - they had never spoken directly and had only met twice, briefly, during the reign of George V - Wallis wrote to her that 'it has always been a source of sorrow and regret to me that I have been the cause of any separation that exists between mother and son and I can't help feel that there must be moments, however fleeting they may be, when you wonder how David is'. After praising Dauglish as 'a delightful man' and suggesting him as a means of first-hand news of her eldest son, she noted that 'the horrors of war and the endless separation of families have in my mind stressed the importance of family ties'. The letter was successful in its aim for Dauglish to be received, but Wallis later wrote that 'when the Bishop mentioned [to Queen Mary] what I was doing with, I judge, some show of appreciation and approval, there was no response. He was met with a stone wall of disinterest.'*[31]

With Wenner-Gren ostracised, the duke and duchess cast

---

* Queen Mary wrote the grand comment that 'I send a kind message to your wife' in a subsequent letter to her son, who was initially thrilled at this apparent acceptance, only to realise what had caused such a gesture.

around for another ally. A meeting with Edward's old supporter Beaverbrook, holidaying in Nassau after his departure from the Cabinet, provided succour. The duke asked the publisher-turned-politician for support, saying, 'a timely word from you may eventually result in the employment of my services in a more useful sphere than my present one'.[32] Yet Beaverbrook was a pragmatist. He had been happy to help Edward when he was king but now saw little benefit to himself in such aid. He promised that he would do all he could, and then did nothing. The governor and his wife remained friendless and alone.

Another American journey offered relief, even if its purpose – for the duke to discuss how the United States and the Bahamas might cooperate on defence – led Wallis to complain to her aunt, 'is it worthwhile for me to attempt the trip? I get so little pleasure with the endless publicity and being gazed at everywhere.' Yet Edward would not let his wife remain at home without him. They left together on 28 May, although Halifax remained unconvinced about the wisdom of the journey. He had sent a telegram to the Foreign Office the previous month stating that while Roosevelt had no objection to the couple's presence, 'for my part I shall regret the [Duke of Windsor's] visit. We are in a wave of anti-British sentiment which shows some signs of receding, but there are plenty of elements that will only too readily seize on anything to whip it up again.' He concluded that 'if the visit is inevitable, [I hope] it may be as unostentatious and limited as possible'.[33] He was more candid to his sister. 'We are at the moment rather feeling the oppression of several imminent visits that will be exacting of time and effort . . . the Duke threatens to stay longer, and I am sure will waste an incredible amount of my time . . . I don't think it is at all a good plan them coming here.'[34]

Meanwhile, a proposed visit to South America was vetoed by Eden, who told Churchill, '[a visit] would certainly arouse suspicions in Washington . . . any prominent visitor to Latin America must be able to speak with authority and first-hand knowledge of what we are doing here in the way of winning the war . . . the

Duke of Windsor could not do this'.[35] It was a recurrent theme amongst official communications at this time that Edward's suggested journeys should if possible be curtailed. Another telegram from the British High Commissioner in South Africa, sounded out about the possibility of him taking an ambassadorial post in the country, stated, 'I cannot but feel that [the duke's] presence in official capacity anywhere in Southern Africa might have the most awkward consequences on public opinion both Afrikaans and British.'*[36]

The king was fully aware of the difficulties his brother presented. He wrote that 'D has written to W asking to leave the Bahamas in August where he has been for 2 years. Where can he go and what job can he do? He cannot come here anyhow, W and I are certain of this, the Dominions don't want him, there is nothing he can do in America, and he wants a temperate climate to live in. W suggests Southern Rhodesia, which is vacant. But would they like it, & [Jan] Smuts† has to be asked as well.' He concluded, with understandable exasperation, 'it is a very difficult problem'.[37]

Edward and Wallis therefore arrived in the United States with the taint of the shop-soiled about them. This arose both from association with Wenner-Gren and from the sense that their visit, important though its intentions were, was taking place at the wrong time. It was compounded by Halifax stating that he was too busy to receive them in Washington, leaving hosting duties to his wife instead. There was an unflattering article about the duchess in one of the papers, which the ambassador called 'pretty unpleasant, but not quite as bad as she thought', but which indicated the opprobrium that both were held in by certain sectors.

Halifax expressed his personal disdain for the duke and his plans to his sister. 'If only such articles would make them realise that people are not all clamouring to see and cheer them, much

---

* Churchill had been keener on the idea, and had in fact discussed it with the king, who did not rule it out initially – 'Much preparation for it is needed if feasible.'

† Smuts was the prime minister of South Africa during the war.

good will have been done.' He remained sceptical about what Edward's further use might be. 'I simply cannot see that young man's future. He can't live for ever in the Bahamas and I don't quite know where else he can live. I have very little doubt that he sees himself as permanent Ambassador in Washington one of these days, but I don't think that would be a terribly good plan!'[38]

Before anything of any diplomatic worth could be achieved, the duke had to return urgently to Nassau, as a riot had broken out there due to dissatisfaction with wages being paid for local work. He was occupied for the next ten days attempting to ameliorate the situation: the longest time he had been apart from Wallis since their marriage. The British government offered little help, but politicians were appalled by a broadcast he made in which he promised the rioters redress for their grievances in the form of a shilling's rise in their wages.

The remainder of the trip was more satisfactory. The duke had an audience with the president, whom he praised as 'the soul of affability' and who spoke candidly to his guest. Decades later, Edward wrote that 'I haven't a clue as to what he really wanted from me . . . I rather suspect [I was there] because he, a man who had achieved on his own the summit of political power within a man's reach, was curious about the motives and reasoning of a man who could give up an inherited position of comparative renown.'[39] And after the duke had fulfilled various requirements of waving and smiling and being photographed, Halifax wrote in his diary, 'I thought that he was in better temper than when he was here last, no doubt due to having been soothed after a week's companionship with the Duchess.'[40]

Nonetheless, there were still moments of embarrassment. An objection was raised by a small group of women to the duchess visiting a United Services Organisation club, to which Wallis angrily responded, 'I don't care whether I see their old Club.' The businessman Walter Hoving* described the matter as 'most unfortunate'[41] to

---

* And subsequent head of Tiffany & Co.

Halifax, who in turn noted to Lord Cranborne, Secretary of State for the Colonies, that 'I had very little doubt that Mr Hoving found himself face to face with some anti-Duchess of Windsor feeling among the elite of Long Island, and thought that the easiest get-out for him was to shove it onto the "British".'

Despite the relative success of the visit, Halifax remained un-happy about the idea of similar embassies in the future. 'I thought you might like to see this minor storm in a teacup as, if I am right, it does furnish some evidence of what the Duke and Duchess are both reluctant to believe, namely that there is still a good deal of feeling against them in American quarters, and that therefore the less publicity they court, the better. I have no doubt that as long as they are in the Bahamas, we shall be subjected to these periodic invasions, but I don't suppose there is anything that you can do about it. He is getting pretty fed up with the Bahamas, as you no doubt know!'[42]

The duke and duchess reluctantly returned to Nassau at the beginning of July. They were accompanied by their friends Herman and Katherine Rogers, who expected a relaxing holiday but who soon wilted in the extreme warmth and had to return home. Wallis told her aunt, 'I am afraid the heat put up Herman's temperature and rather dragged him down … I miss them a lot.'[43] Halifax's activities were regarded with suspicion - 'I hear [he] works continually against the Duke even to putting spokes in the wheels of things he tried to arrange for the Colony' - but Wallis dismissed her husband's tormentors as 'funny people' and expressed her hope that 'they better get on with the war and not be so small'.[44]

After the frustrations and difficulties of the past year, their lives in the Bahamas had settled into a rut. Although Churchill, who had seen them in Washington, described the duke as settling into his work and prepared to divide his time between his role and occasional visits to the United States in a private capacity, this was disingenuous. The governor's responsibilities were far from merely ceremonial, and being regarded with both suspicion and condescension made for difficult working relationships with Britain and America. The risk of the local inhabitants once again rising into violence was ever present, as was the possibility of Government House being targeted by a U-boat. And it was painfully hot. It must have seemed as if matters could not get any worse.

In wartime, they always could.

Chapter Fourteen

'False Rumour and Wild Surmise'

By 1942, the actor, playwright and composer Noël Coward was one of the most popular men in Britain. He had achieved fame in the twenties and thirties with comedies such as *The Vortex* and *Design for Living*, which dared to bring such topics as drug addiction and bisexuality to the stage, and then transferred his talents away from light entertainment towards war work. He had been informally recruited by MI5 in 1940 to act as a conduit between the entertainment industry and British intelligence, and was thrilled to turn his creative talents to low-level espionage. He informed Robert Vansittart on 21 August 1940 that 'I should be only too delighted to register as a government agent and I think it would do away with a lot of the false rumour and wild surmise.'[1]

'False rumour' and 'wild surmise' had dogged Coward throughout most of his life and career. Although he was openly gay in the circles in which he mixed, he never felt obliged to publicly proclaim his sexuality even after homosexuality was legalised in the sixties, quipping, 'There are still a few old ladies in Worthing who don't know.' Yet throughout the twenties and thirties, he was linked with many artistic and cultural figures, including one surprising man: Prince George, the Duke of Kent.

Kent was undoubtedly the most flamboyant member of the royal family. While Bertie and Gloucester were both happily married men,* and Edward's pre-Wallis sexual shenanigans did not conceal his personal inadequacies and peccadilloes,† the youngest of the brothers revelled in the opportunities that his wealth and status offered him. When he was a young naval lieutenant, he was introduced to myriad pleasures‡ by the American socialite Kiki Preston, the so-called 'girl with the silver syringe'. It has even been suggested that he was the father of her son, Michael Canfield, who was born in 1926, although Canfield's death in 1969 dispelled further dissemination of such rumours.

Like Laurence Olivier's character in the film *Spartacus*, Kent's sexual tastes ran to both 'snails and oysters'.§ His female lovers included Preston, the singer Jessie Matthews and the socialite Margaret Campbell, Duchess of Argyll,¶ while men with whom he enjoyed intimate relations included the writer Cecil Roberts, the art historian and future spy Anthony Blunt, and José Uriburu, the son of the Argentine ambassador. Most notoriously, he was said to have been involved with Coward.

Although the playwright's long-term companion Graham Payn cast doubt on the sexual elements of Coward's relationship with the duke, describing their nineteen-year friendship as nothing more than platonic, Coward himself reportedly referred to it to the historian Michael Thornton late in life as 'a little dalliance'. Others were less circumspect. One of the duke's other close friends, the drag artist Douglas Byng, commented that 'Noël and Prince George

---

* Although the Duke of Gloucester's romantic attachment to the aviator Beryl Markham in the late twenties, when she was married, led to considerable controversy.

† See *The Crown in Crisis*, Chapter One, for details. 'Sex meant an awful lot to Edward, but a rather specialised form of sex. He craved to be dominated' (Philip Ziegler).

‡ Cocaine, morphine, group sex . . . the list is long.

§ Channon wrote in his diary of how 'he had a secret of which he rarely talked and was ashamed . . . I was aware of it.'

¶ Who achieved notoriety when photographs of her fellating a 'headless man' were produced at her divorce case in 1963.

were a big item.' They reportedly disported themselves through Soho; an MI5 report grimly noted that they had been seen parading together through the streets of London, dressed and made up as women, and had once been arrested by the police for suspected prostitution. Only the involvement of the long-suffering Lord Stamfordham, private secretary to George V, resulted in this and other incriminating and embarrassing details* never becoming public knowledge.

But Kent was indiscriminate in who he bestowed his favours on. He slept with men, women, aristocrats, actors, comedians, singers and complete strangers, and did so in the knowledge that there would be some functionary or 'little man' who would materialise behind him and tidy up the debris he left in his wake. Like his eldest brother, he led a carefree life in the knowledge that his appetites would be paid for by other people. Despite his parents' distress at his actions, it was hoped that his years of 'sowing his regal oats' would come to an end and that he would assume a responsible position within the royal family.

This proved to be at least half accurate. After he conquered his drug addiction, thanks to the intervention of the Prince of Wales, Kent married the 'lovely, chic creature' Princess Marina in 1934. He became father to two sons and a daughter, and placed himself at the epicentre of a more intellectually elevated social circle than the rest of his family fraternised with. One biographer called him 'the most interesting, intelligent and cultivated member of his generation',[2] and said of him and Marina that 'that dazzling pair dominated London society, gathering around them some of the most brilliant personalities from the arts, entertaining lavishly and generating an interest in their way of life that was unparalleled in the history of the royal family'.[3] Just as the Duke of Windsor had brought glamour and excitement to the role

---

* It has been suggested that love letters between Coward and Kent were stolen by a would-be blackmailer and retrieved by the British diplomat Charles Mendl. When George V became aware of his son's proclivities, he reportedly gasped, 'I thought men like that shot themselves.'

of Prince of Wales in the twenties, so the Duke of Kent gave the impression to his familiars and favourites that he too was a different kind of royal, prizing pleasure and jollity over dull duty and responsibility.

Kent was also an avid aficionado of aviation. He acquired his pilot's licence in 1929 and became a group captain in the RAF by 1937. He was proposed for the role of governor general of Australia, but the outbreak of war led to this becoming impossible. Although he was initially, and perhaps appropriately, assigned the post of rear admiral in the Royal Navy in late 1939, his aeronautical expertise saw him return to the RAF in April 1940. By July 1941, he had moved into the senior non-combatant role of air commodore. He was popular in his dealings with his men as a result of his having moved freely and in wide circles when he was younger. As he remarked to a friend, 'What days we are living in and what changes.'[4]

He threw himself into his responsibilities with aplomb. His playboy years had seen him respond to drug-taking and sexual adventuring with similar abandon, but now he found a new and more respectable vocation in serving his country. He hosted pilots and their crews at his country house, Coppins, and enjoyed the camaraderie of other airmen, taking especial care to attend briefings with them before bombing raids to boost their morale, and often waiting at the airfield until they returned safely. By the time he conducted a tour of America in July 1941, there was a sense that the war had been a good thing for the wildest of the brothers. It was now assumed that he could take his place in whatever post-war settlement could be found, as a pillar of the community. Perhaps he could even bridge the gap between the bohemian artistic community of Cowards and Blunts and the more conservative royal and political establishment.

Unfortunately, it was not to be. Not only was there grumbling that Kent was soaking up a little too much of the limelight for comfort - Hardinge complained to the duke's private secretary, Jack Lowther, that the king was 'far from satisfied' that 'frequent visits are made to industrial centres, dockyards etc. which appear to have the most meagre connection with the RAF'[5] – but his willingness to go the extra mile in support of his country would rebound.* Kent returned triumphantly from the United States in September 1941, remarking, 'it's a gloomy thought to go back to the long blacked out bombing winter. Pray God it's our last.'[6] His words were more apt than he could have imagined. Less than a year later, he was dead.

Ironically, given the efforts that were made to keep the royal family away from the heat of conflict, the Duke of Kent became the first royal to lose his life in active service in nearly half a millennium, after James IV, King of Scotland, was killed at the Battle of Flodden in 1513. The circumstances under which he died have been called everything from a tragic but unforeseeable accident to a carefully orchestrated conspiracy by either German or British secret services. It is the former that is generally believed to be accurate, with the more fanciful rumours swirling around the latter thesis being derided as baseless and hysterical. To date, no firm evidence has emerged that supports any theory that the Duke of Kent was murdered.

Yet there exists a precedent that might make all but the most complacent examine the circumstances of his death afresh. In July 1936, George McMahon attempted to assassinate Edward VIII, but was restrained and arrested before he could do so. McMahon was belittled as a fantasist and attention-seeker who never had any serious intention of doing any harm to the king, and that became the accepted biographical truth for decades. However, with the release of documents from the MI5 archives and the explosive revelation of a hitherto unknown memoir by McMahon, 'He Was My King', from the Walter Monckton papers in Balliol College, Oxford, an unpalatable, even seditious truth began to emerge. MI5 had either

---

* This antipathy went both ways. In January 1942, Kent remarked angrily to Channon that the king and queen were 'inept, ineffectual and inexpert and had no influence in Whitehall, Westminster or anywhere'.

deliberately ignored or, at worst, been actively complicit in the attempted murder of the king.*

If Edward VIII could have been a target for the security services on the grounds that his extramarital affair with Wallis Simpson was seen as a national humiliation and his friendships with Nazis such as von Ribbentrop were potentially compromising to the country's security, then the Duke of Kent epitomised these risks tenfold. Although by 1942 Kent was ostensibly a happily married and patriotic man, taking centre stage in the newsreels and media accounts of the country's air war, there remained two dangers. Firstly, some of the people he had consorted with in former years could not be relied upon to keep quiet about these dangerous liaisons, and their stories were more damaging while he remained alive. Secondly, it was rumoured that he shared something with his eldest brother that was damaging to his country: a sympathy for the nation they were fighting.

Kent's attitude towards Edward was a conflicted one. They had been close as young men, and Kent had been the most sympathetic of all the royal brothers towards Edward during the abdication, in large part because he liked Wallis: she may have reminded him of Kiki Preston. Nonetheless, he tried his best to dissuade his eldest brother from abandoning the throne, knowing the impact it would have upon the Duke of York. When the day of abdication came, he panicked, shouting, 'It isn't possible! It isn't happening!'[7] He made a point of being the first of the royal family to visit his brother – now the Duke of Windsor – in Austria in February 1937, and would certainly have attended his wedding had he been allowed so to do. In the event of his non-attendance, his gift of a Fabergé box was pointedly returned.

By 1939, Kent's attitude towards his brother had shifted from hero worship to something more clear-sighted. He told Betty Lawson-Johnston on 22 September that when Edward had visited

---

* See Chapter Three of *The Crown in Crisis* for the full account of McMahon's actions and their consequences.

the king at Buckingham Palace, 'his interview at BP consisted only of talking about himself', and made it clear that he was no supporter of the exiled pair. 'Thank God tho' they've left the country as it's very tricky having him here & you never know what they're up to – I wonder if you saw them or heard any dirt about them . . .?'[8]

Yet the dirt Kent referred to could also be deflected onto him. He was close to his German relations, Philipp of Hesse and Charles Edward, Duke of Saxe-Coburg, and his wife's sister was married to the German aristocrat Carl Theodor, Count of Toerring-Jettenbach. He was a regular visitor to the Hesse estate in Kronberg in Germany and enjoyed hosting German dignitaries on their visits to London, despite their prominent roles within the Nazi Party. Sometimes his social interactions with these men overshot the boundaries of both propriety and common sense. When he attended the wedding of Princess Irene of Greece to the Duke of Spoleto in Italy on 2 July 1939, he confided his fears about the imminent conflict to Hesse. The intelligence that an invasion of Poland would precipitate a British declaration of war duly found its way to Hitler on 23 August.

It was also possible that when Rudolf Hess arrived in Scotland in May 1941, he hoped to meet Kent as well as Hamilton. The duke was a friend of the Lord Steward and the two men had encountered one another socially several times that year. Unconfirmed but excitable hearsay even suggested that Kent had been nearby on the night of Hess's arrival, and that he, along with like-minded German sympathisers, had wished to broker a peace deal that would then be presented to the king and Churchill as a fait accompli. The most rococo of these conspiracy theories even suggested that MI5 had attempted to blackmail him into drawing out pro-German opinion in Britain, not least to see if the persistent rumours about the Duke of Windsor's wish to return to his former country as a Nazi-backed puppet ruler had any credibility whatsoever.

These stories remain at best extrapolations of circumstantial evidence and at worst fantasies concocted by newspapers and so-called 'historians'.* The rush to sensationalism obscures the need to report the truth dispassionately. Kent had many German friends and relatives, but then so did much of British high society in the pre-war years. Like Hamilton and Buccleuch, he may have had greater personal sympathy for appeasement than the royal family did officially, yet this was hardly proof that he was a crypto-Nazi. He was more a playboy than a political animal, as epitomised by the Prussian prince Louis Ferdinand's description of him as 'artistic and effeminate and [a user of] strong perfume'.[9] Only the strange circumstances of his death continue to invite speculation as to what really happened on 25 August 1942.

When Kent had visited the United States the previous year, it was suggested that he should head to Iceland upon his return to Britain for a morale-boosting trip to the American soldiers stationed in that country. He had visited Portugal in June 1940, ostensibly to celebrate the eight hundredth anniversary of that country's independence but also to act as a reminder of Britain's closeness to Portugal and to suggest that his beleaguered country was by no means beaten. The trip, despite the Nazi influence his brother soon encountered, was fruitful.

Although his Icelandic visit did not take place in 1941 for various reasons, not least some disagreement as to its political wisdom, Lowther, his private secretary, saw to it that the trip was rescheduled after the United States entered the war. He took enormous care with the arrangements. He, Kent and thirteen others would fly from RAF Invergordon in Scotland to RAF Reykjavik on 25 August, returning six days later. It was felt appropriate that Kent should be the intermediary between the two countries as his relationship with the Roosevelts, with whom he had stayed in America, was a warm one. The president had even become godfather to his

---

* I refer to Lynn Picknett and Clive Prince's 2001 book about the Hess landing, *Double Standards*, which posits, amongst other things, that Hess was also killed in the plane crash that fatally injured Kent and that a double posing as him spent decades imprisoned at Spandau. The words 'Up to a point, Lord Copper' barely cover it.

recently born son, Michael George Charles Franklin, something that made Kent 'thrilled and very proud'.[10]

Kent left Coppins early on the morning of 24 August. At around 1 p.m. the next day, he, Lowther and the other men took off from Invergordon in a Short Sutherland Mk III aeroplane. Weather conditions were foggy, but not insurmountably so. It should have been a routine journey of a few hours, but they never reached their destination. Around half an hour later, the plane crashed into Eagle's Rock near Dunbeath in Caithness, to the north of Scotland. Of the fifteen people on board, all but one - Sergeant Andrew Jack, the wireless operator and air gunner - were killed. And as soon as Kent's death became common knowledge, the speculation began.

There are several inconsistencies in the reports of the fate of Flight W-4206 that have never been satisfactorily explained. It seems clear that the plane was flying at far too low an altitude, around 650 feet rather than the 4,000 feet that it should have cleared by then. It is also strange that the plane was only by Eagle's Rock half an hour into the journey, when it should have been well over the North Sea. This could be explained by the pilot, Lieutenant Frank Mckenzie Goyen, making an error of judgement. It has also been suggested, without any hard evidence, that the reason for the delay was that the plane had diverted after take-off to collect a mysterious extra passenger. This theory also suggests that the additional passenger's presence was, directly or indirectly, responsible for the crash.

The official account, as put forward by Sir Archibald Sinclair reporting on the findings of a court of inquiry on 7 October, was that the accident was caused simply by Goyen's error; he described him as 'a flying-boat pilot of long experience on the particular type of aircraft which he was flying that day, and of exceptional ability'. Sinclair told the House of Commons, 'First, that the accident occurred because the aircraft was flown on a track other than that indicated in the flight plan given to the pilot, and at too low an altitude to clear the rising ground on the track; secondly, that the responsibility for this serious mistake in airmanship lies with the captain of the aircraft; thirdly, that the weather encountered should have presented no difficulties to an experienced pilot; fourthly, that the examination of the propellers showed that the engines were under power when the aircraft struck the ground, and fifthly, in accordance with KR & ACI, paragraph 1325, that all the occupants of the aircraft were on duty at the time of the accident.'[11]

'Nothing to see here, let us all move on' might as well have been the subtext. It was enough for the king, who accepted that his brother's death was a tragic accident and attached no blame to anyone else. The circumstances were unpleasant, and hushed up; Halifax wrote to his sister on 17 September that 'Someone tells me that the Duke of Kent was not at all burnt, but that his head was severed from his body. Don't repeat this, but it is pretty grim if true, although merciful compared with the other.'[12] In an earlier letter, he had summarised popular feeling about what had occurred. 'What a tragedy this is about the Duke of Kent, and it seems to be quite inexplicable. I wonder whether we shall ever know what happened.'[13]

Given the paucity of official documents relating to the crash, there is unlikely to be any comprehensive and satisfying explanation as to what really took place on 24 August. The usually authoritative Royal Archives, for instance, contain next to no information about it, and there are no MI5 records that can be consulted. Crawfie summarised the palace's reaction as being one of *omertà*: 'the royal conspiracy of silence had closed about him as it did about so many other uncomfortable things ... in the Palace and the Castle, his name was never mentioned'. However, if one wades through the various conspiracy theories and scraps of half-plausible, half-deranged information, it is possible to come up with counter-explanations that without any definitive information to support or dispel them must remain speculative for the time being.

Despite his good service and popularity, Kent was still a

potential embarrassment to both the royal family and MI5. While a pliant media and a hands-on security service had tried to remove the possibility of blackmail in Britain, his sexual and narcotic adventures earlier in life had left him open to coercion by enemy powers. That he had maintained close contacts with Germans with prominent positions in the Nazi Party, apparently through choice, meant that he was ideally placed to act as a go-between if Hitler or other leading Nazis had wanted to explore a peace deal. And the recent arrival of Hess in Scotland, in an attempt to explore something similar, indicated that others had had the same idea.

This theory presupposes that Kent, whether through choice or due to blackmail, had decided to use the pretext of a trip to Iceland to pursue his own agenda. It has been suggested that a briefcase full of Swedish krona notes was found in the wreckage of the plane, which indicates that the intended destination was the neutral country of Sweden, rather than Iceland. In this scenario, he was acting without the knowledge of Lowther – whose elaborate planning of the trip assumes that he intended the Icelandic visit to go ahead – or any of the remaining crew. If the idea is followed to its logical conclusion, he informed Goyen upon take-off that he would assume the piloting of the aircraft and direct the plane to Sweden rather than its stated destination. Either he engaged Goyen in a fight for the controls that resulted in the plane plummeting through the sky to its destruction, or he took them over but failed to judge the trajectory of an unfamiliar route in poor weather conditions.

It is an intriguing theory, but the logical flaws are clear. Had a member of the royal family deviated from a carefully planned journey on a whim, it could not have been concealed. His unexpected arrival in Sweden, or any other country, would have caused outrage and confusion. If he had been pursuing his own peace mission, it would have achieved no more than Hess's ill-fated attempt. A belief that royalty had autonomy in matters of state had led to Hitler misunderstanding the nature of the abdication and giving the Duke of Windsor more attention on his tour of Germany in 1937 than he had merited, to say nothing of Hess's own free-lance embassy to Britain the previous year. Had Kent arrived in Sweden to meet German operatives, it would have been equally misjudged.

The corollary to this suggestion is that MI5 were aware of Kent's intentions and, rather than attempting to dissuade him from his plans, managed to rig the plane so that it would crash-land shortly after take-off. The argument would be that the security services would countenance the deaths of innocent people to keep an embarrassing development secret. Yet in order that this did not become public knowledge, everybody on board would have had to die, and they did not.

The sole survivor of the crash, Flight Sergeant Andrew Jack, was found wandering several miles away from Eagle Rock by two crofters, covered in burns and in a state of shock. Upon arriving in hospital, he supposedly said, 'I do not know where I am, but I am glad to be in bed.' He never spoke publicly about what happened that day. The only information about what he saw derives from his niece, Margaret Harris. In 2003, Mrs Harris revealed that Jack told her that Kent had been flying the aircraft; that he had been forced to sign the Official Secrets Act while in hospital, where he had been visited by Queen Mary and Princess Marina; and, tantalisingly, that there was somebody on board who should not have been, although he refused to say whether it was a man or a woman. That there were sixteen, rather than fifteen, people on the aircraft was mentioned in passing by Lascelles in his diary, apparently innocent of any further implication. This may have been a simple miscalculation, or a hint at the presence of an anonymous interloper.

Interviewed by the North Wales newspaper *Daily Post*, Mrs Harris said, 'My uncle knew the pilot wasn't to blame yet he couldn't say anything. As a result he felt he'd let his mate down and this had a profound effect on him for the rest of his life. He was never the same after the accident, not because of the injuries he sustained, but because of the terrible injustice he was power-less to put right. The thought of the pilot's family believing he had crashed the aircraft was to erode into his conscience until his dying day.'

She stated that Jack had dragged some of the passengers from the burning aircraft, injuring himself in the process, and it was 'when he returned to the aircraft to try to save [the others] on board that he saw the Duke slumped in the pilot's seat . . . there was no doubt that he had been flying the plane'. Her explanation for Kent serving as the pilot was simple, however. 'The plane was heading for Iceland where the Duke was to inspect Allied forces but had been delayed because of bad weather. The situation hadn't improved much when the Duke and his three associates got tired of waiting and decided they should set off. All three had been drinking and even though the crew had not, the Duke decided to fly the aircraft with fatal consequences.'

She also speculated that the unknown extra passenger was Kent's boyfriend, who was wearing make-up, and concluded, 'There was something there that they wanted to hush up and a scandal of that nature in those days would have been explosive. I recently saw a report suggesting that there was nothing sinister about the accident. It was then that I thought, "I'm not having this", and decided to tell people what I know.'[14]

Margaret Harris cannot be taken as a definitive source on the matter, any more than her uncle's recollections can. There is no public record surviving of the court of inquiry's findings, and any unknown material relating to Kent's death remains locked within an archive somewhere. It is possible that the official account is accurate and he died in an accident en route to Iceland, just as a more complex saga may have unfolded in the half-hour between the plane taking off and its violent destruction. Yet whatever the truth of the end of Flight W-4206, the death of the Duke of Kent did nothing to ease the difficulties the royal family faced.

The king was told the news while dining with Gloucester and their wives at Balmoral on 25 August. When he received an urgent telephone call, his first thought was that his mother had died, but hearing Sinclair's voice made him realise that it was his youngest brother. Returning to the table, white-faced and in distress, he was unable to speak, and had to write a note for the horrified queen. She then broke the news to the other women in the drawing room.

It was a considerable blow to him. He expressed his feelings to Helen Hardinge when he thanked her for her condolences, saying, 'My brother's death has come as a great shock to me. I have lost him & all those qualities which were so apparent in everything he did. He was such a friend & a great help to me in my work. I shall miss him terribly, I know, in so many ways. You have known all of us for many years now & you will realise this more than most people.'[15]

The rest of the family were similarly appalled. Queen Mary had always preferred her wayward youngest son to his brothers, and was grief-stricken by his death. She wrote in her diary in uncharacteristically emotional terms that 'I felt so stunned by the shock I could not believe it.'[16] The queen, meanwhile, described Kent to Osbert Sitwell as 'much more like a brother to me ... he had a quick and sensitive mind & a very good and useful social sense', and said of his death, 'it is really a terrible loss, both to ourselves and to the country'.[17]

Kent's close friend Channon subsequently wrote, 'nobody knew him better than I of recent years'. He called him 'fundamentally frivolous . . . fitful, fretful, both moody and unreliable in small matters' and said 'no man was ever more disloyal in conversation' even as he praised him for his 'painstaking kindness'. He summed up his quixotic character by saying, 'as one began to be fond of him, he would do, or say, some little act that chilled one; and again, just as one began to mistrust or be indifferent to him, he would be so thoughtful, affectionate and disarming that one would genuinely like him once more'.[18]

Lascelles was more measured. He wrote that, 'He was the only one of his family who made any pretensions to be cultured and well-read - and the only one who wrote an educated hand' and praised his 'great social charm' and 'very valuable tour' of Canada. But he also decried him, in a Biblical allusion, as 'unstable as water',* and, although allowing for recent improvements wrought by fatherhood, wrote that 'even when he was at his best, the air of the "spoilt child" never quite deserted him'.[19]

The other member of the royal family who could be thus described discovered his brother's death in grim circumstances. Edward was listening to the BBC Empire Service in his office at Government House when he heard of the accident. Confirmatory telegrams from Halifax and his mother soon dispelled any doubt about the report's accuracy. Kent had been his favourite sibling too. Now, thousands of miles away, he once again saw how distant he had become from his family in this time of adversity. Churchill offered sympathy on his brother's tragic death, and informed Edward that his grief was shared by all of Britain. One can only speculate what the national reaction might have been if the Duke of Windsor had died in similar circumstances.

The funeral was held at St George's Chapel in Windsor almost immediately after Kent's death, on 29 August. Edward, inevitably, could not attend, and was represented by his comptroller, Lionel Halsey. The duke wrote a letter of condolence to the king, which was significantly different to the angry correspondence he had previously sent. He reflected that 'George's death is indeed a terrible loss to us all and especially to you, for with his charm and personality he must have been of the greatest help in the contacts he made in ways and quarters that are denied to you in your position as King. I share with you this irreparable loss and you have my deep and sincere sympathy.'

He spoke from his own experience when he referred to Kent's wild youth. 'I have actually always looked upon George more like a son than a brother for as you know, I took him under my wing and guided him safely through the most difficult period of his life, which might otherwise have turned out disastrously for his future.'

---

* The reference is to Genesis 49:4, when it is said to Reuben - the libidinous son of Jacob and Leah - that 'Unstable as water, thou shalt not excel; because thou wentest up to thy father's bed; then defiledst thou it: he went up to my couch.'

Nevertheless, he could not resist a dig at his family, even in the circumstances. 'It is, therefore, a source of great pain to me now to think that on account of your "attitude" towards me, which has been adopted by the whole family, he and I did not see each other last year when he was so near to me in America.'

Yet most of the letter was peaceable. He praised Queen Mary for writing him a 'wonderful letter' and called her 'a most courageous and noble person . . . it is hard that in her later years, she should have yet another great and bitter blow to bear. Her fortitude is indeed an example to us all.' He then concluded with some general comments about the international situation. 'We hear on all sides praise of the fine job you and Elizabeth are doing in Great Britain and of the loyalty and devotion of your subjects all over the Empire. I can well understand that you have had some difficult times and that it has by no means been easy going - and while there must, I am afraid, still be hard times ahead of us, one prays that a victorious peace may not be too far distant.'[20]

He signed the letter 'David'. Lascelles remarked that '[this was] the first personal communication that he had sent to his brother for some years'.[21] It was not the only one. Thousands of telegrams and letters were sent to the royal family, with the young, handsome Kent's untimely end reminding countless families of their own losses.

Coward was present at the service, along with Channon, who pronounced it 'an exhausting, emotional, hot day', and Buccleuch, still invited to such high-profile events despite his defenestration from the post of Lord Steward.* The playwright later wrote in his diary, 'I tried hard not to cry, but it was useless. When the Duchess came in with the Queen and Queen Mary, I broke down a bit, and when the coffin passed with flowers from the garden at Coppins and Prince George's cap on it, I was finished. I then gave up all pretence and just stood with the tears splashing down my face.' He noted his relief that 'both Dickie [Mountbatten] and the

---

* Churchill, perhaps surprisingly, had not been invited.

King were doing the same thing'.*[22] Channon, meanwhile, called the Duke 'irreplaceable' and described his death as 'the end of an epoch. All elegances are over. Our royalty will become increasingly civic, duty-doing, dour and glamourless.'[23] He did not concede that some in the 'moth-eaten court' might have preferred such a development.†

The king wrote of the ceremony that it was 'short and explicit' and acknowledged that he was greatly affected by it. 'I have attended very many family funerals in the chapel, but none of which have moved me in the same way. Everybody there I knew well but I did not dare to look at any of them for fear of breaking down. His death & the form it took has shocked everybody & I have had countless letters from friends extolling his merits.' His final judgement on his brother acknowledged both his likeability and the accessibility that had led him astray as a younger man. 'The war had brought him out in many ways. Always charming to people, in every walk of life.'[24]

On the same day, Edward held a memorial service for his brother in Nassau. He was deeply moved, breaking down in tears at the beginning and unable to regain his self-control throughout. He was temporarily unable to fulfil his responsibilities, leaving Wallis to reply to the letters of condolence as he retreated into grief. She wrote to her aunt of the 'tragic death', saying that 'I think [Kent's] services will be greatly missed by Great Britain. He was the one with the most charm left at the job . . . We are both greatly shocked and distressed.'[25]

The duke wrote to Sibyl Colefax on 1 October to acknowledge a letter of condolence she sent. As she had known something of both men in their youth, it was a welcome opportunity to be candid. 'As you knew . . . our close relationship in the old days, you will realise that although things had changed, his passing has been a

---

* There is also a more scurrilous rumour that Coward hissed at the mourning Princess Marina, 'I had him first!'

† Subsequently Channon reflected that 'London and life will be more colourless and less gay without . . . that elaborate, eager, excited elf.'

terrible shock and his loss infinitely sad. How bitterly one laments
the cruel waste of the casualties of this second and far more ghastly
war conflict.' He talked of how 'cramped and isolated so far from
the centres of interest' and how detached he and Wallis felt, and
expressed his hope for 'a more interesting job and a better opportunity of pulling one's weight'.²⁶ But such an opportunity lay within
his brother's gift.

Initially, the tragedy seemed to hint at the chance of a rapprochement between the two. Not only did Edward and Queen
Mary exchange atypically warm letters, but the king suggested to
his mother, 'perhaps as you say his grief may now pave the way
for a better understanding in the future'.²⁷ He had visited the crash
site on 14 September, and recorded his impression of what he
saw there. 'The ground for 200 yds long & 100 yds wide had been
scored & scorched by its trail & flame. It hit one side of the slope,
turned over in the air & slid down the other side on its back. The
impact must have been terrific as the aircraft as an aircraft was un-
recognisable when it was found.' It was a difficult thing to see, but
he considered it his duty; as he wrote in his diary, 'I felt I had to do
this pilgrimage.'²⁸

He replied to his brother at the end of October, and praised both
Kent and Edward's tutelage of him. 'I know that George's sudden
& untimely death would cause you a great deal of grief. I am afraid
that the shock must have been great as well. You & George were
always great friends in the old days & he was I know so grateful
to you for helping him in those critical months in his life. When
he lived with you at York House he was making good & after his
marriage he settled down to become a really useful member of the
family & of society. He was such a help & source of encouragement
to me in my work. He was always busy & kept me informed about
things. He found out more facts for me than any other person &
explained them in that downright & humorous way of his. He is a
great loss to me personally & I shall miss him terribly.' But he ended
on a cheerier note. 'We have had to take some heavy knocks but we
are ready now to hit back good & strong. The country has never

been so united as it is now & everybody, men and women alike, are playing their part in industry today & in all forms of war work. The spirit of the people after three years of war is magnificent.'[29]

This rekindled fraternal warmth did not last. Before long, the old grievances of money and Wallis's title were raised, and dealt with dismissively. Kent's death did not lead to a lasting thaw in relations. As his widow mourned him, the country he had served continued the fight against the Axis powers. It seemed as if things would never end.

Chapter Fifteen

'These Years of Tragedy and Glory'

'I feel strongly that nothing written by private secretaries should be published within a considerable time after their principals' deaths.' So Lascelles wrote in his diary on 1 November from Windsor Castle, musing on posterity. Although he acknowledged that 'it would distress me . . . if I thought that any allusion to the present King made in this book would be made public prematurely', he disagreed with Queen Mary, who believed that the role of private secretaries through the ages should be to observe everything and write nothing. 'If those "behind the scenes" were never to put pen to paper, history would lose some of its most informative documents, and literature some of its treasures.' He declared, righteously, 'I don't see how history can arrive at the truth if contemporaries are not allowed to write it.'*1

The first-hand testimonies of Lascelles, Hardinge and Monckton, as well as others in positions of influence with the royal family during World War II, are invaluable not simply from a historical perspective, but from a personal one. Sometimes accounts of battles and conflicts - global or personal - can be revelatory for their far-sightedness, or fascinating in their myopia. Nobody reading

---

* Perhaps appropriately, at the time of writing, Lascelles' full diaries remain embargoed in the keeping of Churchill College, Cambridge until 2027. The only extracts therefore available, and used here, are those that Duff Hart-Davis edited as *King's Counsellor* (W&N, 2006).

Channon's account of the war, for instance, can now do so without heavy doses of dramatic irony.

Yet as Lascelles began writing his day-by-day account of his career, firstly as the king's assistant private secretary and, as of 17 July 1943, as his private secretary proper, he could not know the outcome of the conflict he chronicled. As he alternated between Pooteresque banalities and accounts of death and destruction, he may have wondered whether his diary would become a testament to the end of Britain as he had known it. 1942 had been a chronicle of frustration, with the nadir being the Duke of Kent's death. Despite hoped-for advances in the form of America's entry into the war and Germany being occupied with the Russian front, the long-awaited breakthrough stubbornly refused to take place.

It was therefore with some relief that on 3 November, the king wrote in his diary that 'The Prime Minister came to lunch. He said "I bring you victory" . . . we should know very soon the results of the battle. What rejoicing there will be.'[2] The following day he was able to confirm that it was true - 'A victory at last. How good it is for the nerves'[3] - and national rejoicing began. On 15 November, Lascelles wrote that 'this morning church bells throughout the country, dumb since June 1940, were bidden to ring again in honour of our victory'.[4] The Allied forces had triumphed at the Battle of El Alamein, which had led Churchill to announce that 'This is not the end. It is not even the beginning of the end. But it is, perhaps, the end of the beginning.' With the benefit of many years of hindsight, the prime minister later wrote that 'It may almost be said "Before Alamein we never had a victory. After Alamein we never had a defeat."'[5]

The Allied powers' successful strategy in North Africa owed something to the personal relationship between the king and Dwight D. Eisenhower, Supreme Commander of the Allied Expeditionary Force. When Eisenhower was received at Buckingham Palace in July 1942, he was surprised and relieved to find the king 'most personable and very much "in the know" as to current and prospective plans for Allied operations'.[6] This was repeated in

October that year, when the well-briefed monarch was able to discuss a secret mission that Eisenhower had made to North Africa to liaise with the Vichy French prior to the launch of Operation Torch. The king was by now comfortable enough in such quasi-diplomatic environments to speak with warmth and humour. Addressing Eisenhower's second in command, General Mark Clark, he quipped, 'I know all about you. You're the one who took that fabulous trip. Didn't you, by the way, get stranded on the beach without your trousers?'*[7]

But victory was too welcome to be a joking matter. He conveyed his relief in a letter to Churchill. 'I was overjoyed when I received the news and so was everybody else. In our many talks together over a long period I knew that the elimination of the Afrika Corps, the threat to Egypt, was your <u>one</u> aim, the most important of all the many other operations with which you have had to deal.' He ended the letter with an encomium of thanks to his prime minister. 'When I look back and think of all the many arduous hours of work you have put in, and the many miles you have travelled, to bring this battle to such a successful conclusion you have every right to rejoice; while the rest of our people will one day be very thankful to you for what you have done. I cannot say more.'[8]

Churchill was moved. He thanked his monarch for his 'kind and gracious letter', and said, 'No Minister in modern times, and I daresay in long past days, has received more help and comfort from the King, and this has brought us all thus far with broadening hopes and now I feel to brightening skies.' He struck a personal note by writing, 'It is needless to assure your Majesty of my devotion to yourself and family and to our ancient and cherished Majesty - the true bulwark of British freedom against tyrannies of every kind; but I trust I may have the pleasure of feeling a sense of

---

* Clark had indeed lost his trousers during the operation, although this was a calculated decision to enable him to reach his boat rather than because he fancied becoming a supporting player in a military-themed Aldwych farce. The whole fascinating story is in his memoir, *Calculated Risk*.

personal friendship which is very keen and lively in my heart and has grown strong in these hard times of war.'⁹

However, the king was himself fighting on two fronts. Even as Allied success in North Africa cheered him, there was the pernicious Duke of Windsor to deal with. After the death of the Duke of Kent, Edward felt renewed anger at his removal from his family, and so asked Churchill with icy politeness on 10 November whether the issue of a title for Wallis might be re-examined. The two men had met in June, which had ameliorated what had become poor relations, and the Duke of Windsor now pressed his wife's claim once more.

Addressing the prime minister with passive aggression ('Although I am, in my small way, fully absorbed in handling the problems which affect the wartime lives of some sixty-five thousand British people, I could hardly expect my news to interest one who is guiding the fortunes and destiny of so many millions'), he insisted that 'the hurt both to the Duchess and myself is not healed by time but only aggravated. I therefore feel that, after five and a half years, the question of restoring to the Duchess her royal status should be clarified.' He then requested Churchill's support in asking the king to grant Wallis her HRH title, 'not only as an act of justice and courtesy to his sister-in-law but also as a gesture in recognition of her two years' public service in the Bahamas'.

The duke believed this to be timely and deserved, and again attacked his brother's actions as an 'unwarranted step . . . taken . . . when any action calculated to build up the King's position was considered justifiable, even to the extent of hitting at me where I was most vulnerable, which was to insult the lady who had consented to become my wife'. After thanking Churchill for his condolences – 'Poor George's death under such tragic and seemingly avoidable circumstances was a terrible shock . . . he had the "lighter touch" which would appeal to you as it did to all with whom he came into contact' – he spoke about his distaste for the men he was supposed to be governing ('negroes in the mass are still children both mentally and morally . . . self government for coloured populations and racial equality are psychological adjustments that I personally do not advocate but which must inevitably come to pass')[10] and concluded with his hopes that Churchill's intercession on the duchess's behalf* would be successful.

It was not. The king wrote in his diary on 15 December that 'D has asked Winston to ask me to give the title HRH to his wife. This I cannot do.'[11] Aided by Hardinge, he wrote a formal memorandum to the prime minister in December to say, 'I cannot alter a decision which I made with considerable reluctance at the time of his marriage', and justified this by noting that 'when [Edward] abdicated, he renounced all the rights and privileges of succession for himself and his children - including the title "Royal Highness" in respect of himself and his wife'. Making the point that 'there is therefore no question of the title being "restored" to the Duchess - because she never had it', he concluded, 'there are still large numbers of people in this country, and in the Empire, to whom it would be most distasteful to have to do honour to the Duchess as a member of our family'.

He was weary of the matter. This could be seen both from his statement that 'everything has settled down so well in this unhappy affair that to bring the matter up at this moment would be a tragedy', and in a handwritten note to Churchill: 'I am sure it would be a mistake to reopen this matter at the moment. I am quite ready to leave the question in abeyance for the time being, but I must tell you quite honestly that I do not trust the Duchess' loyalty.'[12] The question of his brother's trustworthiness was not addressed. Churchill telegrammed the duke, acknowledging the sacrifices that had been made but reiterating that neither the king nor the War Cabinet would take the desired action, nor did he intend to raise the matter again. And there, once more, things had to rest.

*

---

* This matter remained of considerably more import to Edward than to Wallis, who seldom expressed much of a preference.

As the momentum of war began to change, so did expectations of how the royal family should behave. The queen, especially, now became a much-sought-after subject for interviews and appearances, because she was felt to offer a warmth and accessibility that her husband did not. This was unpopular with courtiers, who felt that it degraded her station. Lascelles complained, '[American journalists] don't seem to realise that, as long as there is a monarchy in this country, it must conform to *British* standards, and cannot sacrifice them in order to "promote good relations" (which is often only a euphemism for "curry favour") with other nations who have quite other standards.'

Lascelles, who was fifty-five years old at the time, was poised halfway between moderniser and reactionary. As he reflected that 'I am not the least pompous, or courtier-ish, about the monarchy; on the contrary, I take perhaps too pragmatical a view of it', he also noted that there were certain expectations that the country had – 'e.g. not to marry a certain type of woman, as was shown with crystal clearness in 1936'. Hardinge and Lascelles may have had differences in approach, but one area they agreed on was the uselessness of Edward VIII.* In 1927, Lascelles had expressed his hope to Stanley Baldwin that the then Prince of Wales should fall off his horse while riding and break his neck rather than become king, and nothing subsequently had improved his opinion of a man whom he sneered 'thought chatty handiness was the beginning and end of kingship'.[13]

Yet he also refused to be bothered about Wallis being designated HRH, shrugging, 'God knows, [it] is not going to make the world a better or worse place, whichever way it be answered.'[14] The New Year Honours List nevertheless appeared without any reference to Wallis. Meanwhile, the duke wrote to Aunt Bessie to inform her that her niece had suffered 'something of a collapse' over Christmas, although he reassured her by suggesting that his own good health remained constant. 'I on the other hand had a real vacation

---

* As discussed in *The Crown in Crisis*, Chapter One and *passim*.

to which I felt entitled after more than a year without let-up and al-though too short I was able to play golf on those wonderful Florida golf courses and relax and forget all about "governing".'

As the situation improved for the Allies, the Duke of Windsor contemplated his future. He confided in Wallis's aunt that '[She] and I get pretty desperate here at times and wonder how long we can stick it out although as it is essential to have a job at the present time and we will never be offered a better one I guess we could do a lot worse and at least we are together which is vital and all-important to us.'[15] Still, the governor was able to argue that his plans for reform of the Bahamas were far-sighted, even visionary.* If he was still to be ostracised from the royal family, at least he could devote his energies to making a success of his post, however reluctantly acquired it had been.

The question of how long the war was likely to last occupied everyone's thoughts now that events had changed so dramatically. Churchill mused in February 1943 that the European war against Hitler would probably conclude before the end of 1944, but feared that the conflict with Japan would last until mid 1946 at the earliest. Even as the king wrote in his diary on 16 February that 'we must have a cut and dried joint plan for [an assault upon Italy] & that we must be firm & not deal with any of the Fascist regime or Mussolini's people or any kind of quisling',[16] he worried that the advances made so far were too tentative for comfort. He had suggested at the end of 1942 that 'We shall be in a very bad way here in mid-1943 and we shall have to reduce our war effort here, which will prolong the war and put more work for USA to keep us all going', and had written with trepidation that 'all this is not pleasant news to hear. Outwardly one has to be optimistic about the future

---

* The historian Michael Bloch has argued that 'if the Duke had been allowed to depart for good in May 1943 to give more worthwhile service elsewhere, instead of being obliged to stay on for two more bitter years, his time in Nassau would have been recognised as one of the most successful episodes in twentieth-century colonial administration'.

in 1943, but inwardly I am depressed by the present prospect.'[17]

His gloom continued, and he told Churchill that 'I do not feel at all happy about the present political situation in North Africa . . . it looks as if the US Forces have had a sound defeat last week, which will not help them in French eyes, and as if we shall have to do all the fighting there'. He remarked, with concern, 'the state of affairs, according to the telegrams I have seen, looks as if it was deteriorating'.[18] Even his wife was unimpressed, remarking to Queen Mary on 19 February that 'the Americans don't seem to have handled the North African political situation very well, do they? I do wish that they would let us do more there, for at least we have great experience (as a country) in political matters . . . [the Americans] are so very nice, & do make such awful mistakes!'*[19]

The situation in North Africa soon improved, and good spirits were compounded by the lifting of the German siege of Stalingrad on 2 February. The astonishing number of losses on both the Axis and Allied sides demonstrated that Russia under Stalin was a primal force in battle. The king offered Stalingrad the military distinction of the Sword of Honour in recognition of the sacrifices the city's defenders had made, but even as Stalin complained that the Americans and British were not sufficiently committed to joining forces and attacking France, a matter closer to home concerned the king. Churchill's health seemed to be failing, for the first time since he became prime minister.

Although he had managed to conceal his heart attack in December 1941, Churchill had buried himself in work, with a schedule punitive for a man half his age. The stress eventually saw him take to his bed with pneumonia on 12 February. A concerned king wrote to him on the 22nd, 'do please take this opportunity for a rest . . . I trust that you will not forget that you have earned one after your last tour, and you must get your strength back for the strenuous

---

* In the same letter, the queen wrote of Gandhi, then on hunger strike, 'What an old blackmailer he is, practically committing murder to gain his own ends', and decried his actions as 'all very dreadful'.

coming months.' After mentioning various matters of strategic importance, he concluded, 'I should not think of bothering you with
these questions at this moment, but I do feel worried about them,
& I would like an assurance from you that they are being carefully
watched.' The subtext of the letter – *I need you* – was made explicit
by the last line: 'I cannot discuss these vital matters with anyone
but yourself.'[20]

Although Churchill did not return to work until 15 March,
taking time to recuperate at Chequers first, he knew that the king
needed his fears dispelling, and dictated a long letter from his
sickbed. His tone was reassuring – 'I do not feel seriously disturbed
by the course of events in North Africa, either political or even
military' – although he was scathing about Charles de Gaulle, the
leader of Free France, whom he described as both hostile and in-
solent. 'I cannot see any future for the Fighting French Movement
while he remains at their head', he sniffed.* He was more nuanced
about the presence of the Americans. 'I need scarcely say that no
word of mine is intended in disparagement [of them] . . . they are
brave but not seasoned troops, who will not hesitate to learn from
defeat, and who will improve themselves by suffering until all their
strongest martial qualities have come to the front.'[21] Any parallels
between the Americans and the now battle-tested man to whom he
wrote remained implicit.

Without his prime minister by his side, the king turned to his
other close counsellor: his wife. It is hard to overstate the importance he placed on the advice and guidance of the queen, which
put him in a constitutionally difficult situation. Just as he remained
an unanticipated monarch who had arrived on the throne through
circumstance, so her influence, although essentially benign, lacked
accountability. A decade before, the prime minister, Stanley Baldwin, had railed against the influence of the newspaper magnates

---

* De Gaulle later became both prime minister and president of France, and is
today regarded as a national hero. Elsewhere in the letter, Churchill referred
to Gandhi as 'the old humbug', and questioned whether his fast was remotely
genuine.

who opposed him, commenting, 'Power without responsibility – the prerogative of the harlot through the ages.' Few would describe Queen Elizabeth as a harlot. Yet when her rival Wallis sneered that 'the reign of George VI is a split-level matriarchy in pants . . . Queen Mary runs the King's wife, and his wife runs the King',[22] she expressed a truth that could only be half acknowledged by those around the monarch.

There is an irony that both the king and the Duke of Windsor were dominated by the women around them, creating a similarity in their characters where few others existed. Yet as Wallis suggested, this came about from the dominance of Queen Mary within the family. She had influenced George V, had failed to stop Edward VIII from pursuing a course that led to his abdication, and had become the matriarch of the royal family. Even as she remained rusticated within Badminton House in Gloucester, she was able to exert her power, although upon her return to London at the end of the war, she remarked to Lang, 'here I've been anybody to everybody, and back in London I shall have to begin being Queen Mary all over again'.[23] Lang might have replied that she had never ceased to be regal, wherever she dwelt.*

It was, however, her daughter-in-law who remained a practical, rather than symbolic, influence both on her husband and on the direction of the country. Oliver Harvey, Eden's secretary, was scathing about the king, denigrating him as 'fundamentally a weak character and certainly rather a stupid one', but he admired the queen, calling her 'a strong one out of a rather reactionary stable'.[24] Amidst the sentimentality about how the king's wife was his soulmate, confidante and rock, clearer-sighted figures could see the difficulty of her proximity to power. Lascelles, while complimentary about her in his diaries, had a turbulent relationship with her, regarding her as a rival, even unhelpful counsellor. She in turn regarded him as less malleable than she might have hoped.

---

* Crawfie wrote of her that 'there was nobody in the whole of England who went in for austerity to such a degree as Queen Mary'.

Nonetheless, she remained a vital symbolic presence. It was in this capacity that Hardinge asked her to broadcast another morale-lifting talk to the women of the British Empire, as a gesture of thanks and solidarity for all they were doing for the war effort. She remarked to Hardinge on 19 March that 'it is a very difficult proposition, as one would like to congratulate women on the way they are tackling men's jobs, & yet they must be ready to stand down (& by) after the war'.*25 The speech was duly written by Lascelles, Churchill and the Bishop of Lichfield ('a curious trio of collaborationists, who are unlikely ever to be in literary partnership again', Lascelles remarked)† and was broadcast on 11 April.

As with her earlier broadcast on 10 August 1941, the purpose of the queen's speech was to emphasise solidarity and fellowship with her people. The text that the three men devised for her was 'the case of right against wrong', and she spoke of how the women of Britain, 'in these years of tragedy and glory, of crushing sorrow and splendid achievement, have earned the gratitude and admiration of all mankind'.

She tacitly extolled the efforts of herself and the king ('constantly travelling ... through the length and breadth of these Islands, I am fortunate to be able to see a clear picture of the astonishing work that women are doing <u>everywhere</u>'), and exhorted her countrywomen to feel pride in their own achievements, which she described as no less important than those of their menfolk. Her role as a woman in a man's world was not explicitly stated, but in comparison to her husband's often uneasy broadcasts, her fluency

---

* The letter also contained a fine example of her willingness to intervene - or interfere - as she liaised with Hardinge over the king's visit to Orkney to see the Home Fleet, saying, 'I do not hope for much, but must admit that I am not very happy about [the press coverage] ... Please don't say anything about this matter <u>on paper</u> as I am worried about it and would prefer to <u>talk</u> to you some time on this extremely difficult and extremely important and irritating matter.'
† Of which Churchill's contribution, of around ten lines, was the least significant.

indicated to all but the least attuned where the true power behind the monarchy lay.

The speech was well received, and Churchill wrote to the queen to congratulate her on 'an outstanding success'. He praised her voice as 'clear and captivating' and said that 'I have heard from every side nothing but praise and expressions of pleasure and high sentiment.'[26] She herself said of the broadcast that 'some of it was naïve and simple', but her central message of trusting in the 'creative and dynamic power of Christianity'[27] was sufficiently heartfelt to continue goodwill towards her, and to the rest of the royal family.

With the prime minister once again restored to health and vitality,* he could revel in the news of a decisive victory in North Africa on 13 May, something that wittier Americans referred to as 'Tunisgrad'. Although a planned service of thanksgiving at Westminster Abbey had to be cancelled, as the wisdom of assembling the country's leading politicians and the royal family in one place was questionable,† the king remained jubilant and impressed by his prime minister. He gave permission for his telegram of congratulations to Churchill to be published on the front page of *The Times*; in it he praised his premier's 'vision and unflinching determination' in the execution of the campaign, and announced that his work had 'immeasurably increased the debt'[28] his country owed him. Churchill responded with humility ('No Minister of the Crown has ever received more kindness and confidence from his Sovereign . . . this has been a precious aid and comfort to me')‡ and *The Times* lauded the king as 'an unfailing public example of courage, confidence and devoted energy'.[29]

Emboldened by his country's military success, the king prepared

---

* Although he complained about tiredness and weakness in his legs on 16 March.

† It eventually took place at St Paul's on 19 May. Lascelles called it 'not very inspiring . . . the atmosphere was more that of a fashionable wedding'.

‡ Lascelles said admiringly of the reply that 'it might have been written by the elder Pitt; he has evidently given much thought to it'.

to undertake a morale-raising visit to North Africa in June. It would be the first time he had left Britain since December 1940, and it had great symbolic value. Halifax wrote approvingly, 'The news about the King being in Africa has greatly thrilled the Americans as I have no doubt it will have thrilled our own people. Some are inclined to say that it was too great a risk, but my own feeling is that these kind of risks are well worth taking and that the monarchy will clearly be all the better for taking them.'[30]

Six months before, if he had flown to Tunisia, his plane would have been in severe danger of being shot down, but now he could travel unmolested. In Lascelles' words, 'on the twelfth the King . . . flew to Algiers, where he still is, to the great satisfaction of the Allied world'.

At last tragedy seemed to have been superseded by glory. Britain and its allies appeared to be on the verge of total military victory, and the once-unthinkable idea of an unconditional rout of Germany and Hitler now seemed more likely by the day. The king even commented on 28 May that 'The bombing of Germany is to go on with unabated energy, & if German morale gives way at any time a landing will be staged on the Continent at once with the forces available.'[31] Yet the war would continue for a further two years. And even as the country's situation improved, the interpersonal affairs of the royal family and the Duke and Duchess of Windsor would soon plunge into new and hitherto uncharted territory.

Chapter Sixteen

'Never a Dull Day in the Bahamas'

Sir Harry Oakes was – at least after Wenner-Gren's exile into outer darkness – the leading figure in Nassau in July 1943. He had arrived on the island in 1935 and made it his residence for tax reasons. His wealth came from his discovery of a lucrative gold mine in Canada, Lake Shore Mine, which was for a while the most productive in the western hemisphere. To describe him as 'richer than Croesus' was an understatement. His personal fortune was such that he was wealthier than many countries.

Under normal circumstances, he might have been regarded with suspicion, but given his status as a British citizen and philanthropist, he was seen as more useful than his Swedish neighbour had ever been. He had even been knighted by George VI in 1939 for his charitable services to Britain, Canada and the Bahamas, and was a leading member of Nassau's House of Assembly. No taint of Nazi sympathy was attached to him. As his friend Eric Hallinan said, 'he was a small, energetic, rugged man, never happier than when driving a bulldozer. His appearance and style, though rough, was not vulgar; he had a natural dignity. Money had not spoiled him; he remained essentially the plain, single-minded man who had roamed the world in search of gold, and, when he found it, gave most of his wealth away.'[1]

His relationship with the Duke and Duchess of Windsor was warm. In October 1940, he had offered them temporary accommodation while Government House was being refurbished to their exacting specifications, and they were relieved to be his guests in a 'shack by the sea' at his New Providence mansion. His wife, Eunice, became a close friend of Wallis, who was grateful for simpatico and civilised company. And the duke, who was always keen to be associated with the wealthy, found the self-confessed 'rough diamond' millionaire a refreshingly informal presence to be around.

Oakes was a useful figure to the duke in administrative as well as social matters too. He had bought a large proportion of San Salvador, an island 200 miles away from Nassau, and proposed to turn it over to the residents to farm. It was a forward-looking project, and one that the governor approved of. It chimed with his own vision of how his subjects should be given the tools to further their destinies. It was pleasing that Oakes, a man from an affluent but unexceptional background who had become stupendously wealthy through his own efforts, should have been the guiding influence behind such an endeavour.

It was therefore not just a tragedy but a calamity when on 8 July 1943, Harry Oakes was murdered. In addition to his role as governor, the duke now found himself charged with an unexpected and unwelcome responsibility: administering justice.

Before matters had worsened so dramatically, Edward had been offered another job. He had met with Churchill on the prime minister's visit to Washington in May 1943, and indeed had been present when Churchill had addressed Congress. His presence had stolen the show, irritating the politician. Even as Churchill declared that when it came to the conflict against Japan,* 'we will wage that war side by side with you ... while there is breath in our bodies and while blood flows in our veins', it was the Duke of Windsor, watching from the front row, who attracted attention. No wonder he was referred to, without irony, as 'Great Britain's best advertisement in America',[2] with memories of 1937 long since forgotten. Halifax observed that 'the Duke and Duchess got nearly

---

* On 21 October, the king wrote in his diary that 'Japan will be a tough enemy. They work "en masse" like ants, but are stupid individually . . . now we have turned to the offensive from the defensive. Japan brought America into the war just at the right time.'

as good a reception as [Churchill] did when they entered the box to take their seats to hear the speech'.³

The question of Edward's future role inevitably arose during their conversations. No criticism was made of his career as governor of the Bahamas, but his achievements, such as they were, were of little import compared to what was taking place elsewhere in the world. He could have introduced full employment to the islands along with unprecedented economic growth and educational development, and found the next Shakespeare into the bargain, and nobody would have cared. He was therefore offered another position that seemed to befit his talents: the governorship of Bermuda.

The letter that Churchill wrote to the duke to offer him the position did little to sell the role. He mentioned that 'Bermuda is of course a key-point in the relationship between Great Britain and the United States on account of the importance of the naval and air bases', and, with an eye to keeping both Edward and Wallis happy, emphasised, 'it is only a few hours' flying time from Washington and the climate all the year round is greatly superior to Nassau'. Yet no reason was given why Edward should be especially well suited to the job. Churchill talked vaguely about how 'Your Royal Highness would have opportunities of developing American contacts which would be of important service to us at the present time.'⁴

But it was of no interest. The duke turned down the post, and commented to Allen, 'Winston does not seem to have got my meaning of a move.'⁵ Wallis supported him. She wrote to her aunt that 'I am convinced that the Duke was perfectly correct to refuse', and said, 'I can't see much point in island-jumping. I'm for the big hop to a mainland.'⁶ It was clear that they would forever be regarded as second-class citizens without any agency of their own. As the duchess lamented in her memoirs, 'It was now clear beyond all question that David's family were determined to keep him relegated to the furthermost marches of the Empire.'⁷

The only thing Edward could do, more in anger than in

expectation of achieving anything, was to write to his brother and lambast him once again. After the brief reconciliation after the Duke of Kent's death the previous year, normal service had resumed, and the vitriol the Duke of Windsor poured into the letter was only equalled by the familiar manner with which the sentiments were expressed.

Suggesting that '[I write] in an attempt to bring you to your senses with regard to your attitude towards my wife and myself', he portrayed himself as an innocent martyr ('I have taken more than my fair share of cracks and insults at your hands . . . notwithstanding your belligerence, I suffered these studied insults in silence on the supposition that they were a necessary part of the policy of establishing yourself on the throne') and even offered a veiled threat as to what he might be capable of in the future if his wishes were not acceded to. 'The whole world knows we are not on speaking terms which is not surprising in view of the impression you have given via the Foreign Office and in general that my wife and I are to have different official treatment to other royal personages.' He concluded, 'I must frankly admit that I have become very bitter indeed.'[8] Any recipient must have wondered why this truism was worth writing down.

Yet just over a month later, his attention had to be diverted to another matter. As Wallis callously quipped to a friend after Oakes's murder, 'Never a dull day in the Bahamas.'[9]

The initial question when the body was discovered, in bizarre circumstances,* was that of motive. Oakes was wealthy, but unlike many other plutocrats, he was keen to improve the lot of the Bahamians as far as he could. Inevitably he had made many enemies in his business career, not least those who were jealous of his success,

---

* Oakes was discovered on a bed covered in feathers from a mattress, which were being blown around by a nearby fan. He had been stabbed first with an ice pick, then with a miner's hand pick, and then his body had been burnt with insecticide and petrol. The ice pick, naturally, came from Simpsons in the Strand. It was a murder that indicated that whoever had killed Oakes had wished to make a gruesome statement.

but his philanthropy was sincere and consistent. His wife remarked after his death that he would have left little more than £4 million in his estate: a vast sum of money, but hardly the riches that had once been created by the Lake Shore Mine's existence.*

There had been some family drama, in the form of his eighteen-year-old daughter Nancy eloping the previous year with the thirty-two-year-old Count Alfred de Marigny; they had married the day after she turned eighteen, and it was de Marigny's third such union. But nothing had happened that would suggest that any of the immediate family would wish Oakes harm, especially in such a violent and dramatic fashion.

When the duke was informed of his friend's death early the following morning, his first reaction was to impose a news black-out until further details could be known. But Étienne Dupuch, the editor and publisher of the *Nassau Daily Tribune*, could not be silenced as effectively as the British media had been in 1936, and so the story was the talk of the world within moments. Meanwhile, the duke sought conference with Dr H. A. Quackenbush, the island's highest-profile physician and a drily witty man. Upon being asked by the governor what was going on, Quackenbush replied, 'Santa Claus is dead.'

Edward asked for elucidation, and Quackenbush suggested – almost unbelievably in the circumstances – that there was the possibility that Oakes had intended suicide, and that the body's defacement was meant to make the death look like murder. The autopsy later made it clear that the blows above his ear could not have been self-inflicted, confirming that Quackenbush's theory was inaccurate. Yet at the time, a panicking and out-of-his-depth governor needed assistance, and urgently.

Dismissing the idea that he would be able to find competent police in Nassau who could handle an investigation of this

* Between 1924 and 1943, the Lake Shore Gold Mine produced nearly $35 million after tax. Suggestions after Oakes's death that he was worth as much as $200 million were wildly inaccurate.

complexity, Edward telephoned the Miami City Police and asked for the services of Captain W. E. Melchen, chief of the Homicide Bureau. The duke and Wallis had met Melchen on previous visits and believed him to be efficient. Now he was summoned to the Bahamas to investigate what was described as either 'an unusual death' or 'an apparent suicide'. Edward dismissed Quackenbush with the observation that 'For Lady Oakes's sake, I hope it turns out to be murder; for the Colony's sake, suicide.'[10]

The quest for truth duly began. Even as the governor informed London of Oakes's murder ('Deeply regret to report that Sir Harry Oakes has met violent death under circumstances which are not yet known'), he bore in mind Quackenbush's grim observation that 'a body does not remain fresh for long in Nassau'. The usual procedure would have been to send for detectives from Scotland Yard, but even if they had been dispatched immediately, they would not have arrived for at least twenty-four hours, leaving Nassau in a state of anxiety and speculation. It was imperative that the investigation begin immediately, either to prove that Oakes's death was an elaborate suicide, or to find his killer.

Melchen and his assistant, Captain James Barker, liaised with the local police commissioner, Colonel R. A. Erskine-Lindop, whose aim was to resolve the situation as quickly as possible so that his planned transfer to a new job in Trinidad would not be affected by an ongoing murder investigation. The three men agreed with the duke that the killer had to be caught quickly, before further damaging headlines led to panic throughout the island. Soon Barker was able to produce damning evidence of Oakes's son-in-law de Marigny's fingerprints at the scene. With relief, Erskine-Lindop arrested and charged him. The island had the death penalty, and the playboy could expect to hang should he be found guilty.

Yet there was unease about the speed and ease with which the criminal had been caught. Although de Marigny was not a popular figure in the Bahamas, it seemed a stretch to take a rakish philanderer and convict him of murder, especially given that the falling-out between him and Oakes was a matter of historical record. One Cabinet Office functionary, informed by the duke of de Marigny's arrest and the 'most valuable service' rendered by Melchen and Barker, noted that 'the Governor is at some pains to explain why he took the rather unusual step of calling in men from outside, which I must confess I don't very much like. But in the circs I will not question his judgement.'[11]

The court that would try de Marigny was convened with haste. Committal proceedings began in July, and the trial was scheduled for October. Oakes's friend Hallinan would prosecute the case, and it was expected that the suspect would be convicted. Edward headed to Miami on 22 July to give a press conference that he hoped would assuage rumours of poor practice. He called the murder 'a great shock to everybody', and Oakes's death 'a great loss to the Colony . . . [both] in a material way [and] because he was so very popular'.[12] But the governor would not play judge, jury and executioner. Justice was now expected to take its course. And Wallis informed her aunt, 'we are endeavouring to keep as clear from this awful case as is possible . . . I am afraid there is a lot of dirt underneath . . . one wonders how far it will all go . . . I do not think there is a big enough laundry anywhere to take Nassau's dirty linen.'[13]

Edward's role in prosecuting the Oakes case has been overstated by those who would wish to pin any failings of the investigation on him. He wanted justice for his friend, on both a personal and a professional level, but allegations that he colluded with Melchen, Barker and others in deciding on de Marigny's guilt and allowing the trial to come to the same conclusion are not proven by any existing evidence.

He undoubtedly detested the suspect. He referred to de Marigny in an August letter to Oliver Stanley, Secretary of State for the Colonies, as 'a despicable character . . . [he] has the worst possible record, morally and financially, since his adolescence, [and] has insidiously bought his way with his ex-wife's money into the leadership of a quite influential, fast and depraved set of the younger generation'.* However, he also observed that 'whether de Marigny is guilty or not, local opinion is sharply divided for and against him'.

The older population and the black residents all believed his culpability, but 'the unsavoury group of people' de Marigny consorted with wished to see him acquitted. The governor feared civil disobedience in either case, commenting, 'if the coloured people are ever given the slightest reason to suspect the jury, then the consequences may be grave'.[14] Pilate-like, he shrugged off responsibility, and made plans for himself and Wallis to be away from Nassau when the trial commenced in October. He described the whole affair as 'sordid beyond description' and said candidly, 'I will be glad when the trial is over and done with.'

He may not have been. When the so-called 'trial of the century' began in Nassau on 18 October, it initially went against de Marigny, who was damned by the circumstantial evidence of his bad temper and dismal relations with Oakes. It caused especial horror in court, given the circumstances in which his father-in-law was discovered, that he had often threatened to 'smash in' Oakes's head. Yet a week into the trial, it became clear that Barker and Melchen had pursued their own (or the governor's) agenda at the expense of justice. The prosecution's sole piece of real evidence – a fingerprint discovered on a Chinese screen in Oakes's bedroom – was revealed, to the prosecution's dismay, to have been lifted from elsewhere in the property. De Marigny was thereby no longer placed at the scene of the crime at the time he was accused of it, and this wrecked the case beyond repair.

As the defence rubbished the prosecution case as 'a combination of statements of an irrelevant nature and deliberate lying by police officers whose duty is to protect the public', de Marigny's acquittal was now inevitable. It duly came after a two-hour deliberation.

---

* The duke did not make any comparison to the 'Ritz Bar set', with which he consorted as Prince of Wales and king, who were satirised by Osbert Sitwell as 'the nameless, faceless, raucous gang'.

Even the judge in the case described Barker's evidence as 'incredible', and exclaimed, 'one would think an expert would be more careful'. Yet the jury did add one unexpected codicil to their statement, in the form of a recommendation that de Marigny should be deported from the Bahamas immediately.

As the duke remarked to Halifax that he was convinced of the defendant's guilt but doubted that he would be convicted, it was clear that there was no further place for de Marigny in the Bahamas. Edward made considerable, even unprecedented, efforts to follow the jury's advice and deport him, stating that a failure to do so 'would constitute a deplorable evidence of the impotence of the local government and have very serious effect on the Colony's reputation throughout the world'[15] In the event, the acquitted man left voluntarily for Cuba, where he resumed a bacchanalian life that only concluded with his death in 1998, married to his fourth wife.*

Oakes's murder was never solved. It continues to fascinate the curious, and true-crime books based on it appear regularly in bookshops with titles like *Murdered Midas* and *A Serpent in Eden.*[†] Whoever was responsible, it did little for the duke's standing. As his biographer Philip Ziegler – often generously inclined towards his subject – noted, 'The Duke had made a fool of himself . . . there were those who suggested, and still suggest, that he had done far worse.' These suggestions included the idea that Edward and Oakes had been in league with the Mafia in some way, that Oakes's murder was a gangland execution and that a frightened governor attempted to force through a conviction before he could merit the same treatment. But these theories are fanciful. Instead, it is easy to agree with Ziegler's verdict that Edward 'can fairly be accused of impetuosity, and bad judgement, and of allowing his dislike of de Marigny to impair what should have been his complete

---

* De Marigny wrote a memoir of his involvement in the trial, *More Devil than Saint*, that was described in one contemporary review as 'the prissy to hypocritical autobiography of a dandy . . . [a] self-portrait of a lush, with only vicarious values'.

† It was also a pivotal event in William Boyd's excellent novel *Any Human Heart*.

impartiality'.[16] Once again he had failed to rise to an occasion, and pettiness and inadequacy of character had overwhelmed him.

Late 1943 was a miserable time for the governor, who found himself increasingly isolated. He had to sign a blacklist order that meant that Wenner-Gren forfeited his assets in the Bahamas to the American government, and was compelled to give a press conference in which he reluctantly supported their actions. Nor was his presence in the United States a happy one. Halifax commented to Stanley of the 'longish' time the Windsors had spent in America that 'I am not sure that it is very wholesome or healthy for him to keep visiting this country.' Referring to his 'certain misgivings' about the duke and duchess ('His attitude is always quite correct, but I have heard indirectly that hers is sometimes less so'), he reiterated his belief that the governor wanted to usurp his position as ambassador. 'I have not much doubt in my own mind that it is in both of their minds to groom themselves for future occupation of this Embassy.'

Although he stated that 'I don't myself think that would be a very good plan', Halifax allowed that 'it might indeed be quite a popular appointment with Americans'. He saw the dangers of this, especially given that 'in some quarters American thought would almost regard the present King and Queen as place-holders for the in-justice rightful occupant', and recognised the difficulty of what would happen if any organised pro-Edward movement should come into operation. 'This country being what it is, familiarity with him and her is not unlikely to breed a certain kind of sympathy, and from that sympathy the transition to the thought of his having been unjustly treated and therefore of some resentment against those who unjustly treated him is not a very large one.'

Halifax therefore asked Stanley if the duke and duchess could be transported once again. 'The moral therefore to my mind . . . is to get the Prime Minister to move him from the Bahamas or from anywhere within obvious reach of this country. You will know the difficulties of this better than I do and I can imagine them to be great. I can only see it from my angle and write thus frankly to you, not I hope exaggerating my feeling, but with an instinct that you might as well be aware of it.'[17]

Stanley demurred, fearing that such an appointment could be politically disastrous. 'The trouble is that in any larger Colony – and of course he would not be prepared to move to any but one of the largest – the Governor has to be prepared to take part in a political fight which is often extremely bitter and unpleasant. I do not think, in the first instance, that it is desirable that the brother of the King should be involved in controversies of that kind, and in the second place, I doubt whether a man with his training can really stand the give and take of hearty political warfare.'[18] The embarrassment would continue, as Halifax acknowledged when he replied to Stanley that 'If I were in your position, I should feel just the same, but being where I am, I naturally plead for help, even if I realise it is almost impossible to give it to me!'[19] The duke and duchess would stay where they had been sent. But their inconvenience paled in comparison to the predicament that their old friend found himself in.

Charles Bedaux, the industrialist millionaire who had hosted Edward and Wallis for their wedding in 1937, had been in American custody in Algeria since the beginning of the year, awaiting extradition to the United States. It has sometimes been speculated that he was innocent of the charges he was accused of, and that he was the victim of anti-French feeling. Unfortunately, recently released MI5 files have confirmed that Bedaux's links and connections to the Nazi regime meant that the Duke of Windsor's knack for surrounding himself with unsuitable people remained consistent.

When the German naval intelligence officer Erich Pheiffer met Bedaux in Paris in 1940 to discuss ways in which the industrialist might be useful to the Reich, he described him as 'an important but extremely fantastic man, who could see the ideas in his head already worked out as a reality'.[20] Bedaux had already met Ribbentrop in Germany the previous year, but the meeting had not gone smoothly. One associate of Ribbentrop's had been driven to ask him, 'Mr Bedaux, are you an engineer, an economist or a fool?'

Pheiffer, however, was more impressed. The two men discussed the ways in which Iranian oilfields might be mined, and Bedaux asked for German nationality should Pheiffer agree to his plans, on the grounds that he did not wish to be hanged as a spy. Pheiffer noted that 'he had fond hopes of a commission as a General of the German Army, and it was his intention to be parachuted into Iran wearing the full regalia of that rank, down to trousers with a broad red stripe'.[21]

Pheiffer, like Edward, was impressed by Bedaux's chutzpah and vision. 'In him, one saw a true idealist, almost a world reformer and Utopian who well knew, at the time, how to combine with his idealism the ability to promote his own affairs.' Although Bedaux was keen on the idea of a 'Europe Unie' - an EU *avant la lettre* - he was also an admirer of Hitler. Pheiffer wrote that 'Hitler's social measures especially had impressed him, as he also considered himself to be one of the great social performers.' He duly attended 'a rather grim little party' at the Château de Candé, where Bedaux received German citizenship.

Bedaux was not granted his desired rank of general, but was instead given the position of *Sonderführer*. Now ensconced within the German administration, he began to invent wild schemes as a means of helping his new friends, including sending his niece, Betty Halsey, on an espionage mission to America by submarine. His plan was that she should be dropped somewhere off Long Island in her bathing costume and would then contact Bedaux's secretary Mrs Waite claiming that she had lost her clothes in the tide. Although his ideas were discouraged by the Germans, Pheiffer believed that 'his economic plans were fundamentally very sound', and that he should be kept close, even if his 'volatile temperament' and occasional threats to go to Hitler himself had to be managed with suitable tact.

Eventually Bedaux decided that he would head to Algeria in late 1941 in order to ascertain the viability of a pipeline that he wished to build from West Africa to the Mediterranean coastline for the benefit of his new allies. The Germans were delighted to be spared his presence – 'everyone sighed with relief at the thought that they were now well rid of our Charles', Pheiffer noted after a farewell dinner at which 'Bedaux made a long-winded and impassioned speech to which no one paid any great attention'[22] – and ignored him when he arrived in Algeria in early November that year.

Bedaux achieved little during his time in Algeria, and he headed to France in 1942, where he was arrested by the Vichy government on 25 September (something he declared he was 'incensed' about) and interned in a prison camp, before being released on 2 October into German custody. He then returned to Algeria, but was arrested once again on 5 December, this time by the Brigade of Surveillance of the French Territory, and handed over to American custody on 24 January 1943. His FBI file noted, '[Bedaux] apparently does not in any way resent his confinement and philosophises about it, explaining that it is one of those things which occur during a war.' It was a long way from the luxury of the Château de Candé.

During interrogation, Bedaux claimed that he was someone who was not merely *au fait* with current events but possessed the ability to foresee them long in advance. Asked if he had known about the Allied attack on North Africa, he replied, 'I think I had more advance information than either Mr Churchill or Mr Eden.' He stated that he had known about the plans on 30 September 1941, contradicting Churchill's statement to the House of Commons that the attack on North Africa had been decided after Pearl Harbor in December that year. Yet he denied that he was a Nazi, instead suggesting that his motivation for working with the Germans had simply been the pragmatism of a successful businessman who wished to exploit a dangerous situation for economic gain. Unethical, admittedly, but not at all illegal. He suggested that the construction of a pipeline through the Sahara would be an action of positive value, and stated that 'he was very much interested in doing something constructive during the war'.[23] He presented himself as a pacific humanitarian who had allied himself with the dominant political party to further his aims.

His interrogators were unconvinced. The evidence against him in the form of letters and documents was consistently incriminating. He seemed to be at best an amoral profiteer from the Nazi regime's growth and at worst a war criminal. Yet he remembered his friends. A telegram was found, addressed to 'HRH the Duke and Duchess of Windsor, Burma, Bahamas'. It stated, 'You have our fondest wishes with our love. The separation is painful and increases with time.' It was signed, with appropriate informality, 'Charles, Maison des Italiens, Algier'. This belied Bedaux's statement made in April 1941 that although he had been approached by the German authorities and asked to enquire of the Duke of Windsor whether he would be King of England in the event of a German victory, he had declined to do so as he was no longer on close terms with Edward.

This may or may not have been true, but in May 1941, a letter had come into MI5's possession that gave rise to suspicion as to the ongoing relationship between Bedaux and the Windsors. It had been sent from Mme Bedaux to the Duchess of Windsor, and stated elliptically, 'Do you remember a conversation Charles had with . . . in the library at . . . in the spring of 37? We continued the subject the same evening in the . . . and many times after that in our . . . we would come back to the same thing? Well that question is very prominent in the minds of certain powers to-day. We have been asked seriously of the possibility, and we, continuing to believe that both you and . . . are still of the same opinion, can give absolute assurance that it is not only possible but can be counted on. Are we right? I know you understand. I believe that it was the most important thing we ever spoke of. Do try to get word back to me here.'[24]

Although it did not seem a stretch to imagine what 'the most important thing we ever spoke of' was, particularly given the reference to 'certain powers', the ambiguity in Mme Bedaux's account removed the explicit culpability that Edward and Wallis might otherwise have been accused of. Alexander Cadogan's comment on it was that 'The paragraph is certainly capable of the blackest interpretations. But it would be difficult to get a conviction on it.'[25]

Unfortunately for Bedaux, no such escape route remained for him, and his self-assurance began to crumble the longer his interrogation continued. He continued to boast about how 'I control and have access to many persons in many countries . . . including even the Führer', but now offered to make this information available to America, on the condition that his wife, her sister and niece were allowed to remain safely in France. Yet if he had expected gratitude for his potential cooperation, he was disappointed.

FBI intelligence had stated as far back as 20 October 1941 that 'Bedaux is definitely pro-German and has been collaborating with the Germans . . . [he] is said to be doing the Allied cause in France more harm than any other American'. Now that he was in American custody, every single ounce of information would be extracted from him. One interrogator concluded in February 1943 that 'Bedaux himself is under grave suspicion of espionage on behalf of the enemy, and any direct or indirect contact of any of the Bedaux companies with him should be regarded as very dangerous.'

After a year of interrogation, the FBI were satisfied that they had enough information to charge him with the capital offences of consorting with the enemy and treason. He was flown to Miami, and on Valentine's Day was informed of the charges against him. His response was to take a massive overdose of sleeping pills, which killed him, although it took him three days to die. The FBI, disgruntled at being robbed of their prize, noted that 'Bedaux had undoubtedly been engaged in espionage on behalf of Germany and appears to have killed himself in order to avoid facing charges based on his activities.'[26]

His friendship with the Duke and Duchess of Windsor was referred to in many of the news stories that arose after his death, a number of which mentioned that their wedding had been held at the Château de Candé. Yet no newspaper dared connect Bedaux's actions with those of Edward and Wallis, save by the most tenuous of implications. The duke could not have known the full extent of Bedaux's activities, which became more focused on the Nazi regime after the outbreak of war. But the industrialist was not some naïve blunderer, out of his depth amidst worse men. He knew what he was doing when he met Pheiffer and Ribbentrop, just as he hosted the former king and his fiancée at his home in the certainty that he could ask for the favour to be repaid in due course.

Bedaux gambled that the 'right' side would win, and failed. His death dealt another blow to the increasingly tainted reputation of the governor of the Bahamas.

Chapter Seventeen

Liberation

'The majority of the experts collected for "Sextant"* believe that Germany will collapse before the beginning of May; [General Hastings] Ismay† himself thinks not before the autumn, and [he] believes that "Overlord" will be the August 8th battle of this war.'[1] Lascelles began 1944 in a philosophical mood. He had reason to be both optimistic and fearful. After the much-hoped-for advances of the previous year, victory seemed a near inevitability, with the circumstances and timing of such an occurrence the major question. Yet he was himself in a position of power and responsibility that he had spent his working life shirking from: he was now the king's private secretary.

Hardinge, who had segued from reluctantly serving Edward VIII to acting more fulsomely on behalf of George VI, was not seen as an easy figure in the royal household, despite his undeniable dedication to his king and to his work. In January 1939, Chamberlain raised the possibility of him moving to India, with a view to assuming the governorship of Madras.‡ The premier was keen; the monarch less so. He told the prime minister on 3 February, 'It will

---

* A code name for the Cairo conference of November 1943, convened between the United States, Britain and China to discuss the Allied response towards Japan.

† General Ismay was Churchill's chief military assistant.

‡ Hardinge's perennial enemy Channon wrote on 24 July 1941 that 'he ought to have gone to Madras and stayed there when he was offered the Governorship . . . he does infinite harm to the monarchy'.

not be possible for me to let Alec Hardinge go at this moment. I discussed the whole matter with him after Christmas, and though he hopes one day to go to India (he has been here nearly twenty years) your invitation has come a little too early.'

The king knew how difficult his private secretary could be. He acknowledged to Chamberlain that 'there has been I know a good deal of talk and criticism of Alec Hardinge in London', but his reasons for not wishing him to leave his post were twofold. In the first instance, the untested monarch was eager to have a greybeard by his side to guide him, and Hardinge, who had served under both his brother and George V, boasted undeniable expertise. And secondly, as the king acknowledged, 'if he were to leave me now, people would at once say that he and I did not get on, and that he did not agree with the policy of my government'.

Although the sovereign qualified this as 'quite untrue',[2] his hesitancy to take action showed his reluctance to wield executive power by himself. And so Hardinge remained both powerful and influential. Channon summarised this by writing, after Chamberlain's resignation, 'the King is always led by [Hardinge's] apron strings . . . [he] now has a third major victory to his credit, first the abdication, then the fall of [Hore-]Belisha, and now that of Neville'.[3]

Three years later, matters had changed, and Hardinge had been shown to be mortal after all. As Lascelles pithily described it in his diary entry of 17 July, 'Since June 25th, I have been in the throes of a crisis, which has now ended in A. Hardinge tendering his resignation to the King, who instantly accepted it and asked me to fill his place.'

Hardinge may have possessed, in Lascelles' words, 'great administrative and executive talents as a King's secretary', but he was unpopular with everyone in the royal household, including, by this stage, the king himself. Lascelles described this as arising from 'his complete inability to establish friendly, or even civil, relations with the great majority of his fellow-men', something that the politician (and later PM) Harold Macmillan agreed with, describing him as 'idle, supercilious [and] without a spark of imagination or vitality'.*⁴ Even those who had liked him now turned against him. The king's treasurer, Ulick Alexander, remarked to Channon in April 1943 that 'he is ruining the monarchy and always gives the King foolish and misguided advice . . . he is a disaster, a national calamity'.⁵

Channon was no impartial source, and for a while this high-handedness could be endured, but it dawned on Lascelles that the relationship between Hardinge and the monarch threatened to repeat the difficulties that had arisen between the private secretary and Edward VIII. As he described it, '[Hardinge and the King] were so temperamentally incompatible that they were rapidly driving each other crazy.' He compared their relationship to that of Queen Anne and Sarah Churchill, Duchess of Marlborough in its claustro-phobic intensity†, and even feared for Hardinge's mental health, calling him 'a man with no sense of flippancy, and no power to relax' and describing him as 'quite impossible' to work with.

The private secretary had in any case begun to tire of the role, which he had occupied for the past seven years. On 25 July 1942, he had confided to his mother-in-law that he had considered resig-nation, saying, 'I am in rather a different state of mind to what I was a fortnight ago. My balance was quite upset - for some reason or other - a thing that does not often happen with me, luckily!' He had been looking for a new job, but decided to stay put for the time

* This was not limited to his public life. His private letters to his wife are full of apologies for his 'crotchety' behaviour. To his credit, he acknowledged his faults. A typical comment is 'I am too unhappy that I should have upset you so much - and too sorry that I should seem to be intolerant of you.' And like both his masters, he remained uxorious. A touching letter that he wrote in February 1946 offers 'a line of thanks - which cannot possibly be adequate - for the great and unbroken happiness that you have brought me for the last twenty-five years'. Ironically, his nemesis Channon grudgingly admitted that 'his outward manners are always perfect'.
† The Duchess was widely reputed to be the queen's lover, and to exert an influence over her that both her friends and enemies found pernicious. The film *The Favourite* offers a suitably rambunctious and fictionalised account of their relationship.

being: 'I doubt if I am really right - from the point of view of my
family - to take a leap into the unknown.'

However, he then expressed his deep reservations about his
position. 'I am just as convinced that every year that I stay here,
the less chance I have of ever making either a position for myself
in the world - or money. I consider that my life - and any ability
the Lord may have given me - is being wasted here - nothing will
alter my view of that. But in my calmer moments I try to reconcile
myself to the view that all this must be sacrificed to cash.'[6]

Had Hardinge's dissatisfaction been common knowledge, his
departure could have been engineered in a smoother fashion. But
under normal circumstances, compelling the king's private secretary to retire was impossible. Lascelles lamented that 'the Royal
Family themselves are notoriously incapable of cutting that kind
of Gordian knot', and said of the Lord Chamberlain, who should
have been able to take such a decision, '[he] could not be trusted
with negotiating a change of scullery maids, let alone of private
secretaries'.

Yet after a row developed between Hardinge and Lascelles,
both men simultaneously threatened to resign, which would have
caused chaos. Only one could remain, and the king, with little
hesitation, chose to side with Lascelles. He telephoned him to say
that he had accepted Hardinge's resignation, something Lascelles
described as 'remarkable proof that my diagnosis of the intolerable
relationship between him and Alec was even more accurate than I
had suspected'.

The king had mixed reactions to Hardinge's departure. In his
account of events, he wrote, 'Before dinner I received a note from
Alec H in which he tendered his resignation to me as my Private
Secretary', which he called 'a great shock & a great surprise to me'.
He then saw Lascelles, who outlined matters. The king continued,
'Both he and Eric [Miéville]* had been kept so much in the dark
by Alec as to what was going on & they had often complained that

---

* The king's assistant private secretary, who served him from 1936 to 1945.

they had not enough work to do. Matters came to a head over this & Alec who had not been well for some long time & was utterly exhausted from the [North African] tour wrote me the letter from his house.'

It was not unwelcome. 'I replied accepting his resignation as I was not altogether happy with him & had always found him difficult to talk to & to discuss matters with. I knew & felt that he was doing me no good.'* Hardinge was surprised by the alacrity with which his departure was accepted, and the following day he asked the king point blank if he really wanted him to resign. 'I told him that I did, saying that I was very grateful for all that he had done for me in the last 7 years . . . it came as a real shock to him I could see, & I am sure he expected me to say do go on three months sick leave. After that I felt matters would be no better. I know I shall miss him in many ways, but I feel happier now it is over.'7

Hardinge's departure had resolved a dilemma. The king wrote the following day that 'It was difficult for me, but I knew I should not get this opportunity again.'8 The royal household, at a time of international crisis, had been, in Lascelles' description, 'as the sailors say, a very unhappy ship'.† Matters had to be remedied. So 'the old order changeth, yielding place to new'.

Many were delighted. Channon wrote in his diary that 'glorious news awoke me on this gloriously lovely day . . . the monarchy is saved and peace reigns in Buckingham Palace'. He took full credit for Hardinge's departure, in the same fashion as Falstaff's boasts that he had killed Hotspur at the Battle of Shrewsbury. 'For four years I have worked hard to bring about his downfall, and I must say his tactlessness and many enemies were of great assistance.'9 He approved of Lascelles, of whom he wrote, '[he] has moved

---

* Channon also speculated that the king was angered by Hardinge's opposition to Archibald Wavell being made a viscount, and quoted Brendan Bracken saying, 'this small act might prove his undoing, as such acts often do in the end'.
† Hardinge's ever-loyal wife Helen wrote in her memoirs that 'Alec served King George VI until 1943, when his health broke, largely due to the strain of the war years, and he retired.'

about in the world and might look – yet isn't really – hard-nosed'.[10]

The new private secretary assumed his demanding role at the age of fifty-six. He was delighted to be deluged with telegrams and messages of congratulations by everyone from Lord Mountbatten to Cosmo Lang, although less pleased by one press report of his appointment. 'The *Evening Standard*, in a particularly ill-informed paragraph, describes me as having "a thick thatch of black hair", as if I were an Italian organist.'[11]

Hardinge, meanwhile, was coldly courteous towards his successor, with occasional lapses into rudeness that might have been explained by his ill health; the royal doctor, Lord Dawson, thought he would need a break of at least six months to recover from the stress caused by his work. A letter to John Simon of 1 August suggested that 'the machine seems to have been run down – and it will take it some time to get it going perfectly again', even as Hardinge looked forward to his resumption of 'a more normal life'.[12]

The queen was upset by his departure, although more for the loss of a friend and confidante in the form of his wife. She wrote to Helen to ask for a meeting and said that 'I am so <u>very</u> sad about what has happened . . . I do hope that you will be able to keep it all quiet & secret for the moment . . . as you know, whatever "official" things happen . . . I am truly devoted to you & Alec, & eternally grateful for all your marvellous loyalty & unselfish backing of us both.'*[13] She would never display the same warmth towards his successor, marking a rare show of division between king and queen.

Although Lascelles allowed that 'there were some unpleasant phases in the subsequent developments', he claimed that 'there is general recognition on both sides of the fence that all is for the best, and that everyone has behaved with the best intentions'. This was Panglossian in its optimism. As diligent as ever in recording his perceptions of an event, he noted that in his final interview with Hardinge, he expressed his fears of being able to succeed in

---

* Channon summarised her ambivalence by writing, after Hardinge's fall, that 'she was in league with the Black Rat and yet intrigued against him'.

the role. 'Characteristically' Hardinge replied, 'You won't last six months.' Lascelles was able to write, not without satisfaction, 'I lasted nine years.'*[14]

Nonetheless, Lascelles assumed his new responsibility with reluctance. 'For the last twenty years I have said, in jest and in earnest, that the one thing I wished to be spared was being called on to act as the King's private secretary, and as far as my personal inclinations go, this was never more true than now.' He had wished to remain in the less demanding role of assistant private secretary and then to retire in 1947, at the age of sixty, but he was not to be allowed this.

A few months into his appointment, Lascelles would feel the full weight of his office. Churchill remarked to the king on 7 March 1944 that 'with a Bear drunken on victory in the East, and an Elephant lurching about on the West, we the UK were like a donkey in between them which was the only one who knew the way home'. He warned of the dangers the bear could pose ('the War Cabinet were very much alive to the dangerous attitude of Stalin and what a powerful Russia could do in the way of harm to the world. We don't want to have to fight Russia after the defeat of Germany'),[15] but wished to talk of more uplifting matters, namely Operation Overlord.

The code name denoted the planned Allied invasion of Normandy, to be coordinated by Eisenhower, General Bernard 'Monty' Montgomery and Admiral Sir Bertram Ramsay. The logistics of such an attack were formidable. As the king wrote in his diary on 3

---

* There was no subsequent reconciliation between Hardinge and Lascelles. The latter wrote of his former superior that 'Alec died of cancer in 1960. He never really recovered his health, and never took on another job of importance.' Hardinge was subsequently damned with the deadpan remark that 'He spent much time and energy on the Moral Rearmament movement.' The organisation's founder, Frank Buchman, commented, notoriously, 'I thank heaven for a man like Adolf Hitler, who built a front line of defence against the Anti-Christ of Communism.'

February, 'the more I learn, the more alarming [Overlord] becomes in its vastness'.[16] Yet he did not want to be a mere bystander at an event that would dictate the remainder of the course of the war.

Lascelles observed on 3 March that 'two Military Intelligence men called on me yesterday and explained how the King's visits in the next few months could assist the elaborate cover scheme whereby we are endeavouring to bamboozle the German Intelligence regarding the time and place for "Overlord"'.[17] Over the course of the war, the king had been everything from an inspirational leader to a diplomat forced into realpolitik, to say nothing of his role as husband and father. Now he was asked to add espionage to his activities.

During the following months, the king, queen and eighteen-year-old Princess Elizabeth - on her first official tour with her parents, shortly after being made a counsellor of state to deputise for her father in the event of his absence or illness - made a variety of high-profile appearances everywhere from South Wales to Scapa Flow in the Orkney Islands. The king's departure from the latter on 14 May was described in press coverage as his having 'taken leave of his fleet . . . in cold and lonely northern waters'. The intention behind this subterfuge was to persuade German intelligence that the planned target for an Allied invasion was Calais, rather than Normandy, in an operation known as Fortitude. The royals were seen in the south-east on several occasions as part of the stratagem. As the historian Richard Aldrich describes it, 'the King's visits [acted] like a highlighter pen. He identified particular units that later they [wanted] the Germans to follow.'[18]

These visits were not without risk. At least twice the monarch had to appear at locations where U-boats were known to patrol, placing himself in danger. Lascelles remarked of his sangfroid in these situations, which translated into greater public confidence. On 15 May, when the monarch visited Eisenhower's headquarters at St Paul's School in London, Lascelles wrote that 'to my astonishment, [the king] stepped on to the platform and delivered an admirable impromptu speech, in which he said exactly the right things, and said them very well'. The private secretary also noted that given the presence of Eisenhower, Monty, Ramsay, Churchill and other dignitaries, 'there has probably been no single assembly in the last four years the annihilation of which by a single well-directed bomb would affect more profoundly the issue of the war'.[19]

Yet the most elaborate deception the king was involved in turned to the modernist architect Basil Spence for its full effect. Spence, who was serving as a second lieutenant at the time, had designed a vast and entirely fake oil depot near Dover, at the behest of General Patton's First US Army Group. It was an elaborate structure, complete with everything from pipelines to storage tanks, and newsreel footage was filmed of the king inspecting the site and addressing non-existent troops. This was observed by German intelligence, who constructed a 'British Order of Battle' map that formed the basis of their attempts to ascertain where an Allied attack was likely to originate from. It was painstaking, well informed and entirely wrong.

Fired up with excitement and pride at his involvement in the subterfuge, the king now proposed to Churchill that he should take part in Operation Overlord himself. The prime minister, who had a similar aim in mind, was taken aback, but a compromise was agreed upon: the two men would travel into battle together. The king wrote, 'It is a big decision to take on one's own responsibility. W cannot say no if he goes himself, & I don't want to have to tell him he cannot. So? I told Elizabeth about the idea & she was wonderful as always & encouraged me to do it.'[20]

Lascelles was less enthusiastic. He attempted to discourage the king by asking him whether it would be fair to the queen to think of her husband in such perilous circumstances, or whether it was Princess Elizabeth's responsibility to choose a prime minister in the event of both Churchill and her father dying in the invasion attempt. Mindful of the 'paralysing effect' of having the king and/ or Churchill on board for any unfortunate captain thrust into the midst of a fiery maelstrom, he persuaded his monarch against such an endeavour ('which is quite right', the disappointed king observed). It would be heroic, but also ran the risk of being suicidal.

Not without reluctance, the king wrote to Churchill on 31 May to say that 'it would not be right for either you or I to be where we planned to be on D-Day'. He suggested that 'I don't think I need emphasise what it would mean to me personally, and to the whole Allied cause, if at this juncture a chance bomb, torpedo or even a mine would remove you from the scene; equally a change of sovereign at this moment would be a serious matter for the country & Empire.'

Referring to their proposed presence as 'an embarrassment to those responsible for fighting', he decided that 'the right thing to do is . . . to remain at home and wait'. He struck a personal note when he added that 'the anxiety of these coming days would be very greatly increased for me if I thought that . . . there was a risk, however remote, of my losing your help and guidance'.[21]

Churchill refused to withdraw, much to Lascelles' and the King's irritation, and so the unfortunately named 'Operation WC' had to be planned for. As the monarch observed that 'Tommy's face is getting longer and longer', Lascelles remarked, 'I was thinking, Sir, that it is not going to make things easier for you if you have to find a new Prime Minister in the middle of Overlord.' Churchill, who was behaving 'just like a naughty child', with 'sheer selfishness, plus vanity', cheerily said that in the event of his death, 'that's all arranged for',* and that 'I don't think the risk is 100-1.' The king wrote angrily that 'I am very worried over the PM's seemingly selfish way of looking at the matter. He doesn't seem to care about the future, or how much depends on him.'[22]

Lascelles attempted to invoke protocol to frustrate the endeavour, declaring that no minister of the Crown could leave the country without his sovereign's consent, but he was batted back, as Churchill declared that he would not be leaving the country since he would remain on a British man-of-war. Lascelles wrote furiously, 'Just to gratify his love of theatre, and adventure, he is ready

---

* Presumably Churchill would have nominated Anthony Eden as his successor.

to jettison all considerations of what is due to his sovereign, his colleagues, and the state . . . If he should be killed in [Overlord's] early stages, the news of his death might easily have such an effect on the troops as to turn victory into defeat.'[23]

It is not hard to see what attracted Churchill to the idea of taking part in the expedition. The symbolic sight of the prime minister walking onto the Normandy beaches amongst his men and making an impromptu speech of thanks for the much-longed-for victory, to say nothing of the newsreels and photographs that would be taken of such an event, would be nothing less than iconic. Throughout the course of the war, Churchill's actions and speeches had over-shadowed those of his monarch. And now, at literally the eleventh hour, the two men, who had enjoyed such a harmonious relation-ship after initial distrust, once again found themselves at odds. The king was determined that his premier would not leave the country on such a perilous expedition, at any cost. Churchill, meanwhile, had set his heart on participating in it. As Lascelles commented, 'none of those who have access to Winston can influence him once he is set on a course, not even Mrs Churchill; nor, apparently, his anointed King'.[24]

With mere days left before the operation, the king wrote again to Churchill at Lascelles' behest, this time with urgency. 'I am a younger man than you, I am a sailor, & as King I am the head of all the Services. There is nothing I would like better than to go to sea but I have agreed to stay at home; is it fair that you should then do exactly what I should have liked to do myself?' Churchill had spoken to the monarch in romantic terms - 'you said yester-day afternoon that it would be a fine thing for the King to lead his troops into battle, as in old days' - but despite his own sympathy with the idea, the sovereign had to dissuade his prime minister from a potentially ruinous course. The letter stressed that Chur-chill's presence on board ship would be less exciting than antici-pated ('you will see very little, you will seem at considerable risk')[25] as he adopted the tone of a junior partner begging a superior not to take a hazardous course of action. This was not the way a monarch would usually write to a prime minister, even one as popular as Churchill.

The premier, however, remained committed to 'Operation WC'. Although Lascelles wrote optimistically that 'Ismay said this morning that he thought the PM was wobbling'[26] and that Churchill could see the absurdity in his taking part in the operation, having advised the king against so doing, the prime minister possessed a stubborn impulse that would not be dictated to. He wrote with some force to the king to say that while he acknowledged that the monarch heading to war required Cabinet approval, 'as Prime Minister and Minister of Defence, I ought to be allowed to go where I consider it necessary to the discharge of my duty, and I do not admit that the Cabinet have any right to put restrictions on my freedom of movement'. The king remained fearful. 'I have been very worried and anxious over the whole of this business & it is my duty to warn the PM on such occasions. No one else can & should anything dreadful happen I should be asked if I had tried to deter him.'[27]

Yet Churchill was weakening. Eventually, his point made, he admitted defeat. He huffed that 'I rely on my own judgement, invoked in many serious matters, as to what are the proper limits of risk which a person who discharges my duties is entitled to run', but he petulantly acknowledged that 'Since Your Majesty does me the honour to be so much concerned about my personal safety on this occasion, I must defer to Your Majesty's wishes and indeed commands.'[28] He would not go to war. Lascelles wrote triumphantly that 'We have bested him, which not many people have succeeded in doing in the last four years!'[29]

Although Churchill was becalmed, the sea was not. D-Day had been scheduled for 5 June, but bad weather and a growing storm meant that Eisenhower decided to postpone Operation Overlord for twenty-four hours. Therefore, the Allied occupation of Rome, which took place as scheduled on the 4th, seemed momentarily like a one-off incursion rather than a coordinated European assault. Every day Overlord was delayed increased the risk of detection. It seemed extraordinary that German intelligence had not raised the alarm, given that the Allies were about to launch the largest sea invasion ever assembled in history, involving tens of thousands of troops and hundreds of ships. The weather improved, albeit not as much as might have been wished for, but there could be no further postponement. Eisenhower gave the order that Overlord should take place on 6 June.

After months, even years of anticipation, the invasion of Europe went as well as it could possibly have done. Lascelles wrote, 'I was woken at 5 a.m. by streams of aircraft passing across London, the harbingers of "Overlord" . . . the first stage of the adventure has gone well, and surprisingly cheaply. Naval and air casualties are practically negligible, and of the four main landings, only one . . . seems to have met any serious opposition.' Before midday, Monty was able to send a telegram saying that 'I could not wish the situation of this army to be better.' The relief that the king, Churchill and all around them felt at the successful execution of the plan was overwhelming. Lascelles noted that 'all those who have been entrusted with the very well-kept secret look ten years younger'.[30]

It was a magnificent victory. And now that it was clear that it could be billed thus, the king delivered a Churchill-scripted broadcast to the nation that evening. It eschewed triumphalism in favour of optimism, and combined something of both men's best qualities, with the prime minister's ear for a telling phrase ('tested as never before in our history, in God's providence, we survived the test; the spirit of the people, resolute, dedicated, burned like a bright flame') yoked together with the monarch's homespun, man-of-the-people persona. He talked of crusading impulses, called his country to prayer and dedication, and spoke of God, the queen and Empire. The peroration struck a Christian note, as the king cited Psalm 29 and declared, 'The Lord will give strength unto his people; the Lord will give his people the blessing of peace.' Yet peace remained elusive. It would be another year until celebrations could finally take place.

Once it was clear that northern France had been secured, both

Churchill and the king expressed their desire to head there. It was a quirk of the constitutional process that while Churchill could leave for France on 10 June and return on the same day with his monarch's assent, the king had to have a similar visit approved by the entire Cabinet. Churchill granted him permission on 13 June, but took care to emphasise the need for careful action at all times.* Yet he acknowledged that such a visit would be favourable propaganda, and waved it through.

When the king arrived in France early in the morning of Saturday 17 June, it was in grim conditions. Lascelles wrote that Overlord would have been a logistical impossibility if the weather had not been to their advantage. After a good lunch ('with genuine Camembert cheeses', he noted, 'a thing we've not seen in London since 1940'), the king performed an investiture, discussed battle tactics with Monty and had to be dissuaded from going deeper into the battle lines for fear of snipers. Lascelles observed that the French were not entirely delighted by their arrival. 'For four years, they have been selling their farm produce to the Germans, who appear to have treated them well enough; they do not all relish being liberated by an invading army, whose passage must inevitably disturb the even tempo of their lives, even if it don't [sic] actually knock their buildings flat.'[†31]

After all the excitement of Overlord and the king's visit, the next few months proved to be anticlimactic and even disappointing. Hitler's response to the success of D-Day had been to authorise socalled 'Crossbow' air raids. By September that year, the V-2 rocket, a self-propelled, erratic but deadly device, was an ever-present threat to life in Britain, especially given the near-impossibility of being able to shoot them down. The king described them as 'more

---

* Like his elder brother, the king resented the way in which his actions were in the hands of his ministers and not his own. Lascelles recorded how he inveighed 'with some bitterness' against the governmental interference to which he was constitutionally liable.
† He qualified this on 28 June by saying, 'the French population have, in the main, received us very well'.

than a nuisance ... [they are] a threat to our normal life & the effects on people's nerves & energy for their war effort should be impaired should the attacks go on for months'.[32] The only means of destruction was to attack the factories that made them, and so the war of attrition continued.

'Being shut up here is like being a prisoner of war, only worse.'[33] Wallis was miserable when she wrote to her aunt on 5 April. She was tired of life in the Bahamas and frustrated with the pettiness of her official role, the dull responsibilities she faced and the pervasive heat. Oakes's murder with its concomitant publicity* - to say nothing of Bedaux's suicide - had made matters even worse. Yet it still came as a shock to see herself denounced in a magazine as a grasping and insipid clothes horse, less interested in the war her country was participating in than in acquiring seemingly unlimited amounts of jewels, furs and dresses.

In the damning piece in the *American Mercury*, the journalist Helen Worden lambasted Wallis as petty, status-obsessed, in thrall to an outdated perception of her own worth ('She still thinks her public wants display') and responsible for the reduced status of her husband. One anonymous Englishman even suggested that should she return to Britain, she could expect to be stoned to death in the street. It was undeniably a hatchet job, designed to make the duchess - and by extension the duke - look as out of touch and pathetic as possible, even down to the crude caricature of her face on the cover. What it did not warrant, however, was the duke asking J. Edgar Hoover to investigate the *Mercury* and other titles to see if there was a conspiracy to blacken Wallis's name. Edward's latent anti-Semitism came to the fore in his suggestion that this conspiracy was driven by the Jews, as 'he believed that Miss Helen Worden, author of the article, was Jewish'.[†34]

---

* Wallis complained to her friend Rosita Forbes, 'they only murdered Sir Harry Oakes once. They will never stop murdering the Duke of Windsor.' By 'they', she meant, naturally, his ungrateful family.
† She was not.

The duke and duchess were bored of the Bahamas. As Edward complained in an unsent letter to Churchill in March 1944, 'he who is wise senses when he has outgrown his usefulness in any given job, official or otherwise . . . I am fortunate in being able to detect that this has now happened in my own case.'[35] He occupied himself by spreading dissent and cynicism about reports of inevitable victory, remarking to Halifax, 'Although the ultimate outcome of the war is a foregone conclusion, the present military situation is depressing, particularly the fact that the first stages of the seemingly inevitable invasion must involve appalling casualties among the British and American attacking forces. I am afraid that it looks as if the softening up as to the relentless bombing of Germany has not been as successful as we were at one time led to believe.'[36]

He announced his intention of visiting America once again, which a reluctant Halifax complained about to Stanley: 'As you know, I don't like these visits, but neither on compassionate nor on rational grounds can I really bring myself to prohibit them! And it may well be argued that every time he comes, his publicity value will diminish. I hope this is true!'[37]

The duke wished to resign and be rewarded for his years of service with a lucrative sinecure. Unfortunately, this was not a view taken by his family or former associates. Lascelles himself was opposed to the very existence of the duke. 'I don't think any problems in my life have given me so much anxiety as those arising from his.' He tersely outlined the future possibilities for him in a post-war, post-Bahamas milieu. An ambassadorial post; life in Britain as a quasi-younger brother of the king; an anonymous existence in his home country as a wealthy private citizen; or the same in the United States. He believed the first option to be impossible ('I doubt if he would be safe in any ambassadorial post . . . [I base this] on his Rehoboam*-like tendency to take up with undesirable, and dangerous, associates'), the second and third to be impractical,

---

* A Judaic king of notoriously poor and reckless judgement – unlike his father, Solomon – who battled his own brothers.

not least because it would cost Edward around £20,000 a year in tax to return to his home country, which left only the last as remotely suitable, or, in Lascelles' words, 'for the best chance for the Prince's own happiness and for the peace of the world at large'.

Even with the launch of Overlord a few days away, Lascelles remarked that 'the problem of his brother's future (involved as it must be with his brother's past and his own present) probably gives the King deeper and more painful concern than any one of his many responsibilities'.*38 It was unsurprising that the king sent a telegram to Churchill on 16 September before a meeting between the duke and the prime minister in America. It stated baldly, 'In any discussion as to his future perhaps you would put forward my conviction, which you already know, namely that his happiness will be best promoted by his making his home in the USA. Repeat USA.'39

Churchill, despite his own objections to the duke's behaviour, saw matters differently, despite an interview he had had with the king on 30 June in which both men agreed that Edward could not settle in Britain after the end of the war. The prime minister had advised Lascelles in late May that he did not believe Edward could be prevented from returning to Britain, and now he suggested to the king that if he delivered such a blunt message to Edward, it could be counter-productive, and even lead the duke to try and establish a rival court of sorts in England. He would intervene with Edward in person, and hoped to resolve matters satisfactorily.

Shortly before Churchill's visit, the duke and duchess had caused their usual trouble, this time with publicly indiscreet behaviour. A Pennsylvania engineer named William H. Harman wrote to Halifax on 17 August to complain that 'Every daily newspaper has long lists each day of American boys who are being killed or

---

* In a letter written about the same time, Lascelles indicated, 'I do not think that there is any point of difference between the attitude of the King and that of the two Queens as to a meeting with the Duke of Windsor. All of them would be glad to see the Duke; none of them wishes to see the Duchess.'

injured in action in France, Italy, or the Pacific Area. I am sure you can appreciate the reaction of parents, wives and relatives of these boys when they see in the same daily paper, in the midst of their grief, headlines reporting the social activities of the Duke and Duchess of Windsor. For a month now, we have had to read of their night clubbing activities, and at the present the headlines refer to their rounds of gayety [sic] at Newport.'

Harman compared the attitudes of the Americans and the British, to the latter's detriment – 'I am certain that if a Roosevelt boy were engaged in this sort of thing in England that his father would order him home at once' – and added, 'You must appreciate that this is harming tremendously not only the war effort, but the relationship that should exist between our respective countries. If nothing can be done to get them both out of the country, surely somebody could at least see that they both keep their activities under cover.'[40]

Halifax wrote three letters in response to the complaint. He defended the duke and duchess to Harman, suggesting that 'criticism of them for spending time in social relaxation gives them no credit at all for spending, I suppose, ninety per cent of their time . . . in public work and exacting duties in the public service' and adding that 'there is no essential difference, is there, between people taking their pleasure, for example by watching a ball game, and other people finding it in the form of social meetings, except that the position held by the Duke and Duchess of Windsor naturally lends itself more readily to publicity'.[41] He reassured the duke as to the 'injustice' of the letter, while noting that 'there are plenty of unthinking, and perhaps mischievous, people who will be very ready to take unfavourable notice of what Your Royal Highness does, which they would not do in the case of others'.[42] But he offered his most candid reaction to Stanley. 'I suppose one must expect this sort of thing, but you will see the kind of picture which gets into the mind of the American public, and which is very difficult to eradicate.'[43]

Fresh from offending American public opinion, Edward met

Churchill at Roosevelt's summer home of Hyde Park in September. The duke was shocked by the president's shrunken and shrivelled appearance, and described him to Churchill as 'a very sick man', only for the prime minister to counter that he was merely 'tired, very tired'. The pair spoke together *à deux*, the duke reporting it to Allen as 'a long and satisfactory talk - in so far as it went, which was not very far'.[44] It was agreed that Edward would give up the governorship of the Bahamas at the end of the year, that he would then be free to return to his villa in the South of France and that he would not return to England as a full-time resident, although he reserved the right to make informal visits to his former country now and again.

The major point of contention was his future official role. Churchill reported to the king that 'the subject was not raised of his future employment as an Ambassador or Governor', but this was not true. The duke did bring up the idea, which led the prime minister to become evasive and change the subject, but not before saying that the palace would be discomforted if Edward showed an intention of returning to Great Britain as a full-time resident. The duke reported to Allen that '[this] amused me a whole lot', but he was also surprised that 'after eight years absence, I was still considered so formidable a menace to the solidarity of the monarchy'. He caustically remarked that 'hardly a day passes by that British propaganda does not stuff us with the extent to which the King has established himself in the hearts of the people'.[45]

He indicated this in in a milder fashion to Churchill on 3 October. 'I would not wish to remain unemployed if there was any sphere in which it were considered my experience could still be appropriately utilised.' He hoped for, even expected, a well-paid and comfortable ambassadorial post to the United States or France. Here, any responsibilities and duties he faced could be deputed to underlings, and he would be at leisure to pursue the life of a wealthy citizen, bolstered by an official title and the opportunity to wear his decorations at receptions as he smiled for the cameras. This did not materialise.

The prospect of Edward heading anywhere was one that struck discomfort into any country expected to receive him. Eden's private secretary Oliver Harvey reported that René Massigli, the French ambassador to the United Kingdom, was 'embarrassed' at the suggestion that the duke and duchess would return to their villa in the South of France, 'in view of some of the acquaintances which the Duke and Duchess had had [there]'. He asked that they might stay away until at least the conclusion of the war. Harvey observed that '[Massigli] feared that the Duke and Duchess would seek to renew acquaintance with many who had turned out to be collaborators, and this would cause a most embarrassing situation.'

It is tempting to wonder what would have happened to Edward and Wallis had they behaved in the fashion they did without the saving grace of his royal birth. Arrogance, disdain and pig-headedness were hardly character flaws exclusive to those with a certain degree of privilege, and the crass opportunism they both frequently displayed, although regrettable, was not a crime. Yet the flaunting of their associations with Nazis, fascist sympathisers and fellow travellers was too extensive and consistent to be excused merely as poor judgement. It may be overstating the case, as some biographers and historians have done, to call Edward the 'traitor king'. But it is not hard to imagine a situation in which, shorn of the cosseting advantages they enjoyed, the Duke and Duchess of Windsor might have expected to find themselves in Holloway prison, not too far from Oswald Mosley and Diana Mitford, rather than the more salubrious delights of the Château de la Croë.

Edward continued to believe that he was in a stronger position vis-à-vis his family than in fact he was. In his letter to Churchill of 3 October, he reiterated his belief that he and Wallis should be received by the royals for tea, and he explicitly invited the prime minister to take his side in the matter. He acknowledged that 'it could never be a very happy meeting', but suggested that his reason for asking for the 'quite painless' encounter was to silence those

'malicious circles' who speculated about the poor state of royal relations that had existed since the abdication. He wrote, almost triumphantly, 'I will be very surprised if you do not think my remedy
the best cure for this evil situation, and decide to advise the King
and Queen to swallow the "Windsor Pill" just once, however bitter
they may think it is going to taste!'

The royal family did not consider it necessary to swallow the
Windsor Pill at all. Various notes and memoranda that exist from
late 1944 suggest that the king was perfectly happy not to see his
brother for a further decade and had no intention of receiving
Wallis in any formal capacity under any circumstances. Lascelles
wrote on 9 November that 'the King, apart from his recollection
that the D of W has, on more than one occasion, been extremely
rude to, and about, the Queen, Queen Mary and other royal ladies,
thinks that [a gesture of reconciliation] is wrong in principle, and
would imply that the Abdication had all been a mistake'. He also
believed that Churchill's 'sentimental loyalty' to Edward was based
on what he called 'a tragic false premise - viz that he really *knew* the
Duke - which he never did'.[46]

Queen Elizabeth and Queen Mary closed ranks. They signed a
statement refusing to receive the duchess then or at any other time,
and believed this to be consistent with their behaviour in 1936.
It was also made clear that Churchill should either treat this as a
private family matter, in which case his intervention was no longer
welcome, or a state one, in which case he faced the embarrassment
of having to involve the Cabinet. As in the abdication crisis, this
would turn a personal affair into one of national import.

And there, with some tension, the matter was forced to a stale-
mate. Nobody was prepared to compromise or climb down, and
so the persistent ill will that had existed for years was only exa-
cerbated. As the duke prepared to leave his position as governor of
the Bahamas, and the king and queen hoped for a final resolution
to the European war, the conflict between these irreconcilable personalities showed no signs of resolution. Only the most optimistic
of observers might have believed that there was any possibility of

the royal brothers ever exchanging a civil conversation in person again.

Still, it was wartime. Stranger things could, and did, occur, and another event on the horizon took the actions of royalty into the realms not of farce but of tragedy.

Chapter Eighteen

'O Captain! My Captain!'

The noise outside Buckingham Palace was deafening. Tens of thousands of people had gathered in front of the building in a great crush of euphoria and giddiness. They knew that Tuesday 8 May was their day, the desperately looked-for resolution to five and a half years of fear and frustration. Many had lost loved ones, their homes, livelihoods. Yet as they stood there as one entity, all shouted a single sentence with a combination of joy and determination.

'We want the king . . . we want the king.'

Excited, giddy faces, all ideas of protocol or convention abandoned, gazed up at the balcony while they called over and over again for their monarch to appear. As the king finished listening to his prime minister's broadcast, he prepared to satisfy their demands. If he had contemplated the *volte-face* in his fortunes, it might have even amused him. A decade ago, he was the younger brother of the Prince of Wales, with little if any expectation of becoming king. Now he had led his country through the greatest trial it had ever faced, and had done so with courage, humour and good grace.

The once untested and terrified sovereign had, over the previous eight and a half years, established himself as a universally beloved figure, especially at this time of crisis and national suffering. With help from Churchill and others, he had become a unifying presence, and his popularity was such that the reception he and his family received verged on idolatry.

'We want the king . . . we want the king.'

The royal family's appearance had been carefully prepared for. Only the king, queen, Princess Elizabeth and Princess Margaret stepped out onto the balcony, shortly after Churchill's speech to the nation finished. Queen Mary remained in Gloucestershire, the Duke of Gloucester was serving as governor general of Australia, and the Duke of Windsor, naturally, was *persona non grata*. The king was clad, appropriately formally, in his naval outfit, and his elder daughter in the uniform of an officer of the Auxiliary Territorial Service, which she had joined as a subaltern in February 1945.* They received the applause and adulation of the crowd with gratitude, and this continued throughout the day. Their eighth, and final, appearance on the balcony took place after midnight.

Meanwhile, the princesses had escaped the palace and were mingling incognito with the revellers, much to their delight. Two Guards officers escorted them outside, and they were able to have what Crawfie called 'a glorious time'. Elizabeth later recounted how 'We asked my parents if we could go out and see for ourselves. I remember we were terrified of being recognised . . . I remember lines of unknown people linking arms and walking down Whitehall, all of us just swept along on a tide of happiness and relief.'[1] 'Poor darlings, they have never had any fun yet',[2] the king wrote in his diary, with compassionate indulgence.

He addressed his people at 9 p.m. with a mixture of relief, pride and exhaustion. 'Today, we give thanks to Almighty God for a great deliverance.' His broadcast lacked the fluency of many of his previous speeches, although Lascelles called it 'a trifle slow but otherwise excellent.'[†3] The event the country had prayed for since September 1939, the surrender of the German forces, had come to pass. The Second World War in Europe was over. The king praised the 'constancy and courage' of his subjects, and said, 'There is great

---

* It was work that she quickly took to, becoming adept in assembling and dismantling engines; Crawfie described her as 'very grave and determined to get good marks and do the right thing'.
† Harold Nicolson demurred, praising the content of the speech but remarking, 'it is agony to listen to him - like a typewriter that sticks at every third word'.

comfort in the thought that the years of darkness and danger in which the children of our country have grown up are over and, please God, for ever.'

The formal act of military surrender had been signed on 7 May, following the final, chaotic days in Germany. The following day, VE Day, saw exuberant and unchecked celebrations throughout Britain, with spontaneous street parties and national rejoicing as the enormity of the deliverance became clear. Hitler was dead, shot by his own hand in his squalid bunker. Most of his key lieutenants – Himmler, Goebbels, Göring – had either killed themselves in solidarity or been captured by the Allied forces. There had been no compromise, no face-saving final deal. It was the greatest military victory the country had ever seen.

Credit lay with many, but it was Churchill, as prime minister, who was the most obvious recipient of public gratitude. On VE Day, he made a speech at 3 p.m. from Downing Street in which he stated that 'we may allow ourselves a brief period of rejoicing, but let us not forget for a moment the toils and efforts that lie ahead'. He might have been expected to be exultant, but he was not. Not only was he fatigued by his exertions over the previous years, but he was aware that for all the public exuberance, his work was far from done. Japan, by then a more implacable and dangerous enemy than Germany, remained undefeated and with few signs of capitulation. A long-postponed general election awaited. After the harmony of his wartime collaboration with Clement Attlee, normal political business would have to resume. And another, alarming issue had emerged, which he would have preferred to avoid dealing with altogether.

But he was still able to cheer the masses with his statement that 'This is your hour . . . this is not victory of a party or any class. It's a victory of the great British nation as a whole. We were the first, in this ancient island, to draw the sword against tyranny. After a while we were left all alone against the most tremendous military power that has been seen. We were all alone for a whole year.' Amidst roaring and applause, he reminded his listeners of the necessity of defeating 'a foe stained with cruelty and greed' and praised 'our great Russian allies', who were at that moment busily engaged in punitively laying waste to Berlin. He then headed to the House of Commons, where he repeated his statement in a more formal capacity, before joining the king, queen and their children at Buckingham Palace.

Neither the prime minister nor the monarch reacted to VE Day with the giddy excitement of the public, epitomised by Noël Coward describing it as 'the greatest day in our history'.[4] Both had been drained by their responsibilities. Harold Nicolson remarked on the king's 'wizened and lined' face when film of the day was shown in newsreels, and noted that his attempts to control his stammer led him to twitch nervously. The king knew he was unable to present the calm and happy demeanour that might have been expected from him, but he felt it impossible to behave with equanimity.

That night, he wrote, 'The day we have been longing for has arrived at last, and we can look back with thankfulness to God that our tribulation is finally over. No more fear of being bombed at home, & no more living in air raid shelters. But there is still Japan to be defeated & the restoration of our country to be dealt with, which will give us many headaches & hard work in the coming years.'[5] His letters and diary entries struck a similarly downbeat note; he wrote to Gloucester, 'I feel burnt out' and noted that he felt 'rather jaded from it all' and that 'I have found it difficult to rejoice or relax as there is still so much hard work ahead to deal with.'[6]

There were three reasons for his lack of triumphalism. The first was the continuing war with Japan in the Far East, and the second was the death of Roosevelt. Finally, another confrontation with his brother - the very definition of 'hard work' - could not now be avoided.

At the beginning of 1945, with victory in Europe seeming assured, the king's most pressing concern was that Churchill should be granted a suitably fitting honour. He accordingly suggested that he should be awarded the Order of the Garter. The prime minister, while 'touched and honoured', demurred on the grounds that it would be inappropriate for him to accept such a distinction while he served as premier, but qualified this by saying that if he was to agree to it, he should only take it upon his retirement, and if nominated by a succeeding prime minister. The disappointed king replied, 'I feel that the country will expect me to give you a high honour which it will acclaim as a fitting tribute for all your arduous work in this war, and one which will still enable you to remain in the House of Commons',[7] but accepted the point.*

The Duke of Windsor, who was not offered such a distinction, seemed almost disappointed by the prospect of imminent victory, remarking to Halifax on 17 January that 'The European news has been depressing lately and although the situation in Belgium and Luxembourg seems to be well in hand, the German penetration involving heavy allied casualties and loss of material will, I fear, prolong hostilities. I was always afraid that the liberation of France and especially Paris was creating a spirit of optimism both in Great Britain and America which would prove to be premature as soon as we bumped up against the Siegfried line. As things have turned out, my surmise has unfortunately been correct.' Announcing that he intended to leave the Bahamas around the middle of April, he offered Halifax his own perspective on world affairs. 'It is discouraging to observe how the nearer we get to so-called victory, so the breach between the right and left, conservatism and communism, widens in all countries.'[8] Such perspicacious insight would undoubtedly have served him poorly if he had ever attained the ambassadorial position he coveted, but fortunately that would not come to pass.

The ambassador responded robustly to the duke's near defeatism. 'The war news is encouraging and Uncle Joe has really got moving!' Much of his letter could be seen as a coded rebuke to

---

* Churchill would later be awarded the Order of the Garter by Elizabeth II, on 23 April 1953.

Edward's perceived, and lamented, pro-German sympathies. 'I am constantly wondering how the German public - who must have been thinking for years that everything must be coming out all right - can possibly reconcile their present position with their blind faith in the Führer . . . what a retribution it is.' He concluded, pointedly, 'On the whole . . . criticisms of British policy do not seem so far to have had the effect of reviving much of the old fashioned isolationist spirit . . . I hope that when we shall have the pleasure of seeing you again the face of the war will have still further changed in the direction of the right conclusion.'*9

The duke's post-war reception in Britain remained uncertain. Lascelles reported that the king did not want to consider the matter until the start of 1945, and that he was, in any case, implacable about his refusal to receive Wallis. Churchill tried to communicate this in as tactful a fashion as he could, only to receive a haughty letter from Edward on 12 February in which he expressed his intention to avoid his home country. 'The persistence of my mother's attitude towards my wife, which you infer represents the great mass of the British nation . . . makes it preferable not to go to Great Britain for the present. We most certainly do not wish to expose ourselves unnecessarily to insults that can be so simply avoided, by travelling some other way to the Continent of Europe.' He then outlined his planned timetable for his departure from the Bahamas: a formal notice of resignation on 15 March, followed by departure in mid April, when he and Wallis would head to the United States.

Edward's resignation as governor was unnecessary, as his appointment would have terminated on 9 July 1945 in any case, on the five-year anniversary of his assuming the role. But it gave him a sense of being able to assume agency over his own destiny, and inadvertently saved the British government from humiliation. Had his term ended in July, and it had become clear that he was

---

* A chastened duke replied on 20 March, 'The war news is certainly most encouraging; if only the Nazis would throw in the sponge before many more thousands of our people are sacrificed.'

not to be given any other major responsibility or post, it would have laid bare the tensions between the government and the royal couple. As his decision to depart had been taken autonomously, no such embarrassment resulted. It was with relief that Churchill replied to the duke on 18 March, praising him for his efforts over the past five years, with a fulsomeness that failed to fully conceal his disingenuousness.

How had the duke really coped as governor? In some regards, he had executed the role reasonably well. Given that the job had been foisted upon him almost as a punishment, he had behaved reasonably diligently, even as he privately complained about the indignities and inanities he was compelled to suffer. His biographer Michael Bloch gives him credit for bringing an energetic and even fresh approach to a difficult task, citing Sir Philip Rogers, private secretary to the Permanent Head of the Colonial Office, as saying, 'We . . . regarded the Duke of Windsor as a good Governor of the Bahamas . . . he had a sure touch in a colony that was notoriously difficult politically . . . In short, given wartime circumstances and the political circumstances in the Bahamas . . . our feeling in the Colonial Office was that he did a good job.'[10]

Others have been less generous. Another biographer, Frances Donaldson, wrote damningly that '[Edward] had neither the training nor any understanding of the discipline required of His Majesty's representatives in the Colonies' and that 'the Duchess was the more unpopular'. Another biographer - whom Bloch believes produced a 'venomous volume' - simply wrote, 'The Duke had failed . . . at the end of the war, they left the islands quickly . . . in utter disgrace'.[11]

Certainly he was not a trained diplomat, and his half-dismissive, half-contemptuous attitude towards the inhabitants of the Bahamas, although entirely in keeping with a man of his background and class, indicated that his commitment to his role was never overwhelming. Just as he had performed the public aspects of kingship with flair while despising the responsibilities that he believed cramped his personal freedom, he hated being governor and

carried out his tasks under sufferance. That he continued in the
role until virtually the end of the war might be held to his credit,
or alternatively as a reflection of the restricted influence he now
possessed. If he was given a task, he might have grumbled and
complained and been high-handed in its execution, but short of
committing insubordination, there was little else he could do.

Yet as he prepared to depart the Bahamas for the United States,
a tragic event occurred that threatened to overshadow everything
else. On 12 April, Roosevelt remarked, while sitting for a formal
portrait, 'I have a terrific headache.' He then fell unconscious,
and died shortly afterwards. The cause of death was a cerebral
haemorrhage.

His health had been poor for a considerable time – the king had
noted in February that '[the president] has become very feeble'[12]
– but his end was still a shock, especially with the imminent approach of VE Day. The flags flew at half-mast as his bereft nation
dealt with the enormity of their loss. The last president to die in
office, Warren G. Harding, had been a scandal-riddled and diminished figure whose demise from a heart attack in 1921 was an in-
consequential event. Roosevelt's death was a personal and political
blow to the Allied cause. Although his dealings with the king and,
more vitally, Churchill had not been without self-interest – the
monarch mused in July 1944, just before Overlord, that 'FDR is not
always easy'[13] – his support for Britain and British interests had
been unwavering. This particular tolling of the bell diminished all
mankind.

The king and Churchill exchanged glum letters the following
day.* The monarch wrote, 'I cannot tell you how sad I am ... the
news came as a great shock to me. I have lost a friend, but to you
who have known him for so long & so intimately during this war,
the sudden loss to yourself personally of a colleague & helpmate in

---

* The king also remarked to Queen Mary that 'we shall all feel his loss very
much' and put his death down to 'overwork due to the war', a subject he was all
too familiar with.

the framing of far-reaching decisions both for the prosecution of the war & for the future peace of the world must be overwhelming.'[14]

Churchill replied, 'The sudden loss of this great friend and comrade in all our affairs is very hard for me. Ties have been shorn asunder which years had woven. We have to begin again in many ways.' Then he moved from personal to global affairs, contemplating relations with 'the new man', President Truman. He decided against heading to the United States for Roosevelt's funeral, ostensibly because the business of work was so pressing.

The president's death was a huge symbolic blow to the Allies, but it had little practical effect. Mussolini and his mistress were captured and executed by Italian partisans on 28 April, before being strung up on meat hooks: a crude but effective reminder of how a once-powerful man could be defeated and ruined. The Soviet advance through the East continued, and then the troops came across the unimaginable obscenity of Auschwitz. As it became clear, with the discoveries of Bergen-Belsen, Dachau and Buchenwald, that the concentration camp horrors were not a revolting and unlicensed anomaly but a central tenet of the Nazi regime, battle-hardened soldiers who had believed they were fighting an enemy observing the normal rules of warfare were reduced to uncomprehending revulsion.

Eisenhower described it pithily when he wrote, 'I have never felt able to describe my emotional reactions when I first came face to face with indisputable evidence of Nazi brutality and ruthless disregard of every shred of decency. I have never at any other time experienced an equal sense of shock.'[15] This was echoed by the king, who wrote helplessly of how the 'bestial maltreatment' of human beings, of bodies stacked in ovens and littered around the camps, was a sickening display of evil at its most incomprehensible.

His initial response was to ascribe blame to the entire nation, writing, 'the German people are all guilty in allowing these things to happen . . . they have no sense of shame that it is wrong',[16] but he soon retracted this, on the grounds that the ordinary man or woman was unaware of the obscenities committed by the Nazi

high command in the name of racial purity. To have condemned all
of Germany would have seen him disassociate himself from many
members of his extended family, and this was not an estrangement
he wished to undertake. After all, the loss of two of his brothers
had been enough.*

So the king smiled and waved on VE Day, made his broadcast
to the nation and took comfort in the end of the conflict. As the
queen wrote to Osbert Sitwell afterwards, 'it is almost impossible
to believe that the dreadful war is over, and Germany truly beaten
– the sense of relief from bombs and rockets is very agreeable at
the moment, and I hope that people won't forget too soon. They
have shown such a noble and unselfish spirit all through the country during these long years of war, and I long for them to keep at
the same high level in the days to come.'[17]

It was therefore unfortunate from a royal perspective that the
noble and unselfish people showed ingratitude almost immediately. Not two months after VE Day, Churchill was removed from
office by the general election of 5 July. Although the result was
not announced until 26 July, to allow time for overseas votes from
servicemen to be counted, it was a landslide victory for Clement
Attlee and the Labour Party, who had successfully campaigned on
a platform of social change and optimism called 'Let Us Face the
Future'. Although Churchill, as the architect of victory in the war,
remained personally popular, his Conservative Party lost nearly
half their seats, reducing them to 197, while Labour won 393. The
old order had been replaced.

One reason for Churchill's defeat was an ill-judged broadcast he

---

* Halifax was less circumspect. He asked his sister, 'Are not these revelations
of German atrocity concentration camps revolting?' and stated, 'I rejoice to
think of the German civilians being forced to see them with their own eyes.'
The previous year, he had gone further. 'It really does make one feel that for the
sake of ultimate justice and to make these people learn that such things cannot
be done, it is right to look forward to many Germans from the top to bottom
being killed. I do not think in any other way can they be brought to feel the
horror of what they have done to other people.'

made from Chequers on 4 June, in which he decried 'the Socialists' and warned of the chaos and anger that would ensue from their election. To many neutral, even sympathetic voters, his words sounded like an old relic scaremongering, rather than a magnanimous leader trying to find common cause with men with whom up until a few weeks before he had served in a national government. He stated that 'a Socialist policy is abhorrent to the British ideas of freedom', adding hyperbolically that 'no Socialist government conducting the entire life and industry of the country could afford to allow free, sharp or violently worded expressions of public discontent . . . they would have to fall back on some sort of Gestapo'.[18] If there was any doubt that the election was lost before then – Labour had been ahead in the polls since February – it was now dispelled.

Lascelles described the events of 26 July calmly. 'Though I hadn't anticipated as big a swing as this, it don't [sic] surprise me; nor, as I told the King, do I look on it as an unrelieved disaster; in five years' time we may look back on it as the best thing that could have happened, on balance.'[19] His predecessor as private secretary was similarly unsurprised by the result, despite the 'unexpectedly large' majority, but remarked to his mother-in-law, 'What I do think tragic is that the country should have been brought to this state of political chaos, apparently mainly as a result of faulty information to the PM', and continued gloomily that '[the Conservatives] have brought the country to a state when this incarnation of wickedness in some form or another is unavoidable'.[20]

Hardinge's fear of socialist 'wickedness' did not come to pass. The election result was clear and unarguable, and preferable to a ragtag coalition of minor parties vying with one another to implement the post-war settlement in their own image. Churchill professed himself stoic about the result, suggesting that it was a cathartic response by the British people to the horrors and privations of the previous half-decade, and that they had vented their anger and displeasure on the government in charge. Yet it seemed almost unthinkable that with his own triumphs and failings so closely bound up with those of the country, he could cease to be prime

minister. Just as George VI was king for life, so Churchill had assumed the mantle of premier so authoritatively that his departure
from office felt incomprehensible.

Both the king and the queen regarded the election result with
dismay. Churchill had suggested to the sovereign that he would win
a majority of between thirty and eighty seats, but the scale of the
defeat revealed his optimism to be delusional, as well as destroying
any chance of forming a coalition.* The queen pronounced it 'rather
a shock', and called the 'material' of the new Labour administration
'not too inspiring' in a letter to Queen Mary.[21] But her husband saw
the loss as another personal blow. When he received Churchill on
the evening of 26 July and once again offered him the Order of the
Garter, he railed against the ingratitude of the British public with
more vituperation than the now former prime minister might have
expected. The king felt a sense of betrayal, and feared that he was
losing a counsellor and friend at a time when he could not afford
to do so. It was little wonder that he described his encounter with
a 'calm' Churchill in his diary that day as 'a very sad meeting' and
announced, 'I thought that the people were very ungrateful after
the way they had been led in the war.'[22]

It was not the farewell either man had wanted. The king implicitly acknowledged this by writing two letters to his former premier shortly afterwards. The first was as much an apology for his
own behaviour as it was a gesture of regret: 'my heart was too full
to say much at our last meeting . . . I was shocked at the result &
I thought it most ungrateful to you personally after all your hard
work for the people.'[23] He did not acknowledge the sometimes
unpalatable truth that in a democracy, the will of the people is the
correct one, gratitude be damned.

The second letter struck a more contemplative note, as the king

---

* Halifax had written on 23 May that 'I shall be greatly surprised if [Winston]
does not get back pretty satisfactorily', but also suggested that 'I would not like,
though, to see him with a small majority which would result in the Labour
party being pretty tiresome on almost everything . . . Rather than that I would
like to see Labour with a small majority!' His wish was granted, after a fashion.

reflected on the friendship that had grown up between monarch and politician over the previous half-decade. 'We have met on dozens, I may say on hundreds, of occasions . . . I shall always remember our talks with pleasure & only wish they could have continued longer . . . you often told me what you thought of people & matters of real interest which I could never have learnt from anyone else. Your breadth of vision & your grasp of the essential things were a great comfort to me in the darkest days of the war . . . Your conduct as Prime Minister & Minster of Defence has never been surpassed.'

Perhaps the only disingenuous thing he wrote was 'I like to think we have never disagreed on any really important matter.' From the initial *froideur* that existed between the two men to the polite but heated argument that had occurred in the run-up to D-Day, there had been hostility between them. Yet in the context of a harmonious working partnership, it was insignificant.

The relationship between the king and his new prime minister did not begin with any distinction.* Lascelles recorded that an overwhelmed Attlee, the 'poor little man', had arrived in a state of bewilderment at the palace, unsure whether he was the premier the country had voted for, despite the enormity of the landslide. Matters didn't improve. Attlee wished to make Hugh Dalton his Foreign Secretary, but the king asked that he appoint Ernest Bevin instead, which the prime minister agreed to. It was little wonder that the king wrote to Churchill subsequently, 'For myself personally, I regret what has happened more than perhaps anyone else. I shall miss your counsel more than I can say.' He concluded almost pathetically, 'But please remember that as a friend I hope we shall be able to meet at intervals.'[24]

Churchill spent his first days out of office in a morose and detached mood. He had gone from an almost deified figure to being that most dejected of public officials, a former prime minister who

---

* The king complained in his diary that 'the change of government will of course give me a great deal more work and even less leisure'.

had lost an election. Although he remained leader of the Conservative Party, it was an enfeebled and scattershot collection of men
now, blinking into the red dawn of a Labour government. Although
Attlee's personal respect for Churchill remained undiminished,
down to allowing him to hold a farewell dinner party at Chequers,
the former premier felt as if he was yesterday's man. When asked
to add an inscription in the Chequers visitors' book, he did not
contribute the expected aperçu of wisdom, or evocative literary or
historical quotation. Instead he merely wrote 'Finis'.[25]

His reply to the king was composed in a suite at Claridge's. It
would have been an amusing piece of serendipity if it had been the
same one that the Duke of Windsor had chosen for his occasional
visits to Britain: two figures who had once bestridden the world
like colossi now reduced to the very finest of rented lodgings. Yet
Churchill remained poetic as he replied to a man who was both
his king and his friend. There was deep emotional resonance to
his statement that 'It was always a relief to me to lay before my
sovereign all the dread secrets and perils which oppressed my
mind, & the plans which I was forming . . . Your Majesty's grasp
of all matters of state & war was always based upon the most
thorough & attentive study of the whole mass of current documents, and this enabled us to view & to measure everything in due
proportion.'

He concluded by writing in personal terms about their relationship. At the beginning of August 1945, Churchill was seventy and
the king forty-nine. They could almost have been father and son,
although neither man had enjoyed an especially close relationship
with his own father. It would be sentimental to assume that two
Englishmen of a certain background, with a relationship forged
in adversity, would ever declare the strength of their feelings for
one other. Nonetheless, when Churchill wrote, 'Your Majesty has
mentioned our friendship & this is indeed a very strong sentiment
with me, & an honour which I cherish', it is clear that he did so
with deep and sincere emotion.

When Churchill left Edward VIII on the day of his abdication, he recited some lines of Andrew Marvell from his poem 'An Horatian Ode Upon Cromwell's Return from Ireland', specifically:

> He nothing common did or mean
> Upon that memorable scene

It is not recorded whether he took his leave of George VI with any similarly apposite salutation. Yet if he had wished to find an appropriate means of marking the moment - in which a great victory had been achieved, but at significant personal cost - he may have thought of Walt Whitman's 'O Captain! My Captain!' Written after the assassination of President Lincoln, its sentiments of friendship, honour and loss would have resonated with both men, especially with the recent death of Roosevelt.

> O Captain! my Captain! our fearful trip is done,
> The ship has weather'd every rack, the prize we sought is
>   won,
> The port is near, the bells I hear, the people all exulting,
> While follow eyes the steady keel, the vessel grim and
>   daring;
> But O heart! heart! heart!
> O the bleeding drops of red,
> Where on the deck my Captain lies,
> Fallen cold and dead.

Epilogue

The Return of Mr Toad

During 1945, several events occurred that even seasoned observers of political and national actions might once have dismissed as improbable. VE Day was received with the ecstasy it deserved, but Churchill's defeat in the subsequent election was met with surprise. The bombing of Hiroshima and Nagasaki that ended the war with Japan may have been the only viable solution to an intransigent issue, but with the introduction of atomic power into the theatre of battle, it is hard not to agree with its architect J. Robert Oppenheimer's quotation from the *Bhagavad Gita* that 'I am become death, destroyer of worlds'. Less seismically but equally dramatically, 5 October saw an unanticipated return to Britain: that of the Duke of Windsor.

He travelled alone, staying with his mother at Marlborough House, and was received formally by his brother during his visit. He had the chance to meet the leading members of the government, along with his old nemesis Lascelles. But there were no accoutrements of a state reception or the publicity campaign he might have wished for. Even the *Daily Express*, for so long a supporter of both Edward and Wallis, offered no editorial comment or publicity when he arrived. He might once have expected his visit to be a front-page news story, complete with tub-thumping leaders about how 'the Duke of Windsor's presence in our country is a welcome one ... let us hope it becomes a permanent fixture'. But war, and a new government, had distracted people's attention. He was a relic of the previous world now, and treated with the mild interest that shop-soiled antiquities traditionally receive.

The duke had no particular expectations from his visit, which he had announced he would make back in August. Breezily he wrote to his brother to say that 'I will be going to England later on business, and as it has been nearly nine years since I have seen Mama, I have written to ask her if I could spend a few days with her either in London or Badminton ... I have also written the new Prime Minister advising him of my intention of going to Great Britain.'* He then offered his inimitable view on world affairs. 'However, it will be a great relief to get this second World War over and done with, and with the discovery of the atomic bomb, I for one hope I shall have passed on before the next one!'[1] There were those who may have privately wished for his end to have occurred during the most recent conflict.

Before he arrived, he expressed a hope that he might be made ambassador to Buenos Aires, but this was refused, both because Bevin felt unable to recommend such an appointment, and because Wallis's continued unacceptability to the Court of St James's meant that the Argentines would have been within their rights to refuse to acknowledge him. Lascelles characterised this prospect as 'an intolerable insult to our Royal Family, and to our national prestige'.[2]

The private secretary had felt trepidation about his old foe's return to the country, not least because the duke had, as usual, given some ill-advised press interviews, talking up what he expected to achieve from his visit. Nonetheless, as he wrote to the king, 'the only person [these interviews] do any actual harm to is the Duke himself ... the general public are "fed up" with such interviews ... the only reaction of the average man is "Here's the Duke of Windsor talking to the Press again. Why can't he keep quiet?"' He suggested that a blanket ban on speaking to the media

* The Duke's use of American English indicated both his affinity for the country and his wife's pervasive influence.

would inevitably be leaked to the papers, causing further chaos. Therefore his advice was that 'if you mention the Press at all, you might end by saying something to the effect that you hope he won't let the newspapermen be a nuisance to him & that you are sure he realises that it does worry Queen Mary & other members of the Royal Family when they read about the interviews he is supposed to give them . . . as he knows well, the RF never have given interviews in this country, & can't start doing so now'.

He counselled soft treatment - 'if you wrote at all strongly, he might react by taking the line that, when he is about to come to England for the first time for years, in order to see Queen Mary, the first thing that happens to him is to get a "telling off" from the King' - and concluded that the former monarch inevitably marched to the beat of a different drum. 'This would be quite illogical - but then he is a most illogical person!'[3]

Snubbed once again, Edward submitted to the usual treatment. His accent was by now distinctly on the western side of mid-Atlantic - 'more pronouncedly American than many Americans', according to Lascelles - and his voice shriller. He was 'noticeably, almost painfully'[4] thin, and his once-youthful face was much lined, although he seemed still to radiate the untroubled serenity that he had displayed both as Prince of Wales and as king. In contrast, his younger brother was so tired that he quipped to Gloucester, without much humour, that 'I shall be dead before getting [to Balmoral].'[5]

When the two men met for dinner on the evening of 5 October - the first time they had been in a room together since September 1939 - they were joined by the stately presence of Queen Mary, whether as peacemaker or referee. In the event, given the bad blood that had accumulated between the two over the previous six years, it proved to be a largely amicable encounter. Both sides had dreaded it, but the king later remarked that it had 'gone off far better than he had expected'. He noted that 'D was looking very well and talked a great deal about America.' The duke asked Queen Mary if she would be prepared to receive Wallis, and 'after some moments in a strong silence', she answered that she would not, 'as nothing had happened to alter the circumstances which had led to the abdication'. The matter was not raised again, and Edward now accepted that the duchess would never be received formally by his family or be awarded the title Her Royal Highness.

He had a subsequent meeting with his brother the following day, where the two men 'discussed the whole matter very thoroughly and quietly'. The duke stated that he was now happily married and that he would not have been able to carry out his duties as monarch properly without his wife, to which the king replied, not without anger, that 'you have profoundly shocked everybody here and in the Empire . . . you would not listen to your family, friends or advisers, & you have not thought out the consequences of your behaviour'. Edward was then informed that any job under the Crown was now impossible, given his previous status as sovereign, and was told – as if he needed to be – that his role in the Bahamas had been dreamt up to get him out of Europe during wartime.

The king did not note how the duke responded to these statements, nor how he reacted when his former equerry, Ulick Alexander, informed him that his permanent presence elsewhere in the world continued to be a prerequisite of his acceptance, grudging and patronising though it was, on such occasions as the present one.

The most in-depth account of the duke's thoughts and attitudes during his visit came from an interview he had with Lascelles on 9 October. The two men had not met in nearly a decade, and the rancour that had existed between them – although more on the private secretary's side than the former monarch's – was set aside for the 'very friendly' hour and a half that they talked. As with his dealings with the king and others, Edward was courteous, even when Lascelles spelt out harsh home truths to him, rather in the manner of Badger lambasting Mr Toad for his profligacy and irresponsibility.

Lascelles reported to the king that 'I had always tried to tell the Duke the truth . . . though it was not a pleasant thing to say to any man about his wife; my conviction was that, if the Duchess were received by Queen Mary and your Majesty, public opinion would, on balance, react very unfavourably and even dangerously, though I couldn't deny that there would be of course a minority who would think the other way.'[6] Although he acknowledged that 'it was primarily a family matter, on which my opinion didn't matter', he stated that 'if the Duchess were to be formally "received", it would have a very damaging, if not dangerous, effect on public opinion both here and all over the Empire'.

It did not cause Lascelles any particular grief to remind his former employer that 'it was one of the curses of kingship that there is in this world one law for kings and another for commoners'. Edward took this 'quite well', but responded that 'it was unfair to discriminate against his wife - X and Y and Z had all been involved in divorce cases, yet they were received', and claimed that he should now be treated as a private individual. Lascelles answered, 'No, you could never be a private individual. It is one of the hard things about kingship - if you are born a king, you stay a king til the day of your death, even if you have become an ex-king . . . I don't pretend that this is fair and just, but it is so.'[7]

With his wife thus denigrated, the conversation turned to the possibility of the duke's future employment in a British colony. As Lascelles said, 'The British Empire is like the clock on the mantelpiece - it has to be kept ticking away, but the machinery is pretty delicate, & is going to get more so as the years go on; we had, so to speak, taken that clock to pieces a hundred times and tried our damnedest to fit into it an extra wheel - the wheel of an ex-King. We have always found that we couldn't get that wheel in without damaging the works.'

'The wheel fitted in all right in the Bahamas,' the duke replied unabashed.

'As far as your actual running of Governorship went,' Lascelles answered, 'nobody denies that you had been a good Governor, nor that you did remarkably well there. But your appointment to the Bahamas was an emergency solution to the problem of what to do with you in the war. The experiment worked once, but it can't be safely repeated.'[8]

Before Edward could interject, Lascelles continued in a heart-felt manner, 'I have been talking to you quite impersonally, and in general terms. I have said to you exactly what I should say to the present King if he suddenly told me that he proposed to hand over the throne to Princess Elizabeth, and asked me if there was any other job he could do elsewhere in the Empire; but now I am going to make a *personal* appeal to you. In 1936, you made a tremendous sacrifice, on behalf of the lady who is your wife . . . could you not now make another sacrifice on behalf of your brother who, nine years ago, in order that you might lead your own life, took on the toughest job in the world – namely the job of King of England . . . the heaviest possible burden of life-long cares, duties and hard work, a burden for which you had always been prepared, and he not at all: could you not now decide to try and make things easier for him, instead of making them harder? You know that your brother only refuses to receive the Duchess because he is certain that it is his duty to refuse; you know that he can't offer you an official job because he is convinced that it would, in the long run, damage the Empire; you know that your idea of being a "younger brother" under the King simply wouldn't work – wouldn't it just be a good gesture on your part to accept these facts once & for all, and not continually embarrass the King by going on bringing them up for discussion, which can't do anybody any good?'[9]

Lascelles had, inadvertently, exposed the weakness of the royal family. 'The Firm' could belittle the duke, patronise him and write him high-handed letters that refused to grant him the privileges and favours that he asked. But he could not simply be expelled from his position. It might have made matters much more convenient if he had renounced his title and its trappings altogether and lived as a private citizen, but as his great-great-nephew has subsequently discovered, a royal title is a life sentence without the possibility of parole. If its principal members refuse to behave themselves, there is little that can be done with them.

Edward asked if he might go to America and improve Anglo-American relations. Lascelles, refraining from suggesting that his marriage to Wallis had only made such relations worse, replied, 'There is nobody who could have a better opportunity for doing this than yourself. You are past fifty-one, and behind you, you have thirty years of full and varied experience. With your name, and your resources, you could do a great deal of good in that particular direction. If you made your home in America, you could do a very great deal of good . . . you could do it with much greater freedom just because you won't be an official. You could make your house into what the great houses of England used to be – common ground in which all the most interesting people of the day, English or foreign, are continually meeting each other.' He reported that the duke was 'quite interested by the ideas which I had tried to express', but refused to commit himself to anything, and the conversation broke up amicably enough.

Edward telephoned Lascelles two days later, before his departure for Paris, in 'friendly mood', to say that he had spoken to the king on the telephone the previous night and to ask about whether he could be given diplomatic immunity from taxation.* The private secretary now professed himself 'quite impervious' to the old charm. 'I believe I did some good', he wrote. 'It was a very interesting interview . . . [but] I found myself thinking several times during his long soliloquies that I might almost be listening to the Prince Regent of Monday night.'[†10] He reported to the king that Edward spoke 'rather bitterly' of his former friend Churchill, and said, 'I hope Your Majesty will think I took more or less the right line.' He also alluded to the duke's almost compulsive uxoriousness,

---

* Which would generally require a diplomatic post, which the duke did not possess and had no hope of acquiring.

† Lascelles had seen the play *First Gentleman* by Norman Ginsbury, in which the actor Robert Morley offered 'a first-class performance' as the Prince Regent. Edward had implicitly compared himself to the Prince Regent during the abdication crisis, especially given the prince's relationship with his notorious mistress Maria Fitzherbert.

saying, 'A thing that struck me all through my talk with the Duke was his intense devotion to his wife. There is no doubt about that; and, as long as he & she are together, I don't think anybody need worry about his being happy or not. All the more reason, therefore, that, having got what he wants, he should reconcile himself to accepting the drawbacks of his position as well as its advantages.' He concluded philosophically, 'One can't have everything in this life.'[11]

When the duke returned to Paris, he wrote to his brother with warmth, but also pointedly. With a touch of condescension, he praised him for looking 'so well and vigorous after the strain of the last six years of total war' and stated stoutly that 'my admiration for your fortitude knows no bounds'. He was unable to write without extolling his own virtues – 'my life has not been easy-going either . . . I am satisfied that the job I undertook as your representative in a third-class British colony was fulfilled to the best of my ability' – but he was more conciliatory than he had been before, accepting that the 'frank discussion of personal and family matters with special regard to the future' had settled certain issues. There was no talk between them of Wallis's acceptance within the royal family, or her being given HRH status.

Instead, after reiterating his desire to serve both British and American interests in some bespoke quasi-ambassadorial role, the duke struck an almost philosophical note. He acknowledged that he would remain a wandering minstrel, singing for his supper in grand houses throughout the world ('I am frank to admit that I was sorry when your answer was in the affirmative to my question as to whether my taking up residence in Great Britain would be an embarrassment to you, [but] I can see your point . . . I am prepared to put your feelings before my own . . . don't forget that I have suffered many unnecessary embarrassments . . . uncomplainingly during the last nine years'), and then mused about the future he and his brother might face.

'[We are] two prominent personages placed in one of the most unique situations in history, the dignified handling of which is entirely your and my responsibility, and ours alone. It is a situation from which we cannot escape and one that will always be watched with interest by the whole world. I can see no reason why we should not be able to handle it in the best interests of both of us, and I can only assure you that I will continue to play my part to this end.'[12]

It seemed as if, for the first time since the abdication, a truce had been declared between the warring pair. Even if there was no prospect of Edward being readmitted to the fold, if he remained tame and docile this was a more acceptable prospect than having him as an ungovernable and dangerous renegade. But what had not been mentioned at any point during his visit was that earlier in the year, Lascelles, the king and others had been shown all but incontrovertible proof that the former monarch had committed treachery against his country.

The so-called Marburg Files had been found in Germany in May 1945. Their name stemmed from their discovery at Marburg Castle, after which copies were made by the British. It soon became clear that the information within them, revolving around the Duke of Windsor's involvement with the Nazis while in Europe, and specifically Operation Willi, was potentially devastating, both to any remaining reputation Edward possessed and to the wider post-war settlement. It was Bevin's first major test as Foreign Secretary. If he failed, it would be an immediate indictment of Attlee's new and progressive government. But it was far from obvious what the right course of action was.

Bevin communicated his thoughts as undramatically as he could to Attlee on 13 August. 'I believe you will agree that the following exception will have to be made to the release of German documents to other governments . . . I suggest we should try to persuade the United States Government to cooperate with us in suppressing the documents concerned.' He ran through the contents, including the 'second and third hand reports and speculations about the Duke's attitude derived from agents in contact with him'. While he took care to acknowledge that 'the documents have no bearing on war crimes or on the general history of the war', he also recognised that 'they would possess the highest publicity value on account of the personalities involved and the type of intrigues described'. It was no surprise that he warned that 'a disclosure would in my opinion do grave harm to the national interest'.

The files had to be suppressed. Bevin, still a newcomer to his post, trusted that the copy sent to the State Department in Washington would make it no further, but could not say the same for the originals in Marburg. He noted that 'Access to the files there is easily obtained by American service and official personnel and there is therefore risk of the documents being seen and mischief being done by an irresponsible disclosure.'[13] He concluded by suggesting that the United States government should be asked either to destroy their copy of the files, or at the very least hand it over to Britain for safe keeping. The consequences of an English-language copy existing, he implied, would otherwise be ruinous.

Lascelles was shown the files, and his immediate response was to assume that the statements contained within about Edward and Wallis were accurate. As he wrote in his diary, 'If the Windsors' reactions were as implied in this correspondence (which both [Edward's former private secretary] Godfrey Thomas ... and I agree cannot be wholly discounted; internal evidence indicates that there is at any rate a substratum of truth in it) the result is, to say the very least, highly damaging to themselves.'[14]

He arranged for an interview to take place between the king and Bevin on 23 August. Attlee's assistant private secretary, John Peck, recorded that 'the King was much distressed' to discover the news of his brother's untrustworthiness. Monckton and Churchill were also consulted, and Peck noted that 'Both of course agree absolutely that the file should be suppressed and we are so informing the Foreign Office.' Monckton, who had some first-hand experience of the events described due to his involvement with them in August 1940, could only shrug and testify to the accuracy of the files. As Peck concluded, 'it certainly reinforces the desirability of suppressing the Marburg dossier if possible'. Attlee wrote at the bottom of the memorandum, 'I agree'.[15]

So there, uneasily, the matter was allowed to rest. The duke was thus able to sit around in Marlborough House and Buckingham Palace and be treated as an honoured guest. He even accompanied his mother on a tour of the bombed East End docks during his visit. No overt allusion was made to his wartime activities. Maintaining the status quo at all costs was the desired objective. Besides, the Marburg Files were either safely contained within official custody or, at worst, remained little more than an incomprehensible series of German-language documents that only the most curious might have obtained some use from.

It would have been bad luck for the files ever to have made it into the public domain. But luck, good and bad, was what would define the royal family over the next decade. They would meet with tragedy and disaster, as well as renewal and fresh hope for the future. And Edward, the king who had spurned his country and his throne, would continue to lurk in the shadows, an embarrassment to his family and his country alike. Only someone exceptional could manage to neutralise the threat he posed.

Thankfully, it would not be long before she emerged.

Acknowledgements

This book depicts a time of international upheaval and chaos, so it is grimly appropriate that it was researched and written during a pandemic. Nonetheless, there are many who have contributed to its genesis in the kindest and most generous of fashions. The team at Weidenfeld & Nicolson has been consistently professional, including my excellent editors Maddy Price and Ed Lake, my superb project editor Sarah Fortune, my peerless copy-editor Jane Selley, my picture editor Natalie Dawkins and the painstaking campaigns director Elizabeth Allen, and it has been a pleasure to work with them once again.

It has also been an honour to be published by St Martin's Press in the United States, and I would like to thank the brilliant Michael Flamini, editor par excellence, as well as his assistant editor Hannah Phillips, my publicist Sarah Schoof, and SMP's marketing manager Michelle Cashman; it has been an honour to continue our professional association with this book.

My literary agent Ed Wilson has been a committed and supportive advocate of my career for some time, and I thank him on both a personal and professional level for being a sounding board, a cheerleader, a source of invaluable advice and that wonderful thing with an agent, a friend. I am honoured to be his client.

As with *The Crown in Crisis*, there are many distinguished historians and authors whose advice, counsel and insights have been invaluable. I was fortunate enough to talk with Philip Ziegler during the writing of the earlier book. In the course of our lengthy conversation, he offered me the incalculable benefit of his experience and wide-ranging thoughts on the subject, including his own encounters with the Duke of Windsor and Wallis Simpson, which have proved helpful once again here, as did a splendidly entertaining evening with Susan Williams. Marion Milne shared some invaluable material with me that she had discovered in her own research, including a previously unknown letter from the Duke of Windsor to Hitler. I am also grateful to Anne Sebba, Andrew Roberts, Walter Monckton's daughter-in-law Marianna, Richard Aldrich and Rory Cormac, Deborah Cadbury, Tim Bouverie, Sarah Bradford, William Shawcross and Michael Bloch, whose contributions, directly or through their published works, have been hugely useful.

Public and private archival collections have lain at the heart of my research. I would like to thank many people, but especially Bethany Hamblen at the Balliol College Archives, Julie Crocker at the Royal Archives, Mark Ballard at the Kent History and Library Centre, Nick Melia at the Borthwick Institute, Madelin Evans at the Churchill Archives, Emma Quinlan and Ben Copithorne at Nuffield College, Oxford, and Hannah Carson at the Bodleian Library's Special Collections department. Particular gratitude goes to Lord Hardinge and Alex Murray for dealing with all my queries about the Hardinge archive so kindly and courteously. Additionally, I am grateful to the staff of the National Archives, the Oxford Union, the Parliamentary Archive and, in particular, the ever-excellent London Library, whose invaluable care packages of books made it possible for me to continue my research even through national lockdowns in early 2021.

When I'm not in the depths of an archive or library stack, it is conversations with fellow writers and friends both recent and of long standing that steer my thinking in fresh directions. To this end, I owe deep gratitude to many who have stood with me, in some cases *contra mundum*, including Sophie Buchan, Dan Jones, Gustav Temple, Amanda Craig, William Boyd, Simon Sebag Montefiore, Brice Stratford, Thomas Grant, Ben Schott, Catherine Bray, Arabella Byrne, Michael Bhaskar, Mark Atherton, Toby White, Francesca Peacock, 'Boothby' Renshaw, James Douglass, Raymond Stephenson and many others besides.

My greatest thanks must go to my wife Nancy, who has been on a professional level supportive and incisive, and on a personal level the best and kindest of companions. Our magnificent and lovely daughter Rose, meanwhile, continues to enthral and delight, even if I fear that this volume will be joining the (thankfully) growing ranks of 'Daddy's boring books'. I can only trust that one day she enjoys what her father has written.

Finally, it is my honour to dedicate the book to Alan Samson, who commissioned both *The Windsors at War* and *The Crown in Crisis*. Every writer hopes they will have a mentor of Alan's perceptiveness, generosity and boundless good humour, and his guidance throughout the project has been consistently welcome.

Illustration Credits

Page 1
Above – Alamy/piemags
Below – Getty Images/Ivan Dmitri/Michael Ochs Archives

Page 2
Above – Getty Images/Popperfoto
Below – Getty Images/Bettmann

Page 3
Above – Getty Images/Hulton Archive
Centre – Getty Images/Hulton Archive
Below – Alamy/World History Archive

Page 4
Above left – Shutterstock/Gil Friedberg/Associated Press
Above right – Shutterstock/Associated Press
Below left – Bridgeman Images
Below right – Alamy/PJF Military Collection

Page 5
Above – Getty/Hulton-Deutsch Collection/CORBIS
Below left – Alamy/PA Images
Below right – Getty/Hulton Archive

Page 6
Above – Getty Images/Bettmann
Centre – Shutterstock/Carl Mydans/The LIFE Picture Collection

Below - Reproduced by kind permission of the copyright holders and the Master and Fellows of Balliol College

Page 7
Above - Getty Images/Lisa Sheridan/Studio Lisa/Hulton Archive
Below - Getty Images/The Print Collector

Page 8
Full page - Getty Images/Daily Herald Archive/National Science & Media Museum/SSPL

Notes

Prologue: 'We All Wondered Why We Weren't Dead'
1 Bradford, p.424
2 Shawcross, *Counting One's Blessings*, p.295
3 Ibid.
4 Shawcross, *Queen Elizabeth*, p.523
5 Ibid.
6 Ibid., p.524
7 Sir Alec Hardinge to Viscountess Milner, 16 September 1940, Hardinge Papers, U2117 (Acc 2359/224)
8 Aronson, p.46
9 Ziegler, *Crown and People*, p.75
10 Channon, 14 September 1940
11 Aronson, pp.46-7
12 Bradford, p.429
13 George VI diary, 13 September 1940, Royal Archives
14 George VI diary, 19 September 1940, Royal Archives
15 Ibid.

Chapter One: 'The Other One'
1 Jardine, p.16
2 Ibid.
3 Ibid., p.18
4 Ibid., p.54
5 Ibid., p.55
6 Ibid.
7 C. E. Douglas to Monckton, May 1937, Dep Monckton Trustees 9
8 Duke of Windsor to George VI, 17 January 1937, Royal Archives, RA/GVI/PRIV/01/02/04
9 Dep Monckton Trustees 15
10 Hardinge, p.187

11 Ibid., p.185

12 Queen Elizabeth to Viscountess Milner, 7 December 1936, Hardinge Papers, U2117 (Acc 2349/94)

13 17 March 1937, in Nicolson

14 Hardinge, p.188

15 Larman, p.282

16 Monckton to George VI, 10 April 1937, Royal Archives, RA CO42A/037

17 Bradford, p.296

18 Fruity Metcalfe to Alexandra Curzon, 17 February 1937, in Donaldson, p.314

19 Dep Monckton Trustees 15

20 Bradford, p.306

21 Dep Monckton Trustees 15

22 George VI to Duke of Windsor, 2 February 1937, Royal Archives, RA/ CO42A/001A

23 Duke of Windsor to George VI, 21 February 1937, Royal Archives, RA/ GVI/PRIV/01/02/05

24 Wallis Simpson to Duke of Windsor, 3 January 1937, in Bloch, *Wallis and Edward*, pp.245-6

25 George VI to Duke of Windsor, 12 March 1937, Royal Archives, RA/ CO42A/003

26 Wallis Simpson to Duke of Windsor, 30 March 1937, in Bloch, *Wallis and Edward*, pp.302-3

27 Cadbury, p.44

28 Churchill to Chamberlain, 8 April 1937, Churchill Archives, CHAR 2/300

29 Neville Chamberlain to Hilda Chamberlain, 10 April 1937, Chamberlain Papers, NC 18/1/1001, University of Birmingham Special Collections Department

30 Duke of Windsor to Churchill, 16 April 1937, Churchill Archives, CHAR 2/300

31 Ibid.

32 Diana Cooper to Conrad Russell, 16 April 1937, Churchill Archives, DIAC 01/01/10

33 Ibid.

34 Ibid.

35 Ibid.

36 Bradford, p.302

37 Larman, p.265

38 Sitwell, pp.70-1
39 Shawcross, *Counting One's Blessings,* p.397
40 Channon, 7 May 1937
41 Bradford, p.280
42 Ibid., p.283
43 George VI to Duke of Windsor (undated draft but sent 11 April 1937), Royal Archives, RA/C042A/006
44 Ibid., RA/CO42A/007
45 Duke of Windsor to George VI, 13 April 1937, Royal Archives, RA/GVI/PRIV/01/02/06
46 Sir Eric Phipps, Foreign Office memorandum, 4 May 1937, National Archives, FO 954/33A
47 Wallis Windsor, p.296
48 Ibid., p.298
49 Dep Monckton Trustees 15
50 Monckton to George VI, 10 April 1937, Royal Archives, RA CO42A/037
51 Duke of Windsor to Queen Mary, 26 May 1937, Royal Archives, RA DW 1/119
52 Churchill to Duke of Windsor, 17 May 1937, in Cadbury, p.55
53 Ziegler, *King Edward VIII,* p.364
54 Dep Monckton Trustees 15
55 Jardine, p.69
56 Ibid.
57 Ibid., p.74
58 Wallis Windsor, p.323
59 Jardine, p.78
60 Ibid., p.82
61 Ibid., p.87
62 Ibid., pp 88-9
63 Ibid., p.95
64 Duke of Windsor to Jardine, 8 June 1937, in Jardine, p.80
65 Jardine, p.100
66 A. G. Allen to Duke of Windsor, 5 July 1939, Dep Monckton Trustees 15

Chapter Two: 'Germany's No. 1 Gentleman'

1 MEPO 38/155, National Archives
2 Duke of Windsor to Queen Mary, 2 June 1937, Royal Archives, RA/GV/EE/13/14

3 Harold Nicolson diary, 14 July 1937, Balliol College Archives

4 Duke of Windsor to Sibyl Colefax, 6 June 1937, Bodleian Library, ms Eng c5272

5 Dep Monckton Trustees 15

6 Wallis Windsor to Sibyl Colefax, April 1937, Bodleian Library, ms Eng c5272

7 Wallis Windsor to Sibyl Colefax, 21 April 1937

8 George VI to Duke of Windsor, 30 June 1937, Royal Archives, RA/C042A/11

9 Duke of Windsor to George VI, 13 July 1937, Royal Archives, RA/GVI/PRIV/01/02/08

10 Monckton to George VI, 11 August 1937, Royal Archives, RA/C042A/041

11 Duke of Windsor to Monckton, 16 July 1937, Dep Monckton Trustees 15. The letter was sent exactly a year to the day after a failed assassination attempt on Edward (see *The Crown in Crisis*, Chapter Three, for details), and he subsequently referred to his decision to ignore a public proclamation from 'my "would-be" assassin of last year George McMahon' in a letter to Monckton of 17 August.

12 Duke of Windsor to Monckton, 17 August 1937

13 Duke of Kent to George VI, 13 August 1937, Royal Archives, GVI/PRIV/RF/01/08/01

14 Dep Monckton Trustees 15

15 Sir Robert Vansittart to Hardinge, 4 May 1937, National Archives, FO 954/33

16 George VI to Duke of Windsor, 3 June 1937, Dep Monckton Trustees 15

17 Monckton to A. G. Allen, 9 June 1937, Dep Monckton Trustees 15

18 Ziegler, *King Edward VIII*, p.388

19 Dep Monckton Trustees 15

20 Bloch, *Wallis and Edward, Letters, 1931–1937*, p.143

21 Bradford, p.335

22 Shawcross, *Queen Elizabeth*, p.425

23 Phipps telegram to Foreign Office, 5 October 1937, FO 1093

24 George Ogilvie-Forbes to Sir Robert Vansittart, 17 October 1937, National Archives, FO 954/33A

25 Vincent, p.582

26 Ibid., pp.616–21

27 Ibid.

28 Larman, p.280

29 Ullrich, p.689

30 Ziegler, *King Edward VIII*, p.389

31 Foreign Office memorandum to Ogilvie-Forbes, 6 October 1937, National Archives, FO 1093

32 Ziegler, *King Edward VIII*, p.390

33 Bloch, *Wallis and Edward, Letters, 1931–1937*, p.145

34 Valentine Low, 'Duke's Nazi salute pictures for sale', *The Times*, 22 July 2015

35 Bloch, *The Reign & Abdication of Edward VIII* , pp.144–5

36 Ziegler, *King Edward VIII*, p.392

37 Duke of Windsor to Adolf Hitler, 23 October 1937 (copyright Alamy photographic library)

38 Churchill to the Duke of Windsor, 28 October 1937, in Cadbury, p.68

39 Ibid.

40 Foreign Office memorandum to Chamberlain, 22 October 1937, National Archives, FO 1093

41 *The New York Times,* 23 October 1937

42 Bloch, *The Reign & Abdication of Edward VIII*, pp.150–1

43 Ibid.

Chapter Three: 'A Vague Sense of Fear'

1 National Archives, MEPO 10/35

2 Ibid.

3 Ibid.

4 Bloch, *The Reign & Abdication of Edward VIII*, p.121

5 National Archives, MEPO 10/35

6 Ibid.

7 Foreign Office memorandum, 4 March 1938, National Archives, FO 1093

8 Ronald Campbell to Robert Vansittart, 8 November 1937, National Archives, FO 1093

9 Bloch, *The Reign & Abdication of Edward VIII*, p.123

10 Sir Eric Phipps to Sir Alexander Hardinge, 19 January 1938, National Archives, MEPO 10/35

11 Ziegler, *King Edward VIII*, p.368

12 Duke of Windsor to Neville Chamberlain, 22 December 1937, National Archives, FO 1093

13 Ziegler, *King Edward VIII,* p.372

14 King George VI to Duke of Windsor, 22 November 1937, National Archives, FO 1093

15 Neville Chamberlain to Duke of Windsor, 7 January 1938, Dep Monckton Trustees 16

16 Duke of Windsor to Chamberlain, 12 January 1938, Dep Monckton Trustees 16

17 Wallis Simpson to Bessie Merriman, 26 January 1938, in Bloch, *The Reign & Abdication of Edward VIII* pp.124–5

18 Shawcross, *Counting One's Blessings*, p.252

19 Bradford, p.265

20 Ibid., p.266

21 A. G. Allen to Walter Monckton, 15 February 1938, Dep Monckton Trustees 16

22 Horace Wilson to Monckton, 24 February 1938, Dep Monckton Trustees 16

23 Monckton to Horace Wilson, 1 March 1938, Dep Monckton Trustees 16

24 Horace Wilson to Monckton, 3 March 1938, Dep Monckton Trustees 16

25 Monckton to George VI, n.d. (March 1938), Dep Monckton Trustees 16

26 Ziegler, *King Edward VIII*, p.382

27 Bradford, p.269

28 Bloch, *The Reign & Abdication of Edward VIII* , p.128

29 Duke of Windsor to George VI, 30 April 1938, Royal Archives, RA RA/GVI/PRIV/01/02/11

30 Bloch, *The Reign & Abdication of Edward VIII* , p.128

31 Monckton to George VI, 11 May 1938, Dep Monckton Trustees 16

32 Monckton to Duke of Windsor, 20 May 1938, Dep Monckton Trustees 16

33 Bradford, p.271

34 Diana Cooper to Conrad Russell, 20 July 1938, Churchill Archives, DIAC 01/01/10

35 Cooper, *The Light of Common Day*, p.223

36 Ibid.

37 Hardinge to Monckton, 16 August 1938, Dep Monckton Trustees, 16

Chapter Four: 'Humiliation Is Better Than War'

1 Channon, 15 February 1938
2 Neville Chamberlain to Hilda Chamberlain, Chamberlain Papers, NC 18/1/1003
3 Ibid., 30 May 1937, Chamberlain Papers, NC 18/1/1006
4 Chamberlain to George VI, 2 September 1937, Chamberlain Papers, NC 7/3/21
5 Birkenhead, *Life of Lord Halifax*, p.372
6 Channon, 22 June 1938
7 Bouverie, p.233
8 Ibid.
9 Barnes and Nicholson, p.508
10 Bouverie, p.245
11 Channon, 14 September 1938
12 Ibid.
13 Bouverie, p.250
14 Ibid.
15 Bradford, p.275
16 Hardinge to Helen Hardinge, 16 September 1938, Hardinge Papers, U2117 (Acc 2866)
17 Hardinge to Helen Hardinge, 18 September
18 Hardinge to Queen Elizabeth, 19 September 1938, Hardinge Papers, U2117 (Acc 2866)
19 Hardinge to Helen Hardinge, 19 September 1938, Hardinge Papers, U2117 (Acc 2866)
20 Hardinge to Helen Hardinge, 20 September 1938
21 Hardinge to Helen Hardinge, 21 September 1938
22 Hardinge to Helen Hardinge, 22 September 1938
23 Hardinge to Helen Hardinge, 23 September 1938
24 Hardinge memorandum, 23 September 1938, Hardinge Papers, U2117 (Acc 2866)
25 Hardinge to Helen Hardinge, 25 September 1938, Hardinge Papers, U2117 (Acc 2866)
26 Cabinet Minutes, 17 September 1938, CAB 23/95/3/72-86
27 Hardinge to Helen Hardinge, 26 September 1938, Hardinge Papers, U2117 (Acc 2866)
28 Bradford, p.276
29 Hardinge to Helen Hardinge, 28 September 1938, Hardinge Papers, U2117 (Acc 2866)

30 Vickers, p.181

31 Eric Phipps to Walter Monckton, 21 September 1938, Dep Monckton Trustees 16

32 Bloch, *The Reign & Abdication of Edward VIII*, p.133

33 Churchill to Duke of Windsor, 12 September 1938, Churchill Archives, CHAR 1/324/24

34 Dep Monckton Trustees 15

35 Duke of Windsor to George VI, 29 August 1938, Royal Archives, RA/GVI/PRIV/01/02/12

36 Bloch, *The Reign & Abdication of Edward VIII,* p.133

37 Dep Monckton Trustees 15

38 George VI to Duke of Windsor, 17 September 1938, Royal Archives, RA/C042A/014

39 Ibid., n.d. (September 1938), Royal Archives, RA/CO42A/100

40 Bouverie, p.272

41 Bradford, p.277

42 Bouverie, p.273

43 Ibid., p.286

44 Bradford, p.278

45 Ibid.

46 George VI to Lord Halifax, 30 September 1938, Halifax Papers, HALIFAX A2/276/4

47 Bradford, p.279

48 Shawcross, *Counting One's Blessings*, p.258

49 Hardinge to Viscountess Milner, 2 October 1938, Hardinge Papers, U2117 (Acc 2359/224)

50 Duke of Windsor to Walter Monckton, 31 October 1938, Dep Monckton Trustees 16

51 Duke of Windsor to Neville Chamberlain, 18 September 1938, Royal Archives, RA/C042A/079

52 Duke of Windsor to George VI, 23 October 1938, Royal Archives, RA/GVI/PRIV/01/02/13

53 Duke of Windsor to Neville Chamberlain, 23 October 1938, Dep Monckton Trustees 16

54 Chamberlain to Duke of Windsor, November 1938, Dep Monckton Trustees 16

55 Duke of Windsor to Chamberlain, 10 November 1938, Dep Monckton Trustees 16

56 George VI to Duke of Windsor, 28 October 1938, Royal Archives, RA/C042A/015

57 Duke of Windsor to George VI, 30 October 1938, Royal Archives, RA/GVI/PRIV/01/02/14

58 Chamberlain account of Duke of Windsor meeting, 24 November 1938, Royal Archives, RA/C042A/082

59 Chamberlain to Duke of Windsor, 23 December 1938, Dep Monckton Trustees 16

60 Bloch, *The Reign & Abdication of Edward VIII*, p.134

61 George VI to Chamberlain, 14 December 1938, National Archives

Chapter Five: 'Freedom Is Worth Dying For'

1 Hamilton, p.31

2 Ibid., p.58

3 National Archives, MEPO 10/35

4 Duke of Windsor to Monckton, 28 November 1938, Dep Monckton Trustees 16

5 Hardinge to Monckton, 13 December 1938, Dep Monckton Trustees 16

6 National Archives, MEPO 10/35

7 Duke of Windsor to Chamberlain, 9 January 1939, Dep Monckton Trustees 17

8 Duke of Windsor memorandum, 28 January 1939, Dep Monckton Trustees 17

9 Monckton to Chamberlain, 1 February 1939, Dep Monckton Trustees 17

10 Monckton to Duke of Windsor, 22 March 1939, Dep Monckton Trustees 17

11 Robert Boothby, letter to *Daily Telegraph,* 19 March 1939

12 Helen Hardinge, account of conversation with the king and queen, 26 April 1939, Hardinge Papers, U2117 (Acc 2349/89)

13 Vickers, p.184

14 Joseh Israels II, 'Selling George VI to the United States', *Scribner's*, May 1939

15 Bloch, pp.313-14

16 Ibid., p.138

17 Channon, 9 May 1939

18 Duke of Kent to George VI, 16 May 1939, Royal Archives, RA/GVI/PRIV/RF/02

19 Lascelles, p.9

20 Lord Tweedsmuir to Hardinge, 22 May 1939, John Buchan Papers, Queen's University Archives
21 Queen Elizabeth to Princess Elizabeth, 23 May 1939, Royal Archives, RA/QEII/PRIV/RF
22 Dep Monckton Trustees 15
23 Queen Elizabeth to Princess Elizabeth, 27 May 1939, Royal Archives, RA/QEII/PRIV/RF
24 Queen Elizabeth to Queen Mary, 1 June 1939, Royal Archives, RA/QM/PRIV/CC12/99
25 Shawcross, *Counting One's Blessings*, p.270
26 Bradford, p.292
27 Queen Elizabeth to Queen Mary, 11 June 1939, Royal Archives, RA/QM/PRIV/CC12/101
28 Bradford, p.295
29 Ibid., p.296
30 Ibid., p.297
31 Mackenzie King to Roosevelt, 1 July 1939, Roosevelt Library, PSF Great Britain
32 Nicolson, p.405

Chapter Six: 'Not Only Alive, But Very Much So'

1 George VI diary, 2 September 1939, Royal Archives
2 Ziegler, *King Edward VIII*, p.402
3 Bradford, p.303
4 Ibid.
5 Hardinge to Helen Hardinge, 25 August 1939, Hardinge Papers, U2117 (Acc 2866)
6 Dep Monckton Trustees 17
7 Monckton to Horace Wilson, 29 August 1939, Dep Monckton Trustees 15
8 Dep Monckton Trustees 17
9 Ibid.
10 Ziegler, *King Edward VIII*, p.404
11 Queen Elizabeth to Queen Mary, 31 August 1939, Royal Archives, RA GV/CC/12/110
12 Churchill to Duke of Windsor, 10 September 1939, Churchill Archives, CHAR 19/2A/13
13 Hardinge to Helen Hardinge, 5 September 1939, Hardinge Papers, U2117 (Acc 2866)

14 George VI diary, 5 September 1939, Royal Archives

15 George VI to Duke of Kent, 22 September 1939, Royal Archives, RA GV1/342

16 George VI diary, 14 September 1939, Royal Archives

17 Dep Monckton Trustees 17

18 Bloch, *The Reign & Abdication of Edward VIII*, p.144

19 George VI to Kent, 26 September 1939, Royal Archives, RA GVI/342

20 *The Times*, 12 September 1939

21 George VI diary, 15 September, Royal Archives

22 Bloch, *The Reign & Abdication of Edward VIII*, pp.144-5

23 Ibid.

24 George VI diary, 15 September, Royal Archives

25 George VI diary, 16 September, Royal Archives

26 Nicolson, p.168

27 Hardinge to Helen Hardinge, 17 September 1939, Hardinge Papers, U2117 (Acc 2866)

28 Duke of Windsor to Monckton, 2 October 1939, Dep Monckton Trustees 17

29 Alec Hardinge to Sir Richard Howard-Vyse, 20 September 1939, Royal Archives, RA KEVIII, Box 3

30 Bloch, *The Reign & Abdication of Edward VIII*, p.147

31 Ziegler, *King Edward VIII*, p.409

32 Duke of Windsor to Monckton, 31 October 1939, Dep Monckton Trustees 17

33 Henry Pownall, 18 October 1939, *Chief of Staff: 1933-1940*, Leo Cooper, 1972

34 Alec Hardinge memorandum, November 1939, Royal Archives, RA/042A/143

35 Queen Elizabeth to Hardinge, 30 October 1939, Hardinge Papers, U2117 (Acc 2349/94)

36 Duke of Windsor to Monckton, 12 November 1939, Dep Monckton Trustees 17

37 Duke of Windsor to Churchill, 12 November 1939, Dep Monckton Trustees 17

38 Monckton to Duke of Windsor, 14 November 1939, Dep Monckton Trustees 17

39 Churchill to Duke of Windsor, 17 November 1939, in Cadbury, p.78

40 Duke of Windsor to Monckton, 17 November 1939, Dep Monckton Trustees 17

41 Duke of Windsor to Monckton, 19 November 1939, Dep Monckton Trustees 17
42 Bloch, *The Reign & Abdication of Edward VIII*, p.150
43 George VI war diary, 11 October, Royal Archives
44 Hardinge to Helen Hardinge, 5 December 1939, Hardinge Papers, U2117 (Acc 2866)
45 Channon, 8 January 1940
46 2 January 1940, Dep Monckton Trustees 18
47 Ziegler, *King Edward VIII*, p.414

Chapter Seven: 'The Darkest Day in English History'
1 Hardinge to Helen Hardinge, 28 September 1938, Hardinge Papers, U2117 (Acc 2866)
2 Duke of Buccleuch to Duff Cooper, 2 October 1938, Duff Cooper Papers, Churchill Archives, DUFC 2/19
3 Buccleuch to Rab Butler, 24 April 1939, Buccleuch Papers, in Bouverie, p.331
4 Cadbury, p.85
5 Buccleuch to Rab Butler, 24 April 1939, Buccleuch Papers, in Bouverie, p.331
6 Channon, 3 May 1939
7 Ibid., 5 May 1939
8 Chamberlain to Buccleuch, 30 August 1939, Buccleuch Papers, in Bouverie, p.373
9 Buccleuch to George VI, 12 December 1939, Royal Archives, RA/PS/PSO/GVI/C/134/1
10 Channon, 9 February 1940
11 George VI to Buccleuch, n.d. (*c.* May 1940), Royal Archives, RA/PS/PSO/GVI/C/134/1
12 George VI war diary, 26 June 1940, Royal Archives
13 Ziegler, *King Edward VIII*, p.415
14 George VI diary, 25 December 1939, Royal Archives
15 Ibid., p.416
16 Dep Monckton Trustees 15
17 King George VI to Neville Chamberlain, 25 March 1940, Chamberlain Papers NC 7/3/4
18 George VI diary, 17 March 1940, Royal Archives
19 Monckton to Duke of Windsor, 15 April 1940, Dep Monckton Trustees 18

20 Ibid.
21 Channon, 10 May 1940
22 Bradford, pp.310–11
23 George VI diary, 10 May 1940, Royal Archives
24 Churchill, *The Second World War: The Gathering Storm*, p.527
25 King George VI to Winston Churchill, 10 May 1940, Churchill Archives, CHAR 20/11/17–18
26 George VI war diary, 11 May 1940, Royal Archives
27 Frankland, p.185
28 Aronson, p.34

Chapter Eight: 'Anything Except the Right Thing'
1 Wallis Windsor, p.340
2 Philip Ziegler to author, 10 October 2019
3 Winston Churchill draft letter to Commonwealth Prime Ministers, July 1940 Churchill Archives, CHAR 20/9
4 Churchill to Commonwealth Prime Ministers, 4 July 1940, Churchill Archives, CHAR 20/9
5 Ziegler, *King Edward VIII*, p.416
6 Draft Churchill telegram, 1 July 1940, Royal Archives, RA KEVIII Ab Box 3
7 Howard-Vyse to Hardinge, 29 May 1940, Royal Archives, RA KEVIII Ab Box 3
8 Cadbury, p.153
9 Memorandum from Edward Tamm to J. Edgar Hoover, 13 September 1940, FBI HQ 65-31113
10 George VI war diary, 12 June 1940, Royal Archives
11 Edward to Churchill, 21 June 1940, National Archives, FO 800/326
12 Bloch, *Operation Willi*, p.24
13 George VI diary, 23 June 1940, Royal Archives
14 Ziegler, *King Edward VIII*, p.421
15 Duke of Windsor to Churchill, 28 June 1940, Churchill Archives, CHAR 20/9A/11-12
16 Duke of Windsor to Churchill, 24 June 1940, Royal Archives, RA/DW/4512
17 George VI diary, 25 June, Royal Archives
18 Churchill to Duke of Windsor, 28 June 1940, in Gilbert, p.252
19 Cadbury, p.164
20 Duke of Windsor to Churchill, October 1940

21 Bloch, *Operation Willi*, p.58

22 Hoare to Foreign Office, 1 July 1940, National Archives, FO 800/326

23 Hoare to Churchill, 5 July 1940, in Bloch, *Operation Willi*, p.65

24 George VI diary, 29 June 1940, Royal Archives

25 Hardinge to E. A. Seal, 28 June 1940, Churchill Archives, CHAR 20/9A/13-14

26 George VI diary, 3 July 1940, Royal Archives

27 MI5 letter to Sir Alexander Cadogan, 7 July 1940, National Archives, FO 1093/23

28 George VI diary, 7 July 1940, Royal Archives

29 Churchill to Duke of Windsor, 4 July 1940, in Bloch, *Secret File of the Duke of Windsor*, p.143

30 Ziegler, *King Edward VIII*, p.427

31 Duke of Windsor to Walford Selby, 14 August 1957, Bodleian Archive, ms Eng c6590

32 Wallis Windsor, p.342

33 Eccles, p.132

34 Eccles to Hubert Gladwyn Jebb, 4 July 1940, National Archives, FO 1093/23

35 Cadbury, p.177

36 Ribbentrop to Stohrer, 11 July 1940, in Bloch, *Operation Willi*, pp.98-9

37 Bloch, *Operation Willi*, p.102

38 Duke of Windsor to A. G. Allen, 17 July 1940, in Bloch, *Operation Willi*, pp.91-2

39 Sgt D. Morton to Churchill, 19 July 1940, National Archives, FO 1093/23

Chapter Nine: Operation Willi

1 Gerwarth, p.177

2 Schellenberg, pp.127-31

3 Bloch, *Operation Willi*, p.108

4 Ibid., pp.126-7

5 Duke of Windsor to Churchill, 18 July 1940, Churchill Archives, CHAR 20/9A/76

6 George VI diary, 18 July 1940, Royal Archives

7 George VI to Duke of Windsor, 26 July 1940, Royal Archives, RA/EDW/PRIV/MAIN/A/4600

8 Bloch, *Operation Willi*, p.152

9 Ibid., p.169

10 Dep Monckton Trustees 15

11 Bloch, *Operation Willi*, p.172

12 Churchill to Duke of Windsor, 27 July 1940, in Bloch, *Operation Willi*, p.174

13 Dep Monckton Trustees 15

14 Wallis Windsor, pp.342-3

15 Birkenhead, p.180

16 Schellenberg, p.138

17 Bloch, *Operation Willi*, p.178

18 Schellenberg, p.139

19 Bloch, *Operation Willi*, pp.187-8

20 Dep Monckton Trustees 15

21 Duke of Windsor to Churchill, 31 July 1940, Dep Monckton Trustees 18

22 George VI diary, 6 August 1940, Royal Archives

23 Monckton to Churchill, 8 August 1940, Royal Archives, RA/Co42A/074

24 Churchill to Monckton, 9 August 1940, Royal Archives, RA/Co42A/075

Chapter Ten: Team Man or Bloody Buccaneer

1 Queen Elizabeth to Queen Mary, 19 October 1940, in Shawcross, *Counting One's Blessings*, p.298

2 Queen Elizabeth to May Elphinstone, 25 October 1940, in ibid, pp.298-9

3 Monckton to Duchess of Windsor, 16 November 1940, Dep Monckton Trustees 18

4 Monckton to Duke of Windsor, 2 October 1940, Dep Monckton Trustees 18

5 Bradford, p.323

6 George VI diary, 10 September 1940, Royal Archives

7 George VI diary, 5 October 1940, Royal Archives

8 Channon, 10 November 1940

9 Chamberlain diary, 9 September 1940, in Hyde, *Neville Chamberlain*, p.177

10 Hyde, *Neville Chamberlain*, pp.177-8

11 Ibid., p.178

12 George VI diary, 15 October 1940, Royal Archives

13 George VI to Queen Mary, 14 October 1940, Royal Archives

14 George VI diary, 16 November 1940, Royal Archives

15 George VI to Queen Mary, 18 November 1940, Royal Archives, RA QM/PRIV/CC12/143

16 George VI diary, 17 November 1940, Royal Archives

17 Bradford, p.327

18 Monckton to Duke of Windsor, 18 August 1940, Dep Monckton Trustees 18

19 Monckton to Godfrey Thomas, 10 October 1940, National Archives, FO 954/33A

20 Monckton to Duke of Windsor, 26 August 1940, Dep Monckton Trustees 18

21 Bloch, *The Reign & Abdication of Edward VIII* pp.146-7

22 George VI diary, 5 November 1940, Royal Archives

23 Bloch, *The Reign & Abdication of Edward VIII* p.128

24 Ziegler, *King Edward VIII*, p.442

25 Marquess of Lothian to Alexander Cadogan, 4 September 1940, Dep Monckton Trustees 18

26 Ziegler, *King Edward VIII*, p.450

27 Bloch, *The Reign & Abdication of Edward VIII*, p.127

28 Monckton to Duchess of Windsor, 16 November 1940, Dep Monckton Trustees 18

29 Cadbury, p.201

30 Bloch, *The Reign & Abdication of Edward VIII*, p.132

31 FBI documents, 28 January 1940, FBI HQ

32 *Expressen*, 3 July 1940

33 Duke of Windsor to Axel Wenner-Gren, 1 January 1941, in Bloch, *The Reign & Abdication of Edward VIII*, p.176

34 'C' to Henry Hopkinson, 14 December 1940, National Archives

Chapter Eleven: 'The Friend You Used to Be'
1 George VI diary, 11 October 1940, Royal Archives

2 Bradford, p.333

3 Ibid., p.334

4 George VI diary, 24 December 1940, Royal Archives

5 Ibid.

6 George VI diary, 20 January 1941, Royal Archives

7 George VI diary, retrospect of 1940, Royal Archives

8 King George VI to Winston Churchill, 2 January 1941, Churchill Archives, CHAR 20/20/1-2

9 George VI war diary, 9 February 1941, Royal Archives

10 Colville, p.145

11 King George VI to Queen Mary, 27 June 1940, Royal Archives

12 Bradford, p.320

13 Cadbury, p.219

14 Channon, 24 March 1941

15 George VI diary, 7 February 1941, Royal Archives

16 Duke of Windsor to Walter Monckton, 28 January 1941, Dep Monckton Trustees 19

17 Walter Monckton to Duke of Windsor, 19 February 1941, Dep Monckton Trustees 19

18 *Liberty* magazine, 22 March 1941

19 Churchill to Duke of Windsor, 18 March 1941, National Archives, FO 954/33A/189

20 George VI diary, 25 March 1941, Royal Archives

21 Wallis Windsor to Bessie Merriman, 31 March 1941, in Bloch, *The Reign & Abdication of Edward VIII*, p.185

22 Halifax to Mary Wood, 6 March 1941, Halifax Papers, HALIFAX A2/278/26

23 Wallis Windsor to Walter Monckton, 5 March 1941, Dep Monckton Trustees 19

24 Duke of Windsor to Lord Moyne (FAO Churchill), 19 March 1941, Churchill Archives, CHAR 20/31A/22

25 Duke of Windsor to Churchill, 27 March 1941, National Archives, FO 954/33A/190

26 Albrecht Haushofer memorandum, 6 May 1937, National Archives, KV 2/1684

27 Albrecht Haushofer to Douglas Douglas-Hamilton, 23 September 1940, National Archives, KV 2/1684

28 MI5 memorandum B28, 17 November 1940, National Archives, KV 2/1684

29 Thomas Argyll Robertson to F. G. Stammers, 22 January 1941, National Archives, KV 2/1684

30 Douglas Douglas-Hamilton MI5 statement, Air Ministry, 11 March 1941, National Archives, KV2/1684

31 MI5 summary of Hamilton activities, March 1941, National Archives, KV2/1684

32 Report on interview with Rudolf Hess by Duke of Hamilton, Royal Archives, RA/PSO/GVI/C/199/17

33 Churchill, *The Second World War: The Grand Alliance*, p.43

34 George VI diary, 13 May 1941, Royal Archives

35 Rudolf Hess interrogation documents, May 1941, National Archives, CAB 118/56

36 Churchill, *The Second World War: The Grand Alliance*, p.44

37 John Simon, Hess interview report, 11 May 1941, National Archives, CAB 118/56

38 George VI diary, 16 May 1941, Royal Archives

39 Hamilton to George VI, 19 May 1941, Royal Archives, RA/PSO/ GVI/C/199/16

40 George VI diary, 20 May 1941, Royal Archives

41 Alexander Cadogan, 20 June 1941, National Archives, CAB 118/56

42 George VI diary, 11 June 1941, Royal Archives

43 Rudolf Hess statement, 5 September 1941, Royal Archives RA/PSO/ GVI/C/199/03

44 Rudolf Hess statement, 18 September 1941, Royal Archives, RA/PSO/ GVI/C/199/04

45 Colonel M. Rees, minutes, 19 August 1941, National Archives, FO 1093/12

46 Rudolf Hess to George VI, 13 November 1941, Royal Archives, RA/ PSO/GVI/C/199/06

47 Hardinge to Alexander Cadogan, 12 January 1942, Royal Archives, RA/ PSO/GVI/C/199/07

48 J. Edgar Hoover to Adolf A. Berle, 22 April 1942, FBI Archives, FBI HQ 65-31113-26

Chapter Twelve: 'The Hard Sacrifice'

1 Shawcross, *Counting One's Blessings,* pp.313-15

2 Vickers, p.228

3 Bradford, p.336

4 George VI to Halifax, 14 April 1941, Halifax Papers, HALIFAX A2/276/4

5 Halifax to King George VI, 16 May 1941, Halifax Papers, HALIFAX A4.410.1.8/3

6 George VI to President Roosevelt, 3 June 1941, Roosevelt Library, PSF/ GB/Box 82

7 17 February 1941, Halifax Papers, HALIFAX A7.8.19

8 George VI to Queen Mary, 16 August 1941, Royal Archives

9 George VI diary, 19 August 1941, Royal Archives

10 Duke of Kent to Elizabeth Lawson-Johnston, 9 September 1941, in Cadbury, pp.237-8

11 George VI diary, 20 October 1941, Royal Archives

12 Duke of Windsor to Monckton, 11 July 1941, Dep Monckton Trustees 19

13 Halifax to Churchill, 4 October 1941, National Archives, FA 954-33A-202

14 Halifax to Churchill, 19 October 1941, Churchill Archives, CHAR 20/31B/161-163

15 Hansard, 25 November 1941

16 George VI diary, 24 November 1941, Royal Archives

17 George VI diary, 9 December 1941, Royal Archives

18 George VI to Churchill, 7 December 1941, in Bradford, pp.340–1

19 Churchill to George VI, 12 December 1941, in Farrell, p.86

20 Queen Elizabeth to Queen Mary, 9 December 1941, in Shawcross, *Counting One's Blessings*, p.316

21 Halifax to Mary Wood, 10 December 1941, Halifax Papers, HALIFAX A2/278/26

Chapter Thirteen: 'If We Can't Bloody Well Fight, We'd Better Pray'

1 George VI diary, 19 January 1942, Royal Archives

2 George VI diary, 16 February 1942, Royal Archives

3 George VI to Queen Mary, 16 February 1942, Royal Archives

4 Bradford, p.341

5 George VI diary, 17 February 1942, Royal Archives

6 Queen Elizabeth to Helen Hardinge, 10 May 1941, Hardinge Papers, U2117 (Acc 2349/94)

7 George VI diary, 19 February 1942, Royal Archives

8 George VI diary, 24 February 1942, Royal Archives

9 George VI diary, 28 February 1942, Royal Archives

10 Channon, 25 February 1942

11 MS Woolton 2, 29 March 1942, Bodleian Library

12 Crawford, p.150

13 Frankland, p.167

14 Ibid., p.166

15 Channon, 12 April 1942

16 Hardinge to Walter Monckton, 20 March 1942, Dep Monckton Trustees 9

17 Channon, 12 April 1942

18 Churchill, *The Second World War: The Hinge of Fate*, p.397

19 *New Statesman*, 11 April 1942

20 George VI diary, 28 April 1942, Royal Archives

21 George VI to Roosevelt, 11 March 1942, Roosevelt Library PSF
22 Bradford, p.344
23 George VI to Monckton, 1 March 1942, Dep Monckton Trustees 9
24 George VI diary, 31 October 1942, Royal Archives
25 Wallis Windsor to Bessie Merriman, 16 December 1941, in Bloch, *The Reign & Abdication of Edward VIII* p.226
26 Duke of Windsor to George Allen, 13 December 1941, in Bloch, *The Reign & Abdication of Edward VIII,* Ibid
27 Lord Moyne to Halifax, 15 May 1941, National Archives, FO 954/33A
28 Bloch, *The Reign & Abdication of Edward VIII,* p.232
29 Ibid., p.233
30 Ibid., p.238
31 Wallis Windsor, p.356
32 Duke of Windsor to Beaverbrook, 18 April 1942, in Bloch, *The Reign & Abdication of Edward VIII,* p.242
33 Halifax to Foreign Office, 22 April 1942, National Archives, FO 954/33A/208
34 Halifax to Mary Wood, 27 May 1942, Halifax Papers, HALIFAX A2/278/26
35 Eden to Churchill, 14 May 1942, National Archives, FO 954/33A/210
36 United Kingdom High Commissioner in South Africa to Secretary of State for Dominion Affairs, 29 May 1942, Churchill Archives, CHAR 20/75/107
37 George VI diary, 5 May 1942, Royal Archives
38 Halifax to Mary Wood, 4 June 1942, Halifax Papers, HALIFAX A2/278/26
39 Duke of Windsor, *The New York Daily News,* 13 December 1966
40 Halifax diary, 23 June 1942, Halifax Papers
41 Walter Hoving to Halifax, 19 June 1942, Halifax Papers, HALIFAX A4/410/4/18
42 Halifax to Viscount Cranborne, 21 June 1942, Halifax Papers, HALIFAX A4/410/4/18
43 Wallis to Bessie Merriman, 27 July 1942, in Bloch, *The Reign & Abdication of Edward VIII,* p.272
44 Ibid., p.271

Chapter Fourteen: 'False Rumour and Wild Surmise'
1 Noël Coward to Robert Vansittart, 21 August 1940, in *Sunday Telegraph,* 4 November 2007

2 Warwick, p.157

3 Ibid.

4 Watson, p.169

5 Alec Hardinge to Jack Lowther, 14 March 1941, Royal Archives, RA GDKH/ENGT/A40

6 Duke of Kent to Betty Lawson-Johnston, 9 September 1941, in Cadbury, p.238

7 Larman, p.27

8 Duke of Kent to Betty-Lawson Johnston, 22 September 1939, in Cadbury, p.107

9 Aronson, p.54

10 Warwick, p.116

11 Archibald Sinclair to House of Commons, 7 October 1942, Hansard

12 Halifax to Mary Wood, 17 September 1942, Halifax Papers, HALIFAX A2/278/26

13 Halifax to Mary Wood, 27 August 1942, Halifax Papers, HALIFAX A2/278/14

14 'Scandal of a royal death', *Daily Post*, 22 December 2003

15 George VI to Helen Hardinge, 4 September 1942, Hardinge Papers, U2117 (Acc 2349/81)

16 Watson, p.180

17 Queen Elizabeth to Osbert Sitwell, 14 September 1942, in Shawcross, *Counting One's Blessings*, p.324

18 Channon, 6 September 1942

19 Lascelles, 25 August 1942

20 Duke of Windsor to George VI, 15 September 1942, Royal Archives, RA/GVI/PRIV/01/02/16

21 Lascelles, 29 August 1942

22 29 August 1942, in Payn and Morley

23 Channon, 29 August 1942

24 George VI diary, 29 August 1942, Royal Archives

25 Wallis Windsor to Bessie Merriman, 29 August 1942, in Bloch, *The Reign & Abdication of Edward VIII*, p.273

26 Duke of Windsor to Sibyl Colefax, 1 October 1942, Bodleian Archives, ms Eng c5272

27 George VI to Queen Mary, 22 October 1942, Royal Archives, RA/QM/PRIV/CC13/27

28 George VI diary, 14 September 1942, Royal Archives

29 George VI to Duke of Windsor, 30 October 1942, Royal Archives, RA/
Co42A/17

Chapter Fifteen: 'These Years of Tragedy and Glory'

1 Lascelles, 1 November 1942
2 George VI diary, 3 November 1942, Royal Archives
3 George VI diary, 4 November 1942, Royal Archives
4 Lascelles, 15 November 1942
5 Churchill, *The Second World War: The Hinge of Fate*, p.603
6 Bradford, p.349
7 Clark, p.94
8 King George VI to Churchill, 5 November 1942, in Gilbert, p.249
9 Churchill to George VI, 7 November 1942, in ibid., p.251
10 Duke of Windsor to Churchill, 10 November 1942, Churchill Archives,
CHAR 20/63/74-92
11 George VI diary, 15 December, Royal Archives
12 King George VI to Churchill, 9 December 1942, Churchill Archives,
CHAR 20/52/96-100
13 Lascelles, 3 December 1942
14 Ibid., 11 December 1942
15 Duke of Windsor to Bessie Merriman, 24 January 1943, in Bloch, *The
Reign & Abdication of Edward VIII*, pp.287-8
16 George VI diary, 16 February 1943, Royal Archives
17 George VI diary, 31 December 1943, Royal Archives
18 George VI to Churchill, 22 February 1943, in Bradford, p.352
19 Queen Elizabeth to Queen Mary, 19 February 1943, Royal Archives,
RA QM/PRIV/CC13/39
20 George VI to Churchill, 22 February 1943, Churchill Archives, CHAR
20/92/19-20
21 Churchill to King George VI, 22 February 1943, in Gilbert, p.348
22 Aronson, p.103
23 Queen Mary to Lord Lang of Lambeth, 18 June 1945, Lang Papers,
Lambeth Palace Library
24 Harvey, p.275
25 Queen Elizabeth to Alec Hardinge, 19 March 1943, Lady Murray
Papers, in Shawcross, *Counting One's Blessings*, p.343
26 Churchill to Queen Elizabeth, 16 April 1943, in ibid, p 357.
27 Vickers, p.238
28 *The Times*, 15 May 1943

29 Ibid., 18 May 1943

30 Halifax to Mary Wood, 18 June 1943, Halifax Papers, HALIFAX A2/278/26

31 George VI diary, 27 May 1943, Royal Archives

Chapter Sixteen: 'Never a Dull Day in the Bahamas'

1 Bloch, *The Reign & Abdication of Edward VIII*, p.153

2 Ibid., p.294

3 Halifax to Oliver Stanley, 22 November 1943, Halifax Papers, HALIFAX A4/410/4/18

4 Churchill to Duke of Windsor, 10 June 1943, Churchill Archives, CHAR 20/100/10

5 Bloch, *The Reign & Abdication of Edward VIII*, p.295

6 Wallis Windsor to Bessie Merriman, 24 August 1943, in Bloch, *The Reign & Abdication of Edward VIII*, p 303

7 Wallis Windsor, p.355

8 Duke of Windsor to King George VI, 2 June 1943, in Bloch, *The Reign & Abdication of Edward VIII*, p.296 (the letter exists only in draft form, raising the possibility it was never sent)

9 Bloch, *The Reign & Abdication of Edward VIII*, p.303

10 Ibid., p.305

11 National Archives, CO 23/714/5

12 *Miami Herald*, 22 July 1943

13 Wallis Windsor to Bessie Merriman, 24 August 1943, in Bloch, *The Reign & Abdication of Edward VIII*, p.308

14 Duke of Windsor to Oliver Stanley, 10 August 1943, in Ibid, pp.311-2

15 Ziegler, *King Edward VIII*, p.482

16 Ibid., p.483

17 Halifax to Stanley, 22 November 1943, Halifax Papers, HALIFAX A4/410/4/18

18 Stanley to Halifax, 1 December 1943, Halifax Papers, HALIFAX A4/410/4/18

19 Halifax to Stanley, 16 December 1943, Halifax Papers, HALIFAX A4/410/4/18

20 National Archives, KV 2/4412

21 Ibid.

22 Ibid.

23 Ibid.

24 'C' (Sir David Petrie) documents, Royal Archives, RA/042A/298

25 Alexander Cadogan to 'C', 5 May 1941, Royal Archives, RA/042A/297

26 National Archives, KV 2/4412

Chapter Seventeen: Liberation

1 Lascelles, 7 January 1944
2 George VI to Neville Chamberlain, 3 February 1939, National Archives
3 Channon, 10 May 1940
4 Lascelles, p.138
5 Channon, 15 April 1943
6 Hardinge to Viscountess Milner, 25 July 1942, Hardinge Papers, U2117 (Acc 2359/224)
7 George VI diary, 6 July 1943, Royal Archives
8 George VI diary, 7 July 1943, Royal Archives
9 Channon, 17 July 1943
10 Ibid., 20 July 1943
11 Lascelles, 17 July 1943
12 Hardinge to Sir John Simon, 1 August 1943, Bodleian Library, MS Simon 84
13 Queen Elizabeth to Helen Hardinge, 7 July 1943, Hardinge Papers, U2117 (Acc 2349/162)
14 Ibid.
15 George VI diary, 7 March 1944, Royal Archives
16 George VI diary, 3 February 1944, Royal Archives
17 Lascelles, 3 March 1944
18 Richard J. Aldrich, *Daily Express*, 6 June 2020
19 Lascelles, 15 May 1944
20 George VI diary, 30 May 1944, Royal Archives
21 George VI to Churchill, 31 May 1944, Churchill Archives, CHAR 20/136/10
22 George VI diary, 1 June 1944, Royal Archives
23 Lascelles, 1 June 1944
24 Ibid.
25 George VI to Churchill, 2 June 1944, Churchill Archives, CHAR 20/136/4
26 Lascelles, 2 June 1944
27 George VI diary, 2 June 1944, Royal Archives
28 Churchill to George VI, 3 June 1944, in Churchill, *The Second World War: Closing the Ring*, p.550

29 Lascelles, 3 June 1944

30 Ibid., 6 June 1944

31 Ibid., 16 June 1944

32 George VI diary, 4 July 1944, Royal Archives

33 Wallis Windsor to Bessie Merriman, 5 April 1944, in Bloch, *The Reign & Abdication of Edward VIII* p.211

34 E. E. Conroy to J. Edgar Hoover, 1 August 1944, FBI HQ65-31113

35 Bloch, *The Reign & Abdication of Edward VIII*, p.334

36 Duke of Windsor to Halifax, 15 May 1944, Halifax Papers, HALIFAX A4/410/4/18

37 Halifax to Stanley, 22 May 1944, Halifax Papers, HALIFAX A4/410/4/18

38 Lascelles to John Martin, 30 May 1944, Churchill Archives, CHAR 20/148/37-39

39 George VI to Churchill, 16 September 1944, Churchill Archives, CHAR 20/148/45

40 William H. Harman to Halifax, 17 August 1944, Halifax Papers, HALIFAX A4/410/4/18

41 Halifax to Harman, 28 August 1944, Halifax Papers, HALIFAX A4/410/4/18

42 Halifax to Duke of Windsor, 28 August 1944, Halifax Papers, HALIFAX A4/410/4/18

43 Halifax to Stanley, 4 September 1944, Halifax Papers, HALIFAX A4/410/4/18

44 Bloch, *The Reign & Abdication of Edward VIII*, p.344

45 Duke of Windsor to A. G. Allen, 30 September 1944, in ibid.

46 Lascelles, 9 November 1944

Chapter Eighteen: 'O Captain! My Captain!'

1 Pimlott, p.79

2 George VI war diary, 8 May 1945, Royal Archives

3 Lascelles, 8 May 1945

4 Payn and Morley, p.29

5 George VI diary, 8 May 1945, Royal Archives

6 George VI diary, 18 May 1945, Royal Archives

7 George VI to Churchill, 24 December 1944, Churchill Archives, CHAR 20/136/23-24

8 Duke of Windsor to Halifax, 17 January 1945, Halifax Papers, HALIFAX A4/410/4/18

9 Halifax to Duke of Windsor, 28 January 1945, Halifax Papers, HALIFAX A4/410/4/18

10 Bloch, *The Reign & Abdication of Edward VIII*, p.353

11 Pye, p.251

12 George VI diary, 20 February 1945, Royal Archives

13 George VI diary, 3 July 1944, Royal Archives

14 George VI to Churchill, 13 April 1945, Churchill Archives, CHAR 20/199/96

15 Eisenhower, p.298

16 George VI diary, 22 April 1945, Royal Archives

17 Queen Elizabeth to Osbert Sitwell, 14 May 1945, Sitwell Papers, in Shawcross, *Counting One's Blessings*, pp.384-5

18 Jenkins, p.792

19 Lascelles, 26 July 1945

20 Hardinge to Viscountess Milner, 12 December 1945, Hardinge Papers, U2117 (Acc 2349/11)

21 Queen Elizabeth to Queen Mary, 26 July 1945, Royal Archives, RA/QM/PRIV/CC13/133

22 George VI diary, 26 July 1945, Royal Archives

23 George VI to Churchill, 31 July 1945, in Bradford, p.377

24 Ibid., pp.377-8

25 Jenkins, p.800

Epilogue: The Return of Mr Toad

1 Duke of Windsor to George VI, 13 August 1945, Royal Archives, RA/GVI/PRIV/01/02/19

2 Lascelles, 5 October 1945

3 Lascelles to George VI, 19 September 1945, Royal Archives, RA/C042A/343

4 Lascelles to George VI, 9 October 1945, Royal Archives, RA/C042A/343

5 George VI to Duke of Gloucester, 29 May 1945, Royal Archives, RA/HDG/PRIV

6 Lascelles to George VI, 9 October 1945, Royal Archives, RA/042A/350

7 Ibid.

8 Lascelles diary, 9 October 1945

9 Lascelles to George VI, 9 October 1945, Royal Archives, RA/042A/350

10 Lascelles diary, 9 October 1945

11 Lascelles to George VI, 9 October 1945, Royal Archives, RA/042A/349

12 Duke of Windsor to George VI, 18 October 1945, Royal Archives, RA/
GVI/PRIV/01/02/20
13 Ernest Bevin to Clement Attlee, 13 August 1945, National Archives,
FO/800/521
14 Lascelles, 12 August 1945
15 John Peck memoranda, 24 and 28 August 1945, National Archives,
FO/800/521

Bibliography

Aldrich, Richard J., and Cormac, Rory, *The Secret Royals*, Atlantic, 2021

Aronson, Theo, *The Royal Family at War*, John Murray, 1993

Barnes, John, and Nicholson, David, ed., *The Empire at Bay: The Leo Amery Diaries, 1939-1945*, Hutchinson, 1987

Beaken, Robert, *Cosmo Lang: Archbishop in War and Crisis*, I. B. Tauris, 2012

Bew, John, *Citizen Clem*, Riverrun, 2016

Birkenhead, Lord, *Walter Monckton*, Weidenfeld & Nicolson, 1969

——*The Life of Lord Halifax*, Hamish Hamilton, 1965

Blackledge, Catherine, *The Story of V: Opening Pandora's Box*, Weidenfeld & Nicolson, 2003

Bloch, Michael, *Ribbentrop*, Bantam, 1992

——*Secret File of the Duke of Windsor,* Harper Collins, 1990

——*The Reign & Abdication of Edward VIII*, Bantam, 1990

——*The Duchess of Windsor*, Weidenfeld & Nicolson, 1996

——*Operation Willi*, Weidenfeld & Nicolson, 1984

——ed., *Wallis and Edward, Letters, 1931-1937*, Weidenfeld & Nicolson, 1986

Bouverie, Tim, *Appeasing Hitler*, Bodley Head, 2019

Bradford, Sarah, *King George VI*, Weidenfeld & Nicolson, 1989

Brown, W. J., *So Far*, George Allen & Unwin, 1943

Cadbury, Deborah, *Princes at War*, Bloomsbury, 2015

Channon, Henry 'Chips', *The Diaries 1918-38*, ed. Simon Heffer, Hutchinson, 2020

——*The Diaries 1938-43*, ed. Simon Heffer, Hutchinson, 2021

Churchill, Winston, *The Second World War: The Gathering Storm*, Cassell, 1948

——*The Second World War: Their Finest Hour*, Cassell, 1949

——*The Second World War: The Grand Alliance*, Cassell, 1950

——*The Second World War: The Hinge of Fate*, Cassell, 1950

——*The Second World War: Closing the Ring*, Cassell, 1951

——*The Second World War: Triumph and Tragedy*, Cassell, 1953

Clark, Mark, *Calculated Risk*, Harrap, 1951

Colville, John, *The Fringes of Power: Downing Street Diaries 1939-1955*, Hodder & Stoughton, 1989

Cooper, Diana, *Autobiography*, Michael Russell, 1979

——*The Light of Common Day*, Hart-Davis, 1959

Crawford, Marion, *The Little Princesses*, Cassell, 1950

Donaldson, Frances, *King Edward VIII*, Weidenfeld & Nicolson, 1974

Eccles, David, *By Safe Hand*, Bodley Head, 1983

Eisenhower, Dwight, *Crusade in Europe*, Doubleday, 1948

Farrell, Brian, ed., *Churchill and the Lion City*, NUS Press, 2011

Frankland, Noble, *Prince Henry, Duke of Gloucester*, Weidenfeld & Nicolson, 1980

Gerwarth, Robert, *Hitler's Hangman: The Life of Heydrich*, Yale University Press, 2012

Gilbert, Martin, *Prophet of Truth*, Heinemann, 1976

Guedalla, Philip, *The Hundredth Year*, Hodder & Stoughton, 1939

Hamilton, Patrick, *Hangover Square*, Constable, 1941

Hardinge, Helen, *Loyal to Three Kings*, William Kimber, 1967

Harvey, Oliver, *War Diaries*, Collins, 1978

Hesse, Fritz, *Hitler and the English*, Wingate, 1954

Higham, Charles, *Mrs Simpson: Secret Lives of the Duchess of Windsor*, Sidgwick & Jackson, 1998

Hyde, H. Montgomery, *Neville Chamberlain*, Weidenfeld & Nicolson, 1976

——*Walter Monckton*, Sinclair-Stevenson, 1991

Jardine, Rev. R. Anderson, *At Long Last*, Murray & Gee, 1943

Jenkins, Roy, *Churchill*, Macmillan, 2001

Larman, Alexander, *The Crown in Crisis*, Weidenfeld & Nicolson, 2020

Lascelles, Alan, *King's Counsellor: Abdication and War*, Weidenfeld & Nicolson, 2006

Lees-Milne, James, *Harold Nicolson*, Chatto & Windus, 1981

MacDonald, Malcolm, *People and Places*, Collins, 1969

Maxwell, Elsa, *I Married the World*, Heinemann, 1955

Nicolson, Harold, *Diaries and Letters 1930-1939*, ed. Nigel Nicolson, William Collins, 1967

Norwich, John Julius, ed., *The Duff Cooper Diaries: 1915-1951*, Weidenfeld & Nicolson, 2005

Ogilvy, Mabell, *Thatched with Gold*, Hutchinson, 1962

Pasternak, Anna, *Untitled: The Real Wallis Simpson, Duchess of Windsor*, William Collins, 2019

Payn, Graham, and Morley, Sheridan, ed., *The Noël Coward Diaries*, Weidenfeld & Nicolson, 1982

Pimlott, Ben, *The Queen: Elizabeth II and the Monarchy*, HarperCollins, 2001

Powell, Ted, *Edward VIII: An American Life*, OUP, 2018

Pownall, Henry, *Chief of Staff: 1933–1940*, Leo Cooper, 1972

Pye, Michael, *The King Over the Water*, Hutchinson, 1981

Reith, Lord, *The Reith Diaries*, Collins, 1975

Rhodes James, Robert, *Churchill: A Study in Failure 1900–1939*, World Publishing Company, 1970

Rippentrop, Joachim von, *The Ribbentrop Memoirs*, Weidenfeld & Nicolson, 1954

Roberts, Andrew, *Churchill*, Allen Lane, 2018

——*Eminent Churchillians*, Weidenfeld & Nicolson, 1994

Rose, Kenneth, *Kings, Queens and Courtiers*, Weidenfeld & Nicolson, 1985

Schellenberg, Walter, *The Memoirs of Hitler's Spymaster*, Andre Deutsch, 2006

Sebba, Anne, *That Woman*, Weidenfeld & Nicolson, 2011

Shawcross, William, *Queen Elizabeth: The Queen Mother*, Macmillan, 2009

——ed., *Counting One's Blessings: The Selected Letters of Queen Elizabeth, the Queen Mother*, Macmillan, 2012

Sitwell, Osbert, *Queen Mary and Others*, Michael Joseph, 1974

Spoto, Donald, *Dynasty: The Turbulent Saga of the Royal Family from Victoria to Diana*, Simon & Schuster, 1995

Taylor, A. J. P., *Beaverbrook*, Hamish Hamilton, 1972

Templewood, Viscount, *Nine Troubled Years*, Collins, 1954

Ullrich, Volker, *Hitler: Ascent 1889–1939*, Bodley Head, 2016

Vickers, Hugo, *Behind Closed Doors*, Hutchinson, 2011

Vincent, John, ed., *The Crawford Papers*, Manchester University Press, 1984

Warwick, Christopher, *George and Marina: The Duke and Duchess of Kent*, Weidenfeld & Nicolson, 1988

Watson, Sophia, *Marina: The Story of a Princess*, Weidenfeld & Nicolson, 1994

Wheeler-Bennett, John W., *King George VI: His Life and Reign*, Macmillan, 1958

Williams, Susan, *The People's King*, Allen Lane, 2003

Windsor, Duke of, *A King's Story*, Cassell, 1951

Windsor, Wallis, *The Heart Has Its Reasons*, Michael Joseph, 1956

Ziegler, Philip, *King Edward VIII*, Collins, 1990
——*Diana Cooper*, Hamish Hamilton, 1981
——*Crown and People*, Collins, 1978

Index